Diverticulitis

Diet Cookbook for Beginners

Michelle Burns

TABLE OF CONTENTS

EGG FREE AND GLUTEN FREE 119

SAUCES, STEW AND SOUPS 124

VEGAN LUNCH 157

VEGETARIAN DESSERT 174

VEGAN DESSERT 177

BONUS INSTANT POT RECIPES 179

INDEX 191

CONCLUSION AND BONUS 192

INTRODUCTION

As we age, the risks of intestinal problems such as poor digestion, Meteorism, intolerances and above all diverticula also increase. Excruciating pains and the continued sense of inflammation can really make your life uneasy. If you don't know how to cure diverticula, Don't know what to cook or if you feel your colon irritated and don't know how to end all this, This is the book for you.

In this book you can find a guide which will allow you to get to know your intestine and body in depth, learn to listen to it and act accordingly. Very often diverticular diets or anti-inflammatory diets are so poor in tasty foods and interesting recipes that they just throw us even more into despair.

In this book, you will find a lot of tasty and fun recipes that are healthy and good for your intestinal life other than for diverticulitis in particular. You have found an alley in the cure of your intestinal health!

Stop with boring and tasteless diets! Here is your alternative: a healthy but also tasty diet for the well-being of your digestive system and to get rid of your diverticulitis!

How your digestive system works

Suffering from intestinal diseases can be really frustrating, very often the abdominal pains feel acute but generic, they could lead to ask "what's wrong with me, what's wrong with my digestion? A deep knowledge of your digestive system could open your eyes and answer your question.

Digestion is the breakdown of food into molecules or small chemical substances that can be absorbed by the body as nutrients. Most substances in our diet cannot be used by the body in their natural state. It is therefore important that they be broken down into smaller particles, so that they can be absorbed into the blood and then distributed to all body parts. The breakdown and distribution of food to all parts of the body is done by the digestive system. Digestion is both a mechanical and enzymatic process.

The food is broken down into simpler chemical compounds. A healthy adult consumes at least a kilogram of solid food and one or two liters of liquid diet on a daily basis. These food substances have to be digested before they can be absorbed into the blood and distributed to tissues of the body. The gastrointestinal tract, also known as the digestive system plays a very important role in the digestion, distribution, and absorption of food to the various body tissues.

The digestive system includes all organs responsible for the ingestion, degradation, and absorption of food substances, as well as the elimination of waste residues.

Digestion is the fundamental process of ensuring the supply of nutrients and energy to the human body.

Through the action of the digestive system and the organs that compose it, food and fluids are transformed in such a way that they can be absorbed by the cells of the organism.

The organs that make up the digestive system are:

- Mouth and teeth;
- The pharynx;
- The esophagus;
- The stomach;
- The liver;

- The pancreas;
- The small intestine;
- The large intel

Mouth and teeth

The mouth is the cavity through which foods are introduced, that is, the substances from which our body will recover the components for its sustenance, both in terms of matter and energy.

The mouth consists of an upper part, the jaw and a lower part, the jaw, composed of the bones of the skull.

Food modification and then digestion begins in the mouth. Thanks to the action of the teeth, which shred food, the tongue that stirs it and saliva, containing lithic enzymes, foods begin to be processed and made suitable for subsequent processes.

The teeth are hard structures, composed of dentin, a particular bone tissue, very mineralized, covered in its outer portion by enamel, an epithelium also mineralized that allows the strong mechanical shredding action characteristic of chewing.

The teeth are located on both the top and bottom of the mouth, and are complementary to allow a good closure of the mouth and to better allow chewing.

The mouth is the "gateway" of the digestive system, because it is through the oral cavity that we introduce foods into the body and begin to digest them, through chewing and secretion of the first enzymes present in saliva. The mouth is also the organ thanks to which the sense of taste is expressed, directly connected with the act of nutrition, and is an important organ for both breathing and phonation.

Saliva is a hyperosmotic fluid secreted by the salivary glands located in the oral cavity. Like all secretions, saliva is also predominantly water (99%), while only 1% is inorganic and organic substances.

Among the inorganic substances, we find mainly mineral salts, in particular chlorides and baking soda, potassium and calcium. The organic fraction is instead represented by enzymes (amylase, mucin, lysozyme) and immunoglobulins.

Salivary secretion is entrusted to several glands: 60% is produced by the submandibular glands, 30% by the parotid glands and 5% by the sublingual glands. There are also minor salivary glands (5%).

The amount of saliva produced by parotids increases strongly as a result of strong stimulation.

The liquid secreted by the salivary glands does not always have the same characteristics: parotids secrete saliva more fluid and rich in ptyalin; submandibular is secrete mixed saliva, while sublingual's produce a viscous liquid, because it is rich in mucin.

Saliva has numerous and important functions, let's see the main ones.

- Food digestion begins in the mouth, thanks to a mechanical system (chewing) assisted by chemical reactions, made possible by the presence of saliva.
- This liquid turns food into bolus (an almost uniform mixture of shredded and unsalted food), protecting the pharynx and esophagus from any pointed or excessively sized food fragments.

In addition to mechanical means, saliva exerts its digestive properties through enzymes, such as lipase and salivary amylase or ptyalin. The latter begins to digest cooked starch (starch is a polysaccharide, present in bread, pasta, potatoes, chestnuts and other plant foods, consisting of many units of glucose linked together in a linear and branched way). Amylase manages to partially break the bonds inside the amylase molecule, leading to the formation of maltose (disaccharide consisting of the union of two units of glucose), malt triose (this time there are three glucose molecules) and dextrin's (7-9 units of glucose, with the presence of branching).

Due to the reduced time of food in the mouth, amylase fails to digest all starch. However, if we voluntarily chew a piece of bread for a long time, the effective digestive action of saliva will be witnessed by the onset of a sweetish flavor.

Once it arrives in the stomach, bolus-associated amylase is inactivated by the strongly acidic environment, losing its functions. This enzyme is in fact active only under conditions of neutrality (pH 7), guaranteed by the presence in saliva of bicarbonates, substances capable of keeping salivary pH close to neutrality (buffer system). Saliva pH is less than 7 when secretion is poor and shifts to alkalinity as salivary secretion increases.

Amylase digests only cooked starch, as raw starch comes in the form of granules surrounded by an indigestible wall, consisting of cellulose. Cooking instead manages to elide this membrane, releasing starch.

Saliva also has a lubricating function for the oral cavity, thanks to which it facilitates swallowing and phonation (the act of speaking). This property is linked to its content of mucin, a protein that, mixing with the water present in saliva, takes on a sticky consistency.

The mucin straminates along the walls of the oral cavity, protecting it from the abrasions of food fragments. This protein also has a protective action against the larynx and, by surrounding and lubricating the bolus, facilitates swallowing.

The mucin contained in saliva also facilitates phonation: if salivation is reset we struggle to talk precisely because the lubricating action of this liquid is lacking. In Ancient China this assumption was exploited to test the good faith of people suspected of crimes: by forcing the unfortunate to chew dry rice during interrogation, those who could produce enough saliva to swallow it were considered innocent and those who, getting nervous and eliminating salivation, could not ingest it and spoke with difficulty were considered innocent.

Saliva protects the body from microorganisms introduced with food, thanks to an antibacterial agent called lysozyme, whose protective action is enhanced by the simultaneous presence of immunoglobulins (antibodies).

Salivary glands operate in a continuous cycle and saliva is secreted continuously, while varying in quantity (1000-1500 ml per day). About 0.3 ml of saliva per minute is secreted during sleep, while when awake this amount rises to 0.5 ml per minute. Following stimulation salivary secretion can reach 3-4 ml/minute.

The secretory stimulus is mediated by cellular mechanoctors, present on the walls of the oral cavity and sensitive to the presence of food (mortise a pen), and by chemoreceptors activated by particular chemicals (taste pillars). Signals transmitted by these receptors are conveyed to the autonomic nervous system (salivation centers located in the bulb), where they are reprocessed to stimulate glandular secretion. The same result is achieved when the body is subjected to certain stimuli, such as certain odors, the sight of a particularly palatable food or memories that evoke food. The whole mechanism is meant to prepare your mouth to accommodate food.

The efferent nerve fibers that innervate the salivary glands belong primarily to the parasympathetic nervous system. However, a significant contribution is also made by the orthosympathetic system. Both stimulate salivary secretion and this is one of the few, if not the only case, in which, at the same time as the digestive tract, the two systems have the same function (generally the orthosympathetic inhibits, while the sympathetic stimulates). Between these regulatory mechanisms, however, there is a small difference: while under normal conditions both stimulate the salivary glands, in particular situations (strong emotion or fear), the action of the orthosympathetic is reversed and salivary secretion is reset.

Saliva deficiency is called xerostomia and can result from injury to the salivary glands, the use of drugs, psychological disorders, certain diseases such as mumps (mumps) and a state of general dehydration of the body. Excess saliva is instead identified by the term "ptyalism" or "sialorrhea", also due to the use of certain drugs, mental illness, pregnancy, initial laying dental prostheses, inflammatory conditions of the oral cavity, excess interdental tartar and tumors that affect the first tract of the digestive system.

Pharynx

The pharynx is an organ that connects the mouth with the esophagus. The pharynx is also part of the respiratory system, as it flows in the air entered by the nose before passing into the larynx and then to the windpipe and lungs. Given its position, it is therefore part of both the digestive and respiratory systems.

During the swallowing process, i.e. the passage of the bolus (chewed food) and fluids from the mouth to the esophagus through the oral portion of the pharynx, the muscular movement of the soft palate and the closure of the epiglottis, a cartilage structure that extends from the base of the tongue, prevent the transit of the bolus into the airways.

Esophagus

The esophagus is a muscle-membranous canal that thanks to muscle contractions facilitates the descent to the stomach of the food bolus.

It is about 25 cm long and anatomically located behind the windpipe, descending to the entrance of the stomach.

The inner part of the esophagus consists of a mucosa made from epithelial tissue with numerous glands that secrete mucus to facilitate the passage of the bolus. In addition to the mucosa, the walls of the esophagus are made up of muscle cells that provide the contractions necessary for the transit of the bolus.

The esophagus is comparable to a connecting tube - with an almost vertical course similar to an elongated S - which allows food to descend from the mouth to the stomach (anterograde transport) and vice versa (retrograde route during belching and vomiting).

The functions of the esophagus, however, are not limited to simple transport; very important, for example, is the lubricating activity, which allows it to keep its internal walls moist, facilitating the descent of food. The esophagus, moreover, thanks to the presence of a sphincter for the extremities, opposes the entry of air into the stomach during breathing and the ascent of gastric contents in the oral cavity.

The upper esophageal sphincter regulates the passage of the food bolus from the pharynx to the esophagus. The lower esophageal sphincter regulates the passage of the food bolus from the esophagus to the stomach.

A sphincter is a muscle ring with a tone so accentuated that it remains in a state of continuous contraction; this state can be modified by voluntary mechanism (external anal sphint) or reflex (such as the two sphincters of the esophagus).

The upper esophageal sphincter participates in the swallowing function, opening to allow the pharynx to push the bolus into the esophagus; under resting conditions the muscles that constitutes it is contracted and the sphincter remains closed, preventing the passage of air into the digestive tract and the inhalation of food into the airway.

As mentioned, the esophagus has a muscle wall consisting of two structures: a longitudinal outer muscle layer and a circular inner one. It is precisely to the latter that the propulsive activity is entrusted, which allows him to perform very important peristalsis movements. As an upstream musculature segment contracts, the downstream stretch relaxes; then this will contract and so on, with succession from top to bottom until the food bolus is completely descended into the stomach. Esophageal peristalsis is facilitated by the lubricating action of saliva and esophageal secretions.

When the peristaltic wave affects the lower part from the esophagus, relaxation of the lower sphincter (called cardias) occurs resulting in entry of the bolus into the gastric sac. After this phase, the cardias regains normal hyper tone and prevents the gastric contents from rising in the esophagus. If the lower esophageal sphincter does not have sufficient tone, gastric juices and pepsin can rise from the stomach causing so-called gastroesophageal reflux. It is a rather common and annoying disorder, since such substances strongly irritate the esophageal mucosa triggering pain and heartburn (burning sense). The inner walls of the esophagus are lined with musk cassock, a thick multilayered epithelium that protects it from food transit (which may have pointed ends or particularly hard residues). Within certain limits, this effective barrier also repairs it from physiological acid reflux, which appears, especially after meals, a bit in all people.

When cardias, which is normally below the diaphragm, enters the esophageal hiatus going up into the chest cavity, there is talk of a sliding hiatal hernia, a pathology that is constantly increasing especially in people over 45-50 years old; its symptoms are overlapping, but generally more severe, than those of gastroesophageal reflux.

Stomach

The stomach is a sac-shaped organ that welcomes the incoming bolus from the mouth to subject it to the later stages of digestion.

Its main function is to initiate the degradation and solubilization of carbohydrates and proteins, through the attack of gastric juices and digestive enzymes. The passage between the esophagus and stomach is controlled by an opening, cardias, which in addition to regulating the flow of the bolus to the stomach, prevents the contents of the latter, and in particular gastric juices, from refluxing to the esophagus. While the inner wall of the stomach consists of a mucous membrane with epithelial cells that secrete a mucus with the function of lubricating the inner walls facilitating the stirring of food and protecting the walls themselves from the action of gastric acids, such a lining is missing in the esophagus and a reflux of acids would damage it. Gastric juices are secreted by glands also located in the inner wall of the stomach have a strongly acidic pH, being made up of hydrochloric acid and other electrolytes (sodium, potassium, calcium, phosphate, sulfate and baking soda).

The acidic pH of the stomach allows the action of digestive enzymes, whose enzymatic activity is optimal precisely at very low ph.

The final part of the stomach enters the intestine through the pylorus, the connecting opening between the two organs. Outside the innermost wall, a muscle layer allows contractions that ensure the mixing of digested food and favor the passage to the intestine. Outside the muscle cassock, the serous cassock completely coats the organ and provides it with support.

Liver

The liver is the largest gland in our body and performs numerous functions, mainly metabolic, participating in the metabolism of carbohydrates, proteins and fats, the elimination of ammonium through the urea cycle, the detoxification of drugs, cholesterol synthesis and the formation of bile, the emulsion of fats in the digestive process. Bile is collected in a small bag-shaped organ called gallbladder, or gallbladder, located in the lower portion of the liver and is conveyed and poured into the small intestine through the bile ducts.

From an anatomical point of view it occupies the upper right part of the abdomen and partially the left part, and is divided into a right lobe, larger in size, and a left one.

Pancreas

The pancreas is an elongated gland, located behind the stomach, connected to the digestive system that performs decisive functions in regulating digestion and metabolism.

The pancreas secretes digestive enzymes (amylase, lipase and protease), which are fed into the small intestine in order to complete the metabolism of proteins, carbohydrates and fats. The pancreas also has an important endocrine function when the cells constituting the Langherans islands secrete insulin (β cells) and glucagon (α cells), two fundamental hormones for regulating carbohydrate metabolism.

Small intestine

It is the first stretch of the intestinal tube, and also the longest (in an adult individual it measures up to 7 meters). Its main function is to transport and absorb nutrients thanks to the action of digestive enzymes.

The small intestine and divides into: duodenum, fasting; ileo.

Pancreatic juices and bile come to the duodenum level.

The inner wall of the small intestine has numerous cells for absorption into the luminal mucosa, the intestinal villi. The villi are organized into folds of the luminal wall that have the function of increasing the contact surface to promote the absorption and passage of nutrients from the intestinal lumen to the blood. Passage inside the intestine is ensured by concentric and longitudinal contractions of the muscle cells of the parts of the intestine, peristaltic movements.

Large intestine

About 3 meters long, the large intestine is the terminal portion of the intestine, and is divided into: blind, appendix, colon-recto.

It has a larger diameter than that of the small intestine and its tasks are to: absorb water and electrolytes such as sodium and chlorine and complete the digestive function;

Allow the expulsion of feces, waste residues deriving from the breakdown of foods, but also of cells detached from the mucous membrane and residues of bacteria: the latter derive from the high resident microbial population, which with its action helps to metabolize nutrients.

Both the small intestine and the large intestine are considered part of the body's immune system.

The intestine is in fact exposed to a large antigenic load represented by incoming food, with potential pathogenic threat, but also of antigens and allergens present in nutrients. Lymphoid tissue associated with the intestine can provide an effective immune response once it comes into contact with antigens found in the intestinal lumen. An inappropriate response or hyper-reaction can cause an inflammatory reaction and the development of disorders of inflammatory origin such as: Celiac disease; Or chronic bowel diseases (such as Crohn's disease or ulcerative colitis).

Nerve regulation of gastrointestinal functions is ensured by the Enteric Nervous System or met sympathetic system. It is the largest component of the autonomic nervous system, consisting of a dense network of neurons and receptors, which allows the regulation of the gastrointestinal system regardless of the input of the central nervous system.

- Local blood flow;
- Transport and secretion through the mucosa;

- Modulation of immune response and endocrine function are all activities regulated by the enteric nervous system.

Its contribution to the genesis and development of neurological disorders at the systemic level is due to the close connection with nerves of the central nervous system. Some inflammatory diseases affecting the digestion organs also have a strong stressful and psychosomatic component, just think of irritable bowel syndrome (IBS) and spastic colitis.

Medical specialties that deal with treating dysfunctions and diseases that affect the digestive system and its component organs constitute subclasses of the main branch of Gastroenterology.

This specialization is responsible for the prevention, diagnosis and treatment (both pharmacological and endoscopic-surgical type together with general surgery) of the main pathologies affecting the esophagus, stomach, intestines, pancreas, liver, bile ducts, colorectal.

Of the entire digestive system, only the mouth is excluded from this specialized therapeutic area, falling within that of Otolaryngology and Dentistry.

Also with regard to digestive care, interdisciplinary is crucial, since the different organs perform heterogeneous functions and the therapies to be considered can and must include support from other medical specialties, including:

- Dietology;
- Allergology;
- Psychology;

- Endocrinology;
- Oncology;
- Genetic counseling.

The main pathologies of the digestive system

Abnormalities, dysfunctions and pathologies can affect each of the organs that are part of the digestive system, and different health benefits (diagnostics, therapies and surgery) are provided by the National Health System (SSN) to meet different needs.

Esophagus
- Esophageal diverticula: small sac-shaped extroflexions that form on the esophageal wall;

- Reflux: ascent of acidic material (semi-digested food and gastric juices) from the stomach to the esophagus;
- Esophagitis: inflammation of the esophagus (acute or chronic);
- Barrett's Esophagus: moving a portion of the stomach mucosa to that of the esophagus, with consequences such as chronic inflammation and the development of neoplasms;
- Esophagus cancer.

Stomach

- Dyspepsia: difficult and slow digestion;
- Hiatal hernia: sliding of a small portion of the stomach towards the esophagus. This condition can be congenital or acquired;
- Gastritis: chronic or acute inflammation of the mucosa lining the walls of the stomach;
- Peptic ulcer: injury that forms on gastric walls. It can bleed to cause anemia, or open up and become piercing;
- Zollinger-Ellison syndrome: rare disease for which one or more tumors that secrete hormones and cause increased acid production;
- Stomach cancer.

Intestine

- Chronic constipation;
- Appendicitis;
- Irritable bowel syndrome: psychosomatic disorder that manifests itself with symptoms including meteorism, constipation or diarrhea, spasms and abdominal bloating;
- Diverticulitis: inflammation of diverticula, small hollow extroflexions that form along the intestinal mucosa;
- Intestinal polyps: benign neo formations that can evolve into malignant tumors;
- Colon cancer;
- Rectal cancer;
- Crohn's disease and ulcerative rectocolitis: chronic inflammatory diseases of a probable autoimmune nature that manifest themselves with symptoms such as rectal bleeding, diarrhea, slimming, joint pain and general malaise;
- Celiac disease (chronic gluten intolerance) and other types of food intolerances and allergies;
- Inguinal hernia;
- Hemorrhoid

Liver and biliary tract

- Hepatitis (A, B and C);
- Liver steatosis (fatty liver);
- Gallstones: they form in gallbladder (or gallbladder);
- Liver cancer (hepato-carcinoma);
- Liver cirrhosis: change in liver structure that occurs when part of it is damaged (alcohol abuse, hepatitis) and replaced by scar tissue that does not exhibit the same functionality as original liver cells;
- Cholecystitis: inflammation of the gallbladder

Pancreas

- Pancreatitis: acute or chronic inflammation of the pancreas;
- Pancreatic cancer.

Inflammatory bowel disease

IBD

Inflammatory bowel disease (IBD) is a group of chronic phlogistic diseases, which affect the large intestine (ulcerative recto colitis) or any stretch of the digestive tract, from the mouth to the anus (Crohn's disease). There are several types of inflammatory bowel diseases, such as ischemic and lymphocytic colitis, but Crohn's disease and ulcerative colitis are by far the most common diseases.

The etiology of these diseases, that is, the cause of origin, remains unknown, while the evolution of the same (pathogenesis) is considered autoimmune; probably, supported by a genetic predisposition, the immune system tends to "go crazy" - often already at a young age - by throwing its cells excessively and inadequately at those of the digestive system, more frequently than the intestine. In response to this accumulation of immune cells in the walls of the digestive tract, a chronic inflammatory reaction arises that disrupts its normal anatomy and disturbs its function.

Despite chronic adjective, manifestations of inflammatory bowel diseases are not uniform but typically marked by periods of remission and recurrence. The most common symptoms that accompany them are: abdominal pain, vomiting, diarrhea, flatulence, blood in the stool, abundant presence of mucus in the droppings, frequent stimulus to evacuation with a sense of incomplete intestinal emptying (tenesm) and weight loss.

Even important variations in the alve create adaptation problems in many cases and end up influencing social relations and work activity. However, all these symptoms are not exclusive to inflammatory bowel diseases, but common to various conditions - not necessarily morbid - affecting the intestine (spastic colitis, stress colitis, alterations in microbial flora etc.).

What distinguishes chronic inflammatory diseases of the intestine are therefore not the symptoms themselves, but the structural and biochemical alterations encountered by more or less extensive digestive tracts, in particular intestines.

It is no coincidence that the diagnosis of inflammatory bowel disease can generally not ignore colonoscopy, during which a biopsy removal of the mucosa is carried out for the subsequent histological examination, previously flanked by clinical tests (search for inflammatory markers in the blood, such as ESR and PCR, which still remain non-specific and poorly sensitive).

Other instrumental diagnostic tests, such as MRI or soft clema, may be required, for example when Crohn's disease causes digestive lesions that are not endoscopically achievable.

Another distinctive feature between inflammatory bowel diseases and those without a phlogistic component is the frequent detection, in the former, of clinical manifestations also of an extraintestinal nature, especially at the level of the skin (erythema nodosum and granulomatous dermatitis), Liver (primary sclerosing cholangitis), joints (arthritis, ankylosing spondylitis) and eyes.

Currently there is no standardized and universally effective therapeutic protocol; in the acute phases the most powerful anti-inflammatory drugs existing in therapy are generally used, cortisones, but they must be taken only for short periods of time. Salicylates, immunosuppressive drugs or antibodies to TNF alpha (a molecule produced by immune cells) may also be used in the stages of remission, alternatively or in combination with them. In severe cases surgery may be necessary, sometimes with a resolving therapeutic effect.

Digestion and Modern Eating Habits

Digestion is an essential process for the life of humans and many other living organisms. Feeding is not only an instinct, but a pleasure, an indispensable rite aimed at socializing and the very survival of the species. Over the millennia our body has undergone a continuous adaptation process necessary to cope with climate and environmental change. Among these, a primary role has been played by the diet.

As a hunter and collector of berries and tubers, primitive man gradually switched to agriculture and breeding, radically changing both lifestyle and eating habits.

While all this has allowed for greater food availability, it has definitely limited the variety of foods in the diet. Since then, cereals have been the essential basis of human nutrition.

Over the centuries, as social and economic conditions improved, additional foods were associated with these crops. Think, for example, of the introduction of corn and potato in the aftermath of the discovery of America. Despite the evolution of agricultural knowledge, however, it is necessary to wait for the industrial revolution in order to appreciate the first significant changes in the food field.

Since the First World War, the economic wave that has traveled the most industrialized countries has suddenly expanded food availability. Over the course of a few years the food industry has literally revolutionized the dietary habits of millions of people. In addition to the countless benefits of this food boom, however, the foundations have been laid for many of the digestive problems that afflict millions of people around the world every day.

Overeating and poor eating habits are among the main factors underlying digestive problems.

Digestive difficulties, grouped under the generic term dyspepsia (from the Greek "dys-pepsia", meaning "bad digestion"), are responsible for symptoms such as lack of appetite, stomach heaviness, fatigue, drowsiness, belching, bad breath, flatulence.

What is Dyspepsia

The term dyspepsia refers to a condition summarily described by the patient as "bad digestion".

The sharp increase and widespread spread of this problem in industrialized countries testifies how dyspepsia is a disorder related to lifestyle and dietary habits typical of the Western world.

Symptoms

Typical symptoms of dyspepsia are located in the upper abdomen and may include:

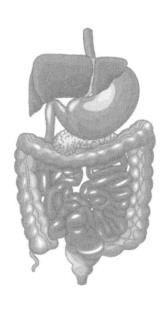

- Heartburn;
- heartburn;
- Acid regurgitation;
- Eruptions;
- Halitosis;
- Pain in the upper abdomen;
- Long and laborious sense of digestion;
- Intolerance to fats, fried meat, meat and eggs.

In order to cure it you should have a specialized medical examination that allows you to obtain a precise diagnosis (e.g. gastroscopy, opaque meal, blood tests, etc.); Cure any organic diseases such as ulcers, gallbladder and bile tract stones, celiac disease etc.

Eliminate or at least reduce risk factors such as NSAID intake, obesity, smoking alcohol, sedentary lifestyle and overweight.

If all these problems are removed, digestive difficulties remain, we speak of functional dyspepsia, that is, a form of disease not linked to organic causes (dyspeptic disorders of a benign nature). In any case, there are very effective drug treatments specific to the symptoms felt.

Excluding food allergies or intolerances, our body is perfectly capable of digesting any food deemed edible. Digestion is still a complex process, which requires a lot of energy from the body (about 15% of daily calorie needs). For this reason, calorie constraint is essential to ensure good food digestion.

The distribution of food into several meals is precisely intended to make digestion easier while preventing the appearance of uncontrollable hunger attacks. Condensing all the food into a single meal would instead be like concentrating the work of a whole day in a few hours, surely the performance would be very low and the nerves would not withstand stress.

On the contrary, taking a regenerating break every now and then would help to regain energy and concentration to better face work commitments.

The same result can be obtained by consuming 3 main meals (breakfast, lunch, dinner) possibly flanked by one or more snacks. In this way digestive problems disappear or at least are considerably reduced.

The maximum amount of food ingestible in a single meal must therefore also be calibrated according to the commitments following food intake. For example, if you feel a strong "stomach hole" an hour before starting a very intense physical or mental activity, it is good to consume a quick snack, easily digestible and not too caloric.

For a 75 kg normal weight, a meal should not indicatively exceed 600-800 kcal. However, a particularly active person such as an athlete may not be able to comply with this constraint even by evenly dividing calories into the three main meals. In this case, snack consumption is the only solution to better redistribute calorie intake throughout the day.

Interestingly, calories are used and not grams to quantify the maximum dose of food that can be consumed with each meal. It is no coincidence that, it is generally precisely the most caloric foods that cause the greatest digestive problems.

Poor digestion and behavioral habits

Sometimes poor digestion is because of some of our habits at the table, let's see some…

The first digestion, you know, takes place in the mouth. That's why eating in a hurry without chewing food for a long time often causes digestive problems. In addition, this behavior prevents you from fully savoring its taste and aromas, inevitably leading to eating more than necessary. The resulting calorie excess is precisely one of the most common causes of the onset of digestive problems.

It must also be considered that digestion, like any other activity of the body, also requires energy that is necessarily subtracted from other metabolic functions at that time less important.

It is no coincidence that during digestive activity the blood supply to the digestive system increases in proportion to the difficulty of the digestive process. Fatigue and drowsiness at the end of a meal are precisely the symptoms of a decrease in blood and oxygen in the brain in favor of the stomach and other organs that form the digestive system.

And if our worker were so willing that he started working immediately after the meal, his performance would still be lower. To promote digestion, it is therefore necessary to eat in total tranquility, perhaps having a chat and maintaining the relaxing condition for at least half an hour after the end of the meal.

Feeling a strong knot in the stomach as a result of a strong emotion is a situation in which everyone, at least once in their life, has found themselves.

Unfortunately, such moods are not always as pleasant as the birth of a new love. Anxiety, stress, dissatisfaction and restrained anger are undoubtedly some of the most influential components of digestive processes.

In these situations, the stomach acts as a real tension accumulator, heavily interfering in normal digestion. In some predisposed people, such problems are accompanied by even rather serious eating disorders such as anorexia or bulimia.

A subject's work habits can strongly affect food digestion. For example, if we think of stress, poor quality fast lunches, too large dinners or the lack of fixed times to have meals, we can easily imagine how these factors often cause dyspepsia.

To keep the situation under control, it is good to choose with criteria the foods to be consumed during lunch break, possibly considering the possibility of taking them from home.

It is also important to eat your meals calmly, possibly sitting, allowing yourself at least 20-30 mins of relaxation before resuming work.

The last, but certainly not least, criterion that can influence digestion concerns the effectiveness of one's digestive system. In fact, all the factors examined so far have a strong subjective component. Just to cite one example, an unfavorable food combination for some might be well digestible for others.

To regularize your digestion you must therefore learn to listen to your body, taking advantage of the signals it sends us.

Physical activity is considered an important means of prevention and treatment for dyspepsia. A little motion improves the functionality of the digestive system and helps keep body weight under control. However, it seems that certain sports such as running, lost lifting and hockey due to high tension and intra abdominal pressure, are indirectly due to esophageal reflux, therefore poor digestion.

A very felt and rather widespread disorder is represented by poor digestion, technically called dyspepsia: often bad digestion is accompanied by heartburn, belching, acid regurgitation, constipation, drowsiness, nausea and slowing gastric and pancreatic functions.

The underlying causes of dyspeptic disorders can be of various kinds: in fact, they range from incorrect, excessive and unbalanced nutrition, to Helicobacter pylori infections, from stress to the abuse of nonsteroidal anti-inflammatory drugs (NSAIDs) with a gastrolesive effect.

Obviously, liver diseases and disorders of the gastro intestinal tract can also result in dyspepsia.

When the cause of poor digestion is not an organic pathology, natural remedies are a valid and effective aid.

Drugs such as gentian, artichoke, ginger, licorice, chamomile, mint and bitter drugs in general (rhubarb, boldo, fennel, cumin, dandelion, chicory etc.) have the ability to to tone the functions of the organs involved in the early stages of digestion: they promote gastric and salivary secretion, help liver and pancreatic functions, and confer gastric tone.

A correct lifestyle, a light and regular diet free of excesses is also recommended; the way you are used to eating should also be correct because, if you tend to eat fast, you engage air that creates swelling and discomfort in the abdominal level.

Herbalism is provided with natural formulations that help the body perform proper digestion: in this article we will analyze two valid products to be considered as a model to counteract dyspepsia.

Chewable tablets are very practical, because they dissolve slowly in the mouth without the need for preparation, as happens with herbal teas and infusions. It is recommended to take the product twice a day after the main meals.

Apple (apple juice extract): it is inserted into an anti-dyspepsia product due to the presence of organic acids - malic, tartaric, succinic and citric - which seem to exert a positive tropism on basal metabolism, improving its expression and favoring the production of digestive juices.

Chicory (Cichorium intybus): despite its very bitter taste, rendered by the presence of inulin, chicory is able to stimulate appetite (taken before meals) and promote digestion, regulating intestinal, liver and kidney functions; it promotes, in fact, diuresis and the production of bile. Its purifying and detoxifying effect is also known.

Ginger (Zingiber officinalis): Some active ingredients with digestive activity are obtained from ginger root. Not surprisingly, ginger, commonly called ginger, is widely exploited for the manufacture of aperitifs and liqueurs. In addition, ginger is considered for its carminative properties, which allow less intestinal gas to be produced and decrease the fermentation process. It should be remembered, however, that ginger is unable to adsorb intestinal gases, as this function is attributed only to clay and coal.

Licorice (Glycyrrhiza glabra): The saponins contained exhibit gastro-productive activity, while flavonoids exert eupeptic activity. Licorice is configured as an aromatic and stomachic drug.

Gentian (Genziana lutea) could not miss gentian, a digestive, tonic and eupeptic drug par excellence, thanks to the iridoids contained, precisely genziopicrina, amarogentin and gentiopicroside.
This natural remedy is not recommended for diabetics (due to the presence of apple extract) and for those suffering from gastric heartburn (because it could boost heartburn). It should not be taken in conjunction with NSAIDs, because being gastrolesive could aggravate the problem.

Digestive herbal tea

Mint and gentian are recommended drugs to lighten disorders related to poor digestion; in particular the presence of anise and caraway, while verbena and yarrow are lesser-known plants in an herbal product of this type. Licorice is a "corrigens" element, therefore flavor corrector.

Mint (Mentha x piperita): it represents an excellent drug with tonic-eupeptic properties thanks to menthol, the active ingredient that characterizes the phytocomplex: it relaxes the muscle tissues of the stomach. It is spasmolytic and is widely used for gastrointestinal disorders. Mint is not recommended in individuals who have gastric ulcers because menthol stimulates the production of acidic juices, enhancing the pre-existing problem.

Gentian (Genziana lutea), as already analyzed, gentian boasts tonic, eupeptic and digestive properties.

Anise (Pimpinella anisum): carminary drug capable of decreasing abdominal bloating thanks to molecules that limit gastric fermentation caused by intestinal flora. The phytocomplex is mainly characterized by anetol, a very volatile terpenoid molecule.

Carvi (Carum carvi): a drug characterized by terpenes and flavonoids, performs a digestive action in synergy with anise: improves liver, intestinal and pancreatic activity, decreases disorders derived from a lazy metabolism, soothes abdominal swelling.

Verbena (Lippia citriodora) is a medicinal plant consisting of verbenin, verbanaloside, verbenone, tannins and other constituents that give the product decidedly appreciated organoleptic properties (corregens" drug, along with licorice). If verbena herbal tea is taken before meals, digestive function is favored: in this regard, it is also used in remedies against gastralgies (stomach pain).

Achillea (Achilea millefolium): Among the active ingredients that make up the phytocomplex we remember lactone sesquiterpenes (achillin, achillicin), flavonoids (apigenin, quercetin), alkaloids, tannins and organic acids;

the essential oil is rich in pinene, bornyl, camphor and eugenol. For internal use, achillea exerts bitter-tonous, choleretic activities and is also used for gastro-intestinal disorders such as gastritis, gastric spasms and digestive difficulties.

Licorice (Glycyrrhiza glabra): In this case, licorice is a "corrigens" drug because it corrects the organoleptic of herbal tea, consisting mainly of bitter drugs.
While considering it "natural", this herbal remedy has some contraindications: for this reason, before buying any "self-medication" product it would be useful to talk to your doctor about it.
In fact, the herbal tea and tablets analyzed are not recommended for those with bile problems, since there are drugs that act on the liver stimulating the gallbladder; consequently they could cause col.
In addition, if these natural remedies are adopted by jets taking tricyclic antidepressants, because they suffer from depression, the contrast between the active ingredients could result in insomnia. Finally, in the presence of chronic dyspepsia, natural products against poor digestion generally fail to bring a substantial benefit.

Ancient remedies

Although there is no scientific foundation, popular tradition has always managed to express its wisdom, for or without reason. Even in the case of difficult digestion, tradition involves the use of some plants such as mallow, lemon balm and sage. Furthermore, the habit of eating garlic seemed to promote digestion, as well as cooked onion, which due to its water content promotes diuresis and supports proper kidney function. Celery also seemed to be a valuable aid for digestion: so much so that we remember a popular saying "if the farmer knew the value of celery, then he would fill his whole garden". In addition to being considered an aphrodisiac plant (still dubious property) and useful for the treatment of open wounds, it also served to promote digestion, relieve abdominal cramps and was considered an excellent diuretic. Finally, horseradish was exploited for its stimulating properties on the production of saliva, gastric juices, as a result it was an excellent natural aid for digestion.

Dissociated diet against digestive problems

At this point it is necessary to introduce the principles underlying the dissociated diet and its variants. In reality, more than real diets, these are food fashions that, due to countless errors of evaluation, have not found a wide consensus among doctors and professionals in the sector.
The composition of the meal in terms of macronutrients is in fact important as the various foods we eat require conflicting or even opposite digestive processes. Studying these associations, a list of unfavorable food combinations has been drawn up, the simultaneous digestion of which creates some problems for the body.

Proteins and carbohydrates

The digestive enzymes that intervene in the digestion of these two classes of nutrients compete with each other. Protein needs an acidic environment to be digested while carbohydrates need a basic environment. Protein intake along with carbohydrates therefore causes a digestion stoppage of both, as carbohydrates, forced to stay longer than necessary in the stomach, give rise to putreffetive processes.
The simpler or high glycemic index carbohydrates (sugar, sugary fruit, sweets, honey, etc.) and the greater the digestive problems will be.

Acids and carbohydrates

Acidic foods and drinks (wine, beer, vinegar, sour fruit, fruit juices and some sugary drinks), tend to lower gastric pH by hindering carbohydrate digestion. These foods are instead indicated to promote the digestion of a protein meal since, as we have already seen, proteins are better digested in an acidic environment.

Fats and Proteins

Especially cooked fats tend to slow down the digestion times of proteins in the intestine giving rise to putrefactive processes that can only be balanced by the simultaneous intake of raw vegetables.

Fruit

We can divide this category of foods into two large groups: sour fruit (lemons, melons, apricots, oranges, apples, cherries) and sugary fruit (cheeks, grapes, figs, dates, chestnuts). Since the first increases gastric acidity by counteracting the digestion of the sugars present in the second, it would be good never to associate these two types of fruit with each other.

Scrupulous observance of these rules necessarily leads to an impoverishment of the diet, both qualitatively and quantitatively.

Those who eat poorly and are overweight are more likely to suffer from digestive problems than a normal-weight who follows a balanced diet. It is therefore necessary to follow some important rules in the dietary field such as the reduction of fats (especially saturated ones) in favor of fiber, vitamins and antioxidants of which raw fruits and vegetables are particularly rich. Fish than meat, in addition to having a better lipid profile, is less rich in connective tissue, therefore more easily digestible.

It is not enough to eat better, you have to strive to eat several times a day and in addition to the three main meals (breakfast, lunch and dinner) possibly insert a snack in the mid-morning and afternoon.

Poor food quality

Today on our tables you can find foods from anywhere in the world at affordable prices.

Unfortunately, in many cases the quality of food does not go hand in hand with the economic possibilities of the consumer or with his dietary knowledge. On the other hand, the food industry, like other commercial activities, is certainly not immune to profit ambitions and this most often comes at the expense of the quality of their products. It often takes puzzling news such as anabolic in meat, mercury in fish, or dioxin in chickens to momentarily awaken the critical spirit of the consumer. In reality, it would be enough to know the real properties of chemical additives or other substances used in the food field to stay away from many of the many existing products on the market.

If these substances taken individually in limited doses are completely harmless, the same cannot be said if their consumption lasts for a long time or if they are taken for years by adding them to other chemical additives.

Frying food develops, for example, numerous toxic substances, depending on the type of oil used and the cooking temperature.

One pound of grilled meat contains roughly the same amount of benzopyrene (an extremely carcinogenic hydrocarbon) found in 600 cigarettes.

The combination of toxic substances, chemical additives and poor quality foods inevitably leads to intoxication of the body whose easily observable symptoms include dermatitis, increased body weight, fatigue, headache and digestive problems.

Regular consumption of fruits and vegetables combined with a little physical activity instead helps to reduce the absorption of these substances while favoring their elimination.

If we ingest two foods that require different digestive processes we inevitably face a slowdown in digestion, which compromises the absorption of various nutrients.

This deficit will be responsible for phenomena such as:

- Sense of heaviness
- Excessive prolongation of digestion
- Partial digestion and fermentation of ingested food
- Partial assimilation of the various nutrients
- Gastrointestinal disorders (stomach acid, bad breath, flatulence, constipation etc.).

WHAT ARE THE CORRECT FOOD PAIRINGS?

Although supporters of the dissociated diet consider single-plate the winning solution to promote digestive processes, there are compatible foods that can be safely matched.
Below are some basic rules for fostering digestive processes:

- Avoid combining different types of protein (milk and meat, eggs and cheese, fish and legumes)
- Avoid pairing carbohydrates with meat
- Avoid combining different types of carbohydrates (simple and complex such as sugar and pasta or grapes and bread, banana and bread)
- Avoid combining protein sources of different kinds (e.g. meat and fish or legumes and dairy products)
- Desert the classic habit of ending the meal with fruit and / or dessert; better to consume these foods alone and at different times of the day
- Body balance is disturbed by the modern lifestyle, which promotes the accumulation of toxins to the point of compromising the functionality of the entire body. To defend against the pitfalls of this dangerous condition, it is necessary to increase the consumption of fruits, vegetables, smoothies and vegetable broths that, together with caloric moderation and correct food associations, promote detoxification of the body.
- If on the one hand the dissociated diet encourages the intake of plant foods, on the other it warns of the dangers of a diet too rich in animal products (cardio circulatory, metabolic diseases and some forms of cancer)
- Then there is the "flexible" indication not to associate different sources of complex carbohydrates with each other, not so much for the digestive problems that derive from them, but to avoid taking excessive caloric intake.
- Carbohydrate consumption must be maximum during the early stages of the day and progressively decrease as you approach dinner
- The most abundant meal should be taken from 1 pm to 4 pm, always being careful not to associate carbohydrates and proteins
- Dinner must be rich in protein foods and almost completely exclude carbohydrates, with the exception of complex ones contained in vegetables or in modest amounts of whole grains

Attention: Learning how to match foods properly is certainly helpful but turning this concept into the most important aspect of your diet is deeply wrong.
The first seven points are the backbone of the dissociated diets most attentive to the health aspect and aimed above all at the prevention of gastrointestinal problems related to poor eating habits (aerophobia, flatulence, fatigue, loss of postprandial concentration, etc.).

Focus on: Diverticulitis

What is diverticula?

Diverticula consists of areas in the intestinal wall that weaken, yield and form small extroflexions (similar to pockets) that swell outwards through the weakest points of the intestinal muscle wall. Colon diverticula are extroflexions, a kind of small sacs that form along the intestinal walls. All sectors of the food channel can give rise to diverticula but the colon is where their presence is most common.

Diverticula can be congenital in nature (present from birth) or acquired. In the first case the extroflexion also includes the muscle wall, in the second it affects only the mucosal cassock and serous.

Diverticular disease was rare before the 20th century. However, it is now one of the commonest health problems in the Western world. Diverticular disease is a group of conditions that can affect your digestive system. Diverticulitis is the most serious type of diverticular disease. Its symptoms are usually very uncomfortable. If left untreated, the complications may trigger chronic health problems.

Probably, the development of diverticula is related to an alteration in intestinal motility, followed by a local increase in pressure that leads to a leakage of the mucosa at the points of least resistance of the intestine.

We are talking about:

- Diverticulosis, when there are one more asymptomatic diverticula in the walls of the intestine, which do not produce any signs or symptoms of the disease. The portion of the intestine predominantly affected by diverticulosis is the colon, especially the sigma and the left colon. Due to the lack of symptoms, most people find that they have diverticula completely randomly, for example in the course of radiological or endoscopic investigations of the colon carried out for other reasons;

- Diverticular disease (Symptomatic Uncomplicated diverticular diseases - SUDD) when diverticula are present in the intestine and, at the same time, non-specific symptoms occur (e.g. abdominal pain, belly cramps, etc.) presumably attributable to diverticula, but in the absence of inflammation (diverticulitis). Diverticular disease can take on both acute and chronic form;

- Diverticulitis when diverticular (per-)inflammation affecting the gut wall is present. This is an important complication that must be kept under strict medical supervision since it can cause various damage to health (major bleeding and subsequent condition of anemia, perforation or fistolization resulting in peritonitis, obstruction followed by an intestinal occlusion, etc.). In case of diverticulitis, antibiotic therapy is necessary and surgery is not excluded, in the most serious cases.

Diverticulitis is the most serious type of diverticular disease. Its symptoms are usually very uncomfortable. If left untreated, the complications may trigger chronic health problems.

The treatment which is prescribed for this condition depends on the severity of your condition.

The uncomplicated form of this disease can easily be treated at home. Your doctor might recommend changes in your diet. In some cases, medications may be prescribed including antibiotics.

If complications develop as a result of the condition (diverticulitis), you'll probably need to visit a health facility for treatment. Treatment may be through intravenous administration of antibiotics or fluids. Depending on the type of complication, you may be required to undergo a surgical procedure.

The condition can be prevented by altering the risk factors such as inactivity, smoking, and obesity.

The diagnosis of diverticulosis, diverticular disease and diverticulitis should be made by the gastroenterologist doctor on the basis of their medical history, objective examination, laboratory tests and image tests (ecography, CT scan and MRI). Diverticulitis, unfortunately, often recurs, so it is very important to periodically undergo specific checks.

What causes diverticulitis

There is no single known cause of diverticular disease. Research and clinical experience have shown that multiple environmental and genetic factors may contribute to its development.

Treatment prescribed for this condition depends on the severity of your condition.

The uncomplicated form of this disease can typically be treated at home.

Your doctor might recommend dietary changes. In some cases, medications may be prescribed including antibiotics.

If complications develop as a result of the condition (diverticulitis), you'll probably need to visit a health facility for treatment. Treatment may be through intravenous administration of antibiotics or fluids. Depending on the type of complication, you may be required to undergo a surgical procedure.

The condition can be prevented by altering the risk factors such as inactivity, smoking, and obesity. Avoiding seeds and nuts as a preventive measure is no longer recommended since there is no scientific evidence that these contribute to inflammation in diverticula.

Studies have shown that up to 35 percent of people in the Western world have diverticulosis. In rural Africa, less than one percent of the population is affected, while 4-15% of these may develop diverticulitis.

The frequency of the disease increases with age, being particularly common in 50 years old people.

Poor eating habits, characterized for example by excessive consumption of refined foods (eg cereals, bread, pasta, rice), meats, fats, preserved foods, etc. and a low intake of fiber-rich foods (fruits, vegetables, legumes, whole grains), represent the first cause of the greatest prevalence of colon diverticular disease.

The primary goal of the diet when diverticula are not inflamed (sense phase) will, therefore, be to promote proper intestinal motility and protect the mucosa of the intestine from inflammatory stimuli. However, in case of diverticulitis, nutrition must be discontinued and artificial nutrition must be used.

Once the acute phase of the disease has been resolved, it is advisable to gradually resume feeding following some particular nutritional measures. In these cases, the right therapy must be set by the gastroenterologist based on the extent of symptoms and may range from an appropriate diet with probiotic supplementation, to specific anti-inflammatory care.

Almost 40% of the population between the ages of 40 and 55 are carriers of diverticula. In the 70- to 80-year-old group, the incidence of diverticulosis reaches almost 70-80% of the population.

Although diverticula can appear at any age among the elderly and the earlier symptoms arise and the greater the risk of complications (recurrent diverticulitis, ulcerations, etc.).

The prevalence of the disease in subjects under 30 despite being very low (1-2%) is set to rise due to the continuous worsening of dietary habits and lifestyle (to take root, read: diet for diverticulosis).

Women are about twice as likely to develop diverticula than men.

Fiber is found in fruits, vegetables, and unrefined (whole meal) grains and is a substance that the body is unable to digest completely. Some fibers, called soluble fibers, dissolve easily in water creating a soft, gelatinous material in the intestine, While the insoluble fiber passes almost unchanged through the intestines.

Both types of fiber help prevent constipation by promoting the formation of soft, easy-to-expel stools.

Constipation manifests itself by forcing the patient to make considerable efforts to defecate; stress can cause increased pressure in the colon which in turn can cause the colon lining to bulge through weak spots in the colon wall. These pockets are diverticula. Lack of exercise can increase the risk of diverticula formation, although this aspect is not considered decisive. Doctors are not sure why diverticula became inflamed, it is hypothesized that the cause is bacteria or feces stagnating inside.

Risks

Diverticulitis can lead to consequences such as bleeding, infections, intestinal perforations, obstructions in the colon. These issues always require medical treatment to prevent them from progressing causing more serious problems.

Rectal bleeding caused by diverticula is a rare complication; it is believed to be caused by a small blood vessel in a diverticulum that weakens until it bursts. When diverticula bleed, the patient usually sees it in the stool and sanitary ware following defecation; bleeding can be abundant and, despite resolving spontaneously without requiring treatment, it is still advisable to evaluate what happened with your doctor.

Colonoscopy is often used to identify the bleeding site and stop bleeding that does not heal spontaneously. If despite all the bleeding does not stop, surgery may be necessary to remove the areas of the colon involved.

Diverticulitis can cause infection, which disappears after a few days of antibiotic treatment.

If the infection worsens, an abscess can form in the colon wall, that is, a collection of localized pus that can cause swelling and destroy the tissue: if the abscess is small and remains in the colon wall following treatment with antibiotics it tends to disappear, if it does not disappear it may be necessary to drain the area with a catheter and a this treatment requires patient sedation.

Infected diverticula can develop perforations, sometimes with pus leakage from the colon due to a large abscess in the abdominal cavity, which is called peritonitis. A person with peritonitis is extremely debilitated and experiences nausea, vomiting, fever, severe abdominal flaccidity.

The situation requires immediate surgery to clean the abdominal cavity and remove the damaged part of the colon. Without treatment, peritonitis can be fatal.

A fistula is an abnormal tissue connection between two organs or between an organ and the skin. When damaged tissues come into contact with each other during infection, they sometimes get sick and the process of subsequent repair can form a fistula.

When diverticulitis is related to an infection, the infection spreads outside the colon with the ability to infect nearby tissues, usually bladder, small intestines, and skin. The most common type of fistula occurs between the bladder and colon, this type of fistula affects men more often than women, and can turn into a serious long-lasting urinary tract infection.

The problem can be solved with surgery to remove the fistula and the affected part of the colon.

Scars caused by infection can lead to partial or total intestinal blockage called intestinal obstruction. When the intestine is blocked the colon is no longer able to move the intestinal contents normally. If the intestine is completely blocked emergency surgery is required, while partial blockage does not normally require surgery.

Chronic inflammation affecting the human body can cause serious diseases such as Alzheimer's, cancer, rheumatoid arthritis and heart diseases.

Normally, inflammation is the body's reaction to infection or injury. Signs of inflammation are swelling, redness and pain.

However, when it lasts longer or when it appears without any apparent reason, it is a sign that the body is taking damage. Lifestyle habits such as smoking, stressful work, lack of exercise and unhealthy meals can trigger chronic inflammation.

For a patient to fight inflammation and to prevent it from getting serious, he/she has to undergo an anti-inflammatory diet. Aside from helping with weight loss, the diet plan can also help prevent diseases. It aids in keeping a patient's health in balance.

Diagnosis

To diagnose diverticular disease, the doctor reconstructs the patient's medical history through an accurate and scrupulous series of questions, continues with an in-depth medical examination and can use one or more diagnostic tests if necessary.

Because most people experience no symptoms, diverticulosis is often diagnosed through tests ordered for another disorder. For example, it can be discovered during a colonoscopy performed for polyps, or to assess the causes of pain or rectal bleeding.Considering the medical history, the doctor can inquire about bowel habits, pain, other symptoms, diet and medications taken by the patient. Physical examination usually involves a digital rectal examination: the doctor inserts a lubricated finger into the rectum to detect flaccidity, blockage, or bleeding. You can check your stool to see if there are signs of bleeding and your blood test to detect signs of infection.

If diverticulitis is suspected, your doctor may order one of the following radiological examinations:

- **Abdominal ultrasound.** Sound waves are sent to the colon through a handheld device that is slipped by a technician into the abdomen. Sound waves bounce in the colon and other organs, and their echo creates electrical impulses that can create an image, called a sonogram, on a monitor. If diverticula are inflamed the sound waves bounce showing their location.

- **Computed tomography.** It is a non-invasive X-ray photograph that produces sections of body images. The doctor may inject a tincture into a vein or may require the patient to ingest the substance while lying on a table flowing inside a shell-shaped machine. The dye helps show complications from diverticulitis, such as perforations and abscesses.

Drug therapy

Treatment for diverticulitis is focused on preventing inflammation and infection, resting the colon, and preventing or reducing complications. If you experience cramps, swelling, constipation and other symptoms your doctor may prescribe a short course of anti-inflammatories, although some pain medications cause constipation.

Some work has shown potential utility related to the administration of lactic acid bacteria, in terms of preventing the symptoms of diverticulosis and developing infections.

Depending on the severity of the symptoms, the doctor may recommend that the patient rest in bed, he may prescribe oral antibiotics, painkillers and a liquid diet. If symptoms disappear after a few days you can gradually increase the amount of high fiber foods. Severe cases of diverticulitis with acute pain and complications may require hospital stay, but most patients are treated with antibiotics and a couple of days of fasting (or drinking) to aid colon rest. Only rarely can surgery be needed. If diverticulitis symptoms are frequent or if the patient does not respond to antibiotics and colon rest, the doctor may recommend surgery.

The surgeon removes the affected part of the colon and joins the remaining sections. This type of surgery, called colon resection, prevents complications and diverticulitis. Your doctor may also recommend surgery for complications such as a fistula or partial intestinal obstruction. Immediate surgery may be necessary when the patient has other complications, such as perforation, a large abscess, peritonitis, complete intestinal obstruction, or severe bleeding. In these cases, two surgeries may be needed as it is not certain that the colon will rejoin immediately.

 During the first surgery the surgeon cleans the infected abdominal cavity, removes the affected part of the colon and performs a temporary colostomy, creating an artificial anus, in the abdomen. The end of the colon is connected to the opening to allow the patient to eat normally during the healing process. Several months later, in the second surgery, the surgeon rejoins the ends of the colon and closes the stomata.

What can you do to avoid diverticulitis

In order to avoid diverticulitis you should take an adequate amount of fiber, about 30-40 grams per day; Moisturize enough, at least 1.5-2 L of fluids per day; Follow the recommendations for proper nutrition in the general population regarding the reduction of especially animal fats, beverages and sugar-rich foods; Cook without adding fat. Prefer simple cooking methods such as steaming, microwave, grill or hotplate, in a pressure cooker and non-stick pan. Avoid frying and boiled meat; On the recommendation of your doctor, or in any case with his approval, you can consume dietary supplements based on fiber powder. During the inflammatory phase, so in the presence of diverticulitis, dietary recommendations change! It is advisable to prefer a liquid or semi-liquid diet with a reduced fiber content. This type of diet, low in fiber and waste, should be followed with the supervision of the doctor and only for limited periods of time.

Symptoms

The risk of diverticula inflamed by evolving into diverticulitis fortunately is quite low. Typically only 20% of people with diverticula experience symptoms, and only 10-15% develop diverticular disease or diverticulitis. Although the percentages are apparently modest, these are still respectable figures since in reality, considering the large incidence of the disease, we are talking about millions of people. Colon diverticulitis is therefore a pathologist with a very high social impact.

The symptoms of diverticular disease are quite varied:

- Feeling of discomfort and abdominal pain
- Abdominal pain at palpation
- Meteorism, flatulence
- Abdominal cramps
- Mass detectable at the abdominal level
- Abdominal pain generally located in the left side

- Alterations of the alvo with alternation of constipation-diarrhea
- Fever and abdominal pain
- Bleeding complication (intestinal bleeding) in 3-5 % of patients

The most common symptom is abdominal pain, while the characteristic sign detected during the medical examination is flaccidity at the bottom left of the belly. The pain is usually severe and manifests itself suddenly, but it can also be mild in principle and gradually worsen over several days, thus increasing in intensity.

Only 20% of diverticula's experience symptoms. Of these, 2% need one or more hospitalizations. Of these, 0.5% require surgery. Mortality from diverticulum-related causes is 1/10,000.

The most common symptom of diverticulitis is abdominal pain. North Americans and Europeans experience abdominal pain on the left lower side (sigmoid colon), while in Asia it is usually on the right (ascending colon).

If you develop any of the symptoms listed above, like blood in your stool or vomiting, then it may be an indication of a serious complication from diverticulitis or any other condition. You should see your doctor right away.

Diverticulosis is often diagnosed randomly, during the execution of tests prescribed for other purposes; for example, it is common to be discovered during the execution of a colonoscopy carried out for the purpose of screening for colorectal cancer.

In the presence of mild symptoms it is often sufficient to adopt a diet rich in fiber and take a slight painkiller as needed, while in case of more severe inflammation it is sometimes necessary to resort to antibiotics. Only in patients who develop severe forms of diverticulitis is surgery eventually considered.

Diverticular disease is common in industrialized countries and particularly those where low-fiber diets apply (United States, England, Australia). The disease is rare in Asia and Africa, where most people follow high-fiber diets.

SHOPPING LIST

A high-fiber diet and the use of painkillers help relieve pain in most cases of diverticulosis: Simple diverticulitis with mild symptoms usually requires the person to rest, take oral antibiotics and follow a liquid diet for a certain period of time. In some cases, the attack of diverticulitis is severe enough to require hospitalization, intravenous antibiotics and possibly surgery.

By increasing the amount of fiber in the diet, you can reduce the symptoms of diverticulosis and prevent complications such as diverticulitis: fiber maintains stool softness and lowers pressure inside the colon so that the intestinal contents can move easily. A consumption of 20 to 35 grams of fiber per day is recommended and possibly the doctor can also recommend taking a fiber supplement to always accompany plenty of water.

Eating high-fiber foods is the only requirement strongly emphasized throughout the medical literature, and although recent work seems to question the benefits in terms of preventing the development of diverticulosis, it is still a shared advice for the prevention of related symptoms and complications.

One observational study found those who ate 25 grams or more of fiber per day had a 41% lower risk of being hospitalized for diverticulitis compared to those who ate less than 14 grams per day.

Another study that followed more than 690,000 women without diverticular disease found that each additional 5 grams of fiber per day was associated with a 15% reduction in risk of diverticulitis.

Considering that fiber has numerous other known benefits for health, particularly in maintaining healthy gut bacteria, it makes sense to recommend a high fiber diet.

Unfortunately today most people only consume half of the recommended amount. Women should aim to get at least 25 grams per day, while the average man should have at least 38 grams per day. Which basically means eat more vegetables
and legumes.

Contrary to popular belief, it is not necessary to eliminate specific foods, maybe just to reduce them for a specific amount of time : the seeds of tomatoes, zucchini, cucumbers, strawberries, raspberries, as well as poppy seeds and others, are generally harmless. Instead, it is advisable to reduce the consumption of red meat, which seems to be linked to the likelihood of diverticulitis.

Decisions regarding diet must be made considering subjective differences, keeping a food diary can help identify foods that cause problems.

Probiotics are really important.

The best food sources of probiotics are fermented foods, such as yogurt, quark, Yakult, sauerkraut, kefir, tempeh, and miso.

Probiotic supplements are also a great option, but recommended dosage has yet to be determined

Food not allowed

- Vegetables that contain very hard and filamentary fiber, such as fennel, artichokes, green beans, etc. If you want to consume vegetables with these characteristics, it is advisable to take them chopped, centrifuged or cooked and sieved;
- Alcoholic (including wine and beer) and spirits, as they can irritate the intestinal wall;
- Tea, coffee, cola and all drinks that contain nerve substances in general (eg: energy drink);
- Spicy spices, such as pepper, chili pepper, curry, etc. ;
- Cocoa;
- sausage, salami, mortadella, cup and all processed meat in general;
- Carbonated drinks (e.g. sparkling water, cola, orangeade, lemonade, etc.) to avoid abdominal bloating;
- Milkshakes, whipped cream, mayonnaise, chewing gum and other foods that can cause flatulence

In the weeks following the inflammatory episode (diverticulitis), temporary intolerance to lactose, i.e. milk sugar, may occur. In these cases, milk and other foods that contain lactose should be eliminated from the diet (click here to consult the diet specifically for lactose intolerance). Milk and dairy products can be gradually reintroduced a few weeks after symptom remission.

Therefore, it is not recommended

- Milk
- Butter
- Fresh cheeses
- Lactose-containing sausages (such as cooked ham and sausages);
- Baked goods containing lactose (biscuits, snacks, cakes, croissants, etc.).

Foods allowed in moderation

- Legumes, to be consumed mainly passed or centrifuged to eliminate the skins;
- Decaffeinated tea and decaffeinated coffee;
- Low-lactose milk and dairy products, such as yogurt and some cheeses such as Grana Padano PDO, which is naturally lactose-free and contains less fat than the whole milk with which it is produced. A couple of teaspoons of grated grapes a day promote the satisfaction of the needs of essential milk nutrients, such as proteins with high biological value, calcium, vitamins and minerals essential for health;
- Meat, preferring white meat (chicken, turkey, rabbit) or the one chosen in the leanest and most deprived cuts of visible fat;

Allowed and recommended foods

- **Water**, drink at least 1.5-2 liters of liquids a day (preferably natural oligo mineral water, but unsweetened herbal teas and infusions or vegetable broth are also fine);
- **Vegetables**, consume at least one portion for lunch or dinner, raw or cooked. The richest vegetables in fiber are: lambs, asparagus, cauliflower, mushrooms, broccoli and chicory. However, since the ability of vegetables to retain water to increase stool volume is also important, lettuce, radicchio, carrots, zucchini and onions (rich inulin) are also very useful. Vegetable extracts are also recommended;
- **Fruit**, consume three fruits each the size of your fist every day. Prefer apples (containing pectin), oranges, pears and bananas (rich in inulin). The fruit should be eaten raw and preferably with the peel (if edible and well washed), to be chewed well before swallowing;
- Refined and whole grains (alternate 50/50), such as bread, pasta, rice, etc. ;
- Potatoes, not to be consumed as a side dish, as they are not vegetables.

Behavioral advice

You should practice physical activity regularly (walk at least 20-30 minutes a day and do gymnastics). Physical activity helps keep abdominal wall muscles toned, improves intestinal motility, and reduces stool stagnation in diverticula. A minimum of 150 minutes per week is recommended, optimal 300;

It is important to achieve a body weight appropriate to your height. In case of overweight or obesity, it is good to eliminate extra pounds through regular physical activity and an adequate diet. If you deal with overweight or obesity, we recommend that you consult a nutritionist to agree on a specific diet. Both in case of diverticulosis and in the presence of diverticulitis, it is important to stop smoking;

Remember to take adequate intakes of vitamin D. The role of this fat-soluble vitamin in diverticular disease has been studied for a long time and optimal values are necessary for prevention. Therefore, a fair daily intake and possible supplementation is recommended if its deficiency in the diet is found.

During the evening meal, to increase the intake of fiber and water, it is good to get used to consuming soups and vegetable purees. Increased fiber consumption can result in a temporary increase in meteorism, but that effect is set to disappear within a few weeks.

Fiber-induced meteorism can be reduced by gradually increasing the introduction of fiber (limiting cauliflower and broccoli), increasing water consumption and at the same time increasing physical activity.

28-DAY MEAL PLAN

The suggested meal plan is based on the de-inflammatory combination of foods, especially in the first two week of your diet, which present a lot of liquid foods. You should always prefer high-fibres dishes, without overdoing it or renounce to tasty recipes.

When you think you haven't really eaten high-fibres meals during the day, you can always rely on our delicious smoothies! They are liquid, fruit or vegetables-based and contain a lot of fibres.

They are also suitable for vegans and vegetarians, try them as a special and delicious snack.

If you have already eaten an heavy and highly-nutrient meal try to eat some carrots or fennels as a snack.

Remember that the key to a successful diet is constance, and in order to achieve it you should not renounce to your favourite meals or desserts. Try our tasty desserts! They are balanced, fruit-based, high in fibres and low in carbs and fats. If you think, it is going to be an heavy day you can also have a dessert for breakfast or snack.

When you finish your 28 days meal plans you can always try to combine the recipes contained in the same section of the one on the plan. In this way, you will have endless combination of meals, all healthy and tasty. Your intestine will be thankful!

Day 1
Breakfast: 6. Cranberry Bulgur Mix
Lunch: 51. Walnuts and Asparagus Combo
Dinner: 117. Mustard and Rosemary Pork Tenderloin

Day 2
Breakfast: 8. Fruit Salad with Yogurt Cream
Lunch: 90. Tomato and Avocado Salad
Dinner: 183. Salmon Skillet Supper

Day 3
Breakfast: 3. Breakfast Toast
Lunch: 279. Green Goddess Sauce
Dinner: 261. Fried Cauliflower Rice

Day 4
Breakfast: 302. The Green Go-Getter Smoothie
Lunch: 128. Tagine of Chicken and Olives
Dinner: 186. Herbed Panini Fillet 'Fish

Day 5
Breakfast: 343. Tofu and Spinach Frittata
Lunch: 411. Avocado Toast with Chickpeas
Dinner: 123. Marinated Balsamic Pork Loin Skillet

Day 6
Breakfast: 335. Hearty Bran Muffins
Lunch: 70. Turkish Appetizer Salad
Dinner: 267. Umami Chicken Burgers

Day 7
Breakfast: 305. Homemade Tomato Juice
Lunch: 284. Lentil and Lemon Soup
Dinner: 180. Miso-Glazed Tuna

Day 8
Breakfast: 318. Lime Vanilla Fudge
Lunch: 147. Vegetable and Beef Steak with Chimichurri
Dinner: 87. Minty Olives and Tomatoes Salad

Day 9
Breakfast: 300. Farmers' Market Smoothie
Lunch: 105. Delicious Rice and Spinach
Dinner: 52. Garlic Lemon Soup

Day 10
Breakfast: 10. Peanut Butter Popcorn
Lunch: 88. Beans and Cucumber Salad
Dinner 159. Stir-Fried Chicken Meal

Day 11
Breakfast: 303. Clementine Smoothie
Lunch: 365. Honey Roasted Cauliflower
Dinner: 168. Cool Greek Chicken Breast

Day 12
Breakfast 1. Hazelnut Pudding
Lunch: 167. Low-Carb Blackened Chicken
Dinner: 240. One pan Broiled Salmon with
Yellow Miso

Day 13
Breakfast: 3. Breakfast Toast
Lunch: 247. Baked Garlic marinade Arctic char
Fillets
Dinner: 143. Tamari Steak Salad

Day 14
Breakfast: 319. Blueberry Cake
Lunch: 370. Zucchini Fries and Sauce
Dinner: 269. Fresh Tomato Vinaigrette

Day 15
Breakfast: 334. Super Nutritious Carrot Cake
Bites
Lunch: 413. Ruby Red Root Beet Burger
Dinner: 70. Turkish Appetizer Salad

Day 16
Breakfast: 5. Fish Eggs
Lunch: 259. Radish Hash Browns with Onion
and Green Pepper
Dinner: 283. Wonton Soup

Day 17
Breakfast: 7. Hummus and Olive Pita Bread
Lunch: 282. "Cream" of Cauliflower Soup
Dinner: 217. Smoked Salmon, Cucumber, and
Avocado Sushi

Day 18
Breakfast: 334. Super Nutritious Carrot Cake
Bites
Lunch: 113. Grilled Burgers with Mushrooms
Dinner: 86. Cashews and Red Cabbage Salad

Day 19
Breakfast: 332. Pecan and Pear Breakfast
Lunch: 377. French Fries
Dinner: 194. Shrimps with Lemon and Pepper

Day 20
Breakfast: 304. Avocado Smoothie
Lunch: 130. Warm Tamari Steak Salad
Dinner: 268. Ultimate Guacamole

Day 21
Breakfast: 324. Banana-Oat Walnut Loaf
Lunch: 374. Vinegar Cucumber, Olives &Shallots
Salad
Dinner: 224. Salmon Meatballs with Garlic

Day 22
Breakfast: 2. Yogurt with Dates
Lunch: 44. Cool Avocado Chips
Dinner: 189. Seafood Stuffing

Day 23
Breakfast 12. Lentil Omelet
Lunch: 109. Raisin Rice Pilaf
Dinner 102. Papaya, Jicama, and Peas Rice Bowl

Day 24
Breakfast: 345. Simple Vegan Breakfast Hash
Lunch: 359. Roasted Jalapeño and Lime
Guacamole
Dinner: 298. Summer Rolls with Peanut Sauce

Day 25
Breakfast: 11. Avocado & Blueberry
Lunch: 97. Cherry, Apricot, & Pecan Brown Rice
Bowl
Dinner: 180. Miso-Glazed Tuna

Day 26
Breakfast: 330. Steamed Artichokes
Lunch: 389. Savory Sweet Potato Casserole
Dinner: 172. Tuna and spinach power bowl

Day 27
Breakfast: 305. Homemade Tomato Juice
Lunch: 152. Pan-Seared Pork Loin and Balsamic
Caramelized Onions
Dinner 241. Lemon Trout

Day 28
Breakfast: 447. Salted Caramel Coconut Balls
Lunch: 384. Cinnamon Cauliflower Rice,
Zucchinis. Spinach
Dinner: 200. Chicken and Apples Mix

BREAKFAST SWEET AND SALT

1. Hazelnut Pudding

Preparation Time: 10 minutes
Cooking Time: 40 minutes
Servings: 8
Ingredients:
- 2 and ¼ cups almond flour
- 3 tablespoons hazelnuts, chopped
- 5 eggs, whisked
- 1 cup stevia
- 1 and 1/3 cups Greek yogurt
- 1 teaspoon baking powder
- 1 teaspoon vanilla extract

Directions:
1. Mix the flour with the hazelnuts plus the other ingredients in a bowl, and pour into a cake pan lined with parchment paper.
2. Introduce in the oven at 350 degrees F, bake for 30 minutes, cool down, slice, and serve.

Nutrition: Calories 178 Fat 8.4 Fiber 8.2 Carbs 11.5 Protein 1.4

2. Yogurt with Dates (FAST)

Preparation time: 10 minutes
Cooking time: 0 minutes
Servings: 4
Ingredients:
- 5 dates, pitted, chopped
- 2 cups plain yogurt
- ½ teaspoon vanilla extract
- 4 pecans, chopped

Directions:
1. Mix up all ingredients in the blender and blend until smooth.
2. Pour it into the serving cups.

Nutrition: Calories 215 Protein 8.7g Carbohydrates 18.5g Fat 11.5g Fiber 2.3g

3. Breakfast Toast (FAST)

Preparation time: 10 minutes
Cooking time: 20 minutes
Servings: 6
Ingredients:
- 2 eggs, beaten
- ½ cup yogurt
- 1 banana, mashed
- ½ teaspoon ground cinnamon
- 6 whole-grain bread slices
- 1 tablespoon olive oil

Directions:
1. In the mixing bowl, mix up eggs, cream, and ground cinnamon, add mashed banana.
2. Coat the bread in the egg mixture. Then heat olive oil.
3. Put the coated bread in the hot olive oil and roast for 3 minutes per side or light brown.

Nutrition: Calories 153 Protein 6.2g Carbohydrates 19.2g Fat 5.6g Fiber 2.6g

4. Bell Pepper Frittata (FAST)

Preparation time: 10 minutes
Cooking time: 15 minutes
Servings: 4
Ingredients:
- 1 cup red bell pepper, chopped
- 1 tablespoon olive oil, melted
- 1 tomato, sliced
- 4 eggs, beaten
- ¼ teaspoon ground black pepper
- ¼ teaspoon salt

Directions:
1. Brush the baking pan with melted olive oil. Then add all remaining ingredients, mix gently and transfer in the preheated to 365F oven. Cook the frittata for 15 minutes.

Nutrition: Calories 105 Protein 6g Carbohydrates 3.3g Fat 7.9g Fiber 0.6g

5. Fish Eggs (FAST)

Preparation time: 5 minutes
Cooking time: 20 minutes
Servings: 4
Ingredients:
- 1 cup sweet potato, chopped, cooked
- 1 tablespoon avocado oil
- 10 oz salmon fillet, chopped
- ¼ cup cauliflower, chopped
- 4 eggs, beaten

Directions:
2. Mash or crush the sweet potato, then mix it with chopped salmon and cauliflower. Then heat avocado oil in the pan.
3. Add mashed sweet potato mixture and cook it for 10 minutes. Stir to from time to time.
4. After this, add eggs, whisk the mixture gently. Close the lid and cook it for 10 minutes more.

Nutrition: Calories 208 Protein 20.5g Carbohydrates 11.2g Fat 9.3g Fiber 2g

6. Cranberry Bulgur Mix (FAST)

Preparation time: 10 minutes
Cooking time: 0 minutes
Servings: 4
Ingredients:
- 1 and ½ cups hot water
- 1 cup bulgur
- Juice of ½ lemon
- 4 tablespoons cilantro, chopped
- ½ cup cranberries, chopped
- 1 and ½ teaspoons curry powder
- ¼ cup green onions, chopped
- ½ cup red bell peppers, chopped
- ½ cup carrots, grated
- 1 tablespoon olive oil
- A pinch of salt and black pepper

Directions:
1. Put bulgur into a bowl, add the water, stir, cover, leave aside for 10 minutes, fluff with a fork, and transfer to a bowl. Add the rest of the ingredients, toss, and serve cold.

Nutrition: Calories 300 Fat 6.4g Fiber 6.1g Carbs 7.6g Protein 13g

7. Hummus and Olive Pita Bread (FAST)

Preparation time: 5 minutes
Cooking time: 0 minutes
Servings: 3
Ingredients:
- 7 pita bread cut into 6 wedges each
- 1 (7 ounces) container plain hummus
- 1 tbsp. Greek vinaigrette
- ½ cup Chopped pitted Kalamata olives

Directions:
1. Spread the hummus on a serving plate — Mix vinaigrette and olives in a bowl and spoon over the hummus. Enjoy with wedges of pita bread.

Nutrition: Calories: 225 Carbs: 40g Fat: 5g Protein: 9g

8. Fruit Salad with Yogurt Cream(FAST)

Preparation Time: 10 minutes
Cooking Time: 0 minutes
Servings: 4
Ingredients:
- 1½ cups grapes, halved
- 1 cup chopped cantaloupe
- 2 plums, chopped
- 1 peach, chopped
- ½ cup fresh blueberries
- 1 cup unsweetened plain nonfat Greek yogurt
- 2 tablespoons honey
- ½ teaspoon ground cinnamon

Directions:
1. In a large bowl, combine the grapes, cantaloupe, plums, peach, and blueberries. Toss to mix. Divide among 4 dessert dishes.
2. In a small bowl, whisk the yogurt, honey, and cinnamon. Spoon over the fruit.

Nutrition: Calories: 159 Protein: 3g Total Carbohydrates: 38g Sugars: 33g Fiber: 2g Total Fat: <1g
Saturated Fat: <1g Cholesterol: 2mg Sodium: 33mg

9. Date Nut Energy Balls (FAST)

Preparation Time: 10 minutes
Cooking Time: 0 minutes
Servings: 24
Ingredients:
- 1 cup walnuts
- 1 cup almonds
- 2 cups Medjool dates, pitted
- 2 tablespoons extra-virgin olive oil
- ¼ cup unsweetened cocoa powder
- ¼ cup shredded unsweetened coconut, plus additional for coating
- Pinch sea salt

Directions:
1. In a blender or food processor, combine the walnuts, almonds, dates, olive oil, cocoa powder, coconut, and sea salt. Pulse for 20 to 30 (1-second pulses) until everything is well chopped. Form the mixture into 24 balls.
2. Spread the additional coconut on a plate and roll the balls in the coconut to coat. Serve, refrigerate, or freeze.

Nutrition: Calories: 164 Protein: 3g Total Carbohydrates: 26g Sugars: 20g Fiber: 3g Total Fat: 6g
Saturated Fat: 1g Cholesterol: 0mg Sodium: 19mg

10. Peanut Butter Popcorn (FAST)

Preparation Time: 15 minutes
Cooking Time: 5 minutes
Servings: 4
Ingredients:
- 2 tbsps. peanut oil
- ½ c. popcorn kernels
- ½ tsp. sea salt
- ⅓ c. chopped peanuts
- ⅓ c. peanut butter
- ¼ c. agave syrup
- ¼ c. wildflower honey

Directions:
1. Combine popcorn kernels and peanut oil in a pot.
2. Over medium heat, shake the pot gently until all corn is popped.

3. In a saucepan, combine the honey and agave syrup. Cook over low heat for 5 min, then add the peanut butter and stir.
4. Coat the popcorn with prepared sauce.

Nutrition: 430 calories 9g protein 20g fat 56g carbs

11. Avocado & Blueberry (FAST)

Preparation Time: 10 minutes
Cooking Time: 0 minutes
Servings: 2
Ingredients:
- 1 frozen banana
- 2 quartered avocados
- 2 c. berries
- Maple syrup

Directions:
1. Blend all ingredients except agave or maple syrup. Add ice water, if needed.
2. Garnish with syrup and serve in smoothie glasses.

Nutrition: 250 calories 4g protein 13g fat 40g carbs

12. Lentil Omelet (FAST)

Preparation Time: 5 minutes
Cooking Time: 10 minutes
Servings: 2
Ingredients:
- 8 Avocado Slices for Garnish
- ½ Cup Grape Tomatoes, Chopped for Garnish
- ½ Cup Lentils, Canned, Drained & Rinsed
- 1 Cup Asparagus, Chopped
- ¼ Cup Onion, Chopped
- 1 Tablespoon Thyme
- 4 Eggs, Whisked

Directions:
1. Get out a bowl and whisk you egg and thyme together. Place it to the side.
2. Heat a skillet using medium heat, and cook your onion and asparagus for two to three minutes. Add in your lentils, cooking for another two minutes. It should be heated all the way through. Reduce the heat to low.
3. Get out a skillet and place it over medium heat, whisking your eggs again before adding them to the skillet. Cook for two to three minutes. They should be set on the bottom.
4. Spread your lentil and asparagus mixture on one half. Cook for another two minutes before folding the egg over the lentil filling. Cook for another two minutes.
5. Repeat with your remaining ingredients to create a second omelet.
6. Garnish with avocado before serving.

Nutrition: Calories: 242 Protein: 19 Grams Fat: 9 Grams Carbs: 22 Grams Sodium: 129 mg

13. Cherry Quinoa Porridge

Preparation time: 15 minutes
Cooking time: 30 minutes
Servings: 8
Ingredients:
- Water (1 cup)
- Dry quinoa (1/2 cup)
- Dried unsweetened cherries (1/2 cup) Vanilla extract (1/2 tsp.)
- Ground cinnamon (1/4 tsp.)
- Honey (1 tsp.)

Directions:
1. Stir Together water, quinoa, cherries, vanilla extract, cinnamon medium-sized saucepan. Bring it to a boil over medium or high heat.
2. Zimmer with the lid covering the sauce pan for 15 minutes. The quinoa is ready when all the water has been absorbed and the porridge is tender.
3. Drizzle With Honey Then Serve.
4. The quinoa porridge makes two servings. Each serving contains 314 calories, 2.8g fat, zero cholesterol and 9 mg sodium.

Nutrition: Calories: 166 Carbs: 27.8g Protein: 3.4g Fat: 4.8g

14. Italian Flat Bread Gluten-Free

Preparation time: 15 minutes
Cooking time: 30 minutes
Servings: 8
Ingredients:
- 1 tbsp. apple cider
- 2 tbsp. water
- ½ cup yogurt
- 2 tbsp. butter
- 2 tbsp. sugar
- 2 eggs
- 1 tsp xanthan gum
- ½ tsp salt
- 1 tsp baking soda
- 1 ½ tsp baking powder
- ½ cup potato starch, not potato flour
- ½ cup tapioca flour
- ¼ cup brown rice flour
- 1/3 cup sorghum flour

Directions:
1. With parchment paper, line an 8 x 8-inch baking pan and grease parchment paper. Preheat oven to 375oF.
2. Mix xanthan gum, salt, baking soda, baking powder, all flours, and starch in a large bowl.

3. Whisk well sugar and eggs in a medium bowl until creamed. Add vinegar, water, yogurt, and butter. Whisk thoroughly.
4. Pour in the egg mixture into a bowl of flours and mix well. Transfer sticky dough into prepared pan and bake in the oven for 25 to 30 minutes.
5. If tops of bread start to brown a lot, cover the top with foil and continue baking until done.
6. Remove from the oven and pan right away and let it cool. Best served when warm.

Nutrition: Calories: 166 Carbs: 27.8g Protein: 3.4g Fat: 4.8g

15. Veggies Avocado Dressing (FAST)

Preparation time: 10 minutes
Cooking time: 0 minutes
Servings: 4
Ingredients:
- 3 tablespoons petites, roasted
- 3 cups water
- 2 tablespoons cilantro, chopped
- 4 tablespoons parsley, chopped
- 1 and ½ cups corn
- 1 cup radish, sliced
- 2 avocados, peeled, pitted and chopped
- 2 mangos, peeled and chopped
- 3 tablespoons olive oil
- 4 tablespoons Greek yogurt
- 1 teaspoons balsamic vinegar
- 2 tablespoons lime juice
- Salt and black pepper to the taste

Directions:
1. In your blender, mix the olive oil with avocados, salt, pepper, lime juice, the yogurt and the vinegar and pulse.
2. In a bowl, mix the pepitas with the cilantro, parsley and the rest of the ingredients, and toss.
3. Add the avocado dressing, toss, divide the mix between plates and serve as a side dish.

Nutrition: Calories 403 Fat 30.5 Fiber 10 Carbs 23.5 Protein 3.5

16. Guacamole (FAST)

Preparation time: 10 minutes
Cooking time: 0 minutes
Servings: 4
Ingredients:
- 3 avocados - peeled, seeded and mashed
- 1 lime, juiced
- 1 teaspoon salt
- 1/2 cup diced onion
- 3 tablespoons chopped fresh coriander
- 2 Roma tomatoes, diced
- 1 teaspoon chopped garlic
- 1 pinch of ground cayenne pepper (optional)

Directions:
1. Puree avocados, lime juice, and salt in a medium bowl.
2. Stir in the onion, coriander, tomatoes, and garlic. Stir in the cayenne pepper.

Nutrition: 262 calories 22.2 g fat 18 grams of carbohydrates 3.7 g of protein 0 mg of cholesterol 596 mg of sodium

17. Sugar-coated Pecans

Preparation time: 15 minutes
Cooking time: 1 hour
Servings: 12
Ingredients:
- 1 egg white
- 1 tablespoon water
- 1 pound pecan halves
- 1 cup white sugar
- 3/4 teaspoon salt
- 1/2 teaspoon ground cinnamon

Directions:
1. Preheat the oven to 120 ° C (250 ° F). Grease a baking tray.
2. In a bowl, whisk the egg whites and water until frothy. Combine the sugar, salt, and cinnamon in another bowl.
3. Add the pecans to the egg whites and stir to cover the nuts. Remove the nuts and mix them with the sugar until well covered. Spread the nuts on the prepared baking sheet.
4. Bake for 1 hour at 250 ° F (120 ° C). Stir every 15 minutes.

Nutrition: 328 calories 27.2 g fat 22 grams of carbohydrates 3.8 g of protein 0 mg of cholesterol 150 mg of sodium

18. Pita Chips (FAST)

Preparation time: 10 minutes
Cooking time: 8 minutes
Servings: 24
Ingredients:
- 12 slices of pita bread
- 1/2 cup of olive oil
- 1/2 teaspoon ground black pepper
- 1 teaspoon garlic salt
- 1/2 teaspoon dried basil
- 1 teaspoon dried chervil

Directions:
1. Preheat the oven to 200 degrees C (400 degrees F).
2. Cut each pita bread into 8 triangles. Place the triangles on the baking sheet.
3. Combine oil, pepper, salt, basil, and chervil in a small bowl. Brush each triangle with the oil mixture.

4. Bake in the preheated oven for about 7 minutes or until light brown and crispy.

Nutrition: 125 calories 5.3 g fat 17.7 g of carbohydrates 3.2 g of protein 0 mg of cholesterol 246 mg of sodium

19. Banana & Tortilla Snacks (FAST)

Preparation time: 5 minutes
Cooking time: 0 minutes
Servings: 1
Ingredients:
- 1 flour tortilla (6 inches)
- 2 tablespoons peanut butter
- 1 tablespoon honey
- 1 banana
- 2 tablespoons raisins

Directions:
1. Lay the tortilla flat. Spread peanut butter and honey on the tortilla. Place the banana in the middle and sprinkle the raisins. Wrap and serve.

Nutrition: 520 calories 19.3 grams of fat 82.9 g carbohydrates 12.8 g of protein 0 mg of cholesterol 357 mg of sodium.

20. Wonton Snacks (FAST)

Preparation time: 20 minutes
Cooking time: 12 minutes
Servings: 48
Ingredients:
- 2 pounds of ground pork
- 2 stalks of celery
- 2 carrots
- 2 cloves of garlic
- 1 small onion
- 1 (8-gram) can water chestnuts
- 1/2 cup of Thai peanut sauce prepared
- 1 package (14-oz.) wonton wraps

Directions:
1. Finely chop celery, carrots, garlic, onion and water chestnuts in a food processor. Parts must be small and fairly uniform, but not liquid.
2. Mix ground pork and chopped vegetables in a large frying pan. Cook over medium heat until the vegetables are soft and the pork is no longer pink. Turn up the heat and let the moisture evaporate, then add the peanut sauce and cook for another 5 minutes before you remove it from the heat.
3. While cooking the pork mixture, preheat the oven to 175 ° C (350 ° F). Press a wonton wrap into each cup of a mini muffin pan, with flared edges on the sides. Place a spoonful of the meat mixture in each cup.

4. Bake in the preheated oven for about 12 minutes or until the outer envelopes are crispy and golden brown.

Nutrition: 86 calories 4.8 g fat6.1 g of carbohydrates4.4 g of protein14 mg of cholesterol67 mg of sodium.

21. Sesame Stick Snacks (FAST)

Preparation time: 15 minutes
Cooking time: 15 minutes
Servings: 10
Ingredients:
- 2 cups biscuit baking mix
- 2/3 cup heavy cream
- 1/4 cup butter, melted
- 1 1/2 tablespoons sesame seeds

Directions:
1. Preheat the oven to 220 ° C. Lightly grease 2 baking trays.
2. Mix the dough mixture and the cream; mix for 30 seconds. Turn the dough on a lightly floured surface and knead 10 times. Roll the dough into a 5 x 10-inch rectangle. Cut the dough into 1/2 inch wide strips.
3. Place the strips on prepared baking trays. Brush the strips with melted butter and sprinkle with sesame seeds.
4. Bake in the preheated oven for 15 minutes, until golden brown.

Nutrition: 201 calories14.8 g of fat15.6 g carbohydrates2.3 g of protein34 mg cholesterol341 mg of sodium.

22. Spiced Popcorn(FAST)

Preparation Time: 5 minutes

23. Baked Spinach Chips(FAST)

Preparation Time: 5 minutes
Cooking Time: 15 minutes
Servings: 4
Ingredients:
- Cooking spray
- 5 ounces baby spinach, washed and patted dry
- 2 tablespoons olive oil
- 1 teaspoon garlic powder
- ½ teaspoon salt
- ⅛ Teaspoon freshly ground black pepper

Directions:
1. Preheat the oven to 350°F. Coat two baking sheets with cooking spray.
2. Place the spinach in a large bowl. Add the olive oil, garlic powder, salt, and pepper, and toss until evenly coated.
3. Spread the spinach in a single layer on the baking sheets. Bake for 12 to 15 minutes, until

the spinach leaves are crisp and slightly browned.
4. Store spinach chips in a resalable container at room temperature for up to 1 week.

Nutrition: Calories: 77 Total Fat: 7g Saturated Fat: 1g Protein: 1g Carbohydrates: 4g Fiber: 2g Sodium: 351 mg

24. Peanut Butter Yogurt Dip with Fruit(FAST)

Preparation Time: 10 minutes
Cooking Time: 0 minutes
Servings: 4
Ingredients:
- 1 cup nonfat vanilla Greek yogurt
- 2 tablespoons natural creamy peanut butter
- 2 teaspoons honey
- 1 pear, cored and sliced
- 1 apple, cored and sliced
- 1 banana, sliced

Directions:
1. In a medium bowl, whisk together the yogurt, peanut butter, and honey.
2. Serve the dip with the fruit on the side.

Nutrition: Calories: 175 Total Fat: 4g Saturated Fat: 1g Protein: 8g Carbohydrates: 29g Fiber: 4g Sodium: 58mg

25. Snickerdoodle Pecans(FAST)

Preparation Time: 10 minutes
Cooking Time: 15 minutes
Servings: 8
Ingredients:
- Cooking spray
- 1½ cups raw pecans
- 2 tablespoons brown sugar
- 2 tablespoons 100% maple syrup
- ½ teaspoon ground cinnamon
- ½ teaspoon vanilla extract
- ⅛ Teaspoon salt

Directions:
1. Preheat the oven to 350°F. Line a baking sheet with parchment paper and coat with cooking spray.
2. In a medium bowl, place the pecans. Add the brown sugar, maple syrup, cinnamon, vanilla, and salt, tossing to evenly coat.
3. Spread the pecans in a single layer on the prepared baking sheet. Bake for about 12 minutes, until pecans are slightly browned and fragrant. Remove and set aside to cool for 10 minutes.

Nutrition: Calories: 151 Total Fat: 13g Saturated Fat: 1g Protein: 2g Carbohydrates: 8g Fiber: 2g Sodium: 38mg

26. Almond-Stuffed Dates (FAST)

Preparation Time: 5 minutes
Cooking Time: 0 minutes
Servings: 4
Ingredients:
- 20 raw almonds
- 20 pitted dates

Directions:
1. Place one almond into each of 20 dates. Serve at room temperature.

Nutrients: Calories: 137 Total Fat: 3g Saturated Fat: 0g Protein: 2g Carbohydrates: 28g Fiber: 4g Sodium: 1mg

27. No-Cook Pistachio-Cranberry Quinoa Bites (FAST

Preparation Time: 15 minutes
Cooking Time: 0 minutes
Servings: 12
Ingredients:
- ½ cup quinoa
- ¾ cup natural almond butter
- ¾ cup gluten-free old-fashioned oats
- 2 tablespoons honey
- ⅛ Teaspoon salt
- ¼ cup unsalted shelled pistachios, roughly chopped
- ¼ cup dried cranberries

Directions:
1. In a blender, add the quinoa and blend until it turns into a flour consistency.
2. Add the almond butter, oats, honey, and salt, and blend until smooth.
3. Transfer the mixture into a medium bowl, and gently fold in the pistachios and cranberries.
4. Spoon out a tablespoon of the batter. Use clean hands to roll into a 2-inch ball, and place into a container. Repeat for the remaining batter, making a total of 12 balls.
5. Place the container in the refrigerator to allow the bites to set, at least 15 minutes.

Nutrition: Calories: 175 Total Fat: 11g Saturated Fat: 1g Protein: 6g Carbohydrates: 16g Fiber: 3g Sodium: 25mg

28. No-Bake Honey-Almond Granola Bars(FAST)

Preparation Time: 15 minutes
Cooking Time: 0 minutes
Servings: 8
Ingredients:
- Cooking spray
- 1 cup pitted dates
- ¼ cup honey
- ¾ cup natural creamy almond butter
- ¾ cup gluten-free rolled oats

- 2 tablespoons raw almonds, chopped
- 2 tablespoons pumpkin seeds

Directions:

1. Line an 8-by-8-inch baking dish with parchment paper, and coat the paper with cooking spray.
2. In a food processor or blender, add the dates and blend until they reach a pastelike consistency. Add the honey, almond butter, and oats, and blend until well combined. Transfer the mixture to a medium bowl.
3. Add the almonds and pumpkin seeds, and gently fold until well combined.
4. Spoon the mixture into the prepared baking dish. Spread the mixture evenly, using clean fingers to push down the mixture so it is compact.
5. Cover with plastic wrap and refrigerate until the bars set, 1 to 2 hours.
6. Remove from the refrigerator and cut into 8 bars. Carefully remove each bar from the baking dish, and wrap individually in plastic wrap. Place bars in the refrigerator until ready to grab and go.

Nutrition: Calories: 296 Total Fat: 16g Saturated Fat: 0g Protein: 8g Carbohydrates: 32g Fiber: 5g Sodium: 1m

29. Curried Veggies and Poached Eggs

Preparation Time: 20 minutes
Cooking Time: 45 minutes
Servings: 4
Ingredients:

- 4 large eggs
- ½ tsp. white vinegar
- 1/8 tsp. crushed red pepper – optional
- 1 cup water
- 1 14-oz. can chickpeas, drained
- 2 medium zucchinis, diced
- ½ lb. sliced button mushrooms
- 1 tbsp. yellow curry powder
- 2 cloves garlic, minced
- 1 large onion, chopped
- 2 tsp.s. extra virgin olive oil

Directions:

1. On medium high fire, place a large saucepan and heat oil.
2. Sauté onions until tender around four to five minutes.
3. Add garlic and continue sautéing for another half minute.
4. Add curry powder, stir and cook until fragrant around one to two minutes.

5. Add mushrooms, mix, cover and cook for 5 to 8 minutes or until mushrooms are tender and have released their liquid.
6. Add red pepper if using, water, chickpeas and zucchini. Mix well to combine and bring to a boil.
7. Once boiling, reduce fire to a simmer, cover and cook until zucchini is tender around 15 to 20 minutes of simmering.
8. Meanwhile, in a small pot filled with 3-inches deep of water, bring to a boil on high fire.
9. Once boiling, reduce fire to a simmer and add vinegar.
10. Slowly add one egg, slipping it gently into the water. Allow to simmer until egg is cooked, around 3 to 5 minutes.
11. Remove egg with a slotted spoon and transfer to a plate, one plate one egg.
12. Repeat the process with remaining eggs.
13. Once the veggies are done cooking, divide evenly into 4 servings and place one serving per plate of egg.
14. Serve and enjoy.

Nutrition: Calories per serving: 215 Protein: 13.8g Carbs: 20.6g Fat: 9.4g

30. Lettuce Stuffed with Eggs 'n Crab Meat (FAST)

Preparation Time: 15 minutes
Cooking Time: 10 minutes
Servings: 8
Ingredients:

- 24 butter lettuce leaves
- 1 tsp. dry mustard
- ¼ cup finely chopped celery
- 1 cup lump crabmeat, around 5 ounces
- 3 tbsp. plain Greek yogurt
- 2 tbsp. extra virgin olive oil
- ¼ tsp. ground pepper
- 8 large eggs
- ½ tsp. salt, divided
- 1 tbsp. fresh lemon juice, divided
- 2 cups thinly sliced radishes

Directions:

1. In a medium bowl, mix ¼ tsp. salt, 2 tsp.s. Juice and radishes. Cover and chill for half an hour.
2. On medium saucepan, place eggs and cover with water over an inch above the eggs. Bring the pan of water to a boil. Once boiling, reduce fire to a simmer and cook for ten minutes.
3. Turn off fire, discard hot water and place eggs in an ice water bath to cool completely.
4. Peel eggshells and slice eggs in half lengthwise and remove the yolks.

5. With a sieve on top of a bowl, place yolks and press through a sieve. Set aside a tablespoon of yolk.
6. On remaining bowl of yolks add pepper, ¼ tsp. salt and 1 tsp. juice. Mix well and as you are stirring, slowly add oil until well incorporated. Add yogurt, stir well to mix.
7. Add mustard, celery and crabmeat. Gently mix to combine. If needed, taste and adjust seasoning of the filling.
8. On a serving platter, arrange 3 lettuce in a fan for two egg slices. To make the egg whites sit flat, you can slice a bit of the bottom to make it flat. Evenly divide crab filling into egg white holes.
9. Then evenly divide into eight servings the radish salad and add on the side of the eggs, on top of the lettuce leaves.
10. Serve and enjoy.

Nutrition: Calories per serving: 121 Protein: 10.0g Carbs: 1.6g Fat: 8.3g

31. Morning Oats (FAST)

Preparation time: 5 minutes
Cooking time: 0 minutes
Servings: 2
Ingredients:
- 1 oz pecans, chopped
- ¼ cup oats
- ½ cup plain yogurt
- 1 date, chopped
- ½ teaspoon vanilla extract

Directions:
1. Mix up all ingredients and leave for 5 minutes.
2. Then transfer the meal to the serving bowls.

Nutrition: Calories 196 Protein 6.5g Carbohydrates 16.5g Fat 11.6g Fiber 2.9g

32. Baked Eggs with Parsley (FAST)

Preparation time: 15 minutes
Cooking time: 20 minutes
Servings: 6
Ingredients:
- 2 green bell peppers, chopped
- 3 tablespoons olive oil
- 1 yellow onion, chopped
- 1 teaspoon sweet paprika
- 6 tomatoes, chopped
- 6 eggs
- ¼ cup parsley, chopped

Directions:
1. Warm a pan with the oil over medium heat, add all ingredients except eggs and roast them for 5 minutes.
2. Stir the vegetables well and crack the eggs.

3. Transfer the pan with eggs in the preheated to 360F oven and bake them for 15 minutes.

Nutrition: Calories 167 Protein .3g Carbohydrates 10.2g Fat 11.8g Fiber 2.6g

33. Flavorful Braised Kale (FAST)

Preparation Time: 15 minutes
Cooking Time: 15 minutes
Servings: 6
Ingredients:
- 1 lb. Kale, Stems Removed & Chopped Roughly
- 1 Cup Cherry Tomatoes, Halved
- 2 Teaspoons Olive Oil
- 4 Cloves Garlic, Sliced Thin
- ½ Cup Vegetable Stock
- ¼ Teaspoon Sea Salt, Fine
- 1 Tablespoon Lemon Juice, Fresh
- 1/8 Teaspoon Black Pepper

Directions:
1. Start by heating your olive oil in a frying pan using medium heat, and add in your garlic. Sauté for a minute or two until lightly golden.
2. Mix your kale and vegetable stock with your garlic, adding it to your pan.
3. Cover the pan and then turn the heat down to medium-low.
4. Allow it to cook until your kale wilts and part of your vegetable stock should be dissolved. It should take roughly five minutes.
5. Stir in your tomatoes and cook without a lid until your kale is tender, and then remove it from heat.
6. Mix in your salt, pepper and lemon juice before serving warm.

Nutrition: Calories: *70* Protein: *4 Grams* Fat: 0.5 Grams *Carbs:* 9 Grams Sodium: *133 mg*

34. Roasted Beet Bites with Orange-Walnut Drizzles (FAST)

Preparation time: 10 minutes
Cooking time: 40 minutes
Servings: 12
Ingredients:
- 3 large beets, trimmed and peeled.
- 1 tablespoon olive oil
- 1/4 cup of walnut oil.
- 1 1/2 cups of finely shredded orange peel
- 1/4 cup of fresh orange juice
- 2 tablespoons of fresh lemon juice
- 2 tablespoons of finely chopped walnuts, toasted.

Directions:

1. Preheat the oven to a temperature of 425F. Cut each beet into eight wedges. Place the beets in a baking dish, drizzle them with olive oil, and then toss to coat. Cover dish with foil paper. Bake with the dish covered for about twenty minutes. Stir beets and roast them uncovered for about twenty minutes.

2. Stir the beets, and then roast them with the dish uncovered for about twenty minutes until the beets are tender. Let the beets cool slightly,

3. For the marinade. Mix walnut oil, orange peel, orange juice, lemon juice in a small bowl. Then, pour the marinade over the beets. Cover and refrigerate for about eight hours or overnight. Then, drain the marinade.

4. Place the beets in a serving bowl and then sprinkle bits of the toasted walnuts over it. Serve with picks.

5. To toast the nuts, spread them in a shallow baking pan. Then, bake them in a 350F oven for about 5 minutes or until they become brown. Ensure that you shake the pan as you toast them.

Nutrition: Calories: 459 Carbs: 43g Fat: 16g Sugar: 0.2g Fiber: 8g Protein: 36g Cholesterol: 44mg

35. Cauliflower Cups with Herb Pesto and Lamb (FAST)

Preparation time: 10 minutes
Cooking time: 15 minutes
Servings: 6
Ingredients:

- 2 tablespoons refined coconut oil, melted.
- 4 cups coarsely chopped fresh cauliflower
- 2 large eggs.
- 1/2 cup of almond meal
- 1/4 teaspoon black pepper.
- 4 scallions
- 12 ounces ground lamb or ground park.
- 3 cloves garlic, minced
- 12 cherry or grape tomatoes, quartered.
- 1 teaspoon Mediterranean Seasoning.
- 3/4 cup of firmly packed fresh cilantro
- 1/2 cup of firmly packed fresh parsley
- 1/4 cup of firmly packed fresh mint.
- 1/3 cup of pine nuts, toasted.
- 1/4 cup of olive oil.

Directions:

1. Preheat oven to a temperature of 425F.

2. Brush the bottom and side of twelve 2 1/2inch muffin cups with coconut oil, and then set it aside.

3. Place cauliflower in a food processor, then cover and blend it until the cauliflower is finely chopped. Fill the large skillet with water to a depth of 1 inch, and then boil it. Set the steamer in a skillet over the basket. Add cauliflower to the steamer basket. Cover and then steam for four minutes until it becomes tender. Remove the steamer basket with cauliflower from the skillet and then set it over a large plate. Let the cauliflower cool slightly.

4. Whisk eggs in a large bowl lightly, stir in cooled cauliflower, almond meal, and pepper. Spoon some cauliflower mix evenly into the prepared muffin cups. Using your fingers and the back of a spoon to press the cauliflower onto the bottoms and the sides of the cups.

5. Bake the cauliflower cups for ten minutes till the center becomes set. Place them on wire racks but ensure that you do not remove the pan.

6. Slice the scallions thinly while ensuring that you keep the white bottom separate from the green tops. In a large skillet, cook the lamb, the sliced white bottoms of the scallions, and the garlic over medium heat until the meat is completely cooked.

7. Drain off the fat, and then add the green parts of scallions, tomatoes, and Mediterranean seasoning. Cook and stir for 1 minute. Spoon lamb mixture evenly into the cauliflower cups.

8. For the herb pesto, mix cilantro, parsley, mint, and pine nuts in a blender. Cover and blend until the mixture is finely chopped. With the blender still running, add oil through the feed tube until the mixture is well mixed.

9. Run a knife about the cauliflower cups' edges, and then carefully remove the cups from the pans. Set on a serving tray. Spoon the herb pesto over the cauliflower cups

Nutrition: Calorie: 464 Carbs: 30.74g Fats: 17.8g Protein: 47.3g

36. Spinach-Artichoke Dip (FAST)

Preparation time: 10 minutes
Cooking time: 20 minutes
Servings: 6

Ingredients:
- 1 tablespoon of extra virgin olive oil
- 1 cup of chopped sweet onions.
- 3 cloves of garlic, minced
- One 9-ounce box of frozen artichoke hearts, thawed.
- 3/4 cup of Paleo Mayo.
- 3/4 cup of cashew cream
- 1/2 teaspoon of finely shredded lemon peel.
- 2 teaspoons of smoky seasonings.
- Two 10-ounce boxes chopped frozen spinach, thawed, and well-drained.

Directions:
1. In a large skillet, heat olive oil over medium heat; add onion, then cook and stir for about 5 minutes or until translucent. Then, add garlic, cook, and 1 minute.
2. Meanwhile, place drained artichokes in a food processor fitted with a mixing blade. Cover and pulse until it gets finely chopped. Then, set it aside.
3. In a small bowl, combine Paleo Mayo and Cashew Cream. Stir in lemon peel, lemon juice, and Smoky seasoning. Set it aside.
4. Add chopped artichokes and spinach to the onion mixture in the skillet. Stir in mayonnaise mixture, heat through. Serve with cut-up vegetables.

Nutrition: Calorie: 376 Carbs: 20g Fats: 34g Protein: 4g

37. Garlic Mushroom Quinoa (FAST)

Preparation Time: 10 Minutes
Cooking Time: 30 Minutes
Servings: 2
Ingredients:
- 1/2 cup quinoa, cooked
- 1/2 tablespoon olive oil
- 1/2-pound cremini mushrooms, thinly sliced
- 3 cloves garlic, minced
- 1/2 teaspoon dried thyme
- Kosher salt and ground black pepper, to flavor
- 1 tablespoon nutritional yeast (optional)

Directions:
1. Place a skillet with olive oil over medium heat.
2. Add mushrooms, garlic, and thyme. Sauté until tender.
3. Add salt, pepper, and quinoa. Mix well.

4. Serve garnished with nutritional yeast, if desired.

Nutrition: Calories: 69 Carbs: 9.6g Fat: 2.7g Sod: 27mg

38. Mixed-Fruit Mini Pies (FAST)

Preparation Time: 15 Minutes
Cooking Time: 20 minutes
Servings: 6
Ingredients:
- 1/2 cup oat flour
- 1/4 cup almond flour
- 1/2 cup chopped toasted hazelnuts
- 1/4 cup shredded coconut
- 1/3 cup coconut oil, melted
- 2 tablespoons maple syrup, divided
- 1/4 teaspoon salt
- 3 medium ripe peaches, peeled and chopped
- 1 cup blueberries
- 1 cup raspberries
- 1 teaspoon vanilla
- 1 tablespoon orange juice

Directions:
1. Preheat oven to 400F. Grease six (1-cup) ovenproof custard cups with coconut oil and set aside.
2. In a medium bowl, merge oat flour, almond flour, hazelnuts, and coconut and toss. Add melted coconut oil, 1 tablespoon maple syrup, and salt and mix until crumbly; set aside.
3. In another medium bowl, combine peaches, blueberries, and raspberries. Sprinkle with vanilla, orange juice and remaining 1 tablespoon maple syrup and toss gently. Divide among prepared custard cups. Top with crumble mixture.
4. Set custard cups on a large rimmed baking sheet and bakes or until fruit is bubbly and tender and topping is browned. Serve warm or cool.

Nutrition: Calories: 325 Carbs: 28g Fat: 23g Sugar: 15g Fiber: 6g Protein: 5g Sodium: 102mg

39. Crustless Apple Pie (FAST)

Preparation Time: 15 Minutes
Cooking Time: 20 minutes
Servings: 8
Ingredients:
- 8 medium apples, peeled, cored, and sliced
- 3 tablespoons orange juice
- 3 tablespoons water

- 1/2 cup chopped pecans
- 1/3 cup maple syrup
- 1/4 cup grass-fed butter, melted
- 1/2 teaspoon cinnamon

Directions:
1. Grease a 4 1/2-quart slow cooker with olive oil. Arrange apple slices to cover the bottom of the slow cooker.
2. In a small bowl or measuring cup, stir orange juice and water to mix. Evenly drizzle over apples.
3. In another small bowl, combine pecans, maple syrup, butter, and cinnamon; mix well. Evenly crumble pecan mixture over apples.
4. Seal and cook on high for 2 hours or on low for 4 hours. Serve warm or chilled.

Nutrition: Calories: 238 Carbs: 35g Fat: 12g Sugar: 27g Fiber: 5g Protein: 1g Sodium: 4mg

40. Blueberry Coconut Crisp

Preparation Time: 15 Minutes
Cooking Time: 45 minutes
Servings 8
Ingredients:
- 4 cups fresh blueberries
- 1/4 cup maple syrup, if needed
- 1 1/2 teaspoons vanilla
- 1 tablespoon lemon juice
- 1 cup chopped pecans
- 1 cup unsweetened shredded coconut
- 1/3 cup coconut flour
- 3 tablespoons coconut oil
- 3 tablespoons grass-fed butter
- 1/8 teaspoon salt

Directions:
1. Preheat oven to 400F. Grease an 8" square glass pan with coconut oil.
2. Combine blueberries, maple syrup (if using), vanilla, and lemon juice in the pan and toss gently; set aside.
3. In a medium bowl, combine pecans, coconut, and coconut flour. Add coconut oil, grass-fed butter, and salt and mix until crumbly. Sprinkle over blueberries.
4. Bake for 35-40 minutes or until blueberry mixture is bubbly. Serve warm or cool.

Nutrition: Calories: 337 Carbs: 24g Fat: 27g Sugar: 15g Fiber: 6g Protein: 3g Sodium: 53mg

41. Plum Blueberry Coconut Crumble

Preparation Time: 15 Minutes
Cooking Time: 45 minutes

Servings 8
Ingredients:
- 8 medium plums, stones removed, sliced
- 2 cups blueberries
- 2 tablespoons maple syrup
- 2 tablespoons lemon juice
- 1 tablespoon arrowroot powder
- 1 cup unsweetened coconut flakes
- 1 cup rolled oats
- 1 cup chopped pecans
- 2/3 cup coconut flour
- 1/4 teaspoon baking soda
- 1/2 teaspoon cream of tartar
- 1/4 teaspoon salt
- 1/3 cup coconut oil, melted

Directions:
1. Preheat oven to 350F. Grease a 9" square baking dish with coconut oil.
2. Combine plums and blueberries in prepared dish. Drizzle with maple syrup, lemon juice, and arrowroot powder and toss to coat.
3. In a medium bowl, combine coconut flakes, oats, pecans, coconut flour, baking soda, cream of tartar, and salt. Add coconut oil and mix until crumbly. Pat mixture on top of fruit in dish.
4. Bake for 40-45 minutes or until fruit is bubbly and topping is golden. Serve warm.

Nutrition: Calories: 387 Carbs: 34g Fat: 28g Sugar: 16g Fiber: 9g Protein: 5g

42. Sweet Potato Chips (FAST)

Preparation Time: 10 Minutes
Cooking Time: 5 Minutes
Servings: 2
Ingredients:
- 2 large sweet potatoes, cut into 1/8-inch slices
- 2 tablespoons olive oil
- Salt to taste
- Pepper to taste

Directions:
1. Set the sweet potato slices in a large baking dish.
2. Sprinkle oil, salt, and pepper.
3. Bake in a preheated oven at 400F for about 25 minutes. Flip sides in between a couple of times.

Nutrition: Calories: 90 Carbs: 8g Fat: 6g Sugar: 4g Fiber: 4g Protein: 2g Sodium: 57mg

43. Lemon Broccoli Roast (FAST)

Preparation Time: 10 minutes
Cooking Time: 15 minutes
Serving: 2

Ingredients

- 2 heads of broccoli, separated into florets
- 2 teaspoons extra virgin olive oil
- 1 teaspoon salt
- ½ teaspoon pepper
- 1 garlic clove, minced
- ½ teaspoon lemon juice

Directions

1. Pre-heat your oven to a temperature of 400 degrees F
2. Take a large bowl and add broccoli florets with some extra virgin olive oil, pepper, sea salt, and garlic
3. Spread the broccoli out in a single even layer on a fine baking sheet
4. Bake in your pre-heated oven for about 15-20 minutes until the florets are soft enough so that they can be pierced with a fork
5. Squeeze lemon juice over them generously before serving
6. Enjoy!

Nutrition Per Serving: Carbohydrates: 4 grams/Fat: 2 grams/Protein: 3 grams/Fiber: 2 grams/Calories: 49

44. Cool Avocado Chips (FAST)

Preparation Time: 5 minutes
Cooking Time: 30 minutes
Servings: 3

Ingredients

- Fresh black pepper
- Salt, as needed
- ½ teaspoon Italian seasoning
- ½ teaspoon garlic powder
- 1 teaspoon lemon juice
- 1 large ripe avocado
- ¾ cup coconut cream

Directions

1. Preheat your oven to 325 degrees F
2. Take two baking sheets and line them with parchment paper
3. Take a medium-sized bowl and add avocado; mash it with a fork until you have a smooth mixture
4. Stir in coconut cream, garlic powder, lemon juice, and seasoning
5. Season more with salt and pepper
6. Place about a heaping teaspoon scoop of the mix on your baking sheet, making sure to leave about a 3-inch distance between each scoop
7. Flatten them to a 3-inch width
8. Bake for about 30 minutes until crispy
9. Serve and enjoy!

Nutrition Per Serving: Carbohydrates: 4 grams/Fat: 10 grams/Protein: 7 grams/Fiber: 1 gram/Calories: 120

45. Roasted Eggplant and Romero rolls (FAST)

Preparation time: 10 minutes
Cooking time: 20 minutes
Servings: 24

Ingredients:

- 3 red sweet peppers, halved, stems removed, and seeded.
- 4 Roma tomatoes, cored.
- One 1-pound eggplant, with the ends, trimmed.
- 1/2 cup of extra virgin olive oil
- 1 tablespoon of Mediterranean seasoning.
- 1/4 cup of almonds, toasted
- 3 tablespoons of roasted garlic vinaigrette
- Extra virgin olive oil.

Directions:

1. To make the Romesco sauce, pre-heat the boiler with the oven rack fixed at a point 4 to 5 inches above the fire. Line a rimmed baking sheet with foil. Then, place sweet peppers with the sides cut down as well as tomatoes on the baking sheet.
2. Broil for ten minutes or till the moment where the skins turn black. Remove the baking sheet from the broiler and then wrap the vegetables with the foil. Then, set it aside.
3. Decrease the temperature of the oven to 400F. Then, use a mandolin to cut the eggplant into slices of 1/4-inch length. You should get about 12 to 14 slices. Line two baking sheets with foil, then place the eggplant slices with olive oil. Sprinkles the rolls with Mediterranean seasoning; then, bake it for about 15 minutes until it becomes soft. Then, flip the slices over once.
4. Set the baked eggplant to cool.
5. Mix the broiled peppers, tomatoes, almonds, and the roasted garlic vinaigrette with a blender, and then blend them until you get a thick paste. Add olive oil to make the sauce smooth.
6. Spread each slice of roasted eggplant with about 1 teaspoon of Romesco sauce. Start from the short end of roasted eggplant

slices, and roll each slice into a spiral. Cut the slice in half while following a cross sign. Secure each roll with a wooden toothpick.

Nutrition: Calories: 240 Carbs: 4.6 g Fat: 25.4 g Protein: 2.7 g

46. Veggie-Beef Wraps (FAST)

Preparation time: 10 minutes
Cooking time: 20 minutes
Servings: 6
Ingredients:
- 1 small red sweet pepper, stemmed, halved, and seeded.
- Two 3-inch pieces of English cucumber halved lengthwise and seeded.
- Two 3-inch pieces of carrot, peeled.
- 1/2 cup daikon radish sprouts.
- 1-pound leftover roast beef tenderloin
- 1 avocado, peeled, seeded, and cut into 12 slices.
- Chimichurri slices.

Directions:
1. Cut the red pepper, cucumber, and carrot into long matchstick-size long.
2. Thinly slice the roast beef. For each wrap, on a clean, dry work surface, place 4 beef slices in a single layer. Then, at the middle of each side, place one slice of avocado, a piece of red pepper, a piece of cucumber, a piece of carrot, and some of the sprouts.
3. Roll beef up and over the vegetables. Then, place the wraps on a platter while ensuring that you seam the sides down. Repeat this technique twice to make 12 wraps in total.
4. Serve the veggie beef wraps with chimichurri sauce for dipping.

Nutrition: Calorie: 513 Carbs: 64.9g Fats: 46.6g Protein: 10.1g

47. Scallop and Avocado Endive Bites (FAST)

Preparation time: 10 minutes
Cooking time: 25 minutes
Servings: 24
Ingredients:
- 1 pound of fresh or frozen bay scallops
- 1 to 2 teaspoons of Cajun seasoning
- 24 medium-sized to large-sized endive leaves
- 1 ripe avocado, peeled, seeded, and chopped.
- 1 red or orange sweet pepper, finely chopped.

- 2 green onions, chopped.
- 2 tablespoons, bright citrus vinaigrette
- 1 tablespoon of extra virgin olive oil

Directions:
1. If scallops are frozen, thaw them. Then, rinse the scallops and pat them dry with paper towels. Then, in a medium-sized bowl, toss the scallops with Cajun seasoning. Then, set them aside.
2. Arrange the endive leaves on a large platter. Then, in a medium-sized bowl, stir these things together—avocado, sweet pepper, green onions, and bright Citrus Vinaigrette. Spoon this mix into endive leaves.
3. In a large skillet, heat the olive oil over medium heat. Then, add scallops before leaving it to cook for one or two more minutes or until it becomes opaque. Ensure that you stir the mix frequently. Spoon the scallops over the avocado mixture on endive leaves.
4. Serve immediately or cover and chill for about two hours.

Nutrition: Calorie: 207 Carbs: 5g Fats: 22g Protein: 3g

48. Exotic Cucumber Sushi (FAST)

Preparation Time: 10 minutes
Cooking Time: 10 minutes
Servings: 2
Ingredients
For Sushi
- 2 small carrots, thinly sliced
- ½ yellow bell pepper, thinly sliced
- ½ red bell pepper, thinly sliced
- ¼ avocado, sliced
- 2 medium cucumbers, halved
- For Sauce
- 1 teaspoon soy sauce
- 1 tablespoon Sirach
- 1/3 cup coconut cream

Directions
1. Take a small spoon, remove the seeds from the center of the cucumber, and hollow them out
2. Press avocado into the center of your cucumber using a butter knife
3. Slide in the sliced bell pepper and carrots until the cucumber shell is full of your vegetables
4. Take a small bowl and add cream, soy sauce, and Sirach; whisk well
5. Slice the cucumber into 1-inch rounds and serve with the sauce

Nutrition Per Serving: Carbohydrates: 9 grams/Fat: 16 grams/Protein: 1 gram/Fiber: 2 grams/Calories: 190

49. Roasted Herb Crackers

Preparation Time: 5 minutes
Cooking Time: 120 minutes
Serving: 75 crackers
Ingredients

- ¼ cup avocado oil
- 10 celery sticks
- 1 sprig fresh rosemary, stem discarded
- 2 sprigs fresh thyme, stems discarded
- 2 tablespoons apple cider vinegar
- 1 teaspoon Himalayan salt
- 3 cups ground flax seeds

Directions

1. Preheat your oven to 225 degrees F
2. Line a baking sheet with parchment paper and set it aside
3. Add oil, herbs, celery, vinegar, and salt to a food processor and pulse until you have an even mixture
4. Add flax and puree
5. Let it sit for 2-3 minutes
6. Transfer batter to your prepared baking sheet and spread evenly, cut into cracker shapes
7. Bake for 60 minutes, flip, and bake for 60 minutes more
8. Enjoy!

Nutrition Per Serving: Carbohydrates: 1 gram/Fat: 5 grams/Protein: 1.3 grams/Fiber: 4 grams/Calories: 34

50. Awesome Cacao Nut Truffles

Preparation Time: 10 minutes + 60 minutes chill time
Cooking Time: 45 minutes
Serving: 16 truffles
Ingredients

- ¼ teaspoon cinnamon, ground
- 2 tablespoons raw honey
- 3 tablespoons coconut oil, melted
- ¼ cup cacao, raw and powdered
- ½ cup creamy almond butter, unsalted
- 1 and ½ cups raw almonds
- Additional shredded coconuts

Directions

1. Take your food processor and add almonds, pulse them until finely ground
2. Add rest of the ingredients to the food processor and pulse until you have a smooth dough with a sticky texture, it should take about 1-2 minutes
3. Scoop about 1 heaping tablespoon of dough at a time and form balls of 1 and ½

inch size. Roll the balls in shredded coconut if desired

4. Transfer the balls to an aluminum foil/parchment paper lined baking sheet
5. Let them chill in your fridge for 60 minutes
6. Serve and enjoy once ready!

Nutrition Per Serving: Carbohydrates: 7 grams/Fat: 12 grams/Protein: 5 grams/Fiber: 1 grams/Calories:148

51. Walnuts and Asparagus Combo (FAST)

Preparation Time: 5 minutes
Cooking Time: 5 minutes
Servings: 2
Ingredients

- 1 and ½ tablespoons olive oil
- ¾ pound asparagus, trimmed
- ¼ cup walnuts, chopped
- Salt and pepper to taste

Directions

1. Place a skillet over medium heat, add olive oil and let it heat up
2. Add asparagus, sauté for 5 minutes until browned
3. Season with salt and pepper
4. Remove from heat
5. Add walnuts and toss
6. Serve warm!

Nutrition Per Serving: Carbohydrates: 2 grams/Fat: 12 grams/Protein: 3 grams/Fiber: 2 grams/Calories: 124

52. Garlic Lemon Soup (FAST)

Preparation Time: 5 minutes
Cooking Time: 10 minutes
Servings: 2
Ingredients

- 1 avocado, pitted and chopped
- 1 cucumber, chopped
- 2 bunches spinach
- 1 and ½ cups watermelon, chopped
- 1 bunch cilantro, roughly chopped
- Juice from 2 lemons
- ½ cup coconut aminos
- ½ cup lime juice

Directions

1. Add cucumber and avocado to your blender and pulse well
2. Add cilantro, spinach, and watermelon; blend
3. Add lemon, lime juice, and coconut amino
4. Pulse a few more times
5. Transfer to a soup bowl and enjoy!

Nutrition Per Serving: Carbohydrates: 6 grams/Fat: 7 grams/Protein: 3 grams/Fiber: 4 grams/Calories: 10

53. Pico De Gallo

Preparation Time: 15 Minutes
Cooking Time: 7 minutes
Servings 2
Ingredients:
- 1 large tomato, diced (about 11/2 cups)
- 1/2 cup chopped white onions
- 2 cloves garlic, minced
- 2 tablespoons lime juice
- 2 tablespoons chopped fresh cilantro
- 1 jalapeño pepper, seeded and finely diced
- 1/2 teaspoon fine sea salt

Directions:
1. Place all of the ingredients in a small bowl and stir until well combined.
2. Set in an airtight container in the refrigerator for up to 5 days.

Nutrition: Calories: 32 Carbs: 2g Fat: 0.1g Fiber: 1g Protein: 1g

54. Citrus Avocado Salsa (FAST)

Preparation Time: 15 Minutes
Cooking Time: 5 minutes
Servings 4
Ingredients:
- 1 cup diced tomatoes
- 1 small avocado, pitted and diced
- 1/4 cup chopped fresh cilantro leaves
- 2 tablespoons avocado oil
- 4 drops orange oil, or 1 teaspoon orange extract
- Juice of 1 lime
- Fine sea salt and ground black pepper

Directions:
1. Place the tomatoes, avocado, and cilantro in a small bowl. Add the avocado oil, orange oil, and lime juice and stir. Season to taste with salt and pepper.
2. Set in an airtight container in the refrigerator for up to 4 days.

Nutrition: Calories: 140 Carbs: 7g Fat: 13g Fiber: 3g Protein: 1g

55. Apple Freeze (FAST)

Preparation Time: 15 Minutes
Cooking Time: 30 minutes
Servings 6
Ingredients:
- 1-pound Golden Delicious apples, peeled, cored, and chopped

- 11/4 cups water
- 1/4 cup maple syrup
- 1/2 teaspoon ground cinnamon
- 1 tablespoon lemon juice

Directions:
1. Place apples, water, maple syrup, and cinnamon in a 2-quart slow cooker. Cover and cook on high for 21/2–31/2 hours. Stir in lemon juice.
2. Process apple and syrup mixture in a blender until smooth. Strain mixture through a sieve, and discard any pulp.
3. Pour liquid into an 11" × 9" baking dish, cover tightly with plastic wrap, and transfer to freezer.
4. Stir every hour with a fork, crushing any lumps as it freezes. Freeze 3–4 hours or until firm. To serve, scoop into six individual small bowls. Set in a tightly sealed container in the freezer for up to several months.

Nutrition: Calories: 78 Carbs: 20g Fat: 0g Sugar: 16g Fiber: 2g Protein: 1g Sodium: 4mg

56. Baked Apples

Preparation Time: 15 Minutes
Cooking Time: 30 minutes
Servings: 6
Ingredients:
- 6 large Pink Lady apples
- 1/2 cup unsweetened coconut flakes
- 1/2 cup rolled oats
- 2 tablespoons maple syrup
- 1/2 teaspoon ground cinnamon
- 3 tablespoons coconut butter

Directions:
1. Preheat oven to 350F.
2. Remove cores from apples, leaving 1/2" intact at the bottom. Place apples in a medium baking dish.
3. In a small bowl, merge together coconut flakes, oats, maple syrup, and cinnamon. Fill cavities with mixture. Top each apple with a spoonful of coconut butter.
4. Bake for 20-30 minutes. Apples are done when they are completely soft and brown on top.

Nutrition: Calories: 217 Carbs: 35g Fat: 9g Sugar: 21g Fiber: 7g Protein: 2g Sodium: 4mg

57. Apples Supreme

Preparation Time: 15 Minutes
Cooking Time: 4-5 hours

Servings 8

Ingredients:

- 4 medium Granny Smith apples, peeled, cored, and sliced
- 4 medium Golden Delicious apples, peeled, cored, and sliced
- 3/4 cup maple syrup
- 1/2 teaspoon ground cinnamon
- 1/2 teaspoon ground cloves
- 1/2 cup coconut butter

Directions:

1. Place apples in a 4-quart slow cooker and toss with remaining ingredients. Seal and cook on low for 4-5 hours. Serve warm.

Nutrition: Calories: 273 Carbs: 47g Fat: 9g Sugar: 35g Fiber: 6g Protein: 2g Sodium: 6mg

58. Roasted Fruit (FAST)

Preparation Time: 15 Minutes
Cooking Time: 20 minutes
Servings: 6

Ingredients:

- 4 medium peaches, pitted and cut into quarters
- 4 medium nectarines, pitted and cut into quarters
- 6 large apricots, pitted and cut in half
- 1 tablespoon olive oil
- 2 tablespoons lemon juice
- 1/2 teaspoon salt
- 1/2 teaspoon dried thyme leaves
- 1/8 teaspoon ground white pepper
- 11/2 cups red grapes

Directions:

1. Preheat oven to 400F. Place peaches, nectarines, and apricots, cut side up, in a large roasting dish. Drizzle with olive oil and lemon juice. Sprinkle with salt, thyme, and white pepper.
2. Roast, uncovered, for 15 minutes. Add grapes to the pan and stir gently. Roast for another 5–10 minutes or until fruit is tender.

Nutrition: Calories: 132 Carbs: 27g Fat: 3g Sugar: 23g Fiber: 4g Protein: 3g Sodium: 197mg

59. Stewed Cinnamon Apples (FAST)

Preparation Time: 15 Minutes
Cooking Time: 20 minutes
Servings: 4

Ingredients:

- 1 teaspoon maple syrup
- 1 tablespoon ground cinnamon

- 2 tablespoons lemon juice
- 2 tablespoons water
- 4 medium apples

Directions:

1. Place maple syrup, cinnamon, lemon juice, and water in a 4-quart slow cooker. Stir until maple syrup dissolves. Add apples.
2. Set on low for up to 8 hours. Stir before serving.

Nutrition: Calories: 101 Carbs: 27g Fat: 0g Sugar: 20g Fiber: 5g Protein: 1g Sodium: 2mg

60. Stewed Cinnamon Plums (FAST)

Preparation Time: 15 Minutes
Cooking Time: 20 minutes
Servings: 4

Ingredients:

- 1/2 cup maple syrup
- 1 cup water
- 1/8 teaspoon salt
- 1 tablespoon fresh lemon juice
- 1 cinnamon stick
- 1-pound fresh ripe plums (about 8 small or 6 medium), pitted

Directions:

1. Combine all ingredients in a 2-4-quart slow cooker and cook on low for about 6 hours, or until plums are tender.
2. Serve warm, chilled, or at room temperature.

Nutrition: Calories: 154 Carbs: 40g Fat: 0g Sugar: 25g Fiber: 2g Protein: 1g

61. Grapefruit Sorbet (FAST)

Preparation Time: 10 minutes
Cooking Time: 25 minutes
Serving: 4

Ingredients

1. 2 grapefruits, peeled and segmented
2. 4 mint leaves.
3. 3 tablespoon clover honey

Directions

1. Place ingredients in a blender and mix until smooth.
2. Pour mixture into a metal container, cover and place in freezer for 2 hours.
3. Remove from freezer and beat for 2 minutes. Return to freezer for 5 more hours.

Nutrition: Calories 17 Fat 0 Sodium 0 (mg) Carbs 4 Sugar 3 Protein 1

62. Peached Grape Bites (FAST)

Preparation Time: 5 minutes

Cooking Time: 0 minutes

Serving: 6

Ingredients

- ½ cup pecans
- 4 cups green grapes
- ½ teaspoon salt

Directions

1. Place pecans and salt in blender, mix until smooth.
2. Slice grapes in half lengthwise, spread a little pecan on one half and place another half on top.

Nutrition: Calories 173 Fat 14 Sodium 195 (mg) Carbs 13 Sugar 11 Protein 2

63. Quinoa Patties

Preparation time: 25 minutes

Total time: 60 minutes

Serving: 4

Ingredients:

- Cooking spray
- 1 green bell pepper, chopped
- 4 garlic cloves, minced
- 1 yellow onion, chopped
- 1 and ½ cups canned black beans, drained
- 1 and ½ cups quinoa, cooked
- 2 tablespoons taco seasoning
- 1 teaspoon sweet paprika
- 1 cup breadcrumbs
- 2 tablespoons flaxseeds, mixed with 6 tablespoons of warm water
- Coconut oil for frying

Direction

1. Spray some cooking spray in a pan, heat over a medium high heat, add onion and bell pepper, stir and cook for 10 minutes.
2. Add garlic, stir, cook for 2 minutes, remove from heat, transfer to a bowl and leave aside for now.
3. Meanwhile, put half of the quinoa and half of the beans in your blender and pulse a few times.
4. Add this mix to onions and stir.
5. Add flax seeds, the rest of the beans, breadcrumbs, taco seasoning, paprika and the rest of the quinoa, stir, leave aside for 5 minutes, shape your patties using your hands and arrange them on a working surface.
6. Heat up a pan with the coconut oil over medium high heat, add quinoa patties and fry them for a few minutes flipping them once.

7. Arrange patties on a platter and serve as an appetizer. Enjoy!

Nutrition: calories 190, fat 13, carbs 20, fiber 3, protein 5

64. Olive Tapenade (FAST)

Preparation Time: 15 Minutes

Cooking Time: 30 Minutes

Servings: 8

Ingredients:

- 1/2 cup pitted green olives
- 3/4 cup pitted black olives
- 2 cloves garlic, peeled
- 1 tablespoon capers
- 2 tablespoons lemon juice
- 2 tablespoons olive oil
- 1/4 teaspoon oregano
- 1/4 teaspoon ground black pepper

Directions:

1. Merge all ingredients in a food processor until almost smooth.

Nutrition: Calories: 65 Carbs: 2g Fat: 7g Fiber: 1g Protein: 0g Sod: 292mg

65. Herbed Oyster Mushroom Chips, Lemon Aioli (FAST)

Preparation time: 10 minutes

Cooking time: 25 minutes

Servings: 4-6

Ingredients:

- 1 pound of oyster mushrooms, stemmed.
- 2 tablespoons of extra virgin olive oil
- 3 tablespoons of snipped fresh rosemary, thyme, sage, or oregano.
- 1/2 cup of Paleo Aioli
- 1/2 teaspoon of finely shredded lemon peel.
- 1 tablespoon of fresh lemon juice

Directions:

1. Preheat the oven to a temperature of 400F. Place a metal rack on a large baking sheet. Then, set it aside. Then, in a large bowl, mix mushrooms, olive oil, and fresh herbs.
2. Spread the mushrooms in a single layer on the rack in the baking sheet.
3. Bake for about thirty minutes until the mushrooms are brown and sizzling.
4. Cool them for about ten minutes before serving them. The mushrooms will become crisp as they cool down.
5. For the lemon aioli, combine Paleo Aioli in a small bowl with lemon juice. Then, serve with mushroom chips.

Nutrition: Calorie: 207 Carbs: 5g Fats: 22g Protein: 3g

66. Basil Pesto Crackers (FAST)

Preparation time: 10 minutes
Cooking time: 25 minutes
Servings: 4-6
Ingredients:

- 1/2 tsp. basil, dried
- 1 garlic clove, chopped
- 2 tbsp. basil pesto
- A pinch of cayenne pepper
- 1/2 tsp. baking grinding grains
- Table salt and black pepper to the taste
- 1 and 1/4 mugs almond flour
- 3 tbsp. ghee

Directions:

1. In a pot, combine table salt, pepper, baking grinding grains and almond flour. Insert garlic, cayenne and basil and shake. Insert pesto and whisk. Also insert ghee and combine your dough with your finger.
2. Scatter this dough on a lined baking sheet, introduce within the oven at 325 degrees F and bake for 17 minutes. Leave aside to cool down, slice your crackers and serve them as a snack.

Nutrition: Calorie: 370 Carbs: 30g Fats: 26g Protein: 9g

67. Salt And Peppery Broccoli (FAST)

Preparation time: 10 minutes
Cooking time:20 minutes
Servings: 4
Ingredients

- 2 medium/ large sized avocados, halve or pitted
- 4 large whole eggs
- ¼ teaspoons fresh ground black pepper

Directions

1. Preheat your oven to 425 degrees F
2. Scoop out some pulp from the avocado halves, leaving enough space to fit an egg
3. Line an 8 by an 8-inch baking pan with foil, place avocado halves in the pan to fit nicely in a single layer
4. Gently fold the foil around the outer edges of the avocados
5. Crack 1 egg into each avocado half, season them with pepper
6. Bake for about 12-15 minutes uncovered until you have your desired doneness
7. Remove from oven and let them rest for 5 minutes
8. Serve and enjoy!

Nutrition: Calories: 62 Fat: 4 g Saturated Fat: 1 g Carbohydrates: 4 g Fiber: 1 g Sodium: 348 mg Protein: 4 g

68. Fancy Avocado Chips (FAST)

Preparation time: 10 minutes
Cooking time:30 minutes
Servings: 4
Ingredients

- Fresh black pepper
- Salt as needed
- ½ teaspoon Italian seasoning
- ½ teaspoon garlic powder
- 1 teaspoon lemon juice
- 1 large ripe avocado
- ¾ cup coconut cream

Directions

1. Preheat your oven to 325 degrees F
2. Take two baking sheets and line them with parchment paper
3. Take a medium-sized bowl and add avocado; mash them with a fork until you have a smooth mixture
4. Stir in coconut cream, garlic powder, lemon juice, and seasoning
5. Season more with salt and pepper
6. Place about a heaping teaspoon scoop of the mix on your baking sheet, making sure to leave about a 3-inch distance between each scoop
7. Flatten them to a 3-inch width
8. Bake for about 30 minutes until crispy
9. Serve and enjoy!

Nutrition: Calories: 120 Fat: 10 g Saturated Fat: 3 g Carbohydrates: 4 g Fiber: 1 g Sodium: 287 mg Protein: 7 g

69. Awesome Cucumber Sushi (FAST)

Preparation time: 10 minutes
Cooking time: 10 minutes
Servings: 4
Ingredients
For Sushi

- 2 small carrots, thinly sliced
- ½ yellow bell pepper, thinly sliced
- ½ red bell pepper, thinly sliced
- ¼ avocado, sliced
- 2 medium cucumbers, halved
- For Sauce
- 1 teaspoon soy sauce
- 1 tablespoon Sirach
- 1/3 cup coconut cream

Directions

1. Take a small-sized spoon, remove the seeds from the center of the cucumber and make them hollow
2. Press avocado into the center of your cucumber using a butter knife
3. Slide in the sliced bell pepper and carrots until the cucumber shell is full of your vegetables
4. Take a small bowl and add cream, soy sauce, and Sirach; whisk well
5. Slice the cucumber into 1-inch rounds and serve with the sauce

Nutrition: Calories: 200 Fat: 16 g Saturated Fat: 4 g Carbohydrates: 9 g Fiber: 2 g Sodium: 247 mg Protein: 1 g

70. Turkish Appetizer Salad (FAST)

Preparation time: 10 minutes
Cooking time: 25 minutes
Serving: 6
Ingredients:
- 3 tablespoons olive oil
- 2 loaves pita bread, toasted
- 1 cucumber, cubed
- 5 tomatoes, roughly chopped
- 1 lettuce head, chopped
- ½ teaspoon sumac
- 1 cup parsley, chopped
- 5 green peppers, chopped
- 5 radishes, sliced
- For the salad dressing:
- 1/3 cup olive oil
- Juice from 1 and ½ limes
- ½ teaspoon cinnamon powder
- 1 teaspoon sumac
- ¼ teaspoon allspice
- Salt and black pepper to the taste

Direction:
1. Heat up a pan with 3 tablespoons olive oil over medium heat, break pita, add to the pan, brown for 2 minutes, add salt, pepper and ½ teaspoon sumac.
2. In a bowl, mix lettuce with onion, cucumber, tomatoes, parsley and radishes and leave aside as well.
3. In another bowl, mix 1/3 cup olive oil with lime juice, salt, pepper, 1 teaspoon sumac, cinnamon and all spice and stir.
4. Mix salad with this dressing, toss to coat, divide into small appetizer bowls and serve with toasted pita on top. Enjoy!

Nutrition: calories 120, fat 0.3, carbs 1, protein 6, fibers 5

71. Tofu Packets (FAST)

Preparation time: 10 minutes
Cooking time: 20 minutes
Serving: 4
Ingredients:
- 20 ounces firm tofu, cut in 16 pieces
- 12 ounces eggplant cut in medium chunks
- 7 tablespoons olive oil
- 2 tablespoons garlic crushed
- 2 tablespoons ginger grated
- ¼ cup soy sauce
- 1 cup dill roughly chopped
- 2 green onions finely chopped
- 1 cucumber cut in chunks
- 2 tablespoons lime juice
- 1 cup cilantro roughly chopped
- 1 red jalapeno pepper sliced
- Sea salt and black pepper to the taste

Direction
1. Place tofu in a zip-top bag, add eggplant pieces, garlic, ginger, soy sauce, green onions, salt, pepper and 5 tablespoons oil, seal, shake well and leave aside for now.
2. Heat up your kitchen grill over medium heat, divide the tofu mix on 4 pieces of high-quality tin foil, wrap them, place on grill, cook for 10 minutes, turning them once, transfer to a platter, unwrap and leave aside to cool down for 1-2 minutes.
3. In a bowl, mix cucumber with cilantro, jalapeno, dill, lime juice, 2 tablespoon oils, season with some salt and pepper and stir well.
4. Serve tofu packets as an appetizer with cucumber mix on the side. Enjoy!

Nutrition: calories 180, fat 10, carbs 20, fiber 0, protein 5

72. Fried Zucchini Sticks (FAST)

Preparation Time: 10 Minutes
Cooking Time: 20 Minutes
Servings: 4
Ingredients:
- 3/4 cup almond flour
- 1/2 teaspoon garlic powder
- 3/4 teaspoon Italian seasoning
- 1/4 teaspoon salt
- 4 medium zucchinis, cut into strips
- 4 tablespoons olive oil

Directions:
1. In a large bowl or pan, combine almond flour, garlic powder, Italian seasoning, and salt.

2. Lightly toss zucchini strips with flour mixture, coating well.
3. Warmth olive oil in a large skillet or frying pan over medium-high heat. When oil is hot, gently add zucchini strips to pan.
4. Fry. Drain on paper towels. Serve warm.

Nutrition: Calories: 263 Carbs: 0g Fat: 23g Sugar: 6g Fiber: 4g Protein: 7g Sodium: 165mg

73. Homemade Tahini

Preparation Time: 30 Minutes
Cooking Time: 20 Minutes
Servings: 20
Ingredients:
- 2 cups sesame seeds
- 1/2 cup olive oil
- 1/2 teaspoon paprika

Directions:
1. Heat oven to 350F.
2. Scatter sesame seeds in a thin layer on a large baking sheet and set in the oven, shaking the sheet once to mix. Cool.
3. Process sesame seeds with oil in a food processor or blender until thick and creamy. Garnish with paprika.

Nutrition: Calories: 142 Carbs: 2gFat: 15g Sugar: 0g Fiber: 2g Protein: 3g Sodium: 7mg

74. Zucchini Appetizer Salad (FAST)

Preparation time: 10 minutes
Cooking time: 10 minutes
Serving: 4
Ingredients:
- 2 pounds zucchinis, sliced with a mandolin
- Salt and black pepper to the taste
- 2 tablespoons lemon juice
- 1/3 cup olive oil
- ½ cup basil, chopped
- ¼ teaspoon red pepper, crushed
- ¼ cup pine nuts, toasted

Direction
1. In a small bowl, mix oil with salt, pepper, red pepper and lemon juice and whisk well.
2. In a salad bowl, mix zucchinis with basil and nuts.
3. Add salad dressing, toss to coat and serve as an appetizer. Enjoy!

Nutrition: calories 100, fat 1, fiber 2, carbs 4, protein 5

75. Classic Guacamole (FAST)

Preparation Time: 10 Minutes
Cooking Time: 20 Minutes

Servings: 4
Ingredients:
- 2 large ripe avocados, pitted, peeled, and coarsely chopped
- 1 small white onion, peeled and diced
- 1 medium tomato, diced
- 1 medium jalapeño pepper, seeded and thinly sliced
- Juice of 1 medium lime

Directions:
1. Gently combine all ingredients in a small serving bowl and serve as a salad or dip.

Nutrition: Calories: 129 Carbs: 10g Fat: 11g Sugar: 2g Fiber: 5g Protein: 2g Sodium: 8mg

76. Asparagus Appetizer Salad (FAST)

Preparation time: 10 minutes
Cooking time: 25 minutes
Serving: 2
Ingredients:
- 1 and ½ tablespoons pea
- 1 teaspoon sesame seed
- 5 ounces asparagus
- 1 teaspoon sesame oil
- 7 ounces courgetti's, sliced
- A handful rocket leaves
- Zest from ½ lemon, grated
- Salt and black pepper to the taste

Direction:
1. Heat up a pan over medium high heat, add sesame seeds, toast them for 1-2 minutes, take off heat and leave aside.
2. Steam asparagus for 3-4 minutes, transfer them to a bowl filled with ice water, drain and leave aside.
3. Put peas in a pot filled with water, bring to a boil and cook for 3 minutes.
4. Drain and leave aside as well.
5. Heat up a grill, brush asparagus and courgetti slices with the oil and cook them for a few minutes.
6. Transfer courgetti slices and asparagus to a bowl, add peas, rocket and lemon zest.
7. Add salt, black pepper, sprinkle sesame seeds on top, toss, divide on appetizer plates and serve. Enjoy!

Nutrition: calories 214, fat 11, carbs 12, fibers 9, protein 15

77. Mushroom Appetizer (FAST)

Preparation time: 5 minutes
Cooking time: 20 minutes
Serving: 2

Ingredients:
- 1 big Portobello mushroom, sliced
- 1 tablespoon water
- ½ tablespoon breadcrumbs
- 1 teaspoon olive oil
- Salt and black pepper to the taste
- 1 teaspoon chives, chopped

Direction:
1. Put mushroom slices in a baking dish, add water, drizzle oil, season with salt and pepper and sprinkle breadcrumbs on top.
2. Place dish on high heated grill and cook for 10 minutes.
3. Take off heat, sprinkle chives on top, divide on appetizer plates and serve. Enjoy!

Nutrition: calories 90, fat 3, carbs 10, protein 7, fibers 5

78. Kale Appetizer (FAST)

Preparation time: 10 minutes
Cooking time: 10 minutes
Serving: 6

Ingredients:
- 4 ounces bulgur wheat
- 4 ounces kale
- A bunch of mint, chopped
- A bunch of spring onions, chopped
- ½ cucumber, chopped
- A pinch of cinnamon powder
- A pinch of allspice
- 6 tablespoons olive oil
- Zest and juice from ½ lemon
- 4 Baby Gem lettuce for serving

Direction:
1. Put bulgur in a bowl, cover with boiling water and leave aside for 10 minutes.
2. Put kale in your food processor and chop.
3. Drain bulgur, put in a bowl and mix with kale, mint, spring onions, cucumber and tomatoes.
4. Add cinnamon and allspice and stir.
5. Add olive oil and lemon juice and toss to coat.
6. Add feta cheese on top and lemon zest.
7. Arrange lettuce leaves on plates and scoop salad into each. Enjoy!

Nutrition: calories 200, fat 9, carbs 12, protein 14, fiber 6

79. No-Sugar Apricot Applesauce (FAST)

Preparation Time: 10 Minutes
Cooking Time: 20 Minutes
Servings: 4

Ingredients:
- 6 medium apples, peeled, cored, and chopped
- 1/3 cup water
- 1/2 cup chopped dried apricots
- 4 large pitted dates, chopped
- 1/4 teaspoon ground cinnamon

Directions:
1. Add apples and water to a large soup pot or stockpot and bring to a low boil over medium-high heat. Set heat to low, secure, and simmer for 15 minutes, stirring occasionally.
2. Add apricots and dates and simmer for another 10–15 minutes.
3. Mash with a large fork until desired consistency is reached, or allow to cool slightly and purée in a blender until smooth.
4. Sprinkle with cinnamon before serving.

Nutrition: Calories: 213 Carbs: 57g Fat: 1g Sugar: 44g Fiber: 9g Protein: 2g Sodium: 5mg

80. Almond Honey Cauliflower Skewers (FAST)

Preparation Time: 10 Minutes
Cooking Time: 12 Minutes
Servings: 4

Ingredients:
- 1/2 cup organic almond butter
- 1 medium head cauliflower
- 2 tablespoons honey
- 1/2 teaspoon salt

Directions:
1. Separate cauliflower into florets, trim stems.
2. Combine almond butter, honey, and salt in a bowl.
3. Add cauliflower, and coat with dressing.
4. Place 4 cauliflower florets per skewer.
5. Heat grill to medium-high.
6. Set skewers on grill and cook for 12 minutes over indirect heat, be sure to turn as required.

Nutrition: Calories: 266 Carbs: 22g Fat: 18g Sugar: 12g Protein: 10g Sodium: 334mg

81. Greek Appetizer (FAST)

Preparation time: 10 minutes
Cooking time: 17 minutes
Serving: 6

Ingredients:
- ½ pounds mushrooms, sliced
- 1 tablespoon extra-virgin olive oil

- 3 garlic cloves, minced
- 1 teaspoon basil, dried
- Salt and black pepper to the taste
- 1 tomato, diced
- 3 tablespoons lemon juice
- ½ cup water
- 1 tablespoons coriander, chopped

Direction:
1. Heat up a pan with the oil over medium heat, add mushrooms, stir and cook for 3 minutes.
2. Add basil and garlic, stir and cook for 1 minute more.
3. Add water, salt, pepper, tomato and lemon juice, stir, cook for a few minutes more, take off heat, divide into small bowls, leave aside to cool down, sprinkle coriander and serve. Enjoy!

Nutrition: calories 140, fat 4, fiber 4, carbs 7, protein 7

82. Colored Halloumi Appetizer (FAST)

Preparation time: 15 minutes
Cooking time: 35 minutes
Serving: 4
Ingredients:
- 7 ounces lentils
- 3 tablespoons capers, chopped
- Juice from 1 lemon
- Zest and juice from 1 lemon, grated
- 1 red onion, sliced
- 3 tablespoons olive oil
- 14 ounces canned chickpeas, drained
- 8 ounces beetroot, cooked and cut in matchsticks
- 1 small hand parsley, chopped
- 8 ounces packed halloumi, cut in 8 slices
- Salt and pepper to the taste

Direction:
1. Put lentils in a pot, cover with water, boil for 20 minutes, drain and leave aside.
2. Put lemon juice from 1 lemon in a bowl, add onion, salt and pepper, stir and leave aside.
3. Put the juice and zest from the second lemon in a bowl, add oil, salt, pepper and the capers, stir well and leave aside.
4. Put lentils and chickpeas in a bowl, add beets, parsley, pickled onions you've prepared and toss to coat.
5. Heat up a grill over medium heat and cook halloumi for 2 minutes on each side.

6. Add this to the salad, add capers along with lemon juice and zest, stir well, divide into appetizer bowls and serve. Enjoy!

Nutrition: calories 400, fat 20, carbs 20, fibers 12, protein 13

83. Garlic Red Bell Pepper Hummus (FAST)

Preparation Time: 10 Minutes
Cooking Time: 10 Minutes
Servings: 4
Ingredients:
- 4 red bell peppers, seeded
- 2 cups cauliflower florets
- 6 cloves garlic
- 1/2 teaspoon salt
- 1/2 teaspoon black pepper
- Extra virgin olive oil

Directions:
1. Set ingredients in a blender and mix until fairly smooth but with some texture.
2. Serve with fresh veggies.

Nutrition: Calories: 117g Carbs: 12g Fat: 7g Sugar: 6g Protein: 3g Sodium: 311g

84. Pollock with Roasted Tomatoes

Preparation Time: 5 minutes
Cooking Time: 40 minutes
Servings: 6
Ingredients:
- 12 plum tomatoes, halved
- 2 shallots, very thinly cut into rings
- 3 garlic cloves, minced
- 3 tablespoons plus 1 teaspoon extra-virgin olive oil, divided
- 1 teaspoon sea salt, divided
- ½ teaspoon freshly ground black pepper, divided
- 1 teaspoon butter (or extra-virgin olive oil)
- ¾ cup whole-wheat bread crumbs
- 6 (4-ounce) Pollock fillets
- ¼ cup chopped fresh Italian parsley leaves

Directions:
1. Preheat the oven to 450°F.
2. In a large bowl, toss the tomatoes, shallots, and garlic with 1 tablespoon of olive oil, ½ teaspoon of sea salt, and ¼ teaspoon of pepper. Transfer to a rimmed baking sheet and arrange in a single layer. Bake for about 40 minutes until the tomatoes are soft and browned.
3. While the tomatoes cook, in a large nonstick skillet over medium-high heat, heat 1 tablespoon plus 1 teaspoon of olive oil until it bubbles.

4. Add the bread crumbs and cook for about 5 minutes, stirring, until they are browned and crunchy. Remove from the pan and set aside, scraping the pan clean.
5. Return the skillet to medium-high heat and add the remaining tablespoon of olive oil.
6. Season the fish with the remaining ½ teaspoon of sea salt and ¼ teaspoon of pepper. Place the fish in the skillet. Cook for about 5 minutes per side until opaque.
7. To assemble, spoon the tomatoes onto four plates. Top with the Pollock and sprinkle with the bread crumbs. Garnish with parsley and serve.

Nutrition: Calories: 286 Protein: 30g Total Carbohydrates: 22g Sugars: 7g Fiber: 3g Total Fat: 9g Saturated Fat: 2g Cholesterol: 64mg Sodium: 419mg

SALADS AND CEREALS

85. Peppers and Lentils Salad (FAST)

Preparation time: 10 minutes
Cooking time: 0 minutes
Servings: 4
Ingredients:
- 14 ounces canned lentils, drained and rinsed
- 2 spring onions, chopped
- 1 red bell pepper, chopped
- 1 green bell pepper, chopped
- 1 tablespoon fresh lime juice
- 1/3 cup coriander, chopped
- 2 teaspoon balsamic vinegar

Directions:
1. In a salad bowl, combine the lentils with the onions, bell peppers, and the rest of the ingredients, toss and serve.

Nutrition: Calories 200 Fat 2.45g Fiber 6.7g Carbs 10.5g Protein 5.6g

86. Cashews and Red Cabbage Salad (FAST)

Preparation time: 10 minutes
Cooking time: 0 minutes
Servings: 4
Ingredients:
- 1-pound red cabbage, shredded
- 2 tablespoons coriander, chopped
- ½ cup cashews halved
- 2 tablespoons olive oil
- 1 tomato, cubed
- A pinch of salt and black pepper
- 1 tablespoon white vinegar

Directions:
1. Mix the cabbage with the coriander and the rest of the ingredients in a salad bowl, toss and serve cold.

Nutrition: Calories 210 Fat 6.3g Fiber 5.2g Carbs 5.5g Protein 8g

87. Minty Olives and Tomatoes Salad (FAST)

Preparation time: 10 minutes
Cooking time: 0 minutes
Servings: 4
Ingredients:
- 1 cup kalamata olives, pitted and sliced
- 1 cup black olives, pitted and halved
- 1 cup cherry tomatoes, halved
- 4 tomatoes, chopped
- 1 red onion, chopped
- 2 tablespoons oregano, chopped
- 1 tablespoon mint, chopped
- 2 tablespoons balsamic vinegar
- ¼ cup olive oil
- 2 teaspoons Italian herbs, dried
- A pinch of sea salt
- black pepper

Directions:
1. In a salad bowl, mix the olives with the tomatoes and the rest of the ingredients, toss, and serve cold.

Nutrition: Calories 190 Fat 8.1g Fiber 5.8g Carbs 11.6g Protein 4.6g

88. Beans and Cucumber Salad (FAST)

Preparation time: 10 minutes
Cooking time: 0 minutes
Servings: 4
Ingredients:
- 15 oz. canned great northern beans
- 2 tablespoons olive oil
- ½ cup baby arugula
- 1 cup cucumber, sliced
- 1 tablespoon parsley, chopped
- 2 tomatoes, cubed
- A pinch of sea salt
- black pepper
- 2 tablespoon balsamic vinegar

Directions:
1. Mix the beans with the cucumber and the rest of the ingredients in a large bowl, toss and serve cold.

Nutrition: calories 233 fat 9g fiber 6.5g carbs 13g protein 8

89. Sun-Dried Tomatoes Salad (FAST)

Preparation time: 15 minutes
Cooking time: 0 minutes
Servings: 4
Ingredients:
- 1 cup sun-dried tomatoes, chopped
- 4 eggs, hard-boiled, peeled, and chopped
- ½ cup olives, pitted, chopped
- 1 small red onion, finely chopped
- ½ cup Greek yogurt
- 1 teaspoon lemon juice
- 1 teaspoon Italian seasonings

Directions:
1. In the salad bowl, mix up all ingredients and shake well.

Nutrition: Calories 120 Protein 8.8g Carbohydrates 5.9g Fat 7.1g Fiber 1.5g

90. Tomato and Avocado Salad (FAST)

Preparation time: 10 minutes
Cooking time: 0 minutes
Servings: 4
Ingredients:
- 1-pound cherry tomatoes, cubed
- 2 avocados, pitted, peeled, and cubed
- 1 sweet onion, chopped
- A pinch of sea salt
- black pepper
- 2 tablespoons lemon juice
- 1 and ½ tablespoons olive oil
- Handful basil, chopped

Directions:
1. Mix the tomatoes with the avocados and the rest of the ingredients in a serving bowl, toss and serve right away.

Nutrition: Calories 148 Fat 7.8g Fiber 2.9g Carbs 5.4g Protein 5.5g

91. Pistachio Arugula Salad (FAST)

Preparation time: 20 minutes
Cooking time: 0 minutes
Servings: 6
Ingredients:
- ¼ Cup Olive Oil
- 6 Cups Kale, Chopped Rough
- 2 Cups arugula
- ½ Teaspoon Smoked Paprika
- 2 Tablespoons Lemon Juice, Fresh
- 1/3 Cup Pistachios, Unsalted & Shelled
- 6 Tablespoons Parmesan, Grated

Directions:
1. Get out a large bowl and combine your oil, lemon juice, kale and smoked paprika. Massage it into the leaves for about fifteen seconds. You then need to allow it to sit for ten minutes.
2. Mix everything together before serving with grated cheese on top.

Nutrition: Calories: *150* Protein: 5 Grams Fat: 12 Grams Carbs: 8 Grams Sodium: 169 mg

92. Potato Salad

Preparation Time: 10 minutes
Cooking Time: 15 minutes
Servings: 6
Ingredients:
- 2 lbs. Golden Potatoes, Cubed in 1 Inch Pieces
- 3 Tablespoons Olive Oil
- 3 tablespoons Lemon Juice, Fresh
- 1 Tablespoon Olive Brine

- ¼ Teaspoon Sea Salt, Fine
- ½ Cup Olives, Sliced
- 1 Cup Celery, Sliced
- 2 Tablespoons Oregano, Fresh
- 2 Tablespoons Mint Leaves, Fresh & Chopped

Directions:
1. Get out a medium saucepan and put your potatoes in cold water. The water should b earn inch above your potatoes. Set it over high heat and bring it to a boil before turning the heat down. You want to turn it down to medium-low. Allow it to cook for twelve to fifteen more minutes. The potatoes should be tender when you pierce them with a fork.
2. Get out a small bowl and whisk your oil, lemon juice, olive brine and salt together.
3. Drain your potatoes using a colander and transfer it to a serving bowl. Pour in three tablespoons of dressing over your potatoes, and mix well with oregano, and min along with the remaining dressing.

Nutrition: Calories: 175 Protein: 3 Grams Fat: 7 Grams Carbs: 27 Grams Sodium: 98 mg

93. Bean Salad (FAST)

Preparation Time: 15 minutes
Cooking Time: 5 minutes
Servings: 6
Ingredients:
- 1 Can Garbanzo Beans, Rinsed & Drained
- 2 Tablespoons Balsamic Vinegar
- ¼ Cup Olive Oil
- 4 Cloves Garlic, Chopped Fine
- 1/3 Cup Parsley, Fresh & Chopped
- ¼ Cup Olive Oil
- 1 Red Onion, Diced
- 6 Lettuce Leaves
- ½ Cup Celery, Chopped Fine/Black Pepper to Taste

Directions:
1. Make the vinaigrette dressing by whipping together your garlic, parsley, vinegar and pepper in a bowl.
2. Add the olive oil to this mixture and whisk before setting it aside.
3. Add in your onion and beans, and then pour your dressing on top. Toss until it's coated together and then cover it. Place it in the fridge until it's time to serve.
4. Place a lettuce leaf on the plate when serving and spoon the mixture in. garnish with celery.

Nutrition: Calories: 218 Protein: 7 Grams Fat: 0 Grams Carbs: 25 Grams Sodium: 160 mg

94. Eggs and fruit salad

Serves 1;
Cooking time: 20 minutes
Ingredients:
- Strawberries, sliced (1/2 cup)
- Mandarin orange sections, unsweetened or fresh (1/2 cup) Blueberries (1/2 cup)
- Egg whites (6 hardboiled eggs, discard yolks)
- Avocado (1/2 cup)
- Salsa (3 tbsp.)

Directions:
1. Prepare the fruit salad in a medium-sized bowl. Slice strawberries, and then gently stir blueberries and mandarin sections in.
2. Boil the eggs for about 10 minutes then allow to cook. Halve the eggs and remove the yolks
3. Dice the hardboiled egg whites and avocado; mix in a separate bowl. Stir the salsa in.
4. Put some fruit salad sidings, and serve.

95. Warm Beef and Lentil Salad (FAST)

Preparation Time: 10 minutes
Cooking Time: 15 minutes
Servings: 4
Ingredients:
- 1 large piece of steak, (rump steak is great), about 1 lb., room temperature
- 1 Tbsp. olive oil
- Salt and pepper
- 3 cups canned brown lentils, (3 cups once drained)
- ½ red onion, finely chopped
- 3 oz. feta cheese, crumbled
- ½ cup finely chopped parsley
- ⅓ cup finely chopped mint
- Juice of 1 lemon
- 3 Tbsp. olive oil

Directions:
1. Place a skillet over a high heat
2. Rub the steak with olive oil and sprinkle with salt and pepper
3. Lay the steak onto the hot skillet and sear on both sides until golden, but still blushing in the center (medium rare), leave to rest while you prepare the salad
4. In a large salad bowl, toss the lentils, onion, feta, parsley, mint, lemon juice, and olive oil
5. Slice the warm steak into thin slices and lay on top of the salad, or divide individually when serving

Nutrition: Calories: 442 Fat: 21.3 grams   Protein: 39.3 grams Total carbs: 24.8 grams Net carbs: 18.4 grams

96. Quinoa and Greens Salad (FAST)

Preparation time: 10 minutes
Cooking time: 0 minutes
Servings: 4
Ingredients:
- 1 cup quinoa, cooked
- 1 medium bunch collard greens, chopped
- 4 tablespoons walnuts, chopped
- 2 tablespoons balsamic vinegar
- 4 tablespoons tahini paste
- 4 tablespoons cold water
- A pinch of salt and black pepper
- 1 tablespoon olive oil

Directions:
1. In a bowl, mix the tahini with the water and vinegar and whisk.
2. In a bowl, mix the quinoa with the rest of the ingredients and the tahini dressing, toss, divide the mix between plates and serve as a side dish.

Nutrition: Calories 175 Fat 3 Fiber 3 Carbs 5 Protein 3

RICE RECIPES

97. Cherry, Apricot, and Pecan Brown Rice Bowl

Preparation time: 15 minutes
Cooking time: 61 minutes
Servings: 2
Ingredients:
- 2 tablespoons olive oil
- 2 green onions, sliced
- ½ cup of brown rice
- 1 cup low -sodium chicken stock
- 2 tablespoons dried cherries
- 4 dried apricots, chopped
- 2 tablespoons pecans, toasted and chopped
- Sea salt
- ground pepper

Directions:
1. Warm-up the olive oil in a medium saucepan over medium-high heat until shimmering.
2. Add the green onions and sauté for 1 minute or until fragrant. Add the rice. Stir to mix well, then pour in the chicken stock.
3. Bring to a boil. Reduce the heat to low. Cover and simmer for 50 minutes or until the brown rice is soft.
4. Add the cherries, apricots, and pecans, and simmer for 10 more minutes or until the fruits are tender.
5. Pour them in a large serving bowl—fluff with a fork. Put sea salt plus ground pepper. Serve immediately.

Nutrition: Calories: 451 Fat: 25.9g Protein: 8.2g Carbs: 50.4g Fiber: 4.6g Sodium: 122mg

98. Curry Apple Couscous with Leeks and Pecans (FAST)

Preparation time: 15 minutes
Cooking time: 8 minutes
Servings: 4
Ingredients:
- 2 teaspoons extra-virgin olive oil
- 2 leeks, white parts only, sliced
- 1 apple, diced
- 2 cups cooked couscous
- 2 tablespoons curry powder
- ½ cup chopped pecans

Directions:
1. Warm-up the olive oil in a skillet over medium heat until shimmering. Add the leeks and sauté for 5 minutes or until soft.

2. Add the diced apple and cook for 3 more minutes until tender. Add the couscous and curry powder. Stir to combine.
3. Transfer them to a large serving bowl, then mix in the pecans and serve.

Nutrition: Calories: 254 Fat: 11.9g Protein: 5.4g Carbs: 34.3g Fiber: 5.9g Sodium: 15mg

99. Lemony Farro and Avocado Bowl (FAST)

Preparation time: 5 minutes
Cooking time: 25 minutes
Servings: 4
Ingredients:
- 1 tbsp & 2 tbsp extra-virgin olive oil, divided
- ½ medium onion, chopped
- 1 carrot, shredded
- 2 garlic cloves, minced
- 1 (6-ounce / 170-g) cup pearled farro
- 2 cups low-sodium vegetable soup
- 2 avocados, peeled, pitted, and sliced
- Zest and juice of 1 small lemon
- ¼ teaspoon of sea salt

Directions:
1. Heat 1 tablespoon of olive oil in a saucepan over medium-high heat until shimmering.
2. Put the onion, then sauté for 5 minutes or until translucent. Add the carrot and garlic and sauté for 1 minute or until fragrant.
3. Add the farro and pour in the vegetable soup. Bring to a boil over high heat. Reduce the heat to low. Put the lid on and simmer for 20 minutes or until the farro is al dente.
4. Transfer it to a large bowl, then fold in the avocado slices. Sprinkle with lemon zest and salt, then drizzle with lemon juice and 2 teaspoons of olive oil. Stir to mix well and serve immediately.

Nutrition: Calories: 210 Fat: 11.1g Protein: 4.2g Carbs: 27.9g Fiber: 7.0g Sodium: 152mg

100. Rice and Blueberry Stuffed Sweet Potatoes (FAST)

Preparation time: 15 minutes
Cooking time: 20 minutes
Servings: 4
Ingredients:
- 2 cups cooked wild rice
- ½ cup dried blueberries
- ½ cup chopped hazelnuts
- ½ cup shredded Swiss chard

- 1 teaspoon chopped fresh thyme
- 1 scallion, white and green parts, peeled and thinly sliced
- Sea salt and freshly ground black pepper, to taste
- 4 sweet potatoes, baked in the skin until tender

Directions:
1. Preheat the oven to 400°F (205°C).
2. Combine all the ingredients, except for the sweet potatoes, in a large bowl. Stir to mix well.
3. Cut the top third of the sweet potato off length wire, then scoop most of the sweet potato flesh out.
4. Fill the potato with the wild rice mixture, then set the sweet potato on a greased baking sheet.
5. Bake in the preheated oven for 20 minutes or until the sweet potato skin is lightly charred. Serve immediately.

Nutrition: Calories: 393 Fat: 7.1g Protein: 10.2g Carbs: 76.9g Fiber: 10.0g Sodium: 93mg

101. Slow-Cooked Turkey and Brown Rice

Preparation time: 15 minutes
Cooking time: 3 hours and 10 minutes
Servings: 6

Ingredients:
- 1 tablespoon extra-virgin olive oil
- 1½ pounds (680 g) ground turkey
- 2 tablespoons chopped fresh sage, divided
- 2 tablespoons chopped fresh thyme, divided
- 1 teaspoon of sea salt
- ½ teaspoon ground black pepper
- 2 cups brown rice
- 1 (14-ounce / 397-g) can stewed tomatoes, with the juice
- ¼ cup pitted and sliced Kalamata olives
- 3 medium zucchinis, sliced thinly
- ¼ cup chopped fresh flat-leaf parsley
- 1 medium yellow onion, chopped
- 1 tablespoon plus 1 teaspoon balsamic vinegar
- 2 cups low-sodium chicken stock
- 2 garlic cloves, minced
- ½ cup grated Parmesan cheese, for serving

Directions:
1. Warm-up the olive oil in a nonstick skillet over medium-high heat until shimmering.
2. Add the ground turkey and sprinkle with 1 tablespoon of sage, 1 tablespoon of thyme, salt, and ground black pepper.
3. Sauté for 10 minutes or until the ground turkey is lightly browned.

4. Pour them into the slow cooker, then pour in the remaining ingredients, except for the Parmesan. Stir to mix well.
5. Cook on high within 3 hours or until the rice and vegetables are tender.
6. Put it into a large bowl, then spread with Parmesan cheese before serving.

Nutrition: Calories: 499 Fat: 16.4g Protein: 32.4g Carbs: 56.5g Fiber: 4.7g Sodium: 758mg

102. Papaya, Jicama, and Peas Rice Bowl

Preparation time: 20 minutes
Cooking time: 45 minutes
Servings: 4

Ingredients:
- Sauce:
- Juice of ¼ lemon
- 2 teaspoons chopped fresh basil
- 1 tablespoon raw honey
- 1 tablespoon extra-virgin olive oil
- Sea salt, to taste

Rice:
- 1½ cups wild rice
- 2 papayas, peeled, seeded, and diced
- 1 jicama, peeled and shredded
- 1 cup snow peas, julienned
- 2 cups shredded cabbage
- 1 scallion, white and green parts, chopped

Directions:
1. Mix the fixings for the sauce in a bowl. Stir to mix well. Set aside until ready to use.
2. Pour the wild rice into a saucepan, then pour in enough water to cover. Bring to a boil.
3. Reduce the heat to low, then simmer for 45 minutes or until the wild rice is soft and plump. Drain, then put in a large bowl.
4. Top the rice with papayas, jicama, peas, cabbage, and scallion. Pour the sauce over and stir to mix well before serving.

Nutrition: Calories: 446 Fat: 7.9g Protein: 13.1g Carbs: 85.8g Fiber: 16.0g Sodium: 70mg

103. Fiber Packed Chicken Rice (FAST)

Preparation Time: 10 minutes
Cooking Time: 16 minutes
Servings: 6

Ingredients:
- 1 lb. chicken breast, skinless, boneless, and cut into chunks
- 14.5 oz canned cannellini beans
- 4 cups chicken broth
- 2 cups wild rice
- 1 tbsp. Italian seasoning
- 1 small onion, chopped
- 1 tbsp. garlic, chopped

- 1 tbsp. olive oil
- Pepper
- Salt

Directions:

1. Warm oil into the pot, then put garlic and onion and sauté for 2 minutes.
2. Add chicken and cook for 2 minutes. Add remaining ingredients and stir well.
3. Cook on high for 12 minutes. Stir well and serve.

Nutrition: Calories 399 Fat 6.4 g Carbohydrates 53.4 g Sugar 3 g Protein 31.6 g Cholesterol 50 mg

104. Wild Rice, Celery, and Cauliflower Pilaf

Preparation time: 15 minutes
Cooking time: 45 minutes
Servings: 4
Ingredients:

- 1 tbsp olive oil
- 1 cup wild rice
- 2 cups low-sodium chicken broth
- 1 sweet onion, chopped
- 2 stalks celery, chopped
- 1 teaspoon minced garlic
- 2 carrots, peeled, halved lengthwise, and sliced
- ½ cauliflower head, cut into small florets
- 1 teaspoon chopped fresh thyme
- Sea salt, to taste

Directions:

1. Warm the oven to 350 F. Line a baking sheet with parchment paper and grease with olive oil.
2. Put the wild rice in a saucepan, then pour in the chicken broth. Bring to a boil. Reduce the heat to low and simmer for 30 minutes or until the rice is plump.
3. Meanwhile, heat the remaining olive oil in an oven-proof skillet over medium-high heat until shimmering.
4. Add the onion, celery, and garlic to the skillet and sauté for 3 minutes or until the onion is translucent. Add the carrots and cauliflower to the skillet and sauté for 5 minutes. Turn off the heat and set aside.
5. Pour the cooked rice into the skillet with the vegetables. Sprinkle with thyme and salt.
6. Set the skillet in the preheated oven and bake for 15 minutes or until the vegetables are soft. Serve immediately.

Nutrition: Calories: 214 Fat: 3.9g Protein: 7.2g Carbs: 37.9g Fiber: 5.0g Sodium: 122mg

105. Delicious Rice and Spinach (FAST)

Preparation Time: 10 minutes

Cooking Time: 15 minutes
Servings: 6
Ingredients:

- 1 onion
- 2 pinch sea salt
- 2 pinch black pepper.
- 1 cup unsalted vegetable broth
- 2 tablespoons olive oil.
- 2 can brown rice
- 4 cups fresh baby spinach
- Juice of orange
- 1 garlic clove
- 1 orange Zest

Directions:

1. In a substantial skillet over medium-high heat the olive oil until it gleams.
2. Include the onion and Directions: for around 5 minutes blending infrequently until delicate.
3. Include the spinach and Directions: for around 2 minutes blending infrequently until it shrivels.
4. Include the garlic and Directions: for 30 seconds blending continually.
5. Blend in the orange juice soup ocean salt and pepper. Convey to a stew.
6. Mix in the rice and Directions: for around 4 minutes mixing until the rice is warmed through and the fluid is consumed.

Nutrition: Calories: 506 Total Fat: 7.5g Sodium: 226mg Total Carbs: 100.3g Fiber: 5g Sugars: 16.9g Protein: 13g

106. Tasty Greek Rice (FAST)

Preparation Time: 10 minutes
Cooking Time: 10 minutes
Servings: 6
Ingredients:

- 1 3/4 cup brown rice, rinsed and drained
- 3/4 cup roasted red peppers, chopped
- 1 cup olives, chopped
- 1 tsp dried oregano
- 1 tsp Greek seasoning
- 1 3/4 cup vegetable broth
- 2 tbsp olive oil
- Salt

Directions:

1. Put rice in a pot with olive oil and cook for 5 minutes.
2. Add remaining ingredients except for red peppers and olives and stir well—cook on high for 5 minutes.
3. Add red peppers and olives and stir well. Serve and enjoy.

Nutrition: Calories 285 Fat 9.1 g Carbohydrates 45.7 g Sugar 1.2 g Protein 6 g Cholesterol 0 mg

107. Raisins, Nuts and Beef on Hashed Rice

Preparation Time: 20 minutes
Cooking Time: 50 minutes
Servings: 8
Ingredients:

- ½ cup dark raisins, soaked in 2 cups water for an hour
- 1/3 cup slivered almonds, toasted and soaked in 2 cups water overnight
- 1/3 cup pine nuts, toasted and soaked in 2 cups water overnight
- ½ cup fresh parsley leaves, roughly chopped pepper and salt to taste
- ¾ tsp. ground cinnamon, divided
- ¾ tsp. cloves, divided
- 1 tsp. garlic powder
- 1 ¾ tsp. allspice, divided
- 1 lb. lean ground beef or lean ground lamb
- 1 small red onion, finely chopped
- Olive oil
- 1 ½ cups medium grain rice

Directions:

1. For 15 to 20 minutes, soak rice in cold water. You will know that soaking is enough when you can snap a grain of rice easily between your thumb and index finger. Once soaking is done, drain rice well.
2. Meanwhile, drain pine nuts, almonds and raisins for at least a minute and transfer to one bowl. Set aside.
3. On a heavy cooking pot on medium high fire, heat 1 tbsp. olive oil.
4. Once oil is hot, add red onions. Sauté for a minute before adding ground meat and sauté for another minute.
5. Season ground meat with pepper, salt, ½ tsp. ground cinnamon, ½ tsp. ground cloves, 1 tsp. garlic powder, and 1 ¼ tsp. allspice.
6. Sauté ground meat for 10 minutes or until browned and cooked fully. Drain fat.
7. In same pot with cooked ground meat, add rice on top of meat.
8. Season with a bit of pepper and salt. Add remaining cinnamon, ground cloves, and allspice. Do not mix.
9. Add 1 tbsp. olive oil and 2 ½ cups of water. Bring to a boil and once boiling, lower fire to a simmer. Cook while covered until liquid is fully absorbed, around 20 to 25 minutes.
10. Turn of fire.
11. To serve, place a large serving platter that fully covers the mouth of the pot. Place platter upside down on mouth of pot, and invert pot. The inside of the pot should now rest on the platter with the rice on bottom of plate and ground meat on top of it.
12. Garnish the top of the meat with raisins, almonds, pine nuts, and parsley.
13. Serve and enjoy.

Nutrition: Calories per serving: 357 Carbs: 39.0g Protein: 16.7g Fat: 15.9g)

108. Beans and Rice

Preparation time: 10 minutes
Cooking time: 55 minutes
Servings: 6
Ingredients:

- 1 tablespoon olive oil
- 1 yellow onion, chopped
- 2 celery stalks, chopped
- 2 garlic cloves, minced
- 2 cups brown rice
- 1 and ½ cup canned black beans, rinsed and drained
- 4 cups water
- Salt and black pepper to the taste

Directions:

1. Heat up a pan with the oil over medium heat, add the celery, garlic and the onion, stir and cook for 10 minutes.
2. Add the rest of the ingredients, stir, bring to a simmer and cook over medium heat for 45 minutes.
3. Divide between plates and serve.

Nutrition: Calories 224 Fat 8.4 Fiber 3.4 Carbs 15.3 Protein 6.2

109. Raisin Rice Pilaf (FAST)

Preparation Time: 7 minutes
Cooking Time: 8 minutes
Servings: 5
Ingredients:

- 1 Tablespoon Olive Oil
- 1 Teaspoon Cumin, 1 Cup Onion, Chopped
- ½ Cup Carrot, Shredded
- ½ Teaspoon Cinnamon
- 2 Cups Instant Brown Rice
- 1 ¾ Cup Orange Juice
- 1 Cup Golden Raisins, ¼ Cup Water
- ½ Cup Pistachios, Shelled
- Fresh Chives, Chopped for Garnish

Directions:

1. Place a medium saucepan over medium-high heat before adding in your oil. Add n your onion, and stir often so it doesn't burn. Cook for about five minutes and then add in your cumin, cinnamon and carrot. Cook for about another minute.

2. Add in your orange juice, water and rice. Bring it all to a boil before covering your saucepan. Turn the heat down to medium-low and then allow it to simmer for six to seven minutes. Your rice should be cooked all the way through, and all the liquid should be absorbed.

3. Stir in your pistachios, chives and raisins. Serve warm.

Nutrition: Calories: 320   Protein: 6 Grams   Fat: 7 Grams Carbs: 61 Grams Sodium: 37 mg

MEAT RECIPES

110. Old-Fashioned Goulash

Preparation time: 15 minutes
Cooking Time: 9 hours 10 minutes
Servings: 4
Ingredients:

- 1 ½ pound pork butt, chopped
- 1 teaspoon sweet Hungarian paprika
- 2 Hungarian hot peppers, deveined and minced
- 1 cup leeks, chopped
- 1 ½ tablespoons lard
- 1 teaspoon caraway seeds, ground
- 4 cups vegetable broth
- 2 garlic cloves, crushed
- 1 teaspoon cayenne pepper
- 2 cups tomato sauce with herbs
- 1 ½ pound pork butt, chopped
- 1 teaspoon sweet Hungarian paprika
- 2 Hungarian hot peppers, deveined and minced
- 1 cup leeks, chopped
- 1 ½ tablespoons lard
- 1 teaspoon caraway seeds, ground
- 4 cups vegetable broth
- 2 garlic cloves, crushed
- 1 teaspoon cayenne pepper
- 2 cups tomato sauce with herbs

Directions:
1. Melt the lard in a heavy-bottomed pot over medium-high heat. Sear the pork for 5 to 6 minutes until just browned on all sides; set aside.
2. Add in the leeks and garlic; continue to cook until they have softened.
3. Place the reserved pork along with the sautéed mixture in your crockpot. Put in the other fixings and stir to combine.
4. Cover with the lid and slow cook for 9 hours on the lowest setting.

Nutrition: Calories 456 Fat 27g Carbs 6.7g Protein 32g Fiber 3.4g

111. Sunday Chicken with Cauliflower Salad (FAST)

Preparation time: 15 minutes
Cooking Time: 20 minutes
Servings: 2
Ingredients:

- 1 teaspoon hot paprika
- 2 tablespoons fresh basil, snipped
- 1/2 cup mayonnaise
- 1 teaspoon mustard
- 2 teaspoons butter
- 2 chicken wings
- 1/2 cup cheddar cheese, shredded
- Sea salt
- ground black pepper
- 2 tablespoons dry sherry
- 1 shallot, finely minced
- 1/2 head of cauliflower

Directions:
1. Boil the cauliflower with salted water in a pot until it has softened; cut into small florets and place in a salad bowl.
2. Melt the butter in a saucepan over medium-high heat. Cook the chicken for about 8 minutes or until the skin is crisp and browned. Season with hot paprika salt, and black pepper.
3. Whisk the mayonnaise, mustard, dry sherry, and shallot and dress your salad. Top with cheddar cheese and fresh basil.

Nutrition: Calories 444 Fat 36g Carbs 5.7g Protein 20.6g Fiber 4.3g

112. Authentic Turkey Kebabs

Preparation time: 15 minutes
Cooking time: 30 minutes
Servings: 6
Ingredients:

- 1 ½ pounds turkey breast, cubed
- 3 Spanish peppers, sliced
- 2 zucchinis, cut into thick slices
- 1 onion, cut into wedges
- 2 tablespoons olive oil, room temperature
- 1 tablespoon dry ranch seasoning

Directions:
1. Thread the turkey pieces and vegetables onto bamboo skewers. Sprinkle the skewers with dry ranch seasoning and olive oil.
2. Grill your kebabs for about 10 minutes, turning them periodically to ensure even cooking.

3. Wrap your kebabs in foil before packing them into airtight containers; keep in your refrigerator for up to 3 to days.

Nutrition: Calories 200 Fat 13.8g Carbs 6.7g Protein 25.8g Fiber 1.2g

113. Grilled Burgers with Mushrooms (FAST)

Preparation time: 15 minutes
Cooking time: 10 minutes
Servings: 4
Ingredients:
- 2 Bibb lettuce, halved
- 4 slices red onion
- 4 slices tomato
- 4 whole wheat buns, toasted
- 2 tbsp olive oil
- ¼ tsp cayenne pepper, optional
- 1 garlic clove, minced
- 1 tbsp sugar
- ½ cup of water
- 1/3 cup balsamic vinegar
- 4 large Portobello mushroom caps, around 5-inches in diameter

Directions:
1. Remove stems from mushrooms and clean with a damp cloth. Transfer into a baking dish with gill-side up.
2. In a bowl, mix thoroughly olive oil, cayenne pepper, garlic, sugar, water, and vinegar. Pour over mushrooms and marinate mushrooms in the ref for at least an hour.
3. Once the one hour is nearly up, preheat grill to medium-high fire and grease grill grate.
4. Grill mushrooms for five minutes per side or until tender. Baste mushrooms with the marinade, so it doesn't dry up.
5. To assemble, place ½ of the bread bun on a plate, top with a slice of onion, mushroom, tomato, and one lettuce leaf.
6. Cover with the other top half of the bun. Repeat process with remaining ingredients, serve, and enjoy.

Nutrition: Calories: 244.1 Carbs: 32g Protein: 8.1g Fat: 9.3g

114. Beef Cacciatore

Preparation Time: 10 minutes
Cooking Time: 40 minutes
Servings: 5
Ingredients:
- 1 lb. beef, cut into thin slices
- 1/4 cup extra virgin olive oil
- 1 onion, chopped
- 2 red bell peppers, chopped

- 1 orange bell pepper, chopped
- Salt and pepper, to taste
- 1 cup tomato sauce

Directions:
1. Place a skillet over a medium heat and add the oil.
2. Add the meat and cook until browned.
3. Add the onions and peppers and cook for 3-5 minutes.
4. Throw in the tomato sauce, salt and pepper, stir well then bring to a simmer.
5. Cover and cook for 40 minutes until the meat is tender.
6. Pour off as much sauce as you can then whizz in a blender.
7. Pour back into the pan and heat again for 5 minutes.
8. Serve with pasta or rice and enjoy.

Nutrition: Calories: 428 Net carbs: 16g Fat: 35g Protein: 12g

115. Balsamic Beef Dish

Preparation Time: 5 minutes
Cooking Time: 55 minutes
Servings: 8
Ingredients:
- 3 pounds chuck roast
- 3 cloves garlic, thinly sliced
- 1 tablespoon oil
- 1 teaspoon flavored vinegar
- ½ teaspoon pepper
- ½ teaspoon rosemary
- 1 tablespoon butter
- ½ teaspoon thyme
- ¼ cup balsamic vinegar
- 1 cup beef broth

Directions:
1. Cut slits in the roast and stuff garlic slices all over.
2. Take a bowl and add flavored vinegar, rosemary, pepper, thyme and rub the mixture over the roast.
3. Set your pot to sauté mode and add oil, allow the oil to heat up.
4. Add roast and brown both sides (5 minutes each side).
5. Take the roast out and keep it on the side.
6. Add butter, broth, balsamic vinegar and deglaze the pot.
7. Transfer the roast back and lock up the lid, cook on HIGH pressure for 40 minutes.
8. Perform a quick release.
9. Remove the lid and serve!

Nutrition: Calories: 393 Protein: 37 g Fat: 15 g Carbohydrates: 25 g

116. Easy Pork Chops

Preparation Time: 10 minutes
Cooking Time: 20 or so minutes
Servings: 4
Ingredients:
- 4 pork chops, boneless
- 1 tablespoon extra-virgin olive oil
- 1 cup chicken stock, low-sodium
- A pinch of black pepper
- 1 teaspoon sweet paprika

Directions:
1. Heat up a pan while using the oil over medium-high heat, add pork chops, brown them for 5 minutes on either sides, add paprika, black pepper and stock, toss, cook for fifteen minutes more, divide between plates and serve by using a side salad.
2. Enjoy!

Nutrition: Calories: 272 Fat: 4 Fiber: 8 Carbs: 14 Protein: 17

117. Mustard and Rosemary Pork Tenderloin (FAST)

Preparation Time: 10 minutes
Cooking Time: 15 minutes plus 5 minutes resting time
Servings: 4
Ingredients:
- ½ cup fresh parsley leaves
- ¼ cup dijon mustard
- 6 garlic cloves
- 3 tablespoons fresh rosemary leaves
- 3 tablespoons extra-virgin olive oil
- ½ teaspoon sea salt
- ¼ teaspoon freshly ground black pepper
- 1 (1½-pound) pork tenderloin

Directions:
1. Preheat the oven to 400°F.
2. In a blender or food processor, combine the parsley, mustard, garlic, rosemary, olive oil, salt, and pepper. Pulse in 1-second pulses, about 20 times, until a paste forms. Rub this paste all over the tenderloin and put the pork on a rimmed baking sheet.
3. Bake the pork for about 15 minutes, or until it registers 165°F on an instant-read meat thermometer.
4. Let rest for 5 minutes, slice, and serve.

Nutrition: Calories: 362 Total Fat: 18g Total Carbs: 5g Sugar: <1g Fiber: 2g Protein: 2g Sodium: 515mg

118. Beef Kofta(FAST)

Preparation Time: 10 minutes
Cooking Time: 15 minutes
Servings: 4

Ingredients:
- 1 lb. ground beef
- 1/2 cup minced onions
- 1 tablespoon olive oil
- 1/2 teaspoon salt
- 1/2 teaspoon ground coriander
- 1/2 teaspoon ground cumin
- 1/4 teaspoon ground cinnamon
- 1/4 teaspoon allspice
- 1/4 teaspoon dried mint leaves

Directions:
1. Grab a large bowl and add all the ingredients.
2. Stir well to combine then use your hands to shape into ovals or balls.
3. Carefully thread onto skewers then brush with oil.
4. Pop into the grill and cook uncovered for 15 minutes, turning often.
5. Serve and enjoy.

Nutrition: Calories: 216 Net carbs: 4g Fat: 19g Protein: 25g

119. Greek Beef and Veggie Skewers (FAST)

Preparation Time: 20 minutes
Cooking Time: 10 minutes
Servings: 6-8
Ingredients:
- For the beef skewers…
- 1 ½ lb. skirt steak, cut into cubes
- 1 teaspoon grated lemon zest
- ½ teaspoon coriander seeds, ground
- ½ teaspoon salt
- 2 garlic cloves, chopped
- 2 tablespoons olive oil
- 2 bell peppers, seeded and cubed
- 4 small green zucchinis, cubed
- 24 cherry tomatoes
- 2 tablespoons extra virgin olive oil
- To serve…
- Store-bought hummus
- 1 lemon, cut into wedges

Directions:
1. Grab a large bowl and add all the ingredients. Stir well.
2. Cover and pop into the fridge for at least 30 minutes, preferably overnight.
3. Preheat the grill to high and oil the grate.
4. Take a medium bowl and add the peppers, zucchini, tomatoes and oil. Season well
5. Just before cooking, start threading everything onto the skewers. Alternate veggies and meat as you wish.
6. Pop into the grill and cook for 5 minutes on each side.
7. Serve and enjoy.

Nutrition: Calories: 938 Net carbs: 65g Fat: 25g Protein: 87g

120. Boneless Pork Chops with Summer Veggies(FAST)

Preparation Time: 10 minutes
Cooking Time: 25 minutes
Servings: 4
Ingredients:

- 8 thin sliced center cut boneless pork chops
- 3/4 teaspoon Montreal chicken seasoning
- 1 small zucchini, julienned
- 1 small yellow squash, julienned
- 1 cup halved grape tomatoes
- 1 tablespoon extra-virgin olive oil
- Salt and pepper, to taste
- ¼ teaspoon oregano
- 3 cloves garlic, thinly sliced
- Extra virgin olive oil, to taste
- 1/4 cup pitted and sliced Kalamata olives
- 1/4 cup crumbled feta cheese
- Juice of ½ lemon
- 1 teaspoon grated lemon rind

Directions:
1. Preheat the oven to 450°F.
2. Grab a medium bowl and add the tomatoes, ½ tablespoon oil, 1/8 teaspoon salt, pepper and oregano. Stir well.
3. Place onto a baking sheet and pop into the oven for 10 minutes.
4. Add the sliced garlic and cook for 5 more minutes.
5. Remove from the oven and transfer to a large bowl.
6. Reduce the oven temperature to 200°F.
7. Place a large skillet over a medium heat, add ½ tablespoon olive oil, the zucchini and a pinch of salt and cook for 5 minutes until tender.
8. Transfer the zucchini to the bowl with the tomatoes and pop into the oven to keep warm.
9. Add more oil to the skillet and cook half the pork chops for about 2 minutes on each side.
10. Pop onto a platter then repeat with the second half. Pop onto a platter.
11. Remove the veggies from the oven then add the olives, lemon and lemon rind. Stir well to combine.
12. Top the pork with the veggies, top with feta then serve and enjoy.

Nutrition: Calories: 230 Net carbs: 9g Fat: 9g Protein: 28g

121. Garlic and Rosemary Pork Roast

Preparation Time: 20 minutes
Cooking Time: 1 hour
Servings: 4
Ingredients:

- 2 - 2 ½ lb. pork sirloin roast
- 3 large garlic cloves, sliced
- Fresh rosemary, to taste
- 1 teaspoon salt
- 1/2 teaspoon pepper
- 2 tablespoons extra virgin olive oil

Directions:
1. Preheat the oven to 250°F.
2. Place the pork onto a flat surface and cut 1-deep slits into the top.
3. Place a sliver of garlic and a leaf of rosemary into each slit.
4. Season well with salt and pepper.
5. Place a skillet over a medium heat and add the olive oil.
6. Add the roast to the skillet and brown on all sides.
7. Grab a small roasting pan, add a rack to the inside and pop the roast on top.
8. Pop into the oven and cook for 1 hours until cooked, turning over halfway through cooking.
9. Remove from the oven, place onto a cutting board and tent with foil. Leave to rest for 15 minutes.
10. Serve and enjoy.

Nutrition: Calories: 198 Net carbs: 8g Fat: 32g Protein: 22g

122. Pork Tenderloin with Roasted Vegetables

Preparation Time: 30 minutes
Cooking Time: 30 minutes
Servings: 8
Ingredients:

- 2 x 1 1/2 lb. pork tenderloins, halved crosswise
- 1 teaspoon ground coriander
- 1 teaspoon dried thyme
- 1 teaspoon granulated or powdered garlic
- 1 teaspoon coarse or kosher salt, plus extra to taste
- 1/2 teaspoon freshly ground black pepper, plus extra to taste
- 10 thyme sprigs
- 4 tablespoons olive oil
- 1 large red or yellow onion, peeled and cut into 1 ½" chunks
- 1 large fennel bulb., trimmed and cut into 1 ½" chunks
- 10 small white or red potatoes, chopped into chunks
- 2 jalapeno peppers, deseeded and sliced

Directions:

1. Preheat the oven to 425°F.
2. Find a small bowl and add the coriander, thyme, garlic, salt and pepper.
3. Stir well together then rub over the pork loins.
4. Pop a heavy skillet over a high heat and add about 2 tablespoons of olive oil.
5. Add the pork and sear on all sides.
6. Find a medium bowl and add the onions, fennel, potatoes, jalapenos and remaining oil.
7. Season well then toss to combine.
8. Place onto a rimmed baking sheet.
9. Top with the pork, tuck in thyme then pop into the oven for 30 minutes.
10. Remove the pork from the oven and place on a plate, covered to keep warm.
11. Spread the vegetables out over the tin and pop back into the oven for another 20 minutes until golden.
12. Slice the pork and serve with the roasted vegetables.
13. Serve and enjoy.

Nutrition: Calories: 401 Net carbs: 40g Fat: 12g Protein: 34g

123. Marinated Balsamic Pork Loin Skillet (FAST)

Preparation Time: 20 minutes
Cooking Time: 15 minutes
Servings: 4-6
Ingredients:

- 1 lb. pork tenderloin, sliced ½" thick
- 1/4 cup balsamic vinegar
- 1/4 cup extra virgin olive oil
- 1/2 teaspoon smoked paprika or regular paprika
- 1 tablespoon honey (optional)
- 1/2 teaspoon minced garlic
- Salt and pepper, to taste
- 1/4 teaspoon oregano
- 1/4 teaspoon dried marjoram or rosemary
- 1 cup sliced red onion
- 2 oz. sliced olives
- 1 zucchini, thinly sliced
- Fresh basil
- To serve…
- Paprika or red pepper flakes
- Mixed leafy greens

Directions:

1. Grab a large bowl and add the balsamic marinade ingredients then stir well to combine.
2. Place the lamb into the bowl, stir well then pop into the fridge for at least 30 minutes to marinate.
3. When you're ready to start cooking, place a skillet over a medium heat. Add a drop of oil to prevent sticking then add the onion and cook for 5 minutes until soft.
4. Add the pork loin and remaining marinade, stir well then cook on medium for 5 minutes.
5. Flip the pork and add the olive and zucchini.
6. Cook for 5 minutes more until the pork is no longer pink.
7. Serve and enjoy.

Nutrition: Calories: 309 Net carbs: 7g Fat: 19g Protein: 26g

124. Chicken With Acorn Squash and Tomatoes

Preparation Time: 20 minutes
Cooking Time: 20 minutes
Servings: 2
Ingredients:

- small acorn squash (about 1 1/2 lb.), 1/4 inch thick, halved, seeded, and sliced
- pint of grape tomatoes, halved 4 garlic cloves, cut
- tbsp. olive oil
- Black pepper and kosher salt
- 6-oz boneless, skinless breasts of chicken One-half tsp. Ground cilantro2 tbsp. of fresh oregano, chopped

Directions:

1. Heat the furnace to 425° F.
2. Toss the squash, tomatoes, and garlic with 2 tablespoons of oil, one-half teaspoon of salt, and one-fourth teaspoon of pepper on a broad-rimmed baking sheet.
3. Roast the vegetables for 20 to 25 minutes until the squash is tender.
4. Meanwhile, over medium heat, heat the remaining tablespoon of oil in a large skillet.
5. Season the coriander, one-half teaspoon salt, and one-fourth teaspoon pepper with the poultry. Cook, 6 to 7 minutes per hand, until golden brown and cooked through.
6. Serve the squash and tomatoes with the chicken and sprinkle with the oregano.

Nutrition: Energy (calories): 877 kcal Protein: 34.11 g Fat: 39.9 g Carbohydrates: 98.08 g Calcium, Ca165 mg Magnesium, Mg144 mg
Mg42 mg

125. Garlic And Citrus Turkey with Mixed Greens (FAST)

Preparation Time: 5 minutes

Cooking Time: 15 minutes
Servings: 4
Ingredients:

- 4 teaspoons (or oil of your choice and fresh chopped garlic) 1 C scallion greens, thinly sliced
- 1 3/4 pounds lean ground turkey
- 1 Tablespoon (or lemon, pepper, garlic, onion, parsley, salt & pepper)
- 8 cups mixed green lettuce
- 1 lemon cut into wedges for garnish

Directions:

1. Heat a large non-stick skillet over medium-high heat with oil and sauté garlic for 1 minute, stirring. Add scallion greens, green onions, ground turkey, and seasonings. Stir and cook for 15 minutes or until meat is thoroughly cooked.
2. Divide greens between 4 plates and top each dish with 1/4 of the meat mixture.
3. Serve with lemon wedges.
4. Enjoy!

Nutrition: Energy (calories): 355 kcal Protein: 38.71 g Fat: 21.33 g Carbohydrates: 3.54 g Calcium, Ca81 mg Magnesium, Mg57 mg Phosphorus, P421 mg

126. Greek Chicken with Yogurt

Preparation Time: 10 minutes
Cooking Time: 20 minutes
Servings: 4
Ingredients:

- oil spray
- 5 oz. plain Greek yogurt 2 tbsp mayonnaise
- 1/2 cup grated parmesan cheese 1 tsp garlic powder
- 1/4 tsp salt
- 1/4 tsp black pepper
- 1.5 lb. chicken tenders (whole) or chicken breasts (cut in quarters) Parsley (chopped, for garnish)

Directions:

1. Fire up the oven to 480 degrees F.
2. Line a baking sheet with parchment paper. Spray oil on parchment, then place chicken on top (the oil will help prevent the chicken from sticking to the parchment paper).
3. In a small mixing bowl, whisk together the yogurt, mayo, parmesan, garlic powder, salt, and pepper. Toss the chicken tenders or breasts with the yogurt mixture and place them on the baking sheet.
4. Repeat with the remaining chicken and yogurt/spices mixture.

5. Bake for 20 minutes. Garnish with extra parsley and serve immediately with extra Greek yogurt, mayo, and grated parmesan sprinkled on top.
6. Enjoy!!!

Nutrition: Energy (calories): 325 kcal Protein: 42.78 g Fat: 14.13 g Carbohydrates: 4.87 g Calcium, Ca189 mg Magnesium, Mg60 mg

127. Sliced Steak with Canadian Crust (FAST)

Preparation Time: 10 minutes
Cooking Time: 20 minutes Servings: 5
Ingredients:

- 1- 10-ounce steaks good for grilling (ask your butcher for suggestions) about
- 1 and one-half thick
- Tablespoon (1 Capful) (or other dry steak seasonings)

Directions:

1. Preheat broiler
2. Sprinkle on both sides of steak dry steak seasonings seasoning
3. Place steak under pre-heated broiler
4. Broil each side to taste (approx. 5 minutes per side for medium-rare)
5. Slice steak in thin, 3/4" slices against the grain.
6. Arrange slices on a serving platter and top with a generous amount of butter.
7. Serve and enjoy with a side salad.

Nutrition: Energy (calories): 51 kcal Protein: 6.58 g Fat: 2.02 g Carbohydrates: 1.03 g Calcium, Ca7 mg Magnesium, Mg8 mg

128. Tagine of Chicken and Olives

Preparation Time: 10 minutes and marinate for 3-4 hours
Cooking Time: 45 minutes
Servings: 4
Ingredients:

- 5 cloves garlic, finely chopped
- One-fourth teaspoon saffron threads, pulverized One-half teaspoon ground ginger
- teaspoon sweet paprika
- One-half teaspoon ground cumin One-half teaspoon turmeric
- Salt and freshly ground black pepper 1 chicken, cut into 8 to 10 pieces
- tablespoons extra virgin olive oil 3 medium onions, sliced thin
- 1 cinnamon stick
- 8 Kalamata olives, pitted and halved
- 8 cracked green olives, pitted and halved

- 1 large or 3 small preserved lemons (sold in specialty food shops) 1 cup chicken stock
- Juice of 1/2 lemon
- 1 tablespoon chopped flat-leaf parsley

Directions:

1. In a large plastic food bag, combine the garlic, saffron, ginger, parsley, paprika, cumin, turmeric, salt, and pepper. Add the chicken and shake the bag to coat the chicken with the spices. Set aside to marinate for 1 hour to 3 hours.
2. Transfer the chicken to a large pot and add the remaining ingredients. If there isn't any liquid in the bag, add enough water to cover the pot's ingredients. Cover and cook until the chicken is tender and the liquid is reduced to about 35 to 45 minutes.
3. Serve garnished with lemon juice and parsley.

Nutrition: Energy (calories): 1090 kcal Protein: 115.01 g Fat: 64.59 g, Carbohydrates: 6.08 g Calcium, Ca111 mg Magnesium, Mg137 mg

129. Delicious Beef and Tomato Squash (FAST)

Preparation time: 10 minutes
Cooking time: 60 minutes
Servings: 4

Ingredients

- 2 pounds acorn squash, pricked with a fork
- Salt and pepper to taste
- 3 garlic cloves, peeled and minced
- 1 onion, peeled and chopped
- 1 Portobello mushroom, sliced
- 28 ounces canned tomatoes, diced
- 1 teaspoon dried oregano
- ¼ teaspoon cayenne pepper
- ½ teaspoon dried thyme
- 1 pound ground beef
- 1 green bell pepper, seeded and chopped

Directions

1. Preheat your oven to 400 degrees F
2. Take acorn squash and transfer to the lined baking sheet, bake for 40 minutes
3. Cut in half and let it cool
4. Deseed them
5. Take a pan and place it over medium-high heat, add meat, garlic, onion, and mushroom, stir cook until brown
6. Add salt, pepper, thyme, oregano, cayenne, tomatoes, green pepper, and stir
7. Cook for 10 minutes
8. Stuff squash halves with beef mix

9. Transfer to oven and bake for 10 minutes more
10. Serve and enjoy!

Nutrition: Calories: 260 Fat: 7 g Saturated Fat: 1 g Carbohydrates: 4 g Fiber: 1 g Sodium: 247 mg Protein: 10 g

130. Warm Tamari Steak Salad (FAST)

Preparation time: 10 minutes
Cooking time:15 minutes
Servings: 4

Ingredients

- 2 large bunches of salad greens
- 8-9 ounces beef steak
- ½ red bell pepper, sliced
- 6-8 cherry tomatoes, cut into halves
- 4 radishes, sliced
- 4 tablespoons olive oil
- ½ tablespoon fresh lemon juice
- 2 ounces gluten-free tamari sauce
- Salt as needed

Directions

1. Marinate steak in tamari sauce
2. Make the salad by adding bell pepper, tomatoes, radishes, salad green, oil, salt, and lemon juice to a bowl, and toss them well
3. Grill the steak to your desired doneness and transfer steak on top of the salad platter
4. Let it sit for 1 minute and cut it crosswise
5. Serve and enjoy!

Nutrition: Calories: 500 Fat: 37 g Saturated Fat: 10 g Carbohydrates: 4 g Fiber: 1 g Sodium: 186 mg Protein: 33 g

131. Healthy Cabbage Fried Beef (FAST)

Preparation time: 10 minutes
Cooking time:15 minutes
Servings: 4

Ingredients

- 1 pound beef, ground
- 1 onion
- 1 garlic clove, minced
- ½ head cabbage, sliced
- Salt and pepper to taste

Directions

1. Take a skillet and place it over medium heat
2. Add beef, and onion until slightly browned
3. Transfer to a bowl and keep it covered
4. Add minced garlic and cabbage to the skillet and cook until slightly browned

5. Return the ground beef mixture to the skillet and simmer for 3-5 minutes over low heat
6. Serve and enjoy!

Nutrition: Calories: 360 Fat: 22 g Saturated Fat: 6 g Carbohydrates: 5 g Fiber: 2 g Sodium: 247 mg Protein: 34 g

132. Mushroom Steak (FAST)

Preparation time: 10 minutes
Cooking time:14 minutes
Servings: 4
Ingredients
- 1-pound boneless beef sirloin steak, ¾ inch thick, cut into 4 pieces
- 1 large red onion, chopped
- 1 cup mushrooms
- 4 garlic cloves, thinly sliced
- 4 tablespoons olive oil
- ½ cup green olives, coarsely chopped
- 1 cup parsley leaves, finely cut

Directions
1. Take a large-sized skillet and place it over medium-high heat
2. Add oil and let it heat p
3. Add beef and cook until both sides are browned, remove beef and drain fat
4. Add rest of the oil to skillet and heat it up
5. Add onions, garlic and cook for 2-3 minutes
6. Stir well
7. Add mushrooms olives and cook until mushrooms are thoroughly done
8. Return beef to skillet and lower heat to medium
9. Cook for 3-4 minutes (covered)
10. Stir in parsley
11. Serve and enjoy!

Nutrition: Calories: 386 Fat: 30 g Saturated Fat: 7 g Carbohydrates: 11 g Fiber: 2 g Sodium: 483 mg Protein: 21 g

133. Muscle Meatballs (FAST)

Preparation Time: 15 minutes
Cooking Time: 20 minutes
Servings: 3
Ingredients:
- 1 1/2 lb. extra-lean ground turkey breast
- 2 egg whites
- 1/2 cup of toasted wheat germ
- 1/4 cup fast-cooking oats
- 1 tbsp. of whole linseed seeds
- 1 tbsp. of grated parmesan cheese
- one-half tsp. All-purpose seasoning

- 1/4 tsp. ground black pepper

Directions:
1. Preheat the furnace to 400° F. Use cooking spray to cover a large baking dish.
2. In a container, mix all the ingredients.
3. Make and place 16 meatballs in the baking dish.
4. Bake the meatballs for 7 minutes and turn them around. Bake for 8–13 minutes longer or until the center is no longer pink.

Nutrition: Energy (calories): 460 kcal Protein: 77.65 g Fat: 9.13 g Carbohydrates: 16.9 g Calcium, Ca78 mg Magnesium, Mg151 mg

134. Orange Chicken

Preparation Time: 15 minutes
Cooking Time: 30 minutes
Servings: 4
Ingredients:
- 1 lb. of skinless, boneless chicken, cut into bite-sized pieces
- 1/2 tsp. Crystal Light Orange Drink
- tsp. of powdered garlic
- 1/2 tsp. Dried ground ginger
- 1/4 tsp. red flakes of pepper
- 1/8 tsp. pepper
- tsp. of olive oil
- 2 tbsp. Of rice vinegar
- 2 tbsp. water
- 1/2 tsp. of sesame oil
- 1 tsp. of medium soy sauce
- 1/2 tbsp. of minced dried onion
- 1/4-1/2 tsp. of dried orange peel

Directions:
1. Preheat the oven to 350° C.
2. Put the chicken in a 13x9 inches baking dish.
3. In a small bowl, mix the remaining ingredients. Pour over the chicken. Bake until done, for 25–30 minutes.

Nutrition: Energy (calories): 171 kcal Protein: 25.78 g Fat: 6.06 g Carbohydrates: 1.42 g Calcium, Ca11 mg Magnesium, Mg35 mg

135. Beef with Vegetables

Preparation time: 10 minutes
Cooking time: 30 minutes
Servings: 4
Ingredients:
- Eight-ounce beef filet – cut into half-inch strips
- Two tablespoons vegetable oil

- One onion – chopped
- One clove garlic – minced
- One teaspoon fresh ginger root – chopped
- One green bell pepper – chopped
- One carrot – chopped
- 10.5-ounce beef broth
- One tablespoon cornstarch
- One teaspoon white sugar
- One tablespoon soy sauce
- One tablespoon oyster sauce
- Salt and pepper – to taste

Direction

1. Add beef slices and oil into the skillet and cook over a medium-high flame and cook for five minutes.
2. Add ginger, garlic, and onion and cook for five minutes.
3. Add beef broth, carrot, and green bell pepper. Decrease the speed of the flame to low and simmer it.
4. During this, mix the oyster sauce, soy sauce, sugar, and corn flour in another bowl.
5. Stir well until smooth.
6. Add this to the vegetables and simmering beef, and stir well.
7. Let simmer until thick – season with pepper and salt.

Nutrition: Calories 267 | fat 20.2g | sodium 537.8mg | carbohydrates 9.3g | fiber 1.6g | sugar 3.9g | protein 12g

136. Mushroom Beef Burgers (FAST)

Preparation time: 15 minutes
Cooking time: 20 minutes
Additional time: 20 minutes
Servings: 8
Ingredients:

- Two pounds ground beef
- 8-ounce mushrooms – chopped
- One onion – chopped
- Three cloves' garlic – minced
- One teaspoon Italian seasoning
- One teaspoon salt
- Half teaspoon ground black pepper
- Cooking spray

Direction:

1. First, remove ground beef from the fridge. Let rest for twenty minutes.
2. Combine the pepper, salt, Italian seasoning, garlic, onion, and mushrooms into the bowl. Combine in beef.
3. Make the beef mixture into patties.

4. Grease indoor grill pan with cooking spray and cook patties until browned for ten minutes.

Nutrition: Calories 216 | fat 13.5g | sodium 358.2mg | carbohydrates 2.8g | fiber 0.7g | sugar 1.1g | Protein 20.1g

137. Dinner-Fast Chicken Salad Sandwich (FAST)

Preparation Time: 20 minutes
Cooking Time: 0 minutes
Servings: 2
Ingredients:

- 2 cans of chicken (3 oz. each), rinsed and drained twice 1 celery stick, finely chopped
- 1 tbsp. Onion, finely chopped 1 tbsp. of pine nuts
- 1 tsp. of spicy brown mustard
- 1 heaping tsp. of sour cream free of fat 1 heaping tsp. of plain yogurt free of fat Ground black pepper pinch
- 4 whole-grain bread slices 2 lettuce leaves

Directions:

1. Combine the celery, onion, pine nuts, vinegar, sour cream, yogurt, and pepper in a dish. Mix the chicken in. On a slice of bread, spread out half of the mixture. Place a lettuce leaf on top and then another slice of bread on top.
2. To make a second sandwich, repeat with the remainder of the mixture.

Nutrition: Energy (calories): 764 kcal Protein: 34.8 g Fat: 50.96 g Carbohydrates: 40.18 g Calcium, Ca131 mg Magnesium, Mg94 mg

138. Feta Chicken with Zucchini

Preparation Time: 20 minutes
Cooking Time: 20 minutes Servings: 2
Ingredients:

- 2 tbsp. olive oil 1 lemon
- 4 boneless, skinless chicken breasts (about 1 1/2 lb.) One-fourth tsp. kosher salt
- 2 mid-sized zucchinis
- One-fourth cup fresh, chopped flat-leaf parsley leaves 13 tsp. of black pepper One-third cup of crumbled Feta (about 2 oz.)

Directions:

1. Heat the furnace to 400° F. In a roasting pan, drizzle one-half tablespoon of the oil. In thin stripes, remove the skin from the lemon; set aside. Slice the lemon thinly. In the pan, place half the slices.

2. On top of the lemon slices, place the chicken and season with 1/8 of a teaspoon of salt.

3. Lengthwise, split each zucchini in half, then split each half into one-fourth inch-thick half-moons. Combine the zucchini, parsley, pepper, the remaining oil, slices of lemon, salt in a bowl; toss.

4. Spread the mixture over the chicken and sprinkle it over the top with the Feta.

5. Roast for 15 to 20 minutes until the chicken is fully cooked. Switch it to a cutting board and cut it into thirds for each piece.

6. Divide the chicken, zucchini mixture, and lemons between individual plates, and sprinkle with the zest.

Nutrition: Energy (calories): 217 kcal Protein: 111.16 g Fat: 88.45 g Carbohydrates: 236.31 g Calcium, Ca819 mg Magnesium, Mg343 mg

139. Cinnamon Chicken

Preparation Time: 20 minutes
Cooking Time: 20 minutes
Servings: 2
Ingredients:

- 4 or 5 (4-6 oz.) boneless chicken breasts without skin 2 tbsp. Italian Dressing
- Low-Calorie
- 1 tsp. of cinnamon
- 1 1/2 tsp. Powdered garlic
- 1/4 tsp. Salt (optional)
- 1/4 tsp. pepper

Directions:
1. Heat the oven the 350° C oven.
2. In a 13x9 baking dish, bring the chicken in. Pour the Italian sauce over it.
3. Blend the remaining ingredients in a small bowl. Sprinkle chicken over it. Bake for 40–45 minutes.

Nutrition: Protein: 94.9 g Fat: 26.29 g Carbohydrates: 6.69 g Calcium, Ca66 mg Magnesium, Mg79 mg Phosphorus, P552 mg

140. Classic Blackened Chicken (FAST)

Preparation time: 10 minutes
Cooking time: 10 minutes
Servings: 4
Ingredients

- ½ teaspoon paprika
- 1/8 teaspoon salt
- ¼ teaspoon cayenne pepper
- ¼ teaspoon ground cumin
- ¼ teaspoon dried thyme

- 1/8 teaspoon ground white pepper
- 1/8 teaspoon onion powder
- 2 chicken breasts, boneless and skinless

Directions
1. Preheat your oven to 350 degrees Fahrenheit
2. Grease baking sheet
3. Take a cast-iron skillet and place it over high heat
4. Add oil and heat it up for 5 minutes until smoking hot
5. Take a small bowl and mix salt, paprika, cumin, white pepper, cayenne, thyme, onion powder
6. Oil the chicken breast on both sides and coat the breast with the spice mix
7. Transfer to your hot pan and cook for 1 minute per side
8. Transfer to your prepared baking sheet and bake for 5 minutes
9. Serve and enjoy!

Nutrition: Calories: 136 Fat: 3 g Carbohydrate: 1 g Protein: 24 g Saturated fat: 0.5 g Fiber: 0.5 g Sodium: 365 mg

141. Beef Zucchini Halves

Preparation Time: 5 minutes
Cooking Time: 35 minutes
Servings: 2
Ingredients

- 2 garlic cloves, peeled and minced
- 1 teaspoon cumin
- 1 tablespoon coconut oil
- 1 pound ground beef
- ½ cup onion, chopped
- 1 teaspoon smoked paprika
- Salt and pepper to taste
- 3 zucchinis, sliced lengthwise, with the insides scooped out
- ¼ cup fresh cilantro, chopped
- ½ cup cheddar cheese, shredded
- 1 and ½ cups enchilada sauce
- Avocado, chopped
- Green onions, chopped
- Tomatoes, cored and chopped

Directions
1. Take a pan and place it over medium-high heat
2. Add oil and heat it up
3. Add onions and stir cook for 2 minutes
4. Add beef and stir for a few minutes
5. Add paprika, salt, pepper, cumin, and garlic; stir cook for 2 minutes

6. Transfer zucchini halves to a baking pan
7. Stuff each with the beef mix and pour the enchilada sauce on top
8. Sprinkle the cheddar on top
9. Bake (covered) for 20 minutes at 350 degrees F
10. Uncover and sprinkle with cilantro
11. Bake for 5 minutes more
12. Sprinkle avocado, green onions, and tomatoes on top
13. Serve and enjoy!

Nutrition Per Serving: Carbohydrates: 8 grams/Fat: 10 grams/Protein: 21 grams/Fiber: 3 grams/Calories: 222

142. Juicy Beef Stuffed Bell Pepper (FAST)

Preparation Time: 5 minutes
Cooking Time: 10 minutes
Servings: 2
Ingredients
- 1 onion, chopped
- 2 tablespoons coconut oil
- 1 pound ground beef
- 1 red bell pepper, diced
- 2 cups spinach, chopped
- Salt and pepper to taste

Directions
1. Take a skillet and place it over medium heat
2. Add onion and cook until slightly browned
3. Add spinach and ground beef
4. Stir fry until done—the whole process should take about 10 minutes
5. Fill up the bell peppers with the mixture
6. Serve and enjoy!

Nutrition Per Serving: Carbohydrates: 4 grams/Fat: 23 grams/Protein: 28 grams/Fiber: 1 gram/Calories: 350

143. Tamari Steak Salad (FAST)

Preparation Time: 5 minutes
Cooking Time: 15 minutes
Servings: 3
Ingredients
- 2 large bunches of salad greens
- 8-9 ounces beef steak
- ½ red bell pepper, sliced
- 6 to 8 cherry tomatoes, cut into halves
- 4 radishes, sliced
- 4 tablespoons olive oil
- ½ tablespoon fresh lemon juice
- 2 ounces gluten-free tamari sauce
- Salt as needed

Directions
1. Marinate steak in tamari sauce

2. Make the salad by adding bell pepper, tomatoes, radishes, salad green, oil, salt, and lemon juice to a bowl and tossing them well
3. Grill the steak to your desired doneness and transfer steak to the top of the salad platter
4. Let it sit for 1 minute and cut it crosswise
5. Serve and enjoy!

Nutrition Per Serving: Carbohydrates: 4 grams/Fat: 37 grams/Protein: 33 grams/Fiber: 1 gram/Calories: 500

144. Zucchini and Beef Sauté

Preparation Time: 5 minutes
Cooking Time: 10 minutes
Servings: 4
Ingredients
- 10 ounces beef, sliced into 1 to2-inch strips
- 1 zucchini, cut into 2-inch strips
- ¼ cup parsley, chopped
- 3 garlic cloves, minced
- 2 tablespoons tamari sauce
- 4 tablespoons avocado oil

Directions
1. Add 2 tablespoons avocado oil in a frying pan over high heat
2. Place in strips of beef and brown for a few minutes on high heat
3. Once the meat is brown, add zucchini strips and sauté until tender
4. Once tender, add tamari sauce, garlic, and parsley; let them sit for a few minutes more
5. Serve immediately and enjoy!

Nutrition Per Serving: Carbohydrates: 5 grams/Fat: 40 grams/Protein: 31 grams/Fiber: 1 gram/Calories: 500

145. Beef Pot Roast

Preparation Time: 5 minutes
Cooking Time: 7 hours
Servings: 4
Ingredients
- 2 pounds beef pot roast, cut up
- 1 tablespoon olive oil
- 1 tablespoon thyme, dried
- ½ teaspoon oregano, dried
- 1 whole bay leaf
- 1 medium onion, sliced
- ½ teaspoon black pepper
- 1 teaspoon salt
- 3 cups of water

Directions
1. Take a bowl and add thyme, oregano, black pepper, and salt

2. Mix them well
3. Rub the mixture all over the cut-up pot roast
4. Place a skillet over heat
5. Put in the marinated pot roast and sear all sides
6. Put the remaining ingredients in the slow cooker
7. Add the seared pot roast
8. Cook for 7 hours
9. Serve and enjoy!

Nutrition Per Serving: Carbohydrates: 0.9 grams/Fat: 9 grams/Protein: 24 grams/Fiber: 0.1 gram/Calories: 181

146. Stir-Fried Ground Beef (FAST)

Preparation Time: 5 minutes
Cooking Time: 15 minutes
Servings: 3
Ingredients

- 1 pound ground beef
- ½ medium onion, chopped
- 1 tablespoon coconut oil
- 1 tablespoon Chinese five spices
- 5 medium-sized mushrooms, sliced
- 2 kale leaves, chopped
- ½ cup broccoli, chopped
- ½ red bell pepper, chopped
- 1 tablespoon cayenne pepper, optional

Directions

1. Take a skillet, add coconut oil
2. Heat the oil over medium-high heat
3. Sauté the onion for one minute and add vegetables
4. Keep stirring constantly
5. Add the ground beef and the spices
6. Cook for 2 minutes and lower the heat
7. Cover the skillet and cook for 10 minutes
8. Now it's ready to serve
9. Enjoy!

Nutrition Per Serving: Carbohydrates: 6 grams/Fat: 17 grams/Protein: 32 grams/Fiber: 4 grams/Calories: 304

147. Vegetable and Beef Steak with Chimichurri (FAST)

Nutrition Per Serving: Carbohydrates: 9 grams/Fat: 34 grams/Protein: 25 grams/Fiber: 2 grams/Calories: 443

148. Bibimbap

Preparation time: 1 hour
Cooking time: 5 minutes
Serving: 4
Meat and Marinade

- 1-pound grass-fed sirloin steaks, very thinly sliced
- 1 small bunch of scallions, green and white parts, thinly sliced
- ¼ cup tamari or gluten-free soy sauce (plus more for vegetables)
- 2 teaspoons grated or minced fresh ginger
- 1 teaspoon maple syrup or artisanal honey
- 2 cloves garlic, minced
- ½ teaspoon red pepper flakes
- 1 tablespoon coconut oil or extra-virgin olive oil
- Cauliflower Rice and Veggies
- 4 cups Easy Cauliflower Rice
- 1 cucumber or zucchini, cut into matchsticks
- 1 carrot, peeled and cut into matchsticks
- ¼ cup bean sprouts, optional
- Optional Garnishes
- Toasted sesame seeds
- Sesame oil
- Sriracha

Directions

1. Add the steaks and marinade ingredients, except for the coconut oil, setting aside one-quarter of the sliced scallions for garnish into a shallow bowl
2. Toss to coat
3. Cover or close and refrigerate for 30 minutes or longer, up to overnight
4. To cook the meat, heat the coconut oil in a large skillet over medium-high heat until melted
5. Add the meat and cook, stirring and flipping frequently
6. Cook for 5 minutes
7. Add the zucchini and carrot matchsticks, standing them up, to another quarter of the bowl and add rice to another side
8. Add the meat to another quarter and the bean sprouts, if you are using, to another quarter
9. Sprinkle with toasted sesame seeds, give a drizzle of sesame oil and/or Sirach, top with a runny egg
10. Serve and enjoy!

Nutrition: Calories: 338 Fat: 20 g Carbohydrate: 14 g Protein: 27 g Saturated fat: 10g Fiber: 4g Sodium: 1106 mg

149. Citrus Chicken

Preparation Time: 10 minutes
Cooking Time: 3-4-hour
Servings: 3

Ingredients:

- 6 bone-in chicken breast halves, skin removed 1 tea. dried oregano
- 1/2 teas seasoned salt 1/4 teas pepper
- Tbsp olive oil
- 1/4 cup water
- Tbsp lemon juice
- 2 garlic cloves, minced
- 1 teas chicken bouillon granule 2 teas minced fresh parsley

Directions:

1. Rinse chicken; pat dry. Place chicken in a 4-qt. Slow cooker.
2. Combine the oregano, seasoned salt, pepper, oil, water, lemon juice, garlic, bouillon, and parsley; pour over the chicken.
3. Cover and cook on low for 3-4 hours or until the chicken is tender.
4. Serve and enjoy it!

Nutrition: Energy (calories): 1379 kcal Protein: 151.74 g Fat: 80.84 g Carbohydrates: 1.75 g Calcium, Ca86 mg Magnesium, Mg140 mg

150. Tender Rosemary Pork Chops (FAST)

Preparation Time: 15 minutes
Cooking Time: 20 minutes
Servings: 4
Ingredients:

- 4 pork loin chops kosher salt
- Freshly ground black pepper
- 1 tbsp. Freshly minced rosemary 2 cloves garlic, minced 1/2 c. (1 stick) butter melted 1 tbsp. extra-virgin olive oil

Directions:

1. Preheat grill or broiler with 1/2 inch of oil in the pan.
2. Pat the chops dry with paper towels and season with salt and pepper to taste.
3. Brush the chops with the melted butter and sprinkle the rosemary and garlic over them on both sides.
4. Grill the chops for 20 minutes or until tenderness comes
5. Serve with a simple carrot and red bell pepper medley.

Nutrition: Energy (calories): 547 kcal Protein: 40.57 g Fat: 41.81 g Carbohydrates: 0.6 g Calcium, Ca49 mg Magnesium, Mg41 mg Phosphorus, P355 mg

151. Cheesy Pepper Taco Bake

Preparation Time: 10 minutes
Cooking Time: 30 minutes
Servings: 4

Ingredients:

- 1 lb. 95-97% lean ground beef (chicken or turkey)
- 1T garlic, cumin, paprika, cayenne, salt, black pepper, onion, and parsley 1C no sugar added, fresh vegetable salsa plus 4 additional Tablespoons for garnish
- 1 1/2 lbs. fresh peppers (green, red, poblano, your choice) stems removed, cut in half lengthwise, and seeded.
- 1/2 C shredded low-fat cheddar cheese 4 T Sour Cream

Directions:

1. Preheat oven to 375 degrees.
2. In a large skillet – brown meat, garlic, spices, and parsley for about 4 min. Over medium heat. Add Fresh salsa and cook for 5 more minutes.
3. Carefully spoon 1/2 cup mixture in each pepper half going up the open side. The goal is to fill up the pepper in an orderly fashion.
4. Pour 1 C of salsa over the stuffed pepper halves in a small baking pan, cover the pepper mixture with the cheese.
5. Bake for about 10-15 min, or until cheese is completely melted.
6. To serve, divide equally into 4 bowls, and pour 1/2 T of sour cream on top of each.

Nutrition: Energy (calories): 362 kcal Protein: 35.6 g Fat: 14.66 g Carbohydrates: 23.03 g Calcium, Ca122 mg Magnesium, Mg84 mg Phosphorus, P397 mg

152. Pan-Seared Pork Loin and Balsamic Caramelized Onions

Preparation Time: 5 minutes
Cooking Time: 25 minutes
Servings: 4
Ingredients:

- on stick cooking spray 1 teaspoon garlic
- 1 teaspoons salt
- 1 teaspoon black pepper 1 teaspoon onion
- 1 teaspoons parsley
- 1 1/2 lbs. pork tenderloin (or beef tenderloin, or chicken breasts)

Directions:

1. Preheat oven to 350 degrees. Lightly spray a shallow baking Pan. Sprinkle steaks with salt and pepper and place in a baking pan.
2. Bake until meat is tender and internal temperature reaches 150 degrees, approximately 15 to 20 minutes.

3. While meat is cooking, prepare your gravy. In a large skillet, sauté onion and garlic in olive oil for 3 to 4 minutes. Add sugar to the pan and let cook until caramelized. Once onions are caramelized, add balsamic vinegar and butter. Allow this to simmer until onions are very soft. Thickens as it simmers.
4. Brush top of pork loin with olive oil. Place the pan under the broiler until the top layer is caramelized, about 1-2 minutes.
5. Remove from the oven and let it rest for 15 minutes.
6. Slice into medallions and top with gravy. Serve.

Nutrition: Energy (calories): 688 kcal Protein: 23.91 g Fat: 61.78 g Carbohydrates: 7.89 g Calcium, Ca29 mg Magnesium, Mg25 mg

153. Roasted Chicken with Lemon Dill Radishes (FAST)

Preparation Time: 5 minutes
Cooking Time: 30 minutes
Servings: 4
Ingredients:
- 2 lbs. chicken thighs (remove skin)
- Pinch Stacey Hawkins Dash of Desperation Seasoning (or garlic, salt, black pepper, onion, and parsley) 1 Tablespoon garlic
- 1 Tablespoon marjoram
- 1 Tablespoon basil
- 1 Tablespoon rosemary 1 Tablespoon onion

Directions:
1. Preheat the oven to 350 degrees.
2. Dice onion.
3. Put the chicken in a deep baking dish.
4. Chop the vegetables. Then put them with some oil on the baking dish.
5. Pour all the seasoning.
6. Bake for 30 minutes, then put the radishes.
7. The radishes cook with the chicken.
8. Serve at room temperature.

Nutrition: Energy (calories): 507 kcal Protein: 37.72 g Fat: 37.74 g Carbohydrates: 1.88 g Calcium, Ca31 mg Magnesium, Mg44 mg Phosphorus, P362 mg

154. Charred Sirloin with Creamy Horseradish Sauce (FAST)

Preparation Time: 5 minutes
Cooking Time: 15 minutes
Servings: 4
Ingredients:
- 1 1/2 pounds sirloin steaks, trimmed & visible fat removed

- 1/2 Tablespoon salt
- 1/2 Tablespoon pepper
- 1/2 Tablespoon garlic and onion to taste
- 6 Tablespoons low-fat sour cream
- 1-3 T horseradish (from the jar)

Directions:
1. Preheat oven to high broil
2. Season your steaks with salt, pepper, garlic, and onion, and then place on a cookie sheet lined with foil.
3. Place your sheet on the top rack of your oven and broil until the steaks are charred to your desired doneness. The steaks will also continue to cook once they are removed from the range.
4. Remove steaks from the oven and let them rest for a few minutes.
5. Warm-up your horseradish sauce in the microwave and set it aside.
6. Meanwhile, in a medium saucepan over medium-high heat, warm up the cream, horseradish, and Worcestershire sauce. Whisk until it is warm and remove from heat. Spoon your horseradish sauce over top of your steak and serve immediately.

Nutrition: Energy (calories): 218 kcal Protein: 35.2 g Fat: 6.38 g Carbohydrates: 2.77 g Calcium, Ca50 mg Magnesium, Mg50 mg Phosphorus, P392 mg

155. Rosemary Beef Tips and Creamy Fauxtatoes (FAST)

Preparation Time: 5 minutes
Cooking Time: 30 minutes
Servings: 4
Ingredients:
- 1 1/2 lbs. top sirloin steak, cubed into one chunk
- 1 T (one capful) fresh rosemary
- 1 T (one capful) sage
- 1 T (one capful) black pepper
- 1 T (one capful) onion and garlic
- 2 1/2 C low sodium beef broth
- 4 C sliced baby Portobello mushrooms
- 1 T fresh minced garlic
- 1 T (one capful) scallions one teaspoon salt and pepper
- 1/2 tsp guar gum & 1/4 C water
- 2 C hot cauliflower mashed potatoes

Directions:
1. Note: To speed up the preparation, all ingredients except steak, mushrooms, and a hint of olive oil for searing/cooking can be

pre-chopped and stored in baggies ahead of time.

2. In a large pot, cook beef over medium to high heat. Add onion, garlic, and mushrooms. Stir occasionally. Add oregano, thyme, parsley, salt, and pepper. Stir.

3. Add chopped rosemary, sage, black pepper, and garlic powder. Stir. Add beef broth. Bring to boil. Lower the heat to simmer.

4. Add half the cooked mushrooms into the pot on top and alongside the beef.

5. When beef is cooked to medium-rare, remove from pan and keep warm—strain broth into a measuring cup to get 4 1/2 cups of broth. Pour broth into a large mixing bowl.

6. Discard solids. Add corn-starch and salt to hot broth and whisk. Add guar gum (or other thickeners) and water and whisk.

7. Bring the water to a boil.

8. Add additional mushrooms and cooked beef to the gravy. Mix. Add chopped garlic and green onions. Mix. Serve sauce alongside beef.

Nutrition: Energy (calories): 492 kcal Protein: 47.47 g Fat: 23.56 g Carbohydrates: 26.14 g Calcium, Ca106 mg Magnesium, Mg70 mg Phosphorus, P606 mg

156. Balsamic-Glazed Chicken Thighs with Broccoli (FAST)

Preparation Time: 5 minutes
Cooking Time: 20 minutes
Servings: 4
Ingredients:
- 4 (~6 ounces) boneless, skinless chicken thighs
- Two teaspoons (one capful) salt and pepper, garlic, onion, and parsley
- 4 Tablespoons balsamic reduction
- 1/4 C low sodium chicken broth
- 4 C broccoli florets, lightly steamed (crisp-tender) non-stick cooking spray

Directions:
1. Mix the chicken thighs to coat with salt, pepper, garlic, onion, and parsley, in a medium bowl. Lightly spray a non-stick skillet with cooking spray to reduce the amount of fat absorbed into the thighs. Heat the skillet to medium-high.

2. Add the thighs to the skillet and cook, uncovered, for about 6 minutes on each side until browned and no longer pink inside.

3. Add the balsamic reduction to deglaze the pan, and cook for one minute. Put the

chicken and balsamic reduction into the slow cooker.

4. Turn the slow cooker to high and add the broth to the chicken. Cook for 15 minutes or until the chicken is tender enough to pull apart with a fork. Stir in the broccoli florets and cook with the chicken for extra 5 minutes or until the broccoli is cooked through but still crisp.

5. Serve hot with a side of wild rice and chopped green onion.

Nutrition: Energy (calories): 823 kcal Protein: 44.87 g Fat: 26.37 g Carbohydrates: 100.81 g Calcium, Ca172 mg Magnesium, Mg121 mg Phosphorus, P476 mg

157. Tender Taco Chicken (FAST)

Preparation Time: 5 minutes
Cooking Time: 10 minutes
Servings: 4
Ingredients:
- 1 1/2 pounds boneless, skinless chicken breast 1 Tablespoon, low salt Tex Mex seasoning
- 1/2 C fresh chopped tomatoes or low carb, no sugar added salsa 1 tsp Stacey
- Hawkins Dash of Desperation Seasoning Your favorite on-program taco condiments

Directions:
1. Cut the chicken into 1/2-inch strips and sprinkle with the Tex Mex and dash of desperation seasoning.

2. In a large pan, heat the over medium and sauté the chicken for about 10 minutes, until cooked through and no longer pink.

3. Remove to a bowl and add tomatoes or salsa and toss to combine.

4. Serve in a bowl with corn chips (or whole grain) and your favorite taco toppings.

5. Enjoy!

Nutrition: Energy (calories): 325 kcal Protein: 16.43 g Fat: 10.65 g Carbohydrates: 40.05 g Calcium, Ca47 mg Magnesium, Mg41 mg Phosphorus, P169 mg

158. Garlic Crusted Baby Back Ribs

Preparation Time: 15 minutes
Cooking Time: 1-hour Servings: 2
Ingredients:
- 11 and 3/4 rack baby back ribs
- Two tablespoons extra-virgin olive oil Kosher salt and freshly ground pepper six clove garlic
- 12 sprig thymes
- Eight sage leaves with stems two sprig rosemary

Directions:

1. For the ribs, trim the excess fat and slice down the middle into one and a half-inch section. Add olive oil and season with salt and pepper.
2. Lay the food grilling rack over a gas or charcoal grill and grill for 1-hour basting with extra-virgin olive oil and coating each side.
3. And then line it in the middle of the grill for 8 minutes.
4. In the meantime, place the garlic and herbs on a large sheet of foil and wrap it tightly.
5. Transfer the ribs and ragout to a platter and drizzle with juices, and top with the foil's garlic and herbs.
6. Enjoy!

Nutrition: Energy (calories): 19328 kcal Protein: 1710.36 g Fat: 1364.22 g Carbohydrates: 76.49 g Calcium, Ca1726 mg Magnesium, Mg2093 mg

159. Stir-Fried Chicken Meal (FAST)

Preparation time: 10 minutes
Cooking time: 15 minutes
Servings: 4
Ingredients

- ½ cup onions, sliced
- 2 tablespoons sesame garlic-flavored oil
- 4 cups Bok-Choy, shredded
- 3 stalks celery, chopped
- 1 and ½ teaspoons garlic, minced
- 1 cup chicken broth
- 2 tablespoons coconut aminos
- 1 tablespoon ginger, minced
- 1 teaspoon arrowroot
- 4 boneless chicken breasts, cooked and sliced

Directions

1. Add bok choy, celery in a skillet alongside 1 tablespoon of garlic oil
2. Stir fry until the bok choy is tender
3. Add the rest of the ingredients except arrowroot
4. If the mixture is too thin, pour a mixture of ½ a cup of cold water and arrowroot into the skillet
5. Bring the whole mixture to a 1-minute boil
6. Remove the heat source
7. Stir in coconut aminos and let it sit for 4 minutes until thick
8. Serve and enjoy!

Nutrition: Calories: 368 Fat: 18 g Carbohydrate: 8 g Protein: 42 g Saturated fat: 3 g Fiber: 2 g Sodium: 475 mg

160. Parsley Chicken Breast

Preparation time: 10 minutes
Cooking time: 40 minutes
Servings: 4
Ingredients

- 1 tablespoon dry parsley
- 1 tablespoon dry basil
- 4 chicken breast halves, boneless and skinless
- ½ teaspoon salt
- ½ teaspoon red pepper flakes, crushed
- 2 tomatoes, sliced

Directions

1. Preheat your oven to 350 degrees F
2. Take a 9x13 inch baking dish and grease it up with cooking spray
3. Sprinkle 1 tablespoon of parsley, 1 teaspoon of basil, and spread the mixture over your baking dish
4. Arrange the chicken breast halves over the dish and sprinkle garlic slices on top
5. Take a small bowl and add 1 teaspoon parsley, 1 teaspoon of basil, salt, basil, red pepper, and mix well. Pour the mixture over the chicken breast
6. Top with tomato slices and cover, bake for 25 minutes
7. Remove the cover and bake for 15 minutes more
8. Serve and enjoy!

Nutrition: Calories: 150 Fat: 4 g Carbohydrate: 4 g Protein: 25 g Saturated fat: 2 g Fiber: 2 g Sodium: 368 mg

161. Asian Chicken Satay (FAST)

Preparation time: 15 mins
Cooking time: 10 mins
Servings: 6
Ingredients

- Juice of 2 limes
- Brown sugar – 2 tbsps.
- Minced garlic – 1 tbsp
- Ground cumin – 2 tsps.
- Boneless, skinless chicken breast – 12, cut into strips

Directions

1. In a bowl, stir together the cumin, garlic, brown sugar, and lime juice.
    1. Add the chicken strips to the bowl and marinate in the refrigerator for 1 hour.
    2. Heat the barbecue to medium-high.
    3. Remove the chicken from the marinade and thread each strip onto wooden

skewers that have been soaked in the water.

4. Grill the chicken for about 4 mins per side or until the meat is cooked through but still juicy.

Nutrition: Calories 78, Carbs 4g, Phosphorus 116mg, Potassium 108mg, Sodium 100mg, Protein 12g

162. Chicken Creole Style (FAST)

Preparation time: 8 minutes
Cooking time: 20 minutes
Servings: 6
Ingredients
- nonstick cooking spray
- 1 lb. boneless, skinless chicken breasts, cut into large chunks
- 1 large onion, chopped
- 1 (14-1/2-ounce) can diced tomatoes
- 1/3 cup tomato paste
- 2 stalks celery, chopped
- 1-1/2 tsps. garlic powder
- 1 tsp onion powder
- 1/4 tsp red pepper flakes
- 1/8 tsp ground black pepper
- 1-1/2 cups broccoli florets

Directions
1. Spray a large skillet with nonstick cooking spray and heat over medium heat.
2. Add chicken and onion; cook, stirring frequently, for 10 mins.
3. Stir in all remaining Ingredients: except broccoli and cook for 5 mins, stirring occasionally.
4. Stir in broccoli, cook for 5 mins more. Serve while hot.

Nutrition: Calories 140, Fat 3g, Sodium 132mg, Carbs 11g, Fiber 1g, Phosphorus 196mg, Potassium 289mg, Protein 18g

163. Healthy Avocado Beef Patties (FAST)

Preparation time: 10 minutes
Cooking time: 15 minutes
Servings: 4
Ingredients
- 1 pound of 85% lean ground beef
- 1 small avocado, pitted and peeled
- 2 slices of yellow cheddar cheese
- Salt as needed
- Fresh ground black pepper as needed

Directions
1. Preheat and prepare your broiler to be high
2. Divide beef into two equal-sized patties

3. Season the patties with salt and pepper accordingly
4. Broil the patties for 5 minutes per side
5. Transfer the patties to a platter and add cheese
6. Slice avocado into strips and place them on top of the patties
7. Serve and enjoy!

Nutrition: Calories: 568 Fat: 43 g Carbohydrate: 9 g Protein: 38 g Saturated fat: 12 g Fiber: 2 g Sodium: 477 mg

164. Sweet & Smoky Pulled Chicken (FAST)

Preparation Time: 10 minutes
Cooking Time: 20 minutes
Servings: 6
Ingredients:
- 750 g chicken breasts, skinless and boneless (1.65 lb.) 400 ml unsweetened tomato passata (sauce) (13.5 fl oz) 100 ml apple cider vinegar (3.5 fl oz)
- 3 tbsp Swerve or Erythritol (30 g/1.1 oz)
- Optional: 1 tbsp molasses (20 g/0.7 oz) - see note above 1 tsp sea salt
- 1 tsp black pepper
- 1 tsp garlic powder
- 1/4 tsp cayenne pepper, or to taste 1 tbsp smoked paprika
- 3 tbsp coconut aminos (45 ml)
- 1/4 cup extra virgin olive oil (60 ml)
- Optional: 1 cup sour cream, full-fat yogurt, or creme fraiche to serve

Directions:
1. In a large bowl, place the chicken breasts and cover them with the tomato passata. To that, add the ground or whole peppercorns, salt, black pepper, and garlic powder. Toss to combine and transfer to the crockpot. Toss again to coat and let it cook on low for 5 hours.
2. Cook the rice according to the package direction and transfer it to a large bowl. Add the sour cream, coconut cream, and Swerve. Whisk until combined.
3. Finely mince the fresh parsley. Mix the parsley and the smoked paprika with the rice. To serve, pile the rice onto the chicken and top with the sour cream or yogurt or creme fraiche.

Nutrition: Energy (calories): 2924 kcal Protein: 85.2 g Fat: 27.19 g Carbohydrates: 515.51 g Calcium, Ca578 mg Magnesium, Mg347 mg Phosphorus, P1475 mg

165. Juicy Rosemary Pulled Pork

Preparation Time: 10 minutes
Cooking Time: 35 minutes
Servings: 4
Ingredients:

- 1 tbsp olive oil 1 tsp sea salt
- 1/2 tsp ground black pepper
- Four boneless center-cut pork chops 6-8 cloves garlic, peeled and whole

Directions:

1. Combine olive oil, salt, and pepper in a small bowl. Rub into the pork chops. Refrigerate for 30 minutes.
2. Rub two cloves of garlic into the pork chops 2. Rub two cloves of garlic into the pork chops3 — Preheat the grill. Grill pork chops 6-8 minutes on each side or until done.
3. Chop the remaining cloves of garlic. Add to a bowl with rosemary, onion, and barbeque sauce. Mix to blend.
4. Preheat the oven to 325-degree F /160 C.
5. Thinly slice the red onion and place it in a bowl. Add enough balsamic vinegar to cover and let marinate for 10 minutes.
6. In the same bowl, add the tomato halves. Sprinkle with garlic salt and olive oil. Stir to coat everything evenly.
7. Place the onions in the bottom of a baking dish. Place the pork chops on top and pour over any leftover marinade.
8. Cook covered for 30-35 minutes.
9. To make the sauce, place all the ingredients into a blender and blend until smooth.
10. Serve pork with sauce and lime wedges on the side.

Nutrition: Energy (calories): 265 kcal Protein: 39.52 g Fat: 10.02 g Carbohydrates: 1.98 g Calcium, Ca44 mg Magnesium, Mg48 mg Phosphorus, P400 mg

166. Slow-Cooked Chicken with Fire-Roasted Tomatoes

Preparation Time: 10 minutes
Cooking Time: 3 hours and 10 minutes
Servings: 4
Ingredients:

- 1 1/2 lbs. boneless, skinless chicken breast
- 15oz can fire-roasted tomatoes (any variety, but make sure no extra added sugar)
- T salt
- 2 T ground black pepper
- 2 T oil

- 2 T (one capful) sage
- 2 T (one capful) black pepper
- 2 T (one capful) onion and garlic

Directions:

1. Add oil and chicken breasts to the slow cooker.
2. Pour a bottle of spices over the chicken and cover.
3. Cook on high for 3 hours.
4. Add fire-roasted tomatoes and cook for additional 10 minutes
5. Using a handheld blender or an upright blender, blend 6 tbsp of the liquid into the chicken.
6. Remove chicken and place on a plate.
7. Shred chicken into smaller pieces using two forks.
8. Serve over white or brown rice.

Nutrition: Energy (calories): 400 kcal Protein: 17.7 g Fat: 17.12 g
Carbohydrates: 45.65 g Calcium, Ca131 mg Magnesium, Mg62 mg Phosphorus, P188 mg

167. Low-Carb Blackened Chicken (FAST)

Preparation time: 10 minutes
Cooking time:10 minutes
Servings: 4
Ingredients

- ½ teaspoon paprika
- 1/8 teaspoon salt
- ¼ teaspoon cayenne pepper
- ¼ teaspoon ground cumin
- ¼ teaspoon dried thyme
- 1/8 teaspoon ground white pepper
- 1/8 teaspoon onion powder
- 2 chicken breasts, boneless and skinless

Directions

1. Preheat your oven to 350 degrees Fahrenheit
2. Grease baking sheet
3. Take a cast-iron skillet and place it over high heat
4. Add oil and heat it up for 5 minutes until smoking hot
5. Take a small bowl and mix salt, paprika, cumin, white pepper, cayenne, thyme, onion powder
6. Oil the chicken breast on both sides and coat the breast with the spice mix
7. Transfer to your hot pan and cook for 1 minute per side
8. Transfer to your prepared baking sheet and bake for 5 minutes
9. Serve and enjoy!

Nutrition: Calories: 136 Fat: 3 g Saturated Fat: 1 g Carbohydrates: 1 g Fiber: 0.2 g Sodium: 173 mg Protein: 24 g

168. Cool Greek Chicken Breast (FAST)

Preparation time: 10 minutes
Cooking time:25 minutes
Servings: 4
Ingredients
- 4 chicken breast halves, skinless and boneless
- 1 cup extra virgin olive oil
- 1 lemon, juiced
- 2 teaspoons garlic, crushed
- 1 and ½ teaspoons black pepper
- 1/3 teaspoon paprika

Directions
1. Cut 3 slits in the chicken breast
2. Take a small bowl and whisk in olive oil, salt, lemon juice, garlic, paprika, pepper, and whisk for 30 seconds
3. Place chicken in a large bowl and pour marinade
4. Rub the marinade all over using your hand
5. Refrigerate overnight
6. Preheat grill to medium heat and oil the grate
7. Cook chicken in the grill until the center is no longer pink
8. Serve and enjoy!

Nutrition: Calories: 644 Fat: 57 g Saturated Fat: 10 g Carbohydrates: 2 g Fiber: 0.2 g Sodium: 325 mg Protein: 27 g

169. Succulent Chicken Dumplings

Preparation time: 25 minutes
Cooking time: 30 minutes
Servings: 8
Ingredients
- 3 cups chicken breast, chopped up and cooked
- 5 tortillas, fat-free and cut up into 2-inch pieces
- 8-ounce chicken broth, fat-free sodium-reduced
- 8-ounce chicken soup, reduced-sodium, and low –fat cream

- ½ teaspoon celery salt
- Salt as needed
- Black pepper as needed

Directions
1. Add chicken broth, cooked chicken breast, and cream of chicken soup into a large-sized saucepan into a large-sized saucepan
2. Bring the mixture to a boil
3. Season with celery, salt, and pepper
4. Once boiling point is reached, drop the tortillas one piece at a time
5. Lower down the heat
6. Simmer for 20-30 minutes
7. Serve and enjoy!

Nutrition: Calories: 105 Fat: 4g Carbohydrates: 0g Protein: 16g Saturated fat: 1g Fiber: 0g Sodium: 147mg

170. Hearty Herbed Chicken (FAST)

Preparation time: 10 minutes
Cooking time: 5 minutes
Servings: 3
Ingredients
- 1-pound large shrimp, peeled and deveined
- 2 tablespoons fresh lemon juice
- 2 tablespoons parsley, chopped
- 2 teaspoons olive oil
- 1 teaspoon salt-free lemon and herb seasoning
- ½ a teaspoon tablespoon salt
- ¼ teaspoon freshly ground black pepper

Directions
1. Take a large-sized skillet and add oil
2. Place it over medium heat
3. Allow the oil to heat up
4. Add shrimp and Sauté for 1 minute
5. Add lemon juice, herb seasoning, salt, and pepper
6. Stir it well to coat the shrimp
7. Sauté for 3 minutes
8. Remove the heat and stir in parsley
9. Serve and enjoy!

Nutrition: Calories- 103 Fat- 3g Carbohydrates- 2g Protein- 16g Saturated fat: 2g Fiber: 1g Sodium: 169 mg

FISH AND SEAFOODS RECIPES

171. Lemon Garlic Salmon with Asparagus (FAST)

Preparation Time: 15 minutes
Cooking Time: 10 minutes
Servings: 3
Ingredients:

- Trimmed asparagus - 1 bunch
- Olive oil - 1 tbsp.
- Minced garlic - 2 cloves
- Salmon - 1 pound
- Salted butter - 1 tbsp.
- Salt and pepper (optional)
- Juice and zest of lemon - 1 small

Directions:

1. Cut the salmon into 3 equal sized fillets
2. Heat a pan and melt the butter and olive oil
3. Place the 3 fillets on the pan.
4. Slowly add the asparagus
5. Cook for 4 minutes on each side then sprinkle salt and pepper
6. Add the lemon zest and garlic in the pan then cook till the garlic is brown.
7. Remove from heat and pour the lemon juice into the meal.
8. Best served hot.

Nutrition: Calories: 162 Total Fat: 12.3g Sodium: 58mg Total Carbs: 1.9g Fiber: 0.7g Sugars: 0.4g Protein: 12.4g

172. Tuna and spinach power bowl (FAST)

Preparation Time: 20 minutes
Cooking Time: 15 minutes
Servings: 6
Ingredients:

- Beans, great northern or cannellini -15oz. (rinsed and drained)
- Chopped spinach - 12 cups
- Tuna in olive oil,-6 oz. (undrained)
- Olive oil - 3 tbsp.
- Onion - 1 cup (chopped)
- Capers - ¼ cup
- Olives - 1/2 cup(sliced and drained)
- Red pepper crushed - ¼ Tsp.
- 3 garlic cloves, minced - 1 ½ Tsp.
- Sugar - 2 Tsp.
- Black pepper - ¼ Tsp.
- Salt - ¼ Tsp.

Directions:

1. In a pot boil, the spinach for 2 minutes to soften it then drain.
2. Heat olive oil in a medium-sized pot and pour the onions in then cook for 5 minutes.
3. Add the garlic and cook for a minute.
4. Take the olives, red pepper and capers and add into the pot for a minute
5. Pour the sugar and spinach into the pot, stir, cover the lip of the pot and cook for 8 minutes.
6. Remove from heat, place in a bowl and mix with beans and tuna.
7. Season as desired and enjoy

Nutrition: Calories: 129 Total Fat: 7.6g Sodium: 138mg Total Carbs: 7.6g Fiber: 2.5g Sugars: 2.8g Protein: 9.5g

173. Soba Noodles with Cucumber, Avocado, and Crab (FAST)

Preparation Time: 15 minutes
Cooking Time: 10 minutes
Servings: 4
Ingredients:

- 8 ounces soba (buckwheat) noodles
- 1 large cucumber, diced
- 1 ripe avocado, pitted, peeled, and diced
- 1 pound canned crabmeat, drained and gently rinsed
- ¼ cup Thai Dressing

Directions:

1. Fill a large pot with water and bring to a boil over high heat. Add the soba noodles and cook until tender, about 8 minutes. Drain in a colander and rinse under cold water. Transfer the noodles to a large bowl and set aside to cool.
2. Once cooled, add the cucumber, avocado, and crabmeat, and toss to combine.
3. Drizzle the Thai Dressing over the noodles, and gently toss to evenly coat.

Nutrition: Calories: 476 Total Fat: 22g Saturated Fat: 3g Protein: 24g Carbohydrates: 51 g Fiber: 7g Sodium: 658mg

174. Greek-Style Fish Pitas(FAST)

Preparation Time: 15 minutes
Cooking Time: 15 minutes
Servings: 4
Ingredients:

- 1 pound tilapia
- 1 teaspoon dried oregano

- ¼ teaspoon salt
- ⅛ teaspoon freshly ground black pepper
- 2 tablespoons olive oil
- Juice of 1 lemon
- 4 (6½-inch) whole-wheat pitas, cut open at the top
- ¼ cup Tahini Yogurt Sauce or store-bought hummus
- 1 cup Mediterranean Chopped Salad

Directions:
1. Preheat the oven to 350°F.
2. Sprinkle both sides of the tilapia with the oregano, salt, and pepper.
3. In a medium skillet over medium heat, heat the olive oil. Add the tilapia and cook for 8 minutes, flipping once halfway through, until the fish is opaque and has reached an internal temperature of 145°F. Add the lemon juice, evenly coating the fish.
4. Remove from heat and allow the fish to slightly cool before cutting it into about 8 equal pieces.
5. On two baking sheets, distribute the pitas in a single layer. Warm in the oven for about 5 minutes. Remove from the oven and allow to slightly cool.
6. Use clean fingers to pry a pita open at the top. Add 2 pieces of fish, 1 tablespoon sauce or hummus, and ¼ cup salad. Repeat with the remaining pitas.

Nutrition: Calories: 392 Total Fat: 14g Saturated Fat: 2g Protein: 32g Carbohydrates: 39g Fiber: 6g Sodium: 634mg

175. Simple Fish Stew (FAST)

Preparation Time: 5 minutes
Cooking Time: 25 minutes
Servings: 4
Ingredients:
- 2 (14-ounce cans) no-added-sodium diced tomatoes, divided
- 2 tablespoons olive oil
- 1 onion, diced
- 3 garlic cloves, minced
- 2 tablespoons herbes de Provence
- 1 (8-ounce) bottle clam juice
- 1¼ pounds cod, cut into 2-inch chunks
- ¼ teaspoon salt
- ⅛ teaspoon freshly ground black pepper

Directions:
1. Pour 1 can of diced tomatoes into a blender. Blend until smooth.
2. In a large saucepan over medium heat, heat the olive oil. Add the onion and cook until soft and translucent, 3 minutes. Add the garlic and

herbes de Provence, and cook until fragrant, 1 minute.
3. Add the blended tomatoes, the remaining can of diced tomatoes, and the clam juice. Bring the mixture to a boil, then reduce heat and simmer for 10 minutes, until the flavors combine.
4. Add the cod, cover, and poach for about 10 minutes, until cooked through and the internal temperature of the fish reaches 145°F.
5. Season with the salt and pepper, and stir to combine.

Nutrition: Calories: 218 Total Fat: 7g Saturated Fat: 1g Protein: 24g Carbohydrates: 13g Fiber: 2g Sodium: 881 mg

176. Braised Cod over Tomatoes (FAST)

Preparation Time: 10 minutes
Cooking Time: 15 minutes
Servings: 4
Ingredients:
- 1¼ pounds cod, cut into 4 equal pieces
- ¼ teaspoon salt
- ⅛ teaspoon freshly ground black pepper
- 2 tablespoons olive oil
- 2 pounds (about 8) Roma or plum tomatoes, cut into ¼-inch-thick slices
- 1 garlic clove, sliced
- 1 tablespoon dried oregano
- ⅛ teaspoon red pepper flakes
- Juice of ½ lemon

Directions:
1. Sprinkle both sides of the cod with the salt and pepper.
2. In a large skillet over medium heat, heat the olive oil. When the oil is shimmering, layer the tomatoes evenly on the bottom of the skillet. Sprinkle with the garlic, oregano, and red pepper flakes. Place the cod evenly over the tomatoes. Cover and cook for about 15 minutes, until the fish is opaque and reaches an internal temperature of 145°F.
3. Transfer the fish to a serving dish, leaving the tomatoes in the skillet. Break up the tomatoes with the back of a spoon, and drizzle them with the lemon juice.
4. Spoon the tomatoes over the fish and serve.

Nutrition: Calories: 204 Total Fat: 8g Saturated Fat: 1g Protein: 24g Carbohydrates: 10g Fiber: 3g Sodium: 589mg

177. Halibut with Carrots, Tomatoes, and Thyme (FAST)

Preparation Time: 10 minutes
Cooking Time: 20 minutes

Servings: 4

Ingredients:

- 4 (5-ounce) skin-on halibut fillets
- ½ teaspoon salt, divided
- 1 tablespoon olive oil
- 1 onion, chopped
- 2 garlic cloves, minced
- 2 medium carrots, peeled into ribbons
- 1 cup cherry tomatoes, halved
- 4 thyme sprigs
- ⅛ teaspoon freshly ground black pepper

Directions:

1. Preheat the oven to 400°F.
2. Sprinkle the flesh side of the fish with ¼ teaspoon of salt.
3. In an ovenproof pan over medium heat, heat the olive oil. When the oil is shimmering, add the onion and cook until translucent, about 3 minutes. Add the garlic and cook until fragrant, an additional 1 minute.
4. Scatter the carrots and tomatoes evenly around the pan, and top with the halibut, skin-side down, and the thyme. Sprinkle with the remaining ¼ teaspoon of salt and the pepper. Cover the pan with a lid or aluminum foil, and bake for about 15 minutes, until the fish is opaque and reaches an internal temperature of 145°F.
5. Remove from the oven and allow to cool for 10 minutes. Serve warm.

Nutrition: Calories: 192 Total Fat: 5g Saturated Fat: 1 g Protein: 27g Carbohydrates: 8g Fiber: 2g Sodium: 415mg

178. Sea Bass with Fennel Sauce (FAST)

Preparation Time: 15 minutes
Cooking Time: 20 minutes
Servings: 4

Ingredients:

- Cooking spray
- 1 medium fennel bulb.
- 1 red onion, thinly sliced
- 4 plum tomatoes, diced
- 2 lemons
- 4 (5-ounce) sea bass fillets
- ¼ teaspoon salt
- ⅛ teaspoon freshly ground black pepper
- 2 tablespoons olive oil
- 1 teaspoon mustard
- 1 garlic clove, minced

Directions:

1. Preheat the oven to 450°F. Coat a baking sheet with cooking spray.

2. Remove the fronds from the fennel bulb. and set aside. Finely chop the fennel bulb. and the fronds separately.
3. Evenly scatter the fennel bulb., onion, and tomatoes on the prepared baking sheet.
4. Bake for 5 minutes, until the vegetables soften.
5. Meanwhile, cut 1 lemon into thin slices. Sprinkle the sea bass with the salt and pepper.
6. Remove the baking sheet from the oven, and top the vegetables with the fish. Place the lemon slices over the fish. Return to the oven and bake for 15 minutes, until the fish is opaque and reaches an internal temperature of 145°F.
7. Meanwhile, juice the second lemon. In a small bowl, whisk together the lemon juice, olive oil, mustard, garlic, and chopped fennel fronds to make a dressing.
8. To serve, place 1 sea bass fillet on each of 4 plates, and top each with ¾ cup of vegetables and 1 tablespoon of dressing.

Nutrition: Calories: 240 Total Fat: 10g Saturated Fat: 2g Protein: 28g Carbohydrates: 10g Fiber: 3g Sodium: 293mg

179. Pistachio-Crusted Flounder (FAST)

Preparation Time: 15 minutes
Cooking Time: 15 minutes
Servings: 4

Ingredients:

- Cooking spray
- ¼ cup gluten-free Dijon mustard
- ½ teaspoon salt, divided
- ⅛ teaspoon freshly ground black pepper
- ½ cup raw shelled pistachios, finely chopped
- 2 tablespoons cornmeal
- ¼ cup chopped fresh parsley
- 4 (5-ounce) flounder fillets

Directions:

1. Preheat the oven to 400°F. Coat a baking sheet with cooking spray.
2. In a small bowl, whisk together the Dijon mustard, ¼ teaspoon of salt, and the pepper. Set aside.
3. In another small bowl, mix together the pistachios, cornmeal, parsley, and remaining ¼ teaspoon of salt.
4. Brush both sides of 1 flounder fillet with the mustard mixture, and then dredge both sides in the pistachio mixture, pressing down with clean fingers to make sure the pistachios stick. Place the flounder on the prepared baking sheet. Repeat with the remaining 3 fillets, leaving ½ inch between pieces.

5. Bake for about 15 minutes, until the fish is cooked through and reaches an internal temperature of 145°F.

Nutrition: Calories: 243 Total Fat: 9g Saturated Fat: 1 g Protein: 30g Carbohydrates: 10g Fiber: 2g Sodium: 573mg

180. Miso-Glazed Tuna

Preparation Time: 10 minutes, plus 30 minutes to chill
Cooking Time: 15 minutes
Servings: 4
Ingredients:
- Cooking spray
- ⅓ cup white miso
- ⅓ cup sake
- ⅓ cup mirin
- 2 tablespoons brown sugar
- 4 (5-ounce) tuna steaks

Directions:
1. Preheat the oven to 400°F. Coat an ovenproof baking dish with cooking spray.
2. In a small saucepan over low heat, whisk together the miso, sake, mirin, and brown sugar. Whisk continuously until the sugar is melted, about 2 minutes.
3. Pour the glaze into a medium bowl. Add the tuna, turning to coat. Cover and place in the refrigerator for at least 30 minutes but no longer than overnight.
4. Remove the tuna from the glaze and place in the prepared baking dish. Discard any remaining glaze. Bake for 12 minutes, or until the fish is opaque and cooked to a minimum internal temperature of 145°F.
5. Serve the fish warm or freeze for later. To freeze, place cooled fish into a freezer-safe container and freeze for up to 2 months. To defrost, refrigerate overnight. Reheat one piece at a time in the microwave on high for 1½ minutes, or in a 350°F oven for about 10 minutes.

Nutrition: Calories: 271 Total Fat: 1g Saturated Fat: 0g Protein: 37g Carbohydrates: 23g Fiber: 2g Sodium: 959mg

181. Crab Cakes with Shaved Fennel Salad (FAST)

Preparation Time: 20 minutes
Cooking Time: 10 minutes
Servings: 6
Ingredients:
- ¾ cup cooked baby shrimp
- 3 tablespoons heavy (whipping) cream
- 1 teaspoon sea salt, divided
- ¼ teaspoon freshly ground black pepper, divided
- 1½ pounds lump crabmeat
- 6 scallions, white and green parts, thinly sliced
- ¼ cup extra-virgin olive oil, divided
- 3 fennel bulbs., cored and very thinly sliced
- 2 tablespoons chopped fennel fronds
- ¼ cup freshly squeezed lemon juice
- ½ teaspoon Dijon mustard
- 1 garlic clove, minced

Directions:
1. In a blender or food processor, blend the shrimp, heavy cream, ½ teaspoon of sea salt, and ⅛ teaspoon of pepper until smooth.
2. In a large bowl, stir together the crabmeat and scallions.
3. Fold in the shrimp mousse until well mixed. Form the mixture into 8 patties. Refrigerate for 10 minutes.
4. In a large, nonstick skillet over medium-high heat, heat 2 tablespoons of olive oil until it shimmers.
5. Add the crab cakes. Cook for about 4 minutes per side until browned on both sides.
6. In a large bowl, combine the fennel and fennel fronds.
7. In a small bowl, whisk the remaining 2 tablespoons of olive oil with the lemon juice, mustard, garlic, and remaining ½ teaspoon of sea salt, and ⅛ teaspoon of pepper. Toss the dressing with the fennel and serve with the crab cakes.

Nutrition: Calories: 379 Protein: 35g Total Carbohydrates: 10g Sugars: <1g Fiber: 3g Total Fat: 20g Saturated Fat: 4g Cholesterol: 250mg Sodium: 1,434mg

182. Swordfish Kebabs (FAST)

Preparation Time: 20 minutes
Cooking Time: 10 minutes
Servings: 6
Ingredients:
- 3 tablespoons extra-virgin olive oil, plus more for the grill
- Juice of 2 oranges
- 1 tablespoon Dijon mustard
- 2 teaspoons dried tarragon
- ½ teaspoon sea salt
- ⅛ teaspoon freshly ground black pepper
- 2 pounds swordfish, cut into 1½-inch pieces
- 2 red bell peppers, cut into pieces

Directions:
1. In a medium bowl, whisk the olive oil, orange juice, mustard, tarragon, sea salt, and pepper.

2. Add the swordfish and toss to coat. Let sit for 10 minutes.

3. Heat a grill or grill pan to medium-high heat and brush it with oil.

4. Thread the swordfish and red bell peppers onto 6 wooden skewers (see tip). Cook for 6 to 8 minutes, turning, until the fish is opaque.

Nutrition: Calories: 326 Protein: 33g Total Carbohydrates: 11g Sugars: 8g Fiber: 2g Total Fat: 18g Saturated Fat: 1g Cholesterol: 0mg Sodium: 187mg

183. Salmon Skillet Supper(FAST)

Preparation Time: 12 minutes
Cooking Time: 15 minutes
Servings: 4
Ingredients:
- 1 tablespoon extra-virgin olive oil
- 2 garlic cloves, minced (about 1 teaspoon)
- 1 teaspoon smoked paprika
- 1 pint grape or cherry tomatoes, quartered (about 1½ cups)
- 1 (12-ounce) jar roasted red peppers, drained and chopped
- 1 tablespoon water
- ¼ teaspoon freshly ground black pepper
- ¼ teaspoon kosher or sea salt
- 1 pound salmon fillets, skin removed, cut into 8 pieces
- 1 tablespoon freshly squeezed lemon juice (from ½ medium lemon)

Directions:
1. In a large skillet over medium heat, heat the oil. Add the garlic and smoked paprika and cook for 1 minute, stirring often. Add the tomatoes, roasted peppers, water, black pepper, and salt. Turn up the heat to medium-high, bring to a simmer, and cook for 3 minutes, stirring occasionally and smashing the tomatoes with a wooden spoon toward the end of the cooking time.

2. Add the salmon to the skillet, and spoon some of the sauce over the top. Cover and cook for 10 to 12 minutes, or until the salmon is cooked through (145°F using a meat thermometer) and just starts to flake.

3. Remove the skillet from the heat, and drizzle lemon juice over the top of the fish. Stir the sauce, then break up the salmon into chunks with a fork. You can serve it straight from the skillet.

Nutrition: Calories: 289 Total Fat: 13g Saturated Fat: 2g Cholesterol: 68mg Sodium: 393mg Total Carbohydrates: 10g Fiber: 2g Protein: 31g

184. Easy Tuna Patties (FAST)

Preparation Time: 15 minutes
Cooking Time: 10 minutes
Servings: 4
Ingredients:
- 2 teaspoons lemon juice
- 3 tablespoons grated Parmesan
- 2 eggs
- 10 tablespoons Italian breadcrumbs
- 3 tuna cans, drained
- 3 tablespoons diced onion
- 1 pinch of ground black pepper
- 3 tablespoons vegetable oil

Directions:
1. Beat the eggs and lemon juice in a bowl. Stir in the Parmesan cheese and breadcrumbs to obtain a paste. Add tuna and onion until everything is well mixed. Season with black pepper. Form the tuna mixture into eight 1-inch-thick patties.

2. Heat the vegetable oil in a frying pan over medium heat; fry the patties until golden brown, about 5 minutes on each side.

Nutrition: 325 calories 15.5 grams of fat 13.9 g of carbohydrates 31.3 g of protein 125 mg cholesterol 409 mg of sodium

185. Salmon Burgers(FAST)

Preparation Time: 10 minutes
Cooking Time: 10 minutes
Servings: 6
Ingredients:
- 16 ounces canned salmon, drained
- 6 scallions, white and green parts, finely chopped
- ¼ cup whole-wheat bread crumbs
- 2 eggs, beaten
- 2 tablespoons chopped fresh Italian parsley leaves
- 1 tablespoon dried Italian seasoning
- Zest of 1 lemon
- 2 tablespoons extra-virgin olive oil
- ¼ cup unsweetened nonfat plain Greek yogurt
- 1 tablespoon chopped fresh dill
- 1 tablespoon capers, rinsed and chopped
- ¼ teaspoon sea salt
- 6 whole-wheat hamburger buns

Directions:
1. In a medium bowl, mix together the salmon, scallions, bread crumbs, eggs, parsley, Italian seasoning, and lemon zest. Form the mixture into 6 patties about ½-inch thick.

2. In a large nonstick skillet over medium-high heat, heat the olive oil until it shimmers.

3. Add the salmon patties. Cook for about 4 minutes per side until browned.
4. While the salmon cooks, in a small bowl, whisk the yogurt, dill, capers, and sea salt. Spread the sauce on the buns. Top with the patties and serve.

Nutrition: Calories: 319 Protein: 28g Total Carbohydrates: 24g Sugars: 6g Fiber: 3g Total Fat: 13g Saturated Fat: 2g Cholesterol: 95mg Sodium: 344mg

186.   Herbed Panini Fillet 'Fish

Preparation time: 15 minutes
Cooking time: 25 minutes
Servings: 4
Ingredients:
- 4 slices thick sourdough bread
- 4 slices mozzarella cheese
- 1 portabella mushroom, sliced
- 1 small onion, sliced
- 6 tbsp oil
- 4 garlic and herb fish fillets

Directions:
1. Prepare your fillets by adding salt, pepper, and herbs (rosemary, thyme, parsley, whatever you like).
2. Then mix in the flour before deep frying in boiling oil. Once nicely browned, remove from oil and set aside.
3. On medium-high fire, sauté for five minutes the onions and mushroom in a skillet with 2 tbsp oil.
4. Prepare sourdough bread by layering the following: cheese, fish fillet, onion mixture, and cheese again before covering with another bread slice.
5. Grill in your Panini press until cheese is melted and bread is crisped and ridged.

Nutrition: Calories: 422 Carbs: 13.2g Protein: 51.2g Fat: 17.2g

187.   Scrambled eggs with Smoked Salmon (FAST)

Preparation Time: 15 minutes
Cooking Time: 8 minutes
Servings: 1
Ingredients:
- 1 tbsp. coconut oil
- Pepper and salt to taste
- 1/8 tsp. red pepper flakes
- 1/8 tsp. garlic powder
- 1 tbsp. fresh dill, chopped finely
- 4 oz. smoked salmon, torn apart
- 2 whole eggs + 1 egg yolk, whisked

Directions:
1. In a big bowl whisk the eggs. Mix in pepper, salt, red pepper flakes, garlic, dill and salmon.
2. On low fire, place a nonstick fry pan and lightly grease with oil.
3. Pour egg mixture and whisk around until cooked through to make scrambled eggs, around 8 minutes on medium fire.
4. Serve and enjoy.

Nutrition: Calories per serving: 366 Protein: 32.0 Carbs: 1.0g Fat: 26.0g

188.   Blackened Salmon Fillets (FAST)

Preparation Time: 15 minutes
Cooking Time: 10 minutes
Servings: 4
Ingredients:
- 2 tablespoons paprika powder
- 1 tablespoon cayenne pepper powder
- 1 tablespoon onion powder
- 2 teaspoons salt
- 1/2 teaspoon ground white pepper
- 1/2 teaspoon ground black pepper
- 1/4 teaspoon dried thyme
- 1/4 teaspoon dried basil
- 1/4 teaspoon dried oregano
- 4 salmon fillets, skin and bones removed
- 1/2 cup unsalted butter, melted

Directions:
1. Combine bell pepper, cayenne pepper, onion powder, salt, white pepper, black pepper, thyme, basil and oregano in a small bowl.
2. Brush salmon fillets with 1/4 cup butter and sprinkle evenly with the cayenne pepper mixture. Sprinkle each fillet with ½ of the remaining butter.
3. Cook the salmon in a large heavy-bottomed pan, until dark, 2 to 5 minutes. Turn the fillets, sprinkle with the remaining butter and continue to cook until the fish easily peels with a fork.

Nutrition: 511 calories 38.3 grams of fat 4.5 grams of carbohydrates 37.4 g of protein 166 mg cholesterol 1248 mg of sodium

189.   Seafood Stuffing

Preparation Time: 25 minutes
Cooking Time: 30 minutes
Servings: 8
Ingredients:
- 1/2 cup butter
- 1/2 cup chopped green pepper
- 1/2 cup chopped onion
- 1/2 cup chopped celery
- Drained and flaky crabmeat

- 1/2 pound of medium-sized shrimp - peeled and deveined
- 1/2 cup spiced and seasoned breadcrumbs
- 1 mixture of filling for cornbread
- 2 tablespoons of white sugar, divided
- 1 can of mushroom soup (10.75 ounces) condensed
- oz. chicken broth

Directions:

1. Melt the butter in a large frying pan over medium heat. Add pepper, onion, celery crabmeat and shrimp; boil and stir for about 5 minutes. Set aside.
2. In a large bowl, mix stuffing, breadcrumbs, and 1 tablespoon sugar. Stir the vegetables and seafood from the pan. Add the mushroom cream and as much chicken broth as you want. Pour into a 9 x 13-inch baking dish.
3. Bake in the preheated oven for 30 minutes or until lightly roasted.

Nutrition: 344 calories 15.7 grams of fat 28.4 g of carbohydrates 22 g of protein 94 mg of cholesterol 1141 mg of sodium.

190.   Heather's Grilled Salmon (FAST)

Preparation Time: 10 minutes
Cooking Time: 10 minutes
Servings: 4
Ingredients:

- 1/4 cup brown sugar
- 1/4 cup olive oil
- 1/4 cup soy sauce
- 2 teaspoons lemon pepper
- 1 teaspoon dried thyme
- 1 teaspoon dried basil
- 1 teaspoon dried parsley
- 1/2 teaspoon garlic powder
- 4 (6 oz.) salmon fillets

Directions:

1. Whisk together the brown sugar, olive oil, soy sauce, lemon pepper, thyme, basil, parsley, and garlic powder in a bowl and pour into a resealable plastic bag.
2. Add the salmon fillets, coat with the marinade, squeeze out excess air, and seal the bag. Marinate in the refrigerator for at least 1 hour, turning occasionally.
3. Preheat an outdoor grill for medium heat, and lightly oil the grate. Remove the salmon from the marinade and shake off excess. Discard the remaining marinade.
4. Grill the salmon on the preheated grill until browned and the fish flakes easily with a fork, about 5 minutes on each side.

Nutrition: 380 calories 19.4 g fat 15.7 g carbohydrates 34.7 g protein 88 mg cholesterol 1251 mg sodium

191.   Brown Butter Perch (FAST)

Preparation Time: 15 minutes
Cooking Time: 10 minutes
Servings: 4
Ingredients:

- 1 cup flour
- 1 teaspoon salt
- 1/2 teaspoon finely ground black pepper
- 1/2 teaspoon cayenne pepper
- 8 oz. fresh perch fillets
- 2 tablespoons butter
- 1 lemon cut in half

Directions:

1. In a bowl, beat flour, salt, black pepper, and cayenne pepper. Gently squeeze the perch fillets into the flour mixture to coat well and remove excess flour.
2. Heat the butter in a frying pan over medium heat until it is foamy and brown hazel. Place the fillets in portions in the pan and cook them light brown, about 2 minutes on each side. Place the cooked fillets on a plate, squeeze the lemon juice, and serve.

Nutrition: 271 calories 11.5 g of fat 30.9 g of carbohydrates 12.6 g of protein 43 mg of cholesterol 703 mg of sodium.

192.   Red Snapper Veracruz (FAST)

Preparation Time: 15 minutes
Cooking Time: 10 minutes
Servings: 2
Ingredients:

- 2 tablespoons olive oil
- 1/2 white onion, diced
- 3 cloves of garlic, minced
- 1 tablespoon capers
- 1 tablespoon caper juice
- 1 cup cherry tomatoes, cut in half
- 1/3 cup pitted and sliced green olives
- 1 jalapeño pepper, seeded and minced
- 2 teaspoons fresh chopped oregano
- 2 teaspoons of olive oil
- 2 red snapper fillets, sliced in half
- salt and pepper to taste
- 1/2 teaspoon cayenne pepper,
- 2 limes, juiced

Directions:

1. Preheat the oven to 220 ° C.
2. Heat the olive oil in a frying pan over medium heat. Stir in the onion; cook and stir until onions begin to become transparent, 6 to 7 minutes.

3. Cook and stir garlic until fragrant, about 30 seconds. Add the capers and the caper juice; stir to combine.
4. Stir in the tomatoes, olives, and jalapeño. Boil and stir for about 3 minutes. Remove from the heat; mix in the oregano.
5. Pour 1 teaspoon of olive oil into a small baking dish. Sprinkle 1 tbsp. of the tomato-olive mixture. Sprinkle with salt, black pepper, and cayenne pepper. Add with more filling and juice of 1 lime. Repeat with the rest of the snapper fillet, herbs, and lime juice in a second baking dish.
6. Bake in the preheated oven until the fish is flaky and no longer translucent, 15 to 20 minutes.

Nutrition: 452 calories 25.2 g fat 16.2 g carbohydrates 43.1 g of protein 73 mg of cholesterol 1034 mg of sodium.

193. Fish in Foil (FAST)

Preparation Time: 10 minutes
Cooking Time: 20 minutes
Servings: 2
Ingredients:
- 2 fillets of rainbow trout
- 1 tablespoon of olive oil
- 2 teaspoons of salt with garlic
- 1 teaspoon ground black pepper
- 1 fresh jalapeño pepper, sliced
- 1 lemon cut into slices

Directions:
1. Preheat the oven to 200 degrees C (400 degrees F). Rinse and dry the fish.
2. Rub the fillets with olive oil and season with garlic salt and black pepper. Lay each on a large sheet of aluminum foil. Garnish with jalapeño slices and squeeze the juice from the lemon onto the fish. Place the lemon slices on the fillets. Carefully seal all edges of the foil to form closed bags. Place the packages on a baking sheet.
3. Bake in the preheated oven for 15 to 20 minutes, depending on the size of the fish. The fish is cooked when it easily breaks with a fork.

Nutrition: 213 calories 10.9 g fat 7.5 grams of carbohydrates 24.3 g of protein 67 mg of cholesterol 1850 mg of sodium

194. Shrimps with Lemon and Pepper (FAST)

Preparation time: 10 minutes
Cooking time: 3 minutes
Servings: 4
Ingredients:

- 40 big shrimp, peeled and deveined
- 6 garlic cloves, minced
- Salt and black pepper to taste
- 3 tablespoons olive oil
- ¼ teaspoon sweet paprika
- A pinch of red pepper flakes, crushed
- ¼ teaspoon lemon zest, grated
- 3 tablespoons sherry
- 1 and ½ tablespoons chives, sliced
- Juice of 1 lemon

Directions:
1. Heat a pan with the oil over medium high heat, add shrimp, season with salt and pepper and cook for 1 minute.
2. Add paprika, garlic and pepper flakes, stir and cook for 1 minute. Add sherry, stir and cook for 1 minute more.
3. Take shrimp off heat, add chives and lemon zest, stir and transfer shrimp to plates.
4. Add lemon juice all over and serve.

Nutrition: Calories 140 Fat 1 Fiber 0 Carbs 1 Protein 18

195. Grilled calamari with lemon juice (FAST)

Preparation Time: 15 minutes
Cooking Time: 5 minutes
Serves: 4
Ingredients:
- ¼ cup dried cranberries
- ¼ cup extra virgin olive oil
- ¼ cup olive oil
- ¼ cup sliced almonds
- ½ lemon, juiced
- ¾ cup blueberries
- 1 ½ pounds calamari tube, cleaned
- 1 granny smith apple, sliced thinly
- 1 tablespoon fresh lemon juice
- 2 tablespoons apple cider vinegar
- 6 cups fresh spinach Freshly grated pepper to taste
- Sea salt to taste

Directions:
1. In a small bowl, make the vinaigrette by mixing well the tablespoon of lemon juice, apple cider vinegar, and extra virgin olive oil. Season with pepper and salt to taste. Set aside.
2. Turn on the grill to medium fire and let the grates heat up for a minute or two.
3. In a large bowl, add olive oil and the calamari tube. Season calamari generously with pepper and salt.
4. Place seasoned and oiled calamari onto heated grate and grill until cooked or opaque. This is around two minutes per side.
5. As you wait for the calamari to cook, you can combine almonds, cranberries, blueberries,

spinach, and the thinly sliced apple in a large salad bowl. Toss to mix.

6. Remove cooked calamari from grill and transfer on a chopping board. Cut into ¼-inch thick rings and throw into the salad bowl.
7. Drizzle with vinaigrette and toss well to coat salad.
8. Serve and enjoy!

Nutrition: Calories per Serving: 567 Fat: 24.5g Protein: 54.8g Carbs: 30.6g

196. Pan-Roasted Salmon with Gremolata(FAST)

Preparation Time: 10 minutes
Cooking Time: 10 minutes
Servings: 6
Ingredients:
- 1½ pounds skin-on salmon fillet, cut into 4 pieces
- 1 teaspoon sea salt, divided
- ¼ teaspoon freshly ground black pepper
- 3 tablespoons extra-virgin olive oil
- 1 bunch fresh Italian parsley leaves, finely chopped
- 1 garlic clove, minced
- Zest of 1 lemon, finely grated (see tip)

Directions:
1. Preheat the oven to 350°F.
2. Season the salmon with ½ teaspoon of salt and the pepper.
3. In a large, ovenproof skillet over medium-high heat, heat the olive oil until it shimmers.
4. Add the salmon to the skillet, skin-side down. Cook for about 5 minutes, gently pressing on the salmon with a spatula, until the skin crisps. Transfer the pan to the oven and cook the salmon for 3 to 4 minutes more until it is opaque.
5. In a small bowl, stir together the parsley, garlic, lemon zest, and remaining ½ teaspoon of sea salt. Sprinkle the mixture over the salmon and serve.

Nutrition: Calories: 214 Protein: 22g Total Carbohydrates: <1g Sugars: <1g Fiber: <1g Total Fat: 14g
Saturated Fat: 2g Cholesterol: 50mg Sodium: 522mg

197. Dijon Mustard and Lime Marinated Shrimp (FAST)

Preparation Time: 10 minutes
Cooking Time: 10 minutes
Servings: 8
Ingredients:
- ½ cup fresh lime juice, and lime zest as garnish

- ½ cup rice vinegar
- ½ teaspoon hot sauce
- 1 bay leaf
- 1 cup water
- 1 lb. uncooked shrimp, peeled and deveined
- 1 medium red onion, chopped
- 2 tablespoon capers
- 2 tablespoon Dijon mustard
- 3 whole cloves

Directions:
1. Mix hot sauce, mustard, capers, lime juice, and onion in a shallow baking dish and set aside.
2. Bring to a boil in a large saucepan bay leaf, cloves, vinegar, and water.
3. Once boiling, add shrimps and cook for a minute while stirring continuously.
4. Drain shrimps and pour shrimps into onion mixture.
5. For an hour, refrigerate the covered shrimps.
6. Then serve shrimps cold and garnished with lime zest.

Nutrition: Calories: 232.2 Protein: 17.8 g Fat: 3 g Carbs: 15 g

198. Dill Relish on White Sea Bass (FAST)

Preparation Time: 10 minutes
Cooking Time: 12 minutes
Servings: 4
Ingredients:
- 1 ½ tablespoon chopped white onion
- 1 ½ teaspoon chopped fresh dill
- 1 lemon, quartered
- 1 teaspoon Dijon mustard
- 1 teaspoon lemon juice
- 1 teaspoon pickled baby capers, drained
- 4 pieces of 4-oz white sea bass fillets

Directions:
1. Preheat oven to 375F.
2. Mix lemon juice, mustard, dill, capers, and onions in a small bowl.
3. Prepare four aluminum foil squares and place 1 fillet per foil.
4. Squeeze a lemon wedge per fish.
5. Evenly divide into 4 the dill spread and drizzle over the fillet.
6. Close the foil over the fish securely and pop in the oven.
7. Bake for 12 minutes or until fish is cooked through.
8. Remove from foil and transfer to a serving platter, serve and enjoy.

Nutrition: Calories: 115 Protein: 7 g Fat: 1 g Carbs: 12 g

199. Lemony Roasted Chicken

Preparation time: 15 minutes
Cooking time: 1 hour + 30 minutes
Servings: 8
Ingredients

- ½ tsp ground black pepper
- ½ tsp mustard powder
- ½ tsp salt
- 1 3-lb whole chicken
- 1 tsp garlic powder
- 2 lemons
- 2 tbsps. olive oil
- 2 tsps. Italian seasoning

Directions

1. In a small bowl, mix black pepper, garlic powder, mustard powder, and salt.
2. Rinse chicken well and slice off giblets.
3. In a greased 9 x 13 baking dish, place chicken on it. Add 1½ tsp of seasoning made earlier inside the chicken and rub the remaining seasoning around the chicken.
4. In a small bowl, mix olive oil and juice from 2 lemons. Drizzle over chicken.
5. Bake chicken in an oven preheated at 3500 F until juices run clear, for around 1½ hour. Occasionally, baste the chicken with its juices.

Nutrition: Calories 190, Fat 7.8 g, Carbs 2g, Protein 37 g, Potassium 439 mg, Sodium 328 mg

200. Chicken and Apples Mix

Preparation Time: 10 minutes
Cooking Time: 40 minutes
Servings: 4
Ingredients:

- ½ cup chicken stock
- 1 red onion, sliced
- ½ cup tomato sauce
- 2 green apples, cored and chopped
- 1-pound breast, skinless, boneless and cubed
- 1 tsp thyme, chopped
- 1 and ½ tbsps. olive oil
- 1 tbsp chives, chopped

Directions:

1. In a roasting pan, combine the chicken with the tomato sauce, apples and the rest of the ingredients except the chives, introduce the pan in the oven and bake at 425 degrees F for 40 mins.

2. Divide the mix between plates, sprinkle the chives on top and serve.

Nutrition: Calories 292, Fat 16.1, Fiber 9.4, Carbs 15.4, Protein 16.4

201. Walnut Turkey and Peaches

Preparation Time: 10 mins
Cooking Time: 1 hour
Servings: 4
Ingredients:

- 2 turkey breasts, skinless, boneless and sliced
- ¼ cup chicken stock
- 1 tbsp walnuts, chopped
- 1 red onion, chopped
- Salt and black pepper to the taste
- 2 tbsps. olive oil
- 4 peaches, pitted and cut into quarters
- 1 tbsp cilantro, chopped

Directions:

1. In a roasting pan greased with the oil, combine the turkey and the onion and the rest of the ingredients except the cilantro, introduce in the oven and bake at 390 degrees F for 1 hours.
2. Divide the mix between plates, sprinkle the cilantro on top and serve.

Nutrition: Calories 500, Fat 14, Fiber 3, Carbs 15, Protein 10

202. Salmon & Pesto Salad   (FAST)

Preparation time:5 mins
Cooking time: 15 mins
Servings:2
Ingredients:
For the pesto:

- 1 minced garlic clove
- ½ cup fresh arugula
- ¼ cup extra virgin olive oi l
- ½ cup fresh basil
- 1 tsp. black pepper
- For the salmon:
- 4 oz. skinless salmon fillet
- 1 tbsp. coconut oil
- For the salad:
- ½ juiced lemon
- 2 sliced radishes
- ½ cup iceberg lettuce
- 1 tsp. black pepper

Direction:

1. Prepare the pesto by blending all the ingredients for the pesto in a food processor or by grinding with a pestle and mortar. Set aside.

2. Add a skillet to the stove on medium-high heat and melt the coconut oil.
3. Add the salmon to the pan.
4. Cook for 7-8 mins and turn over.
5. Cook for a further 3-4 mins or until cooked through.
6. Remove fillets from the skillet and allow to rest.
7. Mix the lettuce and the radishes and squeeze over the juice of ½ lemon.
8. Flake the salmon with a fork and mix through the salad.
9. Toss to coat and sprinkle with a little black pepper to serve.

Nutrition: Calories 221, Protein 13 g, Carbs 1 g, Fat 34 g, Sodium 80 mg, Potassium 119 mg, Phosphorus 158 mg

203. Baked Fennel & Garlic Sea Bass (FAST)

Preparation time:5 minutes
Cooking time:15 minutes
Servings:2
Ingredients:
- 1 lemon
- ½ sliced fennel bulb
- 6 oz. sea bass fillets
- 1 tsp. black pepper
- 2 garlic cloves

Direction:
1. Preheat the oven to 375°F/Gas Mark 5.
2. Sprinkle black pepper over the Sea Bass.
3. Slice the fennel bulb and garlic cloves.
4. Add 1 salmon fillet and half the fennel and garlic to one sheet of baking paper or tin foil.
5. Squeeze in 1/2 lemon juices.
6. Repeat for the other fillet.
7. Fold and add to the oven for 12-15 mins or until fish is thoroughly cooked through.
8. Meanwhile, add boiling water to your couscous, cover and allow to steam.
9. Serve with your choice of rice or salad.

Nutrition: Calories 221, Protein 14 g, Carbs 3 g, Fat 2 g, Sodium 119 mg, Potassium 398 mg, Phosphorus 149 mg

204. Italian Salmon Platter (FAST)

Preparation Time: 5 minutes
Cooking Time: 6 minutes
Servings: 3
Ingredients
- ¾ cup of water
- A few sprigs of parsley, basil, tarragon, basil
- 1 pound of salmon, skin on

- 3 teaspoons of ghee
- ¼ teaspoon of salt
- ½ teaspoon of pepper
- ½ of lemon, thinly sliced
- 1 whole carrot, julienned

Directions
1. Set your pot to sauté mode and put in water and herbs
2. Place a steamer rack inside your pot and place in salmon
3. Drizzle ghee on top of the salmon and season with salt and pepper
4. Cover with lemon slices
5. Lock the lid and cook on HIGH pressure for 3 minutes
6. Release the pressure naturally over 10 minutes
7. Transfer the salmon to a serving platter
8. Set your pot to sauté mode and add vegetables
9. Cook for 1-2 minutes
10. Serve vegetables with the salmon
11. Enjoy!

Nutrition Per Serving: Carbohydrates: 3 grams/Fat: 34 grams/Protein: 15 grams/Fiber: 1 gram/Calories: 464

205. Feisty Grilled Lime Shrimp(FAST)

Preparation Time: 10-20 minutes
Cooking Time: 5 minutes
Servings: 3
Ingredients
- 1-pound medium shrimp, peeled and deveined
- 1 lime, juiced
- ½ cup olive oil
- 3 tablespoons Cajun seasoning

Directions
1. Take a re-sealable zip bag and add lime juice, Cajun seasoning, and olive oil
2. Add shrimp and shake it well; let it marinate for 20 minutes
3. Preheat your outdoor grill to medium heat
4. Lightly grease the grate
5. Remove shrimp from marinade and cook for 2 minutes per side
6. Serve and enjoy!

Nutrition Per Serving: Carbohydrates: 1.2 grams/Fat: 3 grams/Protein: 13 grams/Fiber: 0.1 gram/Calories: 18

206. Smoked Salmon with Capers and Radishes (FAST)

Preparation time: 10 minutes
Cooking time: 0 minutes

Servings: 8
Ingredients:
- 3 tablespoons beet horseradish, prepared
- 1-pound smoked salmon, skinless, boneless and flaked
- 2 teaspoons lemon zest, grated
- 4 radishes, chopped
- ½ cup capers, drained and chopped
- 1/3 cup red onion, roughly chopped
- 3 tablespoons chives, chopped

Directions:
1. In a bowl, combine the salmon with the beet horseradish, lemon zest, radish, capers, onions and chives, toss and serve cold.
2. Enjoy!

Nutrition: calories 254, fat 2, fiber 1, carbs 7, protein 7

207.   Trout Spread

Preparation time: 10 minutes
Cooking time: 0 minutes
Servings: 8
Ingredients:
- 4 ounces smoked trout, skinless, boneless and flaked
- ¼ cup coconut cream
- 1 tablespoon lemon juice
- 1/3 cup non-fat yogurt
- 1 and ½ tablespoon parsley, chopped
- 3 tablespoons chives, chopped
- Black pepper to the taste
- A drizzle of olive oil

Directions:
1. In a bowl mix trout with yogurt, cream, black pepper, chives, lemon juice and the dill and stir.
2. Drizzle the olive oil at the end and serve.
3. Enjoy!

Nutrition: calories 204, fat 2, fiber 2, carbs 8, protein 15

208.   Fish Bone Broth

Preparation Time: 10 minutes
Cooking Time: 1 hour
Serving: 4
Ingredients:
- One tablespoon olive oil
- One onion – peeled and chopped
- One carrot – peeled and chopped
- Two stalks of celery – chopped
- One leek – chopped
- 10 white button mushrooms – sliced
- 35-ounce of fish bones and fish off-cuts
- Four cups of cold water
- Salt
- Parsley – to garnish, chopped

Direction:
1. Add oil into the stockpot or pan. Add mushrooms, leek, celery, carrot, and onions. Cook over medium flame.
2. When softened, add fish bones and add in cold water.
3. Let simmer and cover with a lid. Cook for one hour.
4. Strain the broth through a strainer and season with salt.
5. Serve hot and top with fresh parsley.

Nutrition: Calories 66 | Fat 4g | sodium 254mg | Carbohydrates 8g | Fiber 2g |Sugar 3g | Protein 1g

209.   Broccoli and Tilapia Dish (FAST)

Preparation Time: 5 minutes
Cooking Time: 14 minutes
Serving: 4
Ingredients
- 6 ounces of tilapia, frozen
- 1 tablespoon of butter
- 1 tablespoon of garlic, minced
- 1 teaspoon of lemon pepper seasoning
- 1 cup of broccoli florets, fresh

Directions
1. Preheat your oven to 350 degrees Fahrenheit
2. Put fish into aluminum foil packets
3. Arrange broccoli around the fish
4. Sprinkle lemon pepper on top
5. Close the foil packets and seal
6. Bake for 14 minutes
7. Take a bowl and add garlic and butter, mix well, and set the mixture off to the side
8. Remove the packets from the oven and transfer them to a platter
9. Place butter on top of the fish and broccoli, serve, and enjoy!

Nutrition Per Serving: Carbohydrates: 2 grams/Fat: 25 grams/Protein: 29 grams/Fiber: 1 gram/Calories: 362

210.   Spanish Cod in Sauce

Preparation Time: 10 minutes
Cooking Time: 5.5 hours
Servings:2
Ingredients:
- 1 tsp tomato paste
- 1 tsp garlic, diced
- 1 white onion, sliced
- 1 jalapeno pepper, chopped
- 1/3 cup chicken stock
- 7 oz Spanish cod fillet
- 1 tsp paprika

- 1 tsp salt

Directions:

1. Pour chicken stock in the saucepan.
2. Add tomato paste and mix up the liquid until homogenous.
3. Add garlic, onion, jalapeno pepper, paprika, and salt.
4. Bring the liquid to boil and then simmer it.
5. Chop the cod fillet and add it in the tomato liquid.
6. Close the lid and simmer the fish for 10 mins over the low heat.
7. Serve the fish in the bowls with tomato sauce.

Nutrition: Calories 113, Fat 1.2, Fiber 1.9, Carbs 7.2, Protein 18.9

211. Ginger Shrimp (FAST)

Preparation time: 20 min
Cooking Time: 12 mins
Servings: 4

Ingredients:

- 2 tbsps. of extra-virgin olive oil
- 1 tbsp of minced peeled fresh ginger
- 2 cups of snow peas
- 1½ cups of frozen baby peas
- 3 tbsps. of water
- 1 pound of medium shrimp, shelled and deveined
- 2 tbsps. of low-Sodium soy sauce

Directions:

1. Using a large wok, heat the olive oil over medium heat.
2. Add the ginger and stir-fry for 1 to 2 mins, until the ginger is fragrant.
3. Add the snow peas and stir-fry for 2 to 3 mins, until they are tender-crisp.
4. Add the baby peas and the water and stir. Cover the wok and steam for 2 to 3 mins or until the vegetables are tender.
5. Stir in the shrimp and stir-fry for 3 to 4 mins, or until the shrimp have curled and turned pink.
6. Add the soy sauce and pepper; stir and serve.

Nutrition: Calories 237, Fat 7.3, Fiber 4.6, Carbs 12.9, Protein 32.8 Potassium 504mg Phosphorus 350 mg

212. Baked Halibut (FAST)

Preparation Time: 5 minutes
Cooking Time: 30 minutes
Servings: 4

Ingredients

- 6 ounces halibut fillets
- 1 tablespoon Greek seasoning
- 1 large tomato, chopped
- 1 onion, chopped
- 5 ounces kalamata olives, pitted
- ¼ cup capers
- ¼ cup olive oil
- 1 tablespoon lemon juice
- Salt and pepper, as needed

Directions

1. Preheat your oven to 350 degrees Fahrenheit
2. Transfer the halibut fillets onto a large aluminum foil
3. Season with Greek seasoning
4. Take a bowl and add tomato, onion, olives, olive oil, capers, pepper, lemon juice, and salt
5. Mix well and spoon the tomato mix over the halibut
6. Seal the edges of the foil and fold to make a packet
7. Place the packet on a baking sheet and bake in your oven for 30-40 minutes
8. Serve once the fish flakes off and enjoy!
9. Serve over rice cauliflower, if desired

Nutrition Per Serving: Carbohydrates: 10 grams/Fat: 26 grams/Protein: 36 grams/Fiber: 2 grams/Calories: 429

213. Garlic and Parsley Scallops (FAST)

Preparation Time: 5 minutes
Cooking Time: 25 minutes
Servings: 6

Ingredients

- 8 tablespoons butter
- 2 garlic cloves, minced
- 16 large sea scallops
- Salt and pepper to taste
- 1 and ½ tablespoons olive oil

Directions

1. Season scallops with salt and pepper
2. Take a skillet and place it over medium heat, add oil, and let it heat up
3. Sauté scallops for 2 minutes per side; repeat until all scallops are cooked
4. Add butter to the skillet and let it melt
5. Stir in garlic and cook for 15 minutes
6. Return scallops to skillet and stir to coat
7. Serve and enjoy!

Nutrition Per Serving: Carbohydrates: 5 grams/Fat: 31 grams/Protein: 29 grams/Fiber: 1 gram/Calories: 417

214. Miso-Glazed Pan-Seared Salmon with Bok Choy (FAST)

Preparation time: 10 minutes
Cooking time: 15 minutes
Servings: 2
Ingredients:

- 2 (6-ounce) salmon fillets
- 1/4 cup white or yellow miso
- 2 tablespoons rice or coconut vinegar
- 2 tablespoons sesame oil, divided
- 1 tablespoon gluten-free soy sauce, tamari, or coconut aminos
- 1 tablespoon minced fresh ginger
- 1 clove garlic, minced
- 11/2 pounds (medium bunch) baby bok choy, core removed, sliced into 11/2-inch pieces, white stem and leafy green parts separated
- 2 tablespoons thinly sliced scallion whites (optional)
- 2 tablespoons thinly sliced scallion greens, for garnish (optional)

Directions:

1. Heat the broiler to high.
2. On a baking sheet or broiler pan, place the salmon, skin-side down, and pat it dry. In a small bowl, whisk together the miso, vinegar, 1 tablespoon of the sesame oil, the soy sauce, ginger, and garlic. Spread 2 tablespoons of the glaze evenly over the top of the salmon, setting aside the remainder. Let it stand for 10 minutes, if you have time.
3. Broil the salmon until the glaze is bubbly, 3 to 4 minutes. Cover it loosely with foil and continue to broil until slightly pink in the center, another 3 to 4 minutes. Remove the salmon from the broiler, remove the foil, and let it cool.
4. In a large skillet over medium-high heat, heat the remaining 1 tablespoon sesame oil. Add the bok choy stems and scallion whites (if using) and cook until just tender, 2 to 3 minutes. Stir in the remaining miso glaze and cook until fragrant, 30 to 60 seconds. Add the bok choy greens, cover, and steam until just wilted, 30 seconds. Toss to coat with the sauce.
5. To serve, divide the bok choy evenly between two plates. Top each with a salmon fillet and sprinkle with scallion greens (if using).

Nutrition: Calories: 210 Carbs: 35.1g   Fat: 3.2g Fiber: 13.7g   Protein: 12.2g

215. Miso-Glazed Salmon

Preparation Time: 10 minutes
Cooking Time: 40 minutes
Serving: 4
Ingredients:

- ¼ cup red miso
- ¼ cup's sake
- 1 tablespoon soy sauce
- 1 tablespoon vegetable oil
- 4 salmon fillets

Directions:

1. In a bowl combine sake, oil, soy sauce and miso.
2. Rub mixture over salmon fillets and marinade for 20-30 minutes.
3. Preheat a broiler.
4. Broil salmon for 5-10 minutes.
5. When ready remove and serve.

Nutrition: Calories: 198 Total Carbohydrate: 5 g Cholesterol: 12 mg Total Fat: 10 g Fiber: 2 g Protein: 6 g Sodium: 257 mg

216. Arugula and Sweet Potato Salad

Preparation Time: 10 minutes
Cooking Time: 20 minutes
Serving: 4
Ingredients:

- 1 lb. sweet potatoes
- 1 cup walnuts
- 1 tablespoon olive oil
- 1 cup water
- 1 tablespoon soy sauce
- 3 cups arugula

Directions:

1. Bake potatoes at 400 F until tender, remove and set aside.
2. In a bowl, drizzle walnuts with olive oil and microwave for 2-3 minutes or until toasted.
3. In a bowl, combine all salad ingredients and mix well.
4. Pour over soy sauce and serve.

Nutrition: Calories: 189 Total Carbohydrate: 2 g Cholesterol: 13 mg Total Fat: 7 g Fiber: 2 g Protein: 10 g Sodium: 301 mg

217. Smoked Salmon, Cucumber, and Avocado Sushi (FAST)

Preparation time: 10 minutes
Cooking time: 15 minutes
Servings: 2

Ingredients:
- 2 sheets sushi nori
- 1 medium avocado, pitted and peeled
- 2 tablespoons sesame seeds, divided (optional)
- 4 ounces smoked salmon (about 4 thin slices)
- 1 medium cucumber, cut into matchsticks
- 3 tablespoons pickled ginger (optional)
- 1 teaspoon wasabi paste (optional)
- Gluten-free soy sauce, tamari, or coconut aminos, for dipping

Directions:
1. Lay 1 piece of nori on a sheet of parchment paper or aluminum foil on a flat surface.
2. In a small bowl, mash the avocado with a fork.
3. Spread half of the avocado mixture on the nori sheet, leaving a 1/2-inch strip uncovered along the top edge. Sprinkle 1 tablespoon of the sesame seeds (if using), evenly over the avocado. Arrange 2 pieces of the smoked salmon horizontally, covering the avocado.
4. Arrange the cucumber horizontally, running up the length of the sheet and creating columns to cover the salmon.
5. Wet the tip of your finger and run it along the exposed seam. Roll the nori tightly away from you, using the foil as a guide and pressing firmly to seal. Repeat the process with the remaining nori sheet and ingredients, and refrigerate both for at least 30 minutes to firm up.
6. Using a very sharp or serrated knife, slice each roll into 6 to 8 pieces. Serve with pickled ginger and wasabi (if using) and soy sauce for dipping.

Nutrition: Calories: 457 Carbs: 45.2g   Fat: 18.6g Fiber: 2.8g   Protein: 25.7g

218.   Oil-Poached Whitefish with Lemony Gremolata (FAST)

Preparation time: 10 minutes
Cooking time: 15 minutes
Servings: 4

Ingredients:
- 2 3/4pound skinless Arctic char or other whitefish fillets
- 1 teaspoon kosher salt
- 1 teaspoon freshly ground black pepper
- 1/2 cup extra-virgin olive oil
- 3 cloves garlic, minced
- 3/4 cup fresh parsley leaves, minced, divided

- 1/4 cup grated lemon zest (from 6 small or 4 large lemons), divided

Directions:
1. Place the fish fillets lengthwise in a 13-by-9-inch baking dish and season with the salt and pepper on both sides. In a small bowl, whisk together the olive oil, garlic, half of the parsley, and half of the lemon zest. Pour evenly over the fish, cover, and marinate in the refrigerator for at least 30 minutes and up to overnight.
2. Preheat the oven to 350F.
3. Bake the fish until just cooked through, 15 to 20 minutes. Cut each fillet into 2 pieces, top evenly with the remaining parsley and lemon zest, and serve with Lemony Sautéed Chard with Red Onion and Herbs or another vegetable side or salad.

Nutrition: Calories: 620 Carbs: 89g   Fat: 22g Fiber: 12g   Protein: 18g

219.   Baked Salmon Burger Patty (FAST)

Preparation Time: 15 minutes
Cooking Time: 15 minutes
Serving: 3

Ingredients:
- 1-pound salmon skin removed and chopped into cubes
- 1 Tbsp stone ground mustard
- 1 Tbsp avocado oil
- 1 tsp ground paprika
- 1/2 tsp sea salt
- 3 whole wheat flat bread
- 3 lettuce leaves
- 1 roma tomato sliced into 3 circles
- 3 onion rings

Directions:
1. Preheat oven to 450oF.
2. Lightly grease a cookie sheet with cooking spray.
3. In a food processor, add salmon, mustard, oil, paprika, and salt. Process until you form a thick paste. Scraping sides and bottom.
4. Evenly divide mixture into three and form into equal patties.
5. Place on prepared sheet and bake for 20 mins. Flip burger halfway through cooking time.
6. Assemble burger, serve and enjoy.

Nutrition: Calories 372, Fat 15g, Carbs 17g, Protein 43g, Fiber 3g, Sodium 1097mg, Potassium 591mg

220. Orange Herbed Sauced White Bass

Preparation Time: 15 mins
Cooking Time: 35 mins
Serving: 6
Ingredients:
- 1 ½ tbsp fresh lemon juice
- ¼ cup thinly sliced green onions
- ½ cup orange juice
- 3 tbsp chopped fresh dill
- 6 3-oz skinless white bass fillets
- 1 ½ tbsp olive oil
- 1 large onion, halved, thinly sliced
- 1 large orange, unpeeled, sliced
- Additional unpeeled orange slices

Directions:
1. Grease a 13 x 9-inch glass baking dish and preheat oven to 400oF.
2. Arrange orange slices in single layer on baking dish, top with onion slices, seasoned with pepper and salt plus drizzled with oil.
3. Pop in the oven and roast for 25 mins or until onions are tender and browned.
4. Remove from oven and increased oven temperature to 450oF.
5. Push onion and orange slices on sides of dish and place bass fillets in middle of dish. Season with 1 ½ tbsp dill, pepper and salt. Arrange onions and orange slices on top of fish and pop into the oven.
6. Roast for 8 mins or until salmon is opaque and flaky.
7. In a small bowl, mix 1 ½ tbsp dill, lemon juice, green onions and orange juice.
8. Transfer salmon to a serving plate, discard roasted onions, drizzle with the newly made orange sauce and garnish with fresh orange slices.
9. Serve and enjoy.

Nutrition: Calories 159, Fat 6g, Carbs 10g, Protein 17g, Fiber 2g, Sodium 62mg, Potassium 388mg

221. Ceviche Fish Tacos with Easy Guacamole

Preparation time: 10 minutes
Cooking time: 6 hours minutes
Servings: 2
Ingredients:
- Ceviche:
- 11/4 pounds meaty skinless fresh fish fillets
- 3 tablespoons lime juice
- 3 tablespoons lemon juice
- 1/4 teaspoon salt
- 1/4 teaspoon freshly ground black pepper
- 2 ripe plum or heirloom tomatoes, seeded and chopped (juices reserved)
- 1 tablespoon olive oil
- 3/4 cup chopped red onion
- 1 serrano pepper, seeded and minced (optional)
- Bibb lettuce leaves, for serving
- Guacamole:
- 4 avocados
- Juice from 1/2 lime (reserve remaining half for wedges, for serving)
- 1/2 cup chopped fresh cilantro
- 2 tablespoons chopped red onion
- 1 serrano pepper, seeded and minced
- Additional Taco Fixings:
- Store-bought salsa (without added salt, oil, or sugar)
- Creamy Citrus Slaw
- Chopped fresh cilantro
- Lime wedges
- Quick-Pickled Red Onions

Directions:
1. In a medium bowl, place the fish, lime and lemon juices, salt, and pepper and toss to combine. Cover tightly and chill until the fish turns completely white, tossing occasionally, at least 4 hours and up to 6 hours.
2. Meanwhile, make the guacamole. Cut the avocados in half, then remove the pit and peel. Spoon the avocado into a large bowl and mash it with a large metal spoon. Add the lime juice and continue to mix and mash until mostly smooth with some remaining chunks (this helps prevent the guacamole from browning). Mix in the cilantro, onion, and serrano pepper. Cover tightly and refrigerate until ready to use.
3. Strain the fish, moving it to a clean bowl; discard the marinade. Add the tomatoes, oil, onion, and serrano pepper (if using) and toss gently to combine. Serve wrapped in the Bibb lettuce leaves topped with the guacamole and your choice of additional fixings.

Nutrition: Calories: 253 Carbs: 107g Fat: 5g Fiber: 36g Protein: 32g

222. Baked Haddock with Avocado Mayonnaise

Preparation time: 10 minutes
Cooking time: 30 minutes
Servings: 4

Ingredients:
- 1 pound haddock, boneless
- 3 teaspoons water
- 2 tablespoons lemon juice
- A pinch of salt and black pepper
- 2 tablespoons avocado mayonnaise
- 1 teaspoon dill, chopped
- Cooking spray

Directions:
1. Spray a baking dish with some cooking oil, add fish, water, lemon juice, salt, black pepper, mayo and dill, toss, introduce in the oven and bake at 350 degrees F for 30 minutes.
2. Divide between plates and serve.
3. Enjoy!

Nutrition: calories 264, fat 4, fiber 5, carbs 7, protein 12

223. Basil Tilapia (FAST)

Preparation time: 10 minutes
Cooking time: 10 minutes
Servings: 4

Ingredients:
- 4 tilapia fillets, boneless
- Black pepper to the taste
- ½ cup low-fat parmesan, grated
- 4 tablespoons avocado mayonnaise
- 2 teaspoons basil, dried
- 2 tablespoons lemon juice
- ¼ cup olive oil

Directions:
1. Grease a baking dish with the oil, add tilapia fillets, black pepper, spread mayo, basil, drizzle lemon juice and top with the parmesan, introduce in preheated broiler and cook over medium-high heat for 5 minutes on each side.
2. Divide between plates and serve with a side salad.
3. Enjoy!

Nutrition: calories 215, fat 10, fiber 5, carbs 7, protein 11

224. Salmon Meatballs with Garlic

Preparation time: 10 minutes
Cooking time: 30 minutes
Servings: 4

Ingredients:
- Cooking spray
- 2 garlic cloves, minced
- 1 yellow onion, chopped
- 1-pound wild salmon, boneless and minced
- ¼ cup chives, chopped
- 1 egg
- 2 tablespoons Dijon mustard
- 1 tablespoon coconut flour

- A pinch of salt and black pepper

Directions:
1. In a bowl, mix onion with garlic, salmon, chives, coconut flour, salt, pepper, mustard and egg, stir well, shape medium meatballs, arrange them on a baking sheet, grease them with cooking spray, introduce in the oven at 350 degrees F and bake for 25 minutes.
2. Divide the meatballs between plates and serve with a side salad.
3. Enjoy!

Nutrition: calories 211, fat 4, fiber 1, carbs 6, protein 13

225. Shrimp Scampi with Baby Spinach (FAST)

Preparation time: 10 minutes
Cooking time: 10 minutes
Servings: 2-4

Ingredients:
- 1 pound jumbo shrimp (about 12), peeled and deveined
- 3 tablespoons extra-virgin olive oil, divided
- 6 cloves garlic, minced
- 1 cup unsalted chicken broth or stock
- Grated zest and juice from 1 medium lemon
- 1/2 teaspoon red pepper flakes, or to taste
- 1/4 teaspoon sea salt or Himalayan salt, or to taste
- 1/2 teaspoon freshly ground black pepper, or to taste
- 1/4 cup 1/2 stick) cold unsalted grass-fed butter, cubed
- 6 to 8 cups (6 ounces) baby spinach leaves
- 2 to 3 tablespoons chopped fresh parsley (optional)

Directions:
1. Pat the shrimp very dry with paper towels. Heat 2 tablespoons of the olive oil in a large skillet over medium-high heat. Add the shrimp and cook until pink, flipping once, about 2 minutes per side. Transfer to a large bowl or plate.
2. Reduce the heat to medium and add remaining 1 tablespoon oil. Add the garlic and cook until just fragrant, about 1 minute. Add the broth, lemon zest and juice, red pepper flakes, salt, and black pepper, increase the heat to medium-high, and bring to a simmer. Reduce the sauce by half, scraping up any browned bits from the bottom with a wooden spoon, about 5 minutes.
3. Remove the pan from the heat and allow to cool slightly. Add butter, one cube at a

time, stirring continually with a wooden spoon until the sauce thickens.

4. To serve, divide spinach evenly among four plates. Top each plate with about 4 shrimp. Divide the sauce evenly among the plates and garnish with the parsley (if using).

Nutrition: Calories: 268 Carbs: 40g Fat: 7.4g Fiber: 3.5g Protein: 11g

226. Shrimp Fried Rice (FAST)

Preparation time: 10 minutes
Cooking time: 25 minutes
Servings: 4
Ingredients:
- 3 tablespoons gluten-free soy sauce, tamari, or coconut aminos
- 2 tablespoons minced fresh ginger
- 3 tablespoons sesame oil, divided
- 2 large eggs, lightly beaten
- 2/3-to-3/4-pound medium shrimp, peeled and deveined (about 24)
- 1 shallot, minced
- 1 red bell pepper, seeded and diced
- 1 recipe cooled or chilled Easy Cauliflower Rice
- 3/4 cup frozen peas
- 1/4 cup chopped unsalted cashews
- 2 tablespoons chopped fresh cilantro
- 1/4 teaspoon red pepper flakes (optional)
- Sliced scallion greens, for garnish (optional)

Directions:
1. In a small bowl, whisk the soy sauce and ginger together and set aside.
2. In a wok or large skillet over medium heat, heat 1 tablespoon of the sesame oil. Add the eggs and cook, stirring frequently with a wooden spoon or spatula, until scrambled. Transfer to a small bowl and break up the cooked egg into small pieces using two forks. Set aside.
3. In the same wok over medium-high heat, heat 1 tablespoon of the sesame oil. Add the shrimp and cook, tossing, until bright pink but not browned, 3 to 4 minutes. Transfer the shrimp to a separate plate or bowl and set aside.
4. Add the remaining 1 tablespoon sesame oil and the shallot to the wok and cook until fragrant, tossing frequently, about 30 seconds. Add the bell pepper and cook until just tender, tossing occasionally, about 2 minutes. Add the cauliflower rice and cook, tossing occasionally, until

lightly browned and crisp, about 5 minutes. Stir in the soy sauce mixture. Add the cooked shrimp, cooked eggs, and peas and stir until well combined and heated through, 2 to 3 minutes. Add the cashews, cilantro, and red pepper flakes (if using), tossing to combine.

5. Divide the mixture among four bowls, garnish with scallion greens (if using) and serve.

Nutrition: Calories: 116 Carbs: 24g Fat: 1g Fiber: 4g Protein: 4g

227. Mussels with Lemon-Garlic-Herb Broth (FAST)

Preparation time: 10 minutes
Cooking time: 8 minutes
Servings: 4
Ingredients:
- 2 pounds mussels
- 1 tablespoon extra-virgin olive oil
- 2 shallots, minced
- 3 cloves garlic, minced
- 2 cups chicken or Veggie Trimmings Stock
- 1/4 cup lemon juice (from 2 lemons)
- 1/4 cup chopped fresh parsley, plus more for garnish
- 1/4 cup chopped fresh dill (optional)
- 3 tablespoons chopped fresh thyme
- 1/2 teaspoon salt
- 1/4 teaspoon freshly ground black pepper
- 1/4 teaspoon red pepper flakes (optional)
- 3 cups baby spinach (or spinach leaves torn into smaller pieces)
- 2 tablespoons cold unsalted grass-fed butter, cubed

Directions:
1. Rinse the mussels under cold running water, pulling off their black beards as needed. Place in a strainer to drain and set aside.
2. Heat the oil in a large, deep skillet, stockpot, or Dutch oven over medium-high heat. Add the shallots and cook, stirring, until soft and translucent, about 2 minutes. Add the garlic and cook until fragrant, 30 seconds. Add the stock, lemon juice, herbs, salt, pepper, and red pepper flakes (if using), and stirring to combine. Bring the stock to a boil.
3. Add the mussels, cover, and cook, undisturbed, until the mussels open their shells, about 5 minutes. Reduce the heat to low. Discard any mussels that have not

yet opened. Divide the mussels among four large serving bowls.

4. Add the spinach to the broth, cover, and cook until just wilted, 1 to 2 minutes. Remove the lid and turn off the heat. Let sit for 1 minute, then add the cold butter, one piece at a time, stirring in each one until fully melted before adding the next one.

5. Spoon the broth over the mussels in the bowls, garnish with more parsley if you like, and serve.

Nutrition: Calories: 194 Carbs: 33g   Fat: 3g Fiber: 8g Protein: 10g

228. Crab Cakes with Creamy Citrus Slaw (FAST)

Preparation time: 10 minutes
Cooking time: 7 minutes
Servings: 2
Ingredients:
- 1 (14-ounce) package shredded coleslaw mix
- Grated zest and juice of 1 medium lemon
- Grated zest of 1 medium navel orange
- 2 tablespoons Dijon mustard
- Crab Cakes:
- 2 large eggs
- 1 tablespoon Dijon mustard
- 1/2 teaspoon sea salt
- 1/2 teaspoon Old Bay seasoning or paprika
- 1/4 teaspoon freshly ground black pepper
- 1 (16-ounce) can cooked jumbo lump crab meat, drained and patted dry
- 3/4 cup cooled or chilled cooked Easy Cauliflower Rice, mashed with a fork
- 2 tablespoons chopped fresh parsley
- 2 tablespoons extra-virgin olive oil

Directions:
1. To make the slaw, toss the coleslaw mix with the lemon zest and juice, orange zest, and mustard in a large bowl until evenly coated. Refrigerate for at least 30 minutes.

2. In a medium bowl, whisk together the eggs, mustard, salt, Old Bay seasoning, and pepper. Fold in the crab, cauliflower rice, and parsley until well combined. Refrigerate until slightly firm, about 10 minutes.

3. Remove the crab mixture from the refrigerator and form into four patties about 2 inches thick and 3 inches in diameter.

4. Heat the olive oil in a large skillet or cast-iron pan over medium-high heat. When

the oil is hot, add two of the crab cakes. Cook until golden brown, about 3 minutes per side. Transfer to a paper towel–lined plate. Repeat with the remaining cakes.

5. Place two crab cakes on each plate and serve with the chilled slaw.

Nutrition: Calories: 230 Carbs: 41g Fat: 4g Fiber: 10g Protein: 11g

229. Creamy Salmon Capers with Spiralled Zoodles (FAST)

Preparation time: 10 minutes
Cooking time: 5 minutes
Servings: 2
Ingredients:
- A small shallot, chopped
- 1 Tablespoon of almond flour
- 1 cup sour cream
- 1/2 cup parmesan
- 1/3 cup sliced mushrooms of your choice
- 1 cup broccoli florets
- 1 Tablespoon capers
- 1 Tablespoon chopped chives
- 2 tablespoons s chopped parsley
- 2 fillets of wild Alaskan salmon
- 1 Tablespoon avocado oil
- 3 Tablespoon s pastured butter
- 2 cloves of garlic, minced
- Lemon juice to taste
- Black pepper to taste

Directions:
1. Descale and wash the fish. Fry the salmon with the avocado oil for a few minutes, turning once (do not overcook).

2. Remove its skin and eat it. Add lemon juice on the fish, and set aside.

3. Heat water in a small water and add the mushrooms to boil for a few minutes.

4. Add the broccoli florets for another 1-2 minutes (must remain a little bit crunchy). Strain, set aside.

5. In a large pot heat the butter with the black pepper, garlic and shallot.

6. Add the sour cream and parmesan when browned. Stir to combine, but don't let it get too cooked (no more than 30 seconds on fire, just enough for the parmesan to melt).

7. Cut the salmon in small pieces, add it to the cream.

8. Add the mushrooms, broccoli, and capers, and carefully combine.

9. Sprinkle with chives or parsley; serve with spiralled "zoodles".

Nutrition: Calories: 135 Carbs: 11g Fat: 9.8g Fiber: 4g Protein: 3.9g

230. Garlic and Herb Mussels in Rose Broth (FAST)

Preparation time: 10 minutes
Cooking time: 10 minutes
Servings: 4
Ingredients:

- 32-ounce mussels
- 1 Tablespoon extra-virgin olive oil
- 2 shallots, minced
- 3 cloves garlic, minced
- 2 cups chicken or Veggie Trimmings Stock
- 1/4 cup lemon juice (from 2 lemons)
- 1/4 cup chopped fresh parsley, plus more for garnish
- 1/4 cup chopped fresh dill (optional)
- 3 Tablespoons chopped fresh thyme
- 1/2 Teaspoon salt
- 1/4 Teaspoon freshly ground black pepper
- 1/4 Teaspoon red pepper flakes (optional)
- 3 cups baby spinach (or spinach leaves torn into smaller pieces)
- 2 tablespoons cold unsalted grass-fed butter, cubed

Directions:
1. Rinse the mussels under cold running water, pulling off their black beards as needed. Place in a strainer to drain and set aside.
2. Heat the oil in a large, deep skillet, stockpot, or Dutch oven over medium-high heat.
3. Add the shallots and cook, stirring, until soft and translucent, about 2 minutes. Add the garlic and cook until fragrant, 30 seconds.
4. Add the stock, lemon juice, herbs, salt, pepper, and red pepper flakes (if using), and stirring to combine. Bring the stock to a boil.
5. Add the mussels, cover, and cook, undisturbed, until the mussels open their shells, about 5 minutes.
6. Reduce the heat to low. Discard any mussels that have not yet opened. Divide the mussels among four large serving bowls.
7. Add the spinach to the broth, cover, and cook until just wilted, 1 to 2 minutes. Remove the lid and turn off the heat. Let

sit for 1 minute, then add the cold butter, one piece at a time, stirring in each one until fully melted before adding the next one.
8. Spoon the broth over the mussels in the bowls, garnish with more parsley if you like, and serve.

Nutrition: Calories: 192 Carbs: 14.3g Fat: 9.7g Fiber: 5.2g Protein: 11.4g

231. Tuna-Avo Boat Salad (FAST)

Preparation Time: 10 minutes
Cooking Time: 0 minutes
Serving: 2
Ingredients:

- 2 tbsps. 0% plain Greek yogurt
- 4 tsps. apple cider vinegar
- 1 tsp curry powder
- 1/4 tsp salt
- 1 medium pinch ground cinnamon
- 5-ounce can solid white albacore, drained and flaked
- 1/4 cup finely diced carrot
- 4 tsps. chopped toasted cashews
- 2 tbsps. roughly chopped raisins
- 1 tbsp chopped red onion
- 1 medium avocado, sliced in half and seed removed
- 2 tsps. chopped parsley

Directions:
1. Mix well cinnamon, salt, curry, vinegar, and yogurt in a medium bowl. Whisk in tuna and mix well.
2. Add remaining ingredients in bowl except for parsley and avocado. Mix thoroughly and adjust seasoning to taste.
3. Evenly divide the tuna mixture inside the avocado hole left by the seed.
4. To enjoy, scoop out avocado flesh along with the tuna mixture with each bite.

Nutrition: Calories 241, Fat 13g, Carbs 18g, Protein 18g, Fiber 6g, Sodium 491mg, Potassium 653g

232. Grilled Salmon-Lettuce Wraps (FAST)

Preparation Time: 20 minutes
Cooking Time: 10 minutes
Serving: 6
Ingredients:

- 1/4 cup Avocado Sauce recipe link here
- 2 6-oz fresh salmon fish fillets
- 1 head of butter lettuce
- 2 cup coleslaw mix or shredded cabbage
- 1/4 cup fresh cilantro leaves, chopped
- 1 lime, juiced

- Salt and pepper to taste
- Avocado Sauce Ingredients:
- 1/2 Avocado, pitted
- 1/2 cup Cilantro, fresh
- 1/2 Jalapeño, seeded (adjust to taste)
- 1/2 cup low Fat mayo
- 1/4 cup Water
- 2 tbsp Lime juice, fresh (adjust to taste)
- 1 Garlic clove
- 1/2 tsp Salt

Directions:
1. In a blender, puree all avocado sauce ingredients. Adjust seasoning to taste and puree again. Transfer to a bowl and refrigerate until ready to use.
2. Preheat grill to medium high and lightly grease grate.
3. Season fish with pepper and salt to taste. Grill fish for 3 to 4 mins per side. Transfer to a bowl and shred.
4. In bowl of fish, add shredded cabbage, juice of lime and mix well. If needed, adjust seasoning to taste.
5. To serve, slowly separate butter lettuce into one huge leaf. In one leaf, place a good amount of the salmon filling and a dollop of the avocado sauce. Roll leaf and enjoy.

Nutrition: Calories 247, Fat 10g, Carbs 9g, Protein 31g, Fiber 3g, Sodium 488mg, Potassium 907mg

233. Black Bean and Salmon Salad (FAST)

Preparation Time: 15 minutes
Cooking Time: 0 minutes
Serving: 4
Ingredients:
- 2 cans (5oz each) wild salmon (skinless/boneless), drained and flaked
- 1-15oz can black beans or lentils, drained and rinsed
- 1 clove garlic, minced
- ¼ cup scallions, minced
- ¼ cup celery, finely minced
- 1 tomato or 1cup cherry tomatoes, diced
- ½ lime, juiced
- ¼ tsp. sea salt
- 1 jalapeño, finely minced, ribs and seeds removed
- ¼ cup fresh cilantro, roughly chopped
- 1 ½ tbsp ground flaxseed
- Salad Ingredients:
- 4 cup Spinach leaves
- 4 tsp EVO
- 1 avocado, diced

Directions:
1. In a large bowl, add all ingredients and mix well. Let it rest for 10 mins to let the flavors meld. Mix once again.
2. Evenly divide spinach leaves on to 4 salad bowls.
3. Evenly divide salmon mixture on to each bowl.
4. Top with diced avocado and drizzle with olive oil.
5. Serve and enjoy.

Nutrition: Calories 433, Fat 21g, Carbs 23g, Protein 41g, Fiber 11g, Sodium 727mg, Potassium 1192mg

234. Spicy Crabs with Chilled Coleslaw Mix

Preparation time: 10 minutes
Cooking time: 30 minutes
Servings: 2
Ingredients:
- 1 package shredded coleslaw mix
- Grated zest and juice of 1 medium lemon
- Grated zest of 1 medium navel orange
- 2 tablespoons Dijon mustard
- 2 large eggs
- 1 Tablespoon Dijon mustard
- 1/2 Teaspoon Sea salt
- 1/2 Teaspoon Old Bay seasoning or paprika
- 1/4 Teaspoon freshly ground black pepper
- 1 can cooked jumbo lump crab meat, drained and patted dry
- 3/4 cup cooled or chilled cooked
- Easy Cauliflower Rice, mashed with a fork
- 2 tablespoons chopped fresh parsley
- 2 tablespoons extra-virgin olive oil

Directions:
1. To make the slaw, toss the coleslaw mix with the lemon zest and juice, orange zest, and mustard in a large bowl until evenly coated.
2. Refrigerate it for at least 30 minutes.
3. In a medium bowl, whisk together the eggs, mustard, salt, Old Bay seasoning, and pepper.
4. Fold in the crab, cauliflower rice, and parsley until well combined. Refrigerate until slightly firm, about 10 minutes.
5. Remove the crab mixture from the refrigerator and form into four patties about 2 inches thick and 3 inches in diameter.
6. Heat the olive oil in a large skillet or cast-iron pan over medium-high heat. When the oil is hot, add two of the crab cakes.
7. Cook until golden brown, about 3 minutes per side. Transfer to a paper towel–lined plate. Repeat with the remaining cakes.
8. Place two crab cakes on each plate and serve with the chilled slaw.

Nutrition: Calories: 265 Carbs: 19.8g Fat: 18.4g Fiber: 8.1g Protein: 4.6

235. Coconut Salmon with Scallion Greens (FAST)

Preparation time: 10 minutes
Cooking time: 15 minutes
Servings: 2
Ingredients:

- 2 (6-ounce) salmon fillets
- 1/4 cup white or yellow miso
- 2 tablespoons rice or coconut vinegar
- 2 tablespoons sesame oil, divided
- 1 tablespoon gluten-free soy sauce, tamari, or coconut amino
- 1 tablespoon minced fresh ginger
- 1 clove garlic, minced
- 11/2 pounds (medium bunch) baby bok choy, core removed, sliced into 11/2-inch pieces, white stem and leafy green parts separated
- 2 tablespoons thinly sliced scallion whites (optional)
- 2 tablespoons thinly sliced scallion greens, for garnish (optional)

Directions:

1. Heat the broiler to high.
2. On a baking sheet or broiler pan, place the salmon, skin-side down, and pat it dry.
3. In a small bowl, whisk together the miso, vinegar, 1 tablespoon of the sesame oil, the soy sauce, ginger, and garlic.
4. Spread 2 tablespoons of the glaze evenly over the top of the salmon, setting aside the remainder. Let it stand for 10 minutes, if you have time.
5. Broil the salmon until the glaze is bubbly, 3 to 4 minutes.
6. Cover it loosely with foil and continue to broil until slightly pink in the center, another 3 to 4 minutes.
7. Remove the salmon from the broiler, remove the foil, and let it cool.
8. In a large skillet over medium-high heat, heat the remaining 1 tablespoon sesame oil.
9. Add the bok choy stems and scallion whites (if using) and cook until just tender, 2 to 3 minutes.
10. Stir in the remaining miso glaze and cook until fragrant, 30 to 60 seconds.
11. Add the bok choy greens, cover, and steam until just wilted, 30 seconds. Toss to coat with the sauce.
12. To serve, divide the bok choy evenly between two plates. Top each with a salmon fillet and sprinkle with scallion greens (if using).

Nutrition: Calories: 291 Carbs: 37.2g Fat: 12.4g Fiber: 2.3g Protein: 6.4g

236. Baked Halibut Delight

Preparation time: 10 minutes
Cooking time: 30 minutes
Servings: 4
Ingredients

- 6 ounces halibut fillets
- 1 tablespoon Greek seasoning
- 1 large tomato, chopped
- 1 onion, chopped
- 5 ounces kalamata olives, pitted
- ¼ cup capers
- ¼ cup olive oil
- 1 tablespoon lemon juice
- Salt and pepper as needed

Directions

1. Preheat your oven to 350 degrees Fahrenheit
2. Transfer the halibut fillets on a large aluminum foil
3. Season with Greek seasoning
4. Take a bowl and add tomato, onion, olives, olive oil, capers, pepper, lemon juice, and salt
5. Mix well and spoon the tomato mix over the halibut
6. Seal the edges and fold to make a packet
7. Place the packet on a baking sheet and bake in your oven for 30-40 minutes
8. Serve once the fish flakes off, and enjoy!
9. Serve over rice cauliflower if desired

Nutrition: Calories: 429 Fat: 26 g Carbohydrate: 10 g Protein: 36 g Saturated fat: 5 g Fiber: 5 g Sodium: 400 mg

237. Grilled Shrimp Skewers (FAST)

Preparation time: 5 minutes
Cooking time: 10 minutes
Marinating time: 15 minutes
Servings: 3
Ingredients:

- One-pound large shrimp – peeled and deveined
- 1/4 cup olive oil
- Two tablespoons lemon juice
- 3/4 teaspoon salt
- 1/4 teaspoon pepper
- One teaspoon Italian seasoning
- Two teaspoons' garlic – minced
- One tablespoon parsley – chopped
- Lemon wedges – for serving

Direction:

1. Add garlic, Italian seasoning, pepper, salt, lemon juice, and olive oil into the re-sealable plastic bag. Seal it and shake well.

2. Add shrimp to the bag and again seal. Toss to combine with marinade.
3. Let marinate for fifteen minutes or up to two hours.
4. Next, thread the shrimp onto the skewers. Add on the grill pan over medium-high flame.
5. Place the skewers on the grill and cook for two to three minutes per side.
6. Sprinkle with parsley and garnish with a lemon wedge.

Nutrition: Calories 206 | fat 10g | sodium 1317mg | Carbohydrates 3g | fiber 1g | sugar 0g | protein 23g

238. Garlicky Fish Fillets with Parsley leave (FAST)

Preparation time: 10 minutes
Cooking time: 30 minutes
Servings: 4
Ingredients:
- 2 skinless Arctic char or other whitefish fillets
- 1 Teaspoon kosher salt
- 1 Teaspoon freshly ground black pepper
- 1/2 cup extra-virgin olive oil
- 3 cloves garlic, minced
- 3/4 cup fresh parsley leaves, minced, divided
- 1/4 cup grated lemon zest (from 6 small or 4 large lemons), divided

Directions:
1. Place the fish fillets lengthwise in a 13-by-9-inch baking dish and season with the salt and pepper on both sides.
2. In a small bowl, whisk together the olive oil, garlic, half of the parsley, and half of the lemon zest. Pour evenly over the fish, cover, and marinate in the refrigerator for at least 30 minutes and up to overnight.
3. Preheat the oven to 350F. 3. Bake the fish until just cooked through, 15 to 20 minutes.
4. Cut each fillet into 2 pieces, top evenly with the remaining parsley and lemon zest, and serve with Lemony Sautéed Chard with Red Onion and Herbs or another vegetable side or salad.

Nutrition: Calories: 279.4 Carbs: 45.8 g Fat: 8 g Fiber: 5 g Protein: 10.5 g

239. Butter Shrimp Scampi with Parsley Leaves (FAST)

Preparation time: 10 minutes
Cooking time: 10 minutes
Servings: 3

Ingredients:
- 454 g jumbo shrimp (about 12), peeled and deveined
- 3 Tablespoons extra-virgin olive oil, divided
- 6 cloves garlic, minced
- 1 cup unsalted chicken broth or stock
- Grated zest and juice from
- 1 medium lemon
- 1/2 Teaspoon red pepper flakes, or to taste
- 1/4 Teaspoon Sea salt or Himalayan salt, or to taste
- 1/2 Teaspoon freshly ground black pepper, or to taste
- 1/4 cup (1/2 stick) cold unsalted grass-fed butter, cubed
- 8 cups baby spinach leaves
- 2 to 3 Tablespoons chopped fresh parsley (optional)

Directions:
1. Pat the shrimp very dry with paper towels. Heat 2 tablespoons of the olive oil in a large skillet over medium-high heat.
2. Add the shrimp and cook until pink, flipping once, about 2 minutes per side. Transfer to a large bowl or plate. 2
3. Reduce the heat to medium and add remaining 1 Tablespoon oil. Add the garlic and cook until just fragrant, about 1 minute.
4. Add the broth, lemon zest and juice, red pepper flakes, salt, and black pepper, increase the heat to medium-high, and bring to a simmer.
5. Reduce the sauce by half, scraping up any browned bits from the bottom with a wooden spoon, about 5 minutes.
6. Remove the pan from the heat and allow cooling slightly. Add butter, one cube at a time, stirring continually with a wooden spoon until the sauce thickens.
7. To serve, divide spinach evenly among four plates. Top each plate with about 4 shrimp. Divide the sauce evenly among the plates and garnish with the parsley.

Nutrition: Calories: 147 Carbs: 21.2g Fat: 5g Fiber: 1.5g Protein: 3.8g

240. One pan Broiled Salmon with Yellow Miso (FAST)

Preparation time: 10 minutes
Cooking time: 10 minutes
Servings: 2
Ingredients:
- 2 salmon fillets

- 1/4 cup white or yellow miso
- 2 tablespoons rice or coconut vinegar
- 2 tablespoons sesame oil, divided
- 1 Tablespoon gluten-free soy sauce, tamari, or coconut amino
- 1 Tablespoon minced fresh ginger
- 1 clove garlic, minced
- 680 g (medium bunch) baby bok choy, core removed, sliced into 11/2-inch pieces, white stem and leafy green parts separated
- 2 tablespoons thinly sliced scallion whites (optional)
- 2 tablespoons thinly sliced scallion greens, for garnish (optional)

Directions:
1. Heat the broiler to high.
2. On a baking sheet or broiler pan, place the salmon, skin-side down, and pat it dry.
3. In a small bowl, whisk together the miso, vinegar, 1 Tablespoon of the sesame oil, the soy sauce, ginger, and garlic.
4. Spread 2 tablespoons of the glaze evenly over the top of the salmon, setting aside the remainder. Let it stand for 10 minutes, if you have time.
5. Broil the salmon until the glaze is bubbly, 3 to 4 minutes. Cover it loosely with foil and continue to broil until slightly pink in the center, another 3 to 4 minutes.
6. Remove the salmon from the broiler, remove the foil, and let it cool.
7. In a large skillet over medium-high heat, heat the remaining 1 Tablespoon sesame oil.
8. Add the bok choy stems and scallion whites (if using) and cook until just tender, 2 to 3 minutes.
9. Stir in the remaining miso glaze and cook until fragrant, 30 to 60 seconds.
10. Add the bok choy greens, cover, and steam until just wilted, 30 seconds. Toss to coat with the sauce.
11. To serve, divide the bok choy evenly between two plates.
12. Top each with a salmon fillet and sprinkle with scallion greens (if using).

Nutrition: Calories: 191 Carbs: 22g Fat: 10g Fiber: 3.3g Protein: 4.1g

241. Lemon Trout (FAST)

Preparation time: 10 minutes
Cooking time: 20 minutes
Servings: 4

Ingredients:
- Four cups all-purpose flour
- Two tablespoons lemon pepper
- 1 1/2 tablespoons salt
- Half teaspoon dried thyme
- Half teaspoon cayenne pepper
- One teaspoon onion powder
- ¼ cup grated lemon zest
- 6-ounce fillets rainbow trout
- One lemon
- Half cup lemon juice
- Half cup extra-virgin olive oil

Direction:
1. First, add half of the lemon zest, cayenne, thyme, salt, lemon pepper, and flour into the bowl. Mix the lemon juice with the remaining lemon zest into another bowl. Let soak fish fillets for one minute.
2. Add oil into the big skillet and cook over medium flame.
3. Immerse the trout fillets in the flour mixture until coated.
4. Shake well to remove excess and add fillets in the hot oil and cook for three to four minutes per side until golden brown. Remove the remaining lemon juice.
5. Remove from the skillet and place on the paper towel, and garnish with a lemon wedge.

Nutrition: Calories 979 | fat40.5g | sodium 3401.1mg | carbohydrates 103.1g | fiber 5.7g | sugar 1.8g | protein 48.6g

242. Walnut Encrusted Salmon Meal (FAST)

Preparation time: 10 minutes
Cooking time: 15 minutes
Servings: 4

Ingredients
- ½ cup walnuts
- 2 tablespoons stevia
- ½ tablespoon Dijon mustard
- ¼ teaspoon dill
- 2 Salmon fillets (3 ounces each)
- 1 tablespoon olive oil
- Salt and pepper to taste

Directions
1. Preheat your oven to 350 degrees F
2. Add walnuts, mustard, stevia to a food processor and process until your desired consistency is achieved
3. Take a frying pan and place it over medium heat
4. Add oil and let it heat up
5. Add salmon and sear for 3 minutes
6. Add walnut mix and coat well

7. Transfer coated salmon to the baking sheet, bake in the oven for 8 minutes
8. Serve and enjoy!

Nutrition: Calories: 373 Fat: 43 g Carbohydrate: 4 g Protein:20 g Saturated fat: 10 g Fiber: 2 g Sodium: 600 mg

243. Shrimp with Garlic (FAST)

Preparation Time: 10 minutes
Cooking Time: 25 minutes
Servings: 2
Ingredients:
- 1 lb. shrimp
- ¼ teaspoon baking soda
- 2 tablespoons oil
- 2 teaspoon minced garlic
- ¼ cup vermouth
- 2 tablespoons unsalted butter
- 1 teaspoon parsley

Directions:
1. In a bowl, toss shrimp with baking soda and salt, let it rest for a couple of minutes.
2. In a skillet heat olive oil and add shrimp.
3. Add garlic, red pepper flakes and cook for 1-2 minutes.
4. Add vermouth and cook for another 4-5 minutes.
5. When ready remove from heat and serve.

Nutrition: Calories: 289 Total Carbohydrate: 2 g Cholesterol: 3 mg Total Fat: 17 g Fiber: 2 g Protein: 7 g Sodium: 163 mg

244. Soy dipped Avocado Sushi Roll (FAST)

Preparation time: 10 minutes
Cooking time: 0 minutes
Servings: 2
Ingredients:
- 2 sheets sushi nori
- 1 medium avocado, pitted and peeled
- 2 tablespoons sesame seeds, divided (optional)
- 4 ounces smoked salmon (about 4 thin slices)
- 1 medium cucumber, cut into matchsticks
- 3 tablespoons pickled ginger (optional)
- 1 teaspoon wasabi paste (optional)
- Gluten-free soy sauce, tamari, or coconut amino, for dipping

Directions:
1. Lay 1 piece of nori on a sheet of parchment paper or aluminum foil on a flat surface.
2. In a small bowl, mash the avocado with a fork.
3. Spread half of the avocado mixture on the nori sheet, leaving a 1/2-inch strip uncovered along the top edge.

4. Sprinkle 1 tablespoon of the sesame seeds (if using), evenly over the avocado. Arrange 2 pieces of the smoked salmon horizontally, covering the avocado.
5. Arrange the cucumber horizontally, running up the length of the sheet and creating columns to cover the salmon.
6. Wet the tip of your finger and run it along the exposed seam. Roll the nori tightly away from you, using the foil as a guide and pressing firmly to seal.
7. Repeat the process with the remaining nori sheet and ingredients, and refrigerate both for at least 30 minutes to firm up.
8. Using a very sharp or serrated knife, slice each roll into 6 to 8 pieces. Serve with pickled ginger and wasabi and soy sauce for dipping

Nutrition: Calories: 115 Carbs: 5.3g   Fat: 8.5g Fiber: 2.6g   Protein: 3.3g

245. Tuna-Hummus on Flatbread (FAST)

Preparation Time: 15 minutes
Cooking Time: 0 minutes
Serving: 1
Ingredients:
- 1 whole flat bread, whole wheat or gluten-free
- 1/2 cup spring mix
- 1/2 cup hummus
- 1 packet StarKist Selects Wild-Caught Yellowfin Tuna in E.V.O.O
- 2 mini bell peppers, diced
- 1 tbsp pumpkin seeds, salted
- 1/2 whole lemon, juiced

Directions:
1. Lay flatbread on a plate.
2. Evenly spread hummus on top of bread.
3. Spread spring mix greens on top of hummus.
4. Add the packet of tuna on top and spread evenly.
5. Sprinkle bell pepper and pumpkin seeds.
6. Drizzle lemon juice.
7. Serve and enjoy.

Nutrition: Calories 432, Fat 18g, Carbs 45g, Protein 29g, Fiber 15g, Sodium 509mg, Potassium 914mg

246. Tuna & Sun-Dried Tomato-Wich (FAST)

Preparation Time: 15 mins
Cooking Time: 0 mins
Serving: 1
Ingredients:
- 1 whole flat bread
- 1/2 whole avocado
- 1 packet StarKist Selects Wild Caught Yellowfin Tuna Sun Dried Tomato in E.V.O.O
- 1/4 cup sprouts or microgreens

- 1 tbsp hemp seeds
- 1/2 whole lemon, juiced
- Salt and pepper to taste

Directions:
1. In a small bowl, mash avocado, hemp seeds and lemon juice. Lightly season with pepper and salt.
2. Lay flatbread on a plate.
3. Evenly spread avocado mixture on top of bread.
4. Add the packet of tuna on top and spread evenly.
5. Spread sprouts on top.
6. Serve and enjoy.

Nutrition: Calories 490, Fat 31g, Carbs 23g, Protein 34g, Fiber 7g, Sodium 201mg, Potassium 345mg

247. Baked Garlic marinade Arctic char Fillets

Preparation time: 10 minutes
Cooking time: 30 minutes
Servings: 4

Ingredients:
- 2 3/4pound skinless Arctic char or other whitefish fillets
- 1 teaspoon kosher salt
- 1 teaspoon freshly ground black pepper
- 1/2 cup extra-virgin olive oil
- 3 cloves garlic, minced
- 3/4 cup fresh parsley leaves, minced, divided
- 1/4 cup grated lemon zest (from 6 small or 4 large lemons), divided

Directions:
1. Place the fish fillets lengthwise in a 13-by-9-inch baking dish and season with the salt and pepper on both sides.
2. In a small bowl, whisk together the olive oil, garlic, half of the parsley, and half of the lemon zest.
3. Pour evenly over the fish, cover, and marinate in the refrigerator for at least 30 minutes and up to overnight.
4. Preheat the oven to 350F.
5. Bake the fish until just cooked through, 15 to 20 minutes.
6. Cut each fillet into 2 pieces, top evenly with the remaining parsley and lemon zest and serve.

Nutrition: Calories: 123 Carbs: 13.6g Fat: 7g Fiber: 2g Protein: 1.2g

248. Homemade Shrimp and Pea Bowl with Cashews (FAST)

Preparation time: 10 minutes
Cooking time: 20 minutes
Servings: 4

Ingredients:
- 3 tablespoons gluten-free soy sauce, tamari, or coconut amino
- 2 tablespoons minced fresh ginger
- 3 tablespoons sesame oil, divided
- 2 large eggs, lightly beaten
- 2/3-to-3/4-pound medium shrimp, peeled and deveined (about 24)
- 1 shallot, minced
- 1 red bell pepper, seeded and diced
- 3/4 cup frozen peas
- 1/4 cup chopped unsalted cashews
- 2 tablespoons chopped fresh cilantro
- 1/4 teaspoon red pepper flakes (optional)
- Sliced scallion greens, for garnish (optional)

Directions:
1. In a small bowl, whisk the soy sauce and ginger together and set aside.
2. In a wok or large skillet over medium heat, heat 1 tablespoon of the sesame oil.
3. Add the eggs and cook, stirring frequently with a wooden spoon or spatula, until scrambled.
4. Transfer to a small bowl and break up the cooked egg into small pieces using two forks. Set aside.
5. In the same wok over medium-high heat, heat 1 tablespoon of the sesame oil.
6. Add the shrimp and cook, tossing, until bright pink but not browned, 3 to 4 minutes.
7. Transfer the shrimp to a separate plate or bowl and set aside.
8. Add the remaining 1 tablespoon sesame oil and the shallot to the wok and cook until fragrant, tossing frequently, about 30 seconds.
9. Add the bell pepper and cook until just tender, tossing occasionally, about 2 minutes.
10. Add the cauliflower rice and cook, tossing occasionally, until lightly browned and crisp, about 5 minutes.
11. Stir in the soy sauce mixture. Add the cooked shrimp, cooked eggs, and peas and stir until well combined and heated through, 2 to 3 minutes.
12. Add the cashews, cilantro, and red pepper flakes (if using), tossing to combine.
13. Divide the mixture among four bowls, garnish with scallion greens (if using) and serve.

Nutrition: Calories: 108 Carbs: 3.2g Fat: 9.8g Fiber: 1.8g Protein: 1.1g

249. Mussel Spinach Cold Butter Bowl (FAST)

Preparation time: 10 minutes
Cooking time: 8 minutes
Servings: 4

Ingredients:
- 2 pounds mussels
- 1 tablespoon extra-virgin olive oil
- 2 shallots, minced
- 3 cloves garlic, minced
- 1/4 cup lemon juice (from 2 lemons)
- 1/4 cup chopped fresh parsley, plus more for garnish
- 1/4 cup chopped fresh dill (optional)
- 3 tablespoons chopped fresh thyme
- 1/2 teaspoon salt
- 1/4 teaspoons freshly ground black pepper
- 1/4 teaspoon red pepper flakes (optional)
- 3 cups baby spinach (or spinach leaves torn into smaller pieces)
- 2 tablespoons cold unsalted grass-fed butter, cubed

Directions:
1. Rinse the mussels under cold running water, pulling off their black beards as needed. Place in a strainer to drain and set aside.
2. Heat the oil in a large, deep skillet, stockpot, or Dutch oven over medium-high heat.
3. Add the shallots and cook, stirring, until soft and translucent, about 2 minutes.
4. Add the garlic and cook until fragrant, 30 seconds. Add the stock, lemon juice, herbs, salt, pepper, and red pepper flakes (if using), and stirring to combine. Bring the stock to a boil.
5. Add the mussels, cover, and cook, undisturbed, until the mussels open their shells, about 5 minutes.
6. Reduce the heat to low. Discard any mussels that have not yet opened. Divide the mussels among four large serving bowls.
7. Add the spinach to the broth, cover, and cook until just wilted, 1 to 2 minutes. Remove the lid and turn off the heat. Let sit for 1 minute, then add the cold butter, one piece at a time, stirring in each one until fully melted before adding the next one.
8. Spoon the broth over the mussels in the bowls, garnish with more parsley if you like, and serve.

Nutrition: Calories: 299 Carbs: 48.5g Fat: 7.6g Fiber: 5.4g Protein: 9g

250. Creamy Zucchini Clam Shallow Bowls (FAST)

Preparation time: 10 minutes
Cooking time: 20 minutes
Servings: 4
Ingredients:
- 2 medium zucchinis

- 2 tablespoons extra-virgin olive oil
- 4 cloves garlic, minced
- 4 (6-ounce) cans chopped clams
- 1/2 teaspoon red pepper flakes
- 1/4 cup 1/2 stick cold unsalted grass-fed butter, cubed
- 2 teaspoons grated lemon zest
- Chopped fresh parsley, for garnish
- Freshly ground black pepper
- 2 lemon wedges, for garnish (optional)

Directions:
1. Using a spiralized, cut the zucchini into noodles or use purchased zoodles (thaw if frozen). Set aside.
2. In a large, deep skillet over medium-high heat, heat olive oil and garlic until fragrant, 1 to 2 minutes, taking care that the garlic doesn't brown.
3. Drain the liquid from clams into the skillet, leaving the clams in the cans. Add the red pepper flakes. Bring to a simmer and cook until the liquid is reduced to ¾ cup, about 15 minutes.
4. Add the clams to the broth and cook until heated through, about 1 minute. Turn off the heat and let sit for 1 minute.
5. Add the butter, stirring in each cube until fully melted before adding the next one. Stir in the lemon zest. Add zucchini noodles and toss to coat.
6. To serve, divide between four plates or shallow bowls. Top with parsley and black pepper, and serve with lemon wedges, if desired.

Nutrition: Calories: 267 Carbs: 44.1g Fat: 6.8g Fiber: 7.2g Protein: 7.3g

251. Chicken Mushroom Shrimp Mix Green Onions (FAST)

Preparation time: 10 minutes
Cooking time: 20 minutes
Servings: 4
Ingredients:
- 1/2-pound mushrooms, roughly sliced off
- Table salt and black pepper to the taste
- 1/4 mug mayonnaise
- 2 Tablespoon sriracha
- 1/2 tsp. paprika
- 1/4 tsp. xanthan gum
- 1 green onion stalk, sliced off
- 20 shrimp, raw, peeled and deveined
- 2 chicken breasts, boneless and skinless
- 2 handfuls spinach leaves
- 2 teaspoons lime juice
- 1 tablespoon coconut oil

- 1/2 tsp. red pepper, crushed
- 1 tsp. garlic grinding grains

Directions:

1. Warm up a dish with the oil over moderate gigantic warmth, embed chicken bosoms, season with table salt, pepper, red pepper and garlic pounding grains, plan for 8 minutes, flip and get ready for 6 minutes more.
2. Supplement mushrooms, more table salt and pepper and plan for a couple of moments.
3. Warm up another dish over moderate warmth, embed shrimp, sriracha, paprika, xanthan and mayo, shake and get ready until shrimp turn pink.
4. Eliminate heat, embed lime squeeze and shake everything.
5. Serve spinach on plates, appropriate chicken and mushroom, top with shrimp consolidate, decorate with green onions.

Nutrition: Calories: 171 Carbs: 24g Fat: 6.4g Proteins: 6.2g

EGG FREE AND GLUTEN FREE

252. French Carrot Salad (FAST)

Preparation time: 15 minutes
Cooking time: 0 minute
Serving: 4 to 6
Ingredients:
- 7 medium carrots
- Juice of ½ lime
- 2 tablespoons sunflower oil
- 1 teaspoon Dijon mustard
- ¼ teaspoon salt
- 1/8 teaspoon freshly ground black pepper
- 1 teaspoon dried cilantro or parsley

Direction:
1. 1.Trim off the ends of the carrots and gently scrub them under cool running water. Pat dry with paper towels.
2. 2.Using the smallest holes on a box grater, grate the carrots into a shallow serving bowl.
3. 3.In a small bowl, whisk together the lime juice, oil, mustard, salt, and pepper until smooth. Drizzle the dressing over the carrots, then sprinkle with the cilantro or parsley.
4. 4.Very gently toss the carrots in the dressing and serve immediately.

Nutrition: Calories: 106; Total fat: 7g; Total carbs: 11g; Sugar: 5g; Protein: 1g; Fiber: 3g; Sodium: 235mg

253. Cilantro-Lime Slaw (FAST)

Preparation time: 10 minutes
Cooking time: 0 minute
Serving: 8
Ingredients:
- Zest and juice of 1 lime
- 2 tablespoons extra-virgin olive oil
- 1 teaspoon salt
- ½ cup chopped fresh cilantro
- 1 medium avocado, diced
- 4 cups shredded purple cabbage

Direction:
1. 1.In a large bowl, whisk together the lime zest and juice, oil, and salt.
2. 2.Add the cilantro and avocado, and toss to coat.
3. 3.Add the cabbage and toss gently to coat.
4. 4.Serve immediately, or cover and refrigerate for up to 8 hours.

Nutrition: Calories: 90; Total fat: 9g; Total carbs: 4g; Sugar: 1g; Protein: 1g; Fiber: 3g; Sodium: 299mg

254. Roasted Garlic Smashed Cauliflower (FAST)

Preparation time: 5 minutes
Cooking time: 10 minutes
Serving: 6
Ingredients:
- 1 medium head cauliflower
- 1 cup Homemade Chicken Stock
- ½ teaspoon salt
- 4 garlic cloves, roasted, or ½ teaspoon garlic powder
- 2 tablespoons ghee or dairy-free butter

Direction:
1. 1.Cut out and discard the cauliflower core and any outer leaves or stems. Cut the cauliflower into florets and place them in a 2-quart or larger saucepan.
2. 2.Place the saucepan over high heat and add the stock and salt. Cook, covered, for 5 minutes at a boil.
3. 3.Uncover and cook 5 minutes more on high, or until the cauliflower is tender. Most of the stock will evaporate.
4. 4.Remove from heat and add the garlic and ghee. Use an immersion blender to blend until completely smooth. Alternatively, transfer to a food processor, in batches if necessary, and process until smooth. (Note: Steam builds in the food processor with hot foods, so allow the cauliflower to cool a bit before processing.)

Nutrition: Calories: 66; Total fat: 5g; Total carbs: 6g; Sugar: 2g; Protein: 2g; Fiber: 2g; Sodium: 350mg

255. Persian-Spiced Carrot Hummus

Preparation time: 10 minutes
Cooking time: 25 minutes
Serving: 8
Ingredients:
- 1-pound carrots
- 5 garlic cloves, unpeeled
- ¼ cup tahini
- 2 tablespoons extra-virgin olive oil
- 1 tablespoon freshly squeezed lemon juice
- 1 teaspoon dried cilantro
- ½ teaspoon ground cumin
- ½ teaspoon ground turmeric
- ½ teaspoon salt
- 1/8 teaspoon red pepper flakes

Direction:

1. 1.Preheat the oven to 425°F. Line a roasting pan with aluminum foil.
2. 2.Place the carrots and garlic cloves in the pan and roast for 20 to 25 minutes, until the carrots are tender.
3. 3.When the garlic is cool enough to handle, squeeze the garlic from each clove into the bowl of a food processor. Add the carrots, tahini, olive oil, lemon juice, cilantro, cumin, turmeric, salt, and red pepper flakes. Process until the hummus is smooth. You will need to turn off the processor and scrape down the sides of the bowl a couple of times so that everything blends well.
4. 4.Spoon into a serving dish and serve with Salted Fennel Crackers or Versatile Flatbread, or use as a sandwich spread.

Nutrition: Calories: 102; Total fat: 8g; Total carbs: 8g; Sugar: 3g; Protein: 2g; Fiber: 2g; Sodium: 196mg

256. Tuna with Greens and Blueberries (FAST)

Preparation time: 10 minutes
Cooking time: 5 minutes
Serving: 2

Ingredients

- ¼ cup olive
- 2 (4-ounce) tuna steaks
- Salt
- Freshly ground black pepper
- Juice of 1 lemon
- 4 cups salad greens
- ¼ cup low-carb, diary-free ranch dressing (Tessemae's)
- 2o blueberries

Directions

1. In a large skillet, heat the olive oil over medium-high heat.
2. Season the tuna steaks generously with salt and pepper, and add them to the skillet. Cook for 2 or 2 ½ minutes in each side to sear the outer edges.
3. Squeeze the lemon over the tuna in the pan and remove the fish
4. To serve, arrange the greens on 2 serving plates. Top each plate with one of the tuna steaks, 2 tablespoons of the ranch dressing, and 10 of the blueberries.

Nutritional Information: Calories: 549, Carbs: 7g, Fat: 41g, Fiber: 3g, Protein: 38g

257. Turkey and Orzo Soup (FAST)

Preparation time: 10 minutes
Cooking time: 18 minutes
Serving: 8

Ingredients

- 1 tablespoon coconut oil
- 2 tablespoons finely diced onions
- 2 cups coarsely chopped cauliflower florets
- 6 cups chicken bone broth, homemade or store-bought
- 1½ cups diced roasted turkey or chicken
- Fine sea salt (optional)
- 3 tablespoons chopped fresh dill, plus extra for garnish
- Freshly ground black pepper, for garnish

Directions

1. Melt the coconut oil in a Dutch oven or stockpot over medium-high heat. Add the onions and sauté for 4 minutes or until translucent. Add the cauliflower and sauté for another 3 minutes. Add the broth, turkey, and dill and simmer for 3 minutes or until heated through. Taste and add salt, if needed.
2. Ladle the soup into bowls and garnish with a sprig of dill and some freshly ground pepper before serving.
3. Store in an airtight container in the refrigerator for up to 3 days. To reheat, place the soup in a saucepan over medium heat for a few minutes, until warmed through.

Nutritional Information: Calories: 179, Carbs: 17g, Fat: 18g, Fiber: 2g, Protein: `8g

258. Creamy Spinach with Cardamom (FAST)

Preparation time: 5 minutes
Cooking time: 10 minutes
Serving: 4

Ingredients:

- 1 tablespoon ghee
- 2 garlic cloves, minced
- 10 ounces baby spinach leaves
- ½ cup heavy (whipping) cream
- ¼ teaspoon ground cardamom
- ¼ teaspoon freshly ground black pepper
- ½ cup crumbled goat cheese

Direction:

1. 1.Heat the ghee in a large skillet over medium heat. Add the garlic and sauté for 1 minute.
2. 2.Add the spinach and stir until it wilts completely, about 4 minutes.
3. 3.In a small bowl, whisk together the cream, cardamom, and pepper. Pour this into the skillet and add the cheese. Cook until heated through and serve.

Nutrition: Calories: 160; Total fat: 15g; Total carbs: 4g; Sugar: 0g; Protein: 3g; Fiber: 2g; Sodium: 82mg

259. Radish Hash Browns with Onion and Green Pepper (FAST)

Preparation time: 5 minutes
Cooking time: 25 minutes
Serving: 3
Ingredients
- 5 tablespoons olive oil
- 12 radishes, thinly sliced
- 1 onion, diced
- 1 green bell pepper, seeded and diced
- 6 garlic cloves, minced
- 1 teaspoon cayenne
- 1 teaspoon salt
- ½ teaspoon freshly ground black pepper

Directions
1. In a skillet over medium heat, heat the oil. Add the radishes, onion, bell pepper, and garlic. Cook, stirring frequently, until the vegetables are tender, about 5 minutes.
2. Add the cayenne, salt, and pepper. Continue to cook, stirring occasionally, for about 20 minutes, or until the vegetables are browned and crisp around the edges.

Nutritional Information: Calories: 252, Carbs: 8g, Fat: 24g, Fiber: 2g, Protein: 1g

260. Crispy Oven Fries (FAST)

Preparation time: 10 minutes
Cooking time: 25 minutes
Serving: 4
Ingredients:
- 4 large russet potatoes
- ¼ cup avocado oil or coconut oil
- ½ teaspoon salt
- ½ teaspoon freshly ground black pepper

Direction:
1. 1.Preheat the oven to 425°F. Line a large baking sheet or 2 smaller ones with parchment paper.
2. 2.Scrub the potatoes well and dry completely with clean paper towels. If you prefer, you can peel the potatoes.
3. 3.Cut the potatoes into ¼-inch-thick fries and place them in a large bowl. Pour the oil over the potatoes and toss to coat. Add the salt and pepper and toss again.
4. 4.Place the fries on the baking sheet in a single layer, close to but not touching each other.
5. 5.Bake for about 22 minutes, flipping the potatoes halfway through. The cooking time will vary depending on how thick or thin you cut your fries.

Nutrition: Calories: 373; Total fat: 14g; Total carbs: 58g; Sugar: 4g; Protein: 6g; Fiber: 9g; Sodium: 313mg

261. Fried Cauliflower Rice (FAST)

Preparation time: 5 minutes
Cooking time: 10 minutes
Serving: 2
Ingredients:
- 2 tablespoons gluten-free soy sauce
- 1 tablespoon sesame oil
- ¼ teaspoon red pepper flakes
- ½ tablespoon avocado oil or coconut oil
- 2 cups riced cauliflower
- ½ cup sliced water chestnuts
- ½ cup sliced mushrooms
- ½ cup julienned carrots
- 1/3 cup chopped spring onions
- 1 garlic clove, minced
- 1/3 cup chopped flat-leaf parsley

Direction:
1. 1.In a small bowl, whisk together the soy sauce, sesame oil, and red pepper flakes.
2. 2.Heat the oil in a large skillet over high heat. Add the cauliflower, water chestnuts, mushrooms, carrots, and onions. Cook for 5 to 7 minutes, stirring often, until the vegetables start to become tender.
3. 3.Add the garlic and cook for 1 minute more.
4. 4.Remove the skillet from heat and add the sauce. Stir to coat the vegetables, then stir in the parsley and serve.

Nutrition: Calories: 154; Total fat: 11g; Total carbs: 13g; Sugar: 5g; Protein: 5g; Fiber: 5g; Sodium: 962mg

262. Black Skillet Chicken Thighs with Artichoke Hearts

Preparation time: 10 minutes
Cooking time: 50 Minutes
Serves: 6
Ingredients
- 6 tablespoons olive oil
- 6 boneless, skin-on chicken thighs
- 1 (14-ounce) can artichoke hearts, drained
- 1 onion, diced
- ½ cup bone broth
- 1 teaspoon salt
- 1 teaspoon freshly ground black pepper
- Juice of 1 lemon

Directions
1. Preheat the oven to 400°F.
2. Heat the olive oil in a large cast iron skillet over medium-high heat. Add the chicken and cook until nicely browned on the bottom, about 4 minutes.
3. Once browned, flip the chicken over and add the artichokes, onion, broth, salt, and pepper.

4   Place the skillet in the preheated oven and cook for 40 minutes, or until the chicken is cooked through.

5   Remove the skillet from the oven and squeeze the lemon juice over the top. Serve hot.

Nutritional Information: Calories: 479, Carbs: 6g, Fat: 39g, Fiber: 4g, Protein: 25g

263.   Pan-fried Soft Shell Crab (FAST)

Preparation time: 5 minutes
Cooking time: 10 minutes
Serves: 2
Ingredients
- ½ cup olive oil
- ½ cup almond flour
- 1 teaspoon paprika
- 1 teaspoon garlic salt
- 1 teaspoon freshly ground black pepper
- 2 soft-shell crabs

Directions
1   Fill the bottom of a heavy skillet with the oil and heat over low heat.
2   While the oil is heating, in a medium bowl, mix together the almond flour, paprika, garlic salt, and pepper.
3   Dredge each crab in the flour mixture, coating both sides and shaking off any excess. Put the crabs into the hot oil in the skillet and cook for about 5 minutes per side, or until golden brown.
4   Serve hot.

Nutritional Information: Calories: 489, Carbs: 6g, Fat: 33g, Fiber: 2g, Protein: 42g

264.   Mussels with Lemon-Garlic Sauce and Parsley (FAST)

Preparation time: 10 minutes
Cooking time: 5 minutes
Serves: 5
Ingredients
- 36 live mussels, scrubbed and debearded
- 1 tablespoon olive oil
- 6 tablespoons Lemon-Garlic Dressing
- 2 tablespoons chopped fresh parsley, for garnish

Directions
1   Fill a stockpot halfway with water and bring it to a boil.
2   Add the mussels and olive oil to the boiling water and continue to boil for 4 minutes. Carefully drain off the water.
3   Pour the dressing over the mussels and serve immediately, garnished with the parsley.

Nutritional Information: Calories: 230, Carbs: 3g, Fat: 18g, Fiber: 1g, Protein: 14g

265.   Lobster Tail (FAST)

Preparation time: 5 minutes
Cooking time: 5 minutes
Serves: 2
Ingredients
- 4 cups bone broth (or water)
- 2 lobster tails

Directions
1   In a large pot, bring the broth to a boil.
2   While the broth is coming to a boil, use kitchen shears to cut the back side of the lobster shell from end to end.
3   Place the lobster in the boiling broth and bring it back to a boil. Cook the lobster for 3 minutes.
4   Drain and serve immediately.

Nutritional Information: Calories: 154, Carbs: 0g, Fat: 2g, Fiber: 0g, Protein: 32g

266.   Simple Ham Salad (FAST)

Preparation time: 10 minutes
Cooking time: 0 minute
Serving: 4
Ingredients
- 2 cups diced ham
- ¾ cup low-carb mayonnaise (such as Primal Kitchen)
- 2 celery stalks, diced

Directions
1   In a small bowl, combine the ham, mayonnaise, and celery, and stir to mix well. Serve immediately or store, covered, in the refrigerator for up to 1 week.

Nutritional Information: Calories: 434, Carbs: 3g, Fat: 42g, Fiber: 1g, Protein: 11g

267.   Umami Chicken Burgers (FAST)

Preparation time: 10 minutes
Cooking time: 20 minutes
Serving: 4
Ingredients
- 5 tablespoons olive oil, divided
- 12 ounces spinach
- 1-pound ground chicken
- ¼ cup fish sauce (I like Red Boat; see tip)

Directions
1.   Heat 3 tablespoons of olive oil in a large skillet over medium heat. Add the spinach and sauté until wilted, about 2 minutes. Transfer the spinach to a medium bowl and let cool.
2.   Once the spinach has cooled, add the chicken and fish sauce to it, and mix well with your hands. Form the mixture into 4 patties.

3. Heat the remaining 2 tablespoons of olive oil in the skillet over medium heat. Add the meat patties to the skillet and cook for about 4 minutes per side, or until browned and cooked through. Serve immediately or wrap and refrigerate for up to 1 week.

Nutritional Information: Calories: 351, Carbs: 4g, Fat: 27g, Fiber: 2g, Protein: 23g

268. Ultimate Guacamole (FAST)

Preparation time: 15 minutes
Cooking time: 0 minute
Serving: 6
Ingredients:
- 4 ripe avocados, halved, pitted, and peeled, divided
- Juice of 1 lime
- Zest of 1 lime
- 1 medium tomato, peeled, seeded, cored, and finely diced
- 1 small sweet onion, finely diced (about ⅓ cup)
- 1/3 cup green olives, pitted and diced
- ¼ cup chopped fresh cilantro
- 2 tablespoons minced fresh chives
- 1 garlic clove, finely minced
- 1 to 2 teaspoons minced fresh jalapeño pepper (optional)
- 1 teaspoon ground cumin
- 1/4 teaspoon salt

Direction:
1. 1.On a large plate or shallow bowl with sides at least 2 inches deep, mash 2 avocados. Chop the remaining 2 avocados and add them to the plate. Drizzle the lime juice on top.
2. 2.Add the lime zest, tomato, onion, olives, cilantro, chives, garlic, jalapeño, cumin, and salt, and stir until everything is incorporated.

Nutrition: Calories: 292; Total fat: 27g; Total carbs: 14g; Sugar: 2g; Protein: 3g; Fiber: 10g; Sodium: 168mg

269. Salmon Soup (FAST)

Preparation time: 10 minutes
Cooking time: 20 minutes
Serves: 8
Ingredients
- 1 tablespoon avocado oil or coconut oil
- ¼ cup thinly sliced red onions
- 2 tablespoons minced garlic
- 1-pound skinned salmon fillets, cut into 1-inch chunks
- 1 large tomato, seeded and coarsely chopped

- 1 tablespoon fish sauce
- ¼ teaspoon fine sea salt
- 4 cups fish or chicken bone broth, homemade or store-bought
- 3 tablespoons chopped fresh dill

For Garnish:
- Sprigs of fresh dill Capers
- Sliced fresh chives (optional)
- Freshly ground black pepper

Directions
1. Heat the oil in a saucepan over medium heat. Add the onions and cook for 4 minutes or until soft, stirring occasionally. Add the garlic and sauté for another minute or until fragrant.
2. Add the salmon, tomato, fish sauce (if using), salt, and broth. Bring to a boil over high heat, then reduce the heat to low and simmer gently for 12 minutes or until the salmon is cooked through. Serve immediately, garnished with sprigs of fresh dill, capers, chives (if using), and freshly ground pepper.
3. Store in an airtight container in the refrigerator for up to 3 days. To reheat, place in a saucepan over medium heat for 5 minutes or until warmed through.

Nutritional Information: Calories: 259, Carbs: 4g, Fat: 14g, Fiber: 1g, Protein: 27g

270. Pickled Cucumbers and Onions

Preparation time: 10 minutes
Cooking time: 0 minute
Serving: 6
Ingredients
- 5 or 6 baby cucumbers, diced
- 1 large white onion, diced
- 1 cup white vinegar
- 2 teaspoons chopped fresh dill
- 1½ teaspoons salt
- 1 teaspoon freshly ground black pepper
- 1 teaspoon olive oil

Directions
1. In a mason jar or other airtight container, combine the cucumbers, onion, vinegar, dill, salt, pepper, and olive oil. Serve immediately or cover and store in the refrigerator for up to 2 weeks.

Nutritional Information: Calories: 62, Carbs: 10g, Fat: 2g, Fiber: 2g, Protein: 2g

SAUCES, STEW AND SOUPS

271. <u>White Bean and Cabbage Stew</u>

Preparation Time: 5 minutes
Cooking Time: 8 hours
Servings: 4
Ingredients:
- 3 cups cooked great northern beans
- 1.5 pounds potatoes, peeled, cut into large dice
- 1 large white onion, peeled, chopped
- ½ head of cabbage, chopped
- 3 ribs celery, chopped
- 4 medium carrots, peeled, sliced
- 14.5 ounces diced tomatoes
- 1/3 cup pearled barley
- 1 teaspoon minced garlic
- ½ teaspoon ground black pepper
- 1 bay leaf
- 1 teaspoon dried thyme
- ½ teaspoon crushed rosemary
- 1 teaspoon salt
- ½ teaspoon caraway seeds
- 1 tablespoon chopped parsley
- 8 cups vegetable broth

Directions:
1. Switch on the slow cooker, then add all the ingredients except for salt, parsley, tomatoes, and beans and stir until mixed.
2. Shut the slow cooker with a lid, and cook for 7 hours at a low heat setting until cooked.
3. Then stir in remaining ingredients, stir until combined, and continue cooking for 1 hour.
4. Serve straight away

Nutrition: Calories: 150 Cal Fat: 0.7 g Carbs: 27 g Protein: 7 g Fiber: 9.4 g

272. <u>Spinach and Cannellini Bean Stew (FAST)</u>

Preparation Time: 10 minutes
Cooking Time: 15 minutes
Servings: 6
Ingredients:
- 28 ounces cooked cannellini beans
- 24 ounces tomato passata
- 17 ounces spinach chopped
- ¼ teaspoon ground black pepper
- 2/3 teaspoon salt
- 1 ¼ teaspoon curry powder
- 1 cup cashew butter
- ¼ teaspoon cardamom

- 2 tablespoons olive oil
- 1 teaspoon salt
- ¼ cup cashews
- 2 tablespoons chopped basil
- 2 tablespoons chopped parsley

Directions:
1. Take a large saucepan, place it over medium heat, add 1 tablespoon oil and when hot, add spinach and cook for 3 minutes until fried.
2. Then stir in butter and tomato pasta until well mixed, bring the mixture to a near boil, add beans, and season with ¼ teaspoon curry powder, black pepper, and salt.
3. Take a small saucepan, place it over medium heat, add remaining oil, stir in cashew, stir in salt and curry powder and cook for 4 minutes until roasted, set aside until required.
4. Transfer cooked stew into a bowl, top with roasted cashews, basil, and parsley, and then serve.

Nutrition: Calories: 242 Cal Fat: 10.2 g Carbs: 31 g Protein: 11 g Fiber: 8.5 g

273. <u>Quick-and-Easy **Pumpkin** Soup</u>

Ingredients:
- Chopped onion (1 cup)
- Peeled and minced ginger root (1 1-inch pc.)
- Minced garlic (1 clove)
- Vegetable stock (6 cups)
- Pumpkin puree (4 cups)
- Salt (1 tsp.)
- Chopped thyme (1/2 tsp.)
- Half-and-half milk (1/2 cup)
- Chopped parsley (1 tsp.)

Procedures:
1. Put garlic, ginger and onion in a large soup pot. Add 1/2 cup of vegetable stock and cook for 5 minutes or until onion is tender.
2. Add Thyme,salt,5 ½ cups of vegetables tock and pumpkin purée into the pot. Cook the soup. Cook the soup for 30 minutes.
3. Put the soup in a blender and blend until become smooth
4. Take out the soup from the stove and add half-and-half milk. Stir it well, then add chopped parsley as garnish. Serve.

This pumpkin soup yields eight servings. One serving has 120 calories, 4.0 g fat, 11 mg cholesterol and 700 mg sodium.

274. Turkey Parsley Soup (FAST)

Preparation Time: 5 Minutes
Cooking Time: 20 Minutes
Servings: 2
Ingredients:
- 6 mugs turkey stock
- Table salt and black pepper to the taste
- 1/4 mug parsley, sliced off
- 3 mugs baked spaghetti squash, sliced off
- 3 celery stalks, sliced off
- 1 yellow onion, sliced off
- 1 tablespoon ghee
- 3 mugs turkey, prepared and shredded

Directions:
1. Warm up a pot with the ghee over moderate immense heat, insert celery and onion, shake and prepare for 5 minutes. Insert parsley, stock, turkey meat, table salt and pepper, shake and prepare for 20 minutes.
2. Insert spaghetti squash, shake and prepare turkey soup for 10 minutes more. Distribute into pots and serve.

Nutrition: Calories: 213 Carbs: 9g Fat: 5g Sodium: 213mg

275. Gooseberry Sauce (FAST)

Preparation Time: 30 minutes
Cooking Time: 5 minutes
Servings: 4
Ingredients
- 5 cups gooseberries, rinsed, topped and tailed
- 5 garlic cloves, crushed
- 1 cup fresh dill, rinsed, stems removed
- Salt to taste

Directions
1. Combine gooseberries and dill in a blender and pulse until smooth.
2. Add garlic and salt.
3. Let stand for 30 minutes, covered.

Nutrition: Carbs: 8 g / Fat: 2 g / Protein: 1 g / Calories: 35

276. Fresh Tomato Vinaigrette (FAST)

Preparation Time: 5 minutes
Cooking Time: 0 minutes
Serving: 5
Ingredients:
- 1 fresh tomato, chopped
- ¾ cup olive oil
- ¼ cup apple cider vinegar

- 1 clove of garlic, chopped
- ½ tsp dried oregano
- Salt and pepper to taste

Directions:
1. Place all ingredients in a food processor and pulse until a smooth paste is formed.
2. Place in containers and store in the fridge until ready to use.

Nutrition: Calories 298, Fat 32g, Carbs 2g, Protein 0.2g, Fiber 0.4g, Sodium 3mg, Potassium 75mg

277. Cabbage & Beet Stew (FAST)

Preparation Time: 20 minutes
Cooking Time: 10 minutes
Servings: 4
Ingredients:
- 2 Tablespoons Olive Oil
- 3 Cups Vegetable Broth
- 2 Tablespoons Lemon Juice, Fresh
- ½ Teaspoon Garlic Powder
- ½ Cup Carrots, Shredded
- 2 Cups Cabbage, Shredded
- 1 Cup Beets, Shredded
- Dill for Garnish
- ½ Teaspoon Onion Powder
- Sea Salt & Black Pepper to Taste

Directions:
1. Heat oil in a pot, and then sauté your vegetables.
2. Pour your broth in, mixing in your seasoning. Simmer until it's cooked through, and then top with dill.

Nutrition: Kcal: 263 Carbohydrates: 8 g Protein: 20.3 g Fat: 24

278. Root Vegetable Soup (FAST)

Preparation Time: 5 Minutes
Cooking Time: 15 Minutes
Servings: 6
Ingredients:
- 1/4 cup olive oil
- 2 medium onions, peeled and chopped
- 6 cloves garlic, peeled and minced
- 1 small butternut squash, divided, seeded, and cubed
- 3 large carrots, peeled and sliced
- 1 medium rutabaga, peeled and chopped
- 5 cups Basic Vegetable Stock
- 1 teaspoon dried marjoram leaves
- 1 teaspoon dried thyme leaves
- 1 teaspoon salt
- 1/4 teaspoon ground black pepper

Directions:

1 1n large soup pot or Dutch oven, heat olive oil over medium heat. Add onions and garlic; cook and stir for 4 minutes.
2 Add squash, carrots, and rutabaga; cook and stir for about 10 minutes or until vegetables start to brown.
3 Add stock, marjoram, thyme, salt, and black pepper and bring to a simmer. Set heat to low, cover, and simmer for 45-55 minutes or until vegetables are tender. Correct seasoning if needed, and serve.

Nutrition: Calories: 205 Carbs: 30g Fat: 10g Sugar: 11g Fiber: 8g Protein: 3g Sodium: 476mg

279. Green Goddess Sauce (FAST)

Preparation Time: 5 minutes
Cooking Time: 0 minutes
Serving: 8
Ingredients:

- 1 cup basil, chopped
- 1 cup flat leaf parsley, chopped
- ¼ cup green onion
- 1 clove of garlic, minced
- 1 tsp apple cider vinegar
- 2 tbsps. lemon juice, freshly squeezed
- ¼ cup olive oil
- 1 cup plain non-Fat Greek yogurt
- 1/8 tsp salt
- 1/8 tsp black pepper
- 1/8 tsp cayenne pepper

Directions:

1 Place all ingredients in a food processor and blend until smooth.
2 Place in containers and store in the fridge until ready to use.

Nutrition: Calories 78, Fat 7g, Carbs 2g, Protein 3g, Fiber 0.4g, Sodium 13mg, Potassium 90mg

280. Garlicky Vegetable Soup (FAST)

Preparation Time: 5 Minutes
Cooking Time: 20 Minutes
Servings: 4
Ingredients:

- 5 medium heads garlic, peeled (each clove peeled)
- 6 cups Roasted Vegetable Stock
- 1 (6-ounce) can tomato paste
- 1 large yellow onion, peeled and diced
- 1/4 teaspoon lemon juice
- 2 tablespoons olive oil
- 2 tablespoons chopped basil

Directions:

1 Place all ingredients except olive oil and basil into a 4–6-quart slow cooker. Stir.
2 Secure and cook on low for 8 hours or on high for 5 hours.
3 Add olive oil. Set an immersion blender or blend soup in batches in a standard blender until smooth.
4 Garnish with basil and serve.

Nutrition: Calories: 223 Carbs: 37g Fat: 8g Sugar: 16g Fiber: 9g Protein: 6g Sodium: 73mg

281. Peach Stew (FAST)

Preparation Time: 10 minutes
Cooking Time: 10 minutes
Servings: 6
Ingredients:

- 3 tbsp coconut sugar
- 5 cups peeled and cubed peaches
- 2 cup water
- 1 tsp grated ginger

Directions:

1 In a pot, combine the peaches while using the sugar, ginger and water, toss, provide a boil over medium heat, cook for 10 mins, divide into bowls and serve cold.

Nutrition: Calories 142, Fat 1.5g, Carbs 7.8g, Protein 2.4g, Phosphorus 127mg, Potassium 199mg, Sodium 134g

282. "Cream" of Cauliflower Soup (FAST)

Preparation Time: 5 Minutes
Cooking Time: 20 Minutes
Servings: 4
Ingredients:

- 1 large head cauliflower, chopped
- 3 large stalks celery, chopped
- 1 medium carrot, peeled and chopped
- 2 cloves garlic, peeled and minced
- 1 medium onion, peeled and chopped
- 2 teaspoons ground cumin
- 1/2 teaspoon ground black pepper
- 1 tablespoon chopped parsley
- 1/4 teaspoon dill

Directions:

1 1In a large soup pot, combine cauliflower, celery, carrot, garlic, onion, cumin, and black pepper. Add water to just cover ingredients in pot. Bring to a boil over high heat.
2 Set heat to low. Simmer until vegetables are tender. Stir in parsley and dill before serving.

Nutrition: Calories: 62 Carbs: 13g Fat: 1g Sugar:5g Fiber: 5g Protein: 4g Sodium: 94mg

283. Wonton Soup (FAST)

Preparation Time: 5 minutes
Cooking Time: 15 minutes
Servings: 8
Ingredients:
- 4 sliced scallions
- ¼ tsp. ground white pepper
- 2 cup sliced fresh mushrooms
- 4 minced garlic cloves
- 6 oz. dry whole-grain yolk-free egg noodles
- ½ lb. lean ground pork
- 1 tbsp minced fresh ginger
- 8 cup low-Sodium chicken broth

Directions:
1. 1Place a stockpot over medium heat. Add the ground pork, ginger, and garlic and sauté for 5 mins. Drain any excess Fat, then return to stovetop.
2. Add the broth and bring to a boil. Once boiling, stir in the mushrooms, noodles, and white pepper. Cover and simmer for 10 mins.
3. Remove pot from heat. Stir in the scallions and serve immediately.

Nutrition: Calories 143, Fat 4g, Carbs 14g, Protein 16g, Fiber 3g, Sodium 55mg, Potassium 125mg

284. Lentil And Lemon Soup

Preparation Time: 10 minutes
Cooking Time: 40 minutes
Servings: 4
Ingredients:
- 2 tsp olive oil
- 1 large onion finely chopped
- 5 oz red lentils
- 2 tsp tomato puree
- 1 garlic clove, peeled
- 1 pint vegetable stock
- 14 oz tin chopped tomatoes
- juice of 1/2 lemon

Directions:
1. Heat the oil and cook onion and garlic for 10 mins. Add the lentils and the stock and bring to the boil.
2. Add the tinned tomatoes and tomato puree and bring back to the boil (covered 15 mins). Taste for seasoning and serve.

Nutrition: Calories 104, Fat 12g, Carbs 12g, Protein 11g

285. Halibut Soup (FAST)

Preparation Time: 5 Minutes
Cooking Time: 15 Minutes
Servings: 2

Ingredients:
- Table salt and black pepper to the taste
- 2 tbsp. ginger, chopped
- 1 mug water
- 1 yellow onion, sliced off
- 1-pound carrots, sliced
- 1 tablespoon coconut oil
- 1-pound halibut, slice into moderate chunks
- 12 mugs chicken stock

Directions:
1. Warm up a pot with the oil over moderate heat, insert onion, shake and prepare for 6 minutes. Insert ginger, carrots, water and stock, shake bring to a simmer, reduce tempera and prepare for 20 minutes.
2. Merge soup using an immersion blender, season with table salt and pepper and insert halibut pieces. Shake gently and simmer soup for 5 minutes more. Distribute into pots and serve.

Nutrition: Calories: 132 Carbs: 5g Fat: 6g Sod: 234mg

286. Egg Soup with Scallions and Bok Choy (FAST)

Preparation Time: 5 Minutes
Cooking Time: 20 Minutes
Servings: 3
Ingredients:
- 1 2-inch piece fresh ginger, peeled and slice into very thin matchstick-size strips
- 1-star anise
- 1-pound shiitake mushrooms, stemmed and sliced
- 1 tsp. five-spice grinding grains
- 1/4 mug fresh lemon juice
- 3 large eggs
- 6 scallions, thinly sliced
- 2 heads baby book choy, slice into 1/4-inch-thick slices
- 0.5-ounce sun-dried wakame
- 3 tbsp. unrefined coconut oil
- 2 shallots, chopped
- 1/4 tsp. black pepper
- 8 mugs Beef Bone Broth

Directions:
1. In a very moderate pot Wrap up wakame with warm water. Let indicate 10 minutes or till soft and pliable. Drain well; rinse well and drain again. Slice strips of wakame into 1-inch items; put aside. In a very large pot warmth coconut oil over moderate heat. Insert shallots, ginger, and star anise.

2   Prepare and shake for regarding a pair of minutes or till shallots are translucent. Insert mushrooms; prepare and shake for two minutes.

3   Garnish 5-spice grinding grains and pepper over mushrooms; prepare and shake for one minute. Insert reserved wakame, Beef Bone Broth, and lemon juice. Bring combine to simmering. In an exceedingly little pot beat egg. Drizzle overwhelmed eggs into simmering broth, swirling broth in an exceedingly figure-eight motion. Remove soup from heat. Shake in scallions. Distribute book choy among large, warmed pots. Ladle soup into pots; serve instantly.

Nutrition: Calories: 123 Carbs: 5 g Fat: 11 g Fiber: 3 g Protein: 5 g Sodium: 16 mg

287.   Chunky Tomato Sauce (FAST)

Preparation Time: 5 minutes
Cooking Time: 15 minutes
Serving: 6
Ingredients:
- ¼ cup extra virgin olive oil
- 2 onions, chopped
- 5 cloves of garlic, minced
- 2 red bell peppers, chopped
- ½ cup sliced Portobello mushrooms
- 3 cups diced tomatoes
- 1 tsp dried oregano
- 2 tsps. honey
- 2 tsps. balsamic vinegar
- 1 tsp dried basil
- ½ cup fresh spinach, chopped

Directions:
1   In a heavy pan, heat oil over medium flame.
2   Stir in the onions, garlic, and bell pepper until fragrant.
3   Add in the mushrooms, tomatoes, oregano, honey, balsamic vinegar, and basil. Season with salt and pepper to taste.
4   Close the lid and bring to a simmer for 10 mins until the tomatoes have wilted.
5   Add in the spinach last and cook for another 5 mins.
6   Place in containers and store in the fridge until ready to use.

Nutrition: Calories 86, Fat 4g, Carbs 11g, Protein 2g, Fiber 2g, Sodium 88mg, Potassium 358mg

288.   Homemade Tzatziki Sauce (FAST)

Preparation Time: 20 minutes
Cooking Time: 0 minutes
Servings: 1

Ingredients:
- 2 ounces (57 g) raw, unsalted cashews (about ½ cup)
- 2 tablespoons lemon juice
- 1/3 cup water
- 1 small clove garlic
- 1 cup chopped cucumber, peeled
- 2 tablespoons fresh dill

Directions:
1   In a blender, add the cashews, lemon juice, water, and garlic. Keep it aside for at least 15 minutes to soften the cashews.
2   Blend the ingredients until smooth. Stir in the chopped cucumber and dill, and continue to blend until it reaches your desired consistency. It doesn't need to be totally smooth. Feel free to add more water if you like a thinner consistency.
3   Transfer to an airtight container and chill for at least 30 minutes for best flavors.
4   Bring the sauce to room temperature and shake well before serving.

Nutrition: Calories: 208 Fat: 13.5g Carbs: 15.0 g Protein: 6.7g Fiber: 2.8g

289.   Lemon Celery Soup with Herb Oil (FAST)

Preparation Time: 5 Minutes
Cooking Time: 15 Minutes
Servings: 4
Ingredients:
- 1/2 of a head cauliflower, cored and broken into florets
- 1/4 mug packed Italian (flat leaf) parsley
- 1/4 mug packed basil leaves
- 1/4 mug olive oil
- 1 tablespoon fresh lemon juice
- 1 tablespoon olive oil
- 1 leek, sliced
- 4 mugs Chicken Bone Broth
- 1/2 of a moderate celery root (about 10 ounces), peeled and slice into 1-inch cubes
- 1/4 tsp. black pepper

Direction:
1   In an exceedingly large sauce dish heat the one tablespoon olive oil over moderate heat. Insert leek; prepare for four to 5 minutes or till tender. Insert Chicken Bone Broth, celery root, and cauliflower. Bring to boiling; reduce heat. Wrap up and simmer for 20 to twenty-five minutes or till vegetables are tender. Remove from heat; cool slightly.
2   Meanwhile, for herb oil, in a food processor or blender combine the parsley, basil, and also the 1/4 mug olive oil. Wrap up and method or

blend till well combined and herbs are in very little items. Set oil through a fine-mesh strainer into a small pot, pressing herbs with the back of a spoon to extract as abundant oil as possible.

3   Remove herbs; set herb oil aside. Shift half of the celery root combine   to the food processor or blender. Wrap up and process or blend till sleek. Pour into a large pot. Repeat with remaining celery root mix. Return all of the combine   back to the sauce dish. Shake in lemon juice and pepper, heat through. Ladle soup into pots. Drizzle with herb oil.

Nutrition: Calories: 143 Carbs: 6 g Fat: 8 g Fiber: 4 g Protein: 3 g Sodium: 58 mg

290.   Tangy Orange Shrimp (FAST)

Preparation Time: 15 minutes
Cooking Time: 15 minutes
Servings: 4
Ingredients:

- ½ cup of freshly squeezed orange juice
- ½ tsp of cornstarch
- ¼ tsp of freshly grated orange zest
- 1 tsp of olive oil
- 12 ounces (26/30 count) of shrimp, peeled and deveined, tails left on
- 1 cup of broccoli florets
- 1 tsp of unsalted butter
- ½ cup of orange segments
- Freshly ground black pepper

Directions:

1   In a small bowl, whisk together the orange juice, cornstarch, and orange zest and set aside.
2   In a large skillet over medium-high heat, heat the olive oil.
3   Add the shrimp and sauté until just cooked through and opaque, about 5 mins. Transfer the cooked shrimp to a plate. Add the broccoli and sauté until tender, about 4 mins. Transfer to the plate with the shrimp.
4   Pour the orange juice mixture into the skillet, and whisk until the sauce has thickened and is glossy about 3 mins.
5   Whisk in the butter, and add the orange segments, shrimp, and broccoli to the skillet.
6   Toss to combine and season with pepper. Serve immediately.

Nutrition: Calories 140, Fat 3g, Sodium 132mg Carbs 8g Fiber 1g Phosphorus 196mg Potassium 329mg Protein 18g

291.   Salmon and Cauliflower (FAST)

Preparation Time: 10 minutes
Cooking Time: 20 minutes
Servings: 4
Ingredients:

- 4 boneless salmon fillets
- 2 tbsp Coconut aminos
- 1 sliced big red onion
- ¼ cup coconut sugar
- 1 head separated cauliflower florets
- 2 tbsp Olive oil

Directions:

1   In a smaller bowl, mix sugar with coconut aminos and whisk.
2   Heat up a pan with half the oil over medium-high heat, add cauliflower and onion, stir and cook for 10 mins.
3   Put the salmon inside baking dish, drizzle the remainder inside oil, add coconut aminos, toss somewhat, season with black pepper, introduce within the oven and bake at 400 0F for 10 mins.
4   Divide the salmon along using the cauliflower mix between plates and serve.

Nutrition: Calories 227, Fat 3g, Sodium 96mg, Carbs 12g, Fiber 1g, Phosphorus 151mg, Potassium 242g, Protein 9g

292.   Sirloin Carrot Soup

Preparation Time: 30 minutes
Cooking Time: 20 minutes
Servings: 4
Ingredients:

- 1 lb. chopped carrots and celery mix
- 32 oz. low-Sodium beef stock
- 1/3 cup whole-wheat flour
- 1 lb. ground beef sirloin
- 1 tbsp olive oil
- 1 chopped yellow onion

Directions:

1   Heat up the olive oil in a saucepan over medium-high flame; add the beef and the flour.
2   Stir well and cook to brown for 4-5 mins.
3   Add the celery, onion, carrots, and stock; stir and bring to a simmer.
4   Turn down the heat to low and cook for 12-15 mins.
5   Serve warm.

Nutrition: Calories 140, Fat 4g, Carbs 17g, Protein 9g, Sugar: 12g, Fiber 3g, Sodium 86mg, Potassium 184mg

293. Vegetable Lentil Soup (FAST)

Preparation Time: 10 minutes
Cooking Time: 25 minutes
Servings: 4
Ingredients:
- 1 tbsp of extra-virgin olive oil
- ½ sweet onion, diced
- 2 carrots, diced
- 2 celery stalks, diced
- ½ cup of lentils
- 5 cups of Simple Chicken Broth or low-Sodium store-bought chicken stock
- 2 cups of sliced chard leaves
- Freshly ground black pepper
- 1 lemon

Directions:
1. In a medium stockpot over medium-high heat, heat the olive oil.
2. Add the onion and stir until softened, about 3 to 5 mins.
3. Add the carrots, celery, lentils, and broth.
4. Bring to a boil, reduce the heat, and simmer, uncovered, for 15 mins, until the lentils are tender.
5. Add the chard and cook for 3 additional mins, until wilted—season with the pepper and lemon juice.

Nutrition: Calories 19, Fat 6g, Carbs 25g, Protein 13g, Phosphorus 228mg, Potassium 707mg, Sodium 157mg

294. Tender Beef and Cabbage Soup (FAST)

Preparation Time: 5 Minutes
Cooking Time: 20 Minutes
Servings: 14
Ingredients:
- 1 pound 85% lean ground beef
- 1 small head cabbage, cored and chopped
- 2 green onions
- 1 medium red bell pepper
- 1 medium bunch celery, chopped
- 1 cup chopped carrots
- 4 cups Basic Vegetable Stock
- 4 cups water
- 3 cloves garlic, peeled and minced
- 1/4 teaspoon crushed red pepper flakes
- 1/4 teaspoon dried basil
- 1/4 teaspoon dried oregano
- 1/4 teaspoon dried thyme
- 1/4 teaspoon onion powder

Directions:
1. Heat a large skillet over medium-high heat. Add beef and cook, breaking up the lumps, until the meat is cooked through and just beginning to brown, 8–10 minutes. Drain excess fat.
2. Place beef, cabbage, green onions, bell pepper, celery, and carrots in a 6-quart slow cooker.
3. Pour in stock and water.
4. Stir in garlic, pepper flakes, basil, oregano, thyme, and onion powder. Secure and cook on low for 8-10 hours.

Nutrition: Calories: 107 Carbs: 8g Fat: 5g Sugar: 4g Fiber: 3g Protein: 8g Sodium: 69mg

295. Blueberry Soup

Preparation Time: 5 Minutes
Cooking Time: 15 Minutes
Servings: 4
Ingredients:
- 3 cups fresh blueberries, divided
- 2 cups water, divided
- 1/2 cup freshly squeezed orange juice
- 2 tablespoons lemon juice
- 1 cinnamon stick
- 2 tablespoons honey
- 1/4 teaspoon salt
- 2 tablespoons quick-cooking tapioca, ground in a food processor or blender
- 1 teaspoon vanilla

Directions:
1. In a large saucepan, combine 21/2 cups blueberries, 1 cup water, orange juice, lemon juice, cinnamon stick, honey, and salt. Bring to a simmer over medium heat.
2. Set heat to low and simmer until blueberries pop.
3. Purée soup in batches in blender or food processor and return to pan.
4. Dissolve tapioca in remaining 1 cup water and add to the soup. Simmer for another 5 minutes until thickened.
5. Cool soup for 30 minutes, and then stir in vanilla. Cover and refrigerate until cold. Stir in remaining 1/2 cup blueberries before serving.

Nutrition: Calories: 128 Carbs: 33g Fat: 0g Sugar: 23g Fiber: 3g Protein: 1g Sodium: 150mg

296. Baked Eggplants in Tomato Sauce

Preparation time: 10 minutes
Cooking time: 40 minutes
Servings 4
Ingredients:
- 4 eggplants
- 4 tomatoes, quartered
- 3 cups tomato puree

- 1 onion, finely chopped
- 4 cloves garlic, minced
- 1 teaspoon oregano
- Salt
- Black pepper
- Olive oil

Directions:

1 Slice eggplants in half and sprinkle with salt. Let the eggplants rest at room temperature for 20-30 minutes, until they have sweat some water out. Pat dry with paper towel, detach all excess water and salt.
2 Preheat oven to 400F, brush a casserole dish with olive oil.
3 Mix tomato with salt, and black pepper to taste. Add oregano, garlic, and onion, and pour into casserole dish.
4 Place eggplants in casserole dish, face down, and bake in oven for 20 minutes.
5 Remove from oven, turn eggplant over, cover with aluminum foil, and bake for another 20 minutes or until the eggplants are fork tender.

Nutrition: Calories: 308 Carbs: 58g   Fat: 9g Sugar: 30g Protein: 10g Sodium: 362mg

297. Spaghetti with Tomato Sauce (FAST)

Preparation Time: 5 Minutes
Cooking Time: 15 Minutes
Servings: 2

Ingredients:

- 4 ounces' spaghetti
- 2 green onions, greens, and whites separated
- 1/8 teaspoon coconut sugar
- 3 ounces' tomato sauce
- 1 tablespoon olive oil
- 1/3 teaspoon salt
- 1/4 teaspoon ground black pepper

Directions:

1 Prepare the spaghetti, and for this, cook it according to the Directions on the packet and then set aside.
2 Then take a skillet pan, place it over medium heat, add oil and when hot, attach white parts of green onions and cook.
3 Add tomato sauce, season with salt and black pepper and bring it to a boil.

4 Switch heat to medium-low level, simmer sauce for 1 minute, then add the cooked spaghetti and toss until mixed.
5 Divide spaghetti between two plates, and then serve.

Nutrition: Calories: 265 Carbs: 8g Fat: 2g Protein: 7g

298. Summer Rolls with Peanut Sauce (FAST)

Preparation time: 15 minutes
Cooking time: 0 minutes
Servings: 4-6

Ingredients:

- 6 to 8 Vietnamese/Thai round rice paper wraps
- 1 (13-ounce) package organic, extra-firm smoked or plain tofu, drained, cut into long, thin slices
- 1 cucumber, cored, cut into matchsticks (about 1 cup)
- 1 cup carrot, cut into matchsticks
- 1 cup mung bean or soybean sprouts
- 4 to 6 cups of spinach
- 12 to 16 basil leaves
- 3 to 4 mint sprigs
- Sweet Peanut Dressing

Directions:

1 Place the rice paper wrap under running water or in a large bowl of water for a moment, then set it on a plate or cutting board to absorb the water for 30 seconds. The wrap should be transparent and pliable.
2 Place your desired amount of filling on each wrap, being careful not to overfill because they will be hard to close.
3 Tightly fold the bottom of the wraps over the ingredients, and then fold in each side. Continue rolling each wrap onto itself to form the rolls. Enjoy your rolls dipped in sweet peanut dressing.

Nutrition: Calories: 216 Fat: 6g Carbohydrate: 32g Protein: 13g

DRINK AND SMOOTHIES

299. Zucchini Apple Smoothie (FAST)

Preparation Time: 10 Minutes
Cooking Time: 0 Minutes
Servings: 2
Ingredients:
- 1 cup spinach
- 1 medium zucchini, chopped
- 3 medium carrots, peeled and chopped
- 2 medium apples, cored and peeled
- 2 cups water, divided

Directions:
1 Place spinach, zucchini, carrots, apples, and 1 cup water in a blender and blend until thoroughly combined.
2 Add remaining water while blending until desired texture is achieved.

Nutrition: Calories: 163 Carbs: 40g Fat: 1g Sugar: 28g Fiber: 9g Protein: 4g Sodium: 90mg

300. Farmers' Market Smoothie (FAST)

Preparation Time: 10 Minutes
Cooking Time: 0 Minutes
Servings: 2
Ingredients:
- 1 cup chopped romaine lettuce
- 2 medium tomatoes
- 1 medium zucchini, chopped
- 2 medium stalks celery, chopped
- 1 medium cucumber, chopped
- 1/2 cup chopped green onions
- 2 cloves garlic, peeled
- 2 cups water, divided

Directions:
1 Place romaine, tomatoes, zucchini, celery, cucumber, green onions, garlic, and 1 cup water in a blender and blend until thoroughly combined.
2 Add remaining 1 cup water, if needed, while blending until desired texture is achieved.

Nutrition: Calories: 86 Carbs: 17g Fat: 1g Sugar: 11g Fiber: 6g Protein: 5g Sodium: 59mg

301. Sweet Citrus Smoothie (FAST)

Preparation Time: 10 Minutes
Cooking Time: 0 Minutes

Servings: 2
Ingredients:
- 1 cup chopped watercress
- 1 large grapefruit, peeled
- 2 medium oranges, peeled
- 1 (1/2) piece gingerroot, peeled
- 1/2 medium lemon, peeled
- 1 cup water, divided

Directions:
1 Place watercress, grapefruit, oranges, gingerroot, lemon, and 1/2 cup water in a blender and blend until thoroughly combined.
2 Add remaining water while blending until desired texture is achieved.

Nutrition: Calories: 136 Carbs: 35g Fat: 0g Sugar: 24g Fiber: 7g Protein: 3g Sodium: 7mg

302. The Green Go-Getter Smoothie (FAST)

Preparation Time: 10 Minutes
Cooking Time: 0 Minutes
Servings: 1
Ingredients:
- 1 cup spinach
- 2 medium green apples, peeled and cored
- 1/2 medium banana, peeled
- 1 cup water, divided

Directions:
1 Place spinach, apples, banana, and 1/2 cup water in a blender and blend until thoroughly combined.
2 Continue adding remaining water while blending until desired texture is achieved.

Nutrition: Calories: 241 Carbs: 63g Fat: 1g Sugar: 44g Fiber: 11g Protein: 2g Sodium: 29mg

303. Clementine Smoothie (FAST)

Preparation Time: 5 Minutes
Cooking Time: 5 minutes
Servings 1
Ingredients:
- 4 oz. clementine juice
- 2 oz. oats
- 2 oz. blueberries
- 2 pears
- 1 tablespoon honey
- 1 tsp. mixed spice

Directions:
1 In a blender merge all ingredients and blend until smooth
2 Pour smoothie in a glass and serve

Nutrition: Calories: 86 Carbs: 17g Fat: 1g Fiber: 6g Protein: 5g Sod: 59mg

304. Avocado Smoothie (FAST)

Preparation Time: 5 Minutes
Cooking Time: 5 minutes
Servings: 1
Ingredients:
- 1 banana
- 2 tablespoons cacao powder
- 1 tsp. coconut oil
- 1 avocado
- 1 tsp. vanilla extract
- 2 tablespoons honey
- 1 cup ice

Directions:
1 In a blender merge all ingredients and blend until smooth
2 Pour smoothie in a glass and serve

Nutrition: Calories: 185 Carbs: 29g Fat: 7g Fiber: 15g Protein: 3g Sodium: 309mg

305. Homemade Tomato Juice

Preparation Time: 10 Minutes
Cooking Time: 4 Hours
Servings: 4
Ingredients:
- 10 large tomatoes, seeded and sliced
- 1 teaspoon lemon juice
- 1/4 teaspoon ground black pepper
- 1 tablespoon maple syrup

Directions:
1 Place tomatoes in a 2-quart slow cooker. Cover; cook on low for 4–6 hours.
2 Press cooked tomatoes through a sieve. Add remaining ingredients and chill.

Nutrition: Calories 95 Fat 1g Protein 4g Sodium 23mg Fiber 6g Carbohydrates 21g Sugar 15g

306. Raspberry Muffins (FAST)

Preparation time: 10 minutes
Cooking time: 25 minutes
Servings: 12
Ingredients:
- ½ cup and 2 tablespoons whole-wheat flour
- 1 ½ cup raspberries, fresh and more for decorating
- 1 cup white whole-wheat flour
- 1/8 teaspoon salt
- ¾ cup of coconut sugar
- 2 teaspoons baking powder
- 1 teaspoon apple cider vinegar
- 1 ¼ cups water
- ½ cup olive oil

Directions:
1 Switch on the oven, then set it to 400 degrees f and let it preheat.
2 Meanwhile, take a large bowl, place both flours in it, add salt and baking powder and then stir until combined.
3 Take a medium bowl, add oil to it, and then whisk in the sugar until dissolved.
4 Whisk in vinegar and water until blended, slowly stir in flour mixture until smooth batter comes together, and then fold in berries.
5 Take a 12-cups muffin pan, grease it with oil, fill evenly with the prepared mixture and then put a raspberry on top of each muffin.
6 Bake the muffins for 25 minutes until the top golden brown, and then serve.

Nutrition: Calories: 109 Cal; Fat: 3.4 g; Protein: 2.1 g; Carbs: 17.6 g;

307. Banana Muffins

Preparation time: 10 minutes
Cooking time: 30 minutes
Servings: 12
Ingredients:
- 1 ½ cups mashed banana
- 1 ½ cups and 2 tablespoons white whole-wheat flour, divided
- ¼ cup of coconut sugar
- ¾ cup rolled oats, divided
- 1 teaspoon ginger powder
- 1 tablespoon ground cinnamon, divided
- 2 teaspoons baking powder
- ½ teaspoon salt
- 1 teaspoon baking soda
- 1 tablespoon vanilla extract, unsweetened
- ½ cup maple syrup
- 1 tablespoon rum
- ½ cup of coconut oil

Directions:
1 Switch on the oven, then set it to 350 degrees f and let it preheat.
2 Meanwhile, take a medium bowl, place 1 ½ cup flour in it, add ½ cup oars, ginger, baking powder and soda, salt, and 2 teaspoons cinnamon and then stir until mixed.
3 Place ¼ cup of coconut oil in a heatproof bowl, melt it in the microwave oven and then whisk in maple syrup until combined.
4 Add mashed banana along with rum and vanilla, stir until combined, and then whisk this mixture into the flour mixture until smooth batter comes together.
5 Take a separate medium bowl, place remaining oats and flour in it, add cinnamon, coconut sugar, and coconut oil and then stir with a fork until crumbly mixture comes together.
6 Take a 12-cups muffin pan, fill evenly with prepared batter, top with oats mixture, and then bake for 30 minutes until firm and the top turn golden brown.
7 When done, let the muffins cool for 5 minutes in its pan and then cool the muffins completely before serving.

Nutrition: Calories: 240 Cal; Fat: 9.3 g; Protein: 2.6 g; Carbs: 35.4 g; Fiber: 2 g

308. No-Bake Cookies (FAST)

Preparation time: 30 minutes
Cooking time: 0 minutes
Servings: 9
Ingredients:
- 1 cup rolled oats
- ¼ cup of cocoa powder
- 1/8 teaspoon salt
- 1 teaspoon vanilla extract, unsweetened
- ¼ cup and 2 tablespoons peanut butter, divided
- 6 tablespoons coconut oil, divided
- ¼ cup and 1 tablespoon maple syrup, divided

Directions:
1   Take a small saucepan, place it over low heat, add 5 tablespoons of coconut oil and then let it melt.
2   Whisk in 2 tablespoons peanut butter, salt, 1 teaspoon vanilla extract, and ¼ cup each of cocoa powder and maple syrup, and then whisk until well combined.
3   Remove pan from heat, stir in oats and then spoon the mixture evenly into 9 cups of a muffin pan.
4   Wipe clean the pan, return it over low heat, add remaining coconut oil, maple syrup, and peanut butter, stir until combined, and then cook for 2 minutes until thoroughly warmed.
5   Drizzle the peanut butter sauce over the oat mixture in the muffin pan and then let it freeze for 20 minutes or more until set.
6   Serve straight away.

Nutrition: Calories: 213 Cal; Fat: 14.8 g; Protein: 4 g; Carbs: 17.3 g; Fiber: 2.1 g

309. Peanut Butter, Nut, And Fruit Cookies (FAST)

Preparation time: 30 minutes
Cooking time: 0 minutes
Servings: 25
Ingredients:
- ¾ cup rolled oats
- ¼ cup chopped peanuts
- ½ cup coconut flakes, unsweetened
- ¼ cup and 2 tablespoons chopped cranberries, dried
- ¼ cup sliced almonds
- ¼ cup and 2 tablespoons raisins
- ¼ cup maple syrup
- ¾ cup peanut butter

Directions:
1   Take a baking sheet, line it with wax paper, and then set it aside until required.
2   Take a large bowl, place oats, almonds, and coconut flakes in it, add ¼ cup each of cranberries and raisins, and then stir until combined.
3   Add maple syrup and peanut butter, stir until well combined, and then scoop the mixture on the prepared baking sheet with some distance between them.
4   Flatten each scoop of cookie mixture slightly, press remaining cranberries and raisins into each cookie, and then let it chill for 20 minutes until firm.
5   Serve straight away.

Nutrition: Calories: 140 Cal; Fat: 7 g; Protein: 3 g; Carbs: 18 g; Fiber: 5 g

310. Garlic and Herb Oodles (FAST)

Preparation Time: 5minutes
Cooking time: 2minutes
Servings: 3
Ingredients:
- 1 teaspoon extra-virgin olive oil or 2 tablespoons vegetable broth
- 1 teaspoon minced garlic (about 1 clove)
- 4 medium zucchinis, spiraled
- 1/2 teaspoon dried basil
- 1/2 teaspoon dried oregano
- 1/41/4 to 1/2 teaspoon red pepper flakes, to taste
- 1/4 teaspoon salt (optional)
- 1/4 teaspoon freshly ground black pepper

Directions:
1   Heat the olive oil. Add the garlic, zucchini, basil, oregano, red pepper flakes, salt (if using), and black pepper. Sauté for 1 to 2 minutes, until barely tender.
2   Divide the oodles evenly among 4 storage containers. Let cool before sealing the lids.

Nutrition: Calories: 120 Protein: 10g Fat: 44g Carbs: 32g Fibers: 5g

311. Lemon Cashew Tart

Preparation Time: 3 hours and 15 minutes
Cooking Time: 0 minute
Servings: 12
Ingredients:
For the Crust:
- 1 cup almonds
- 4 dates, pitted, soaked in warm water for 10 minutes in water, drained
- 1/8 teaspoon crystal salt
- 1 teaspoon vanilla extract, unsweetened
- For the Cream:
- 1 cup cashews, soaked in warm water for 10 minutes in water, drained
- 1/4 cup water
- 1/4 cup coconut nectar
- 1 teaspoon coconut oil
- 1 teaspoon vanilla extract, unsweetened
- 1 lemon, Juiced
- 1/8 teaspoon crystal salt
- For the Topping:
- Shredded coconut as needed

Directions:
1.   Prepare the cream and for this, place all its ingredients in a food processor, pulse for 2

minutes until smooth, and then refrigerate for 1 hour.

2. Then prepare the crust, and for this, place all its ingredients in a food processor and pulse for 3 to 5 minutes until the thick paste comes together.

3. Take a tart pan, grease it with oil, place crust mixture in it and spread and press the mixture evenly in the bottom and along the sides, and freeze until required.

4. Pour the filling into the prepared tart, smooth the top, and refrigerate for 2 hours until set.

5. Cut tart into slices and then serve.

Nutrition: Calories: 166 Cal Fat: 10 g Carbs: 15 g Protein: 5 g Fiber: 1 g

312. Mango Bowls (FAST)

Preparation time: 30 minutes
Cooking time: 0 minutes
Servings: 4
Ingredients:
- 3 cups mango, cut into medium chunks
- ½ cup of coconut water
- ¼ cup stevia
- 1 teaspoon vanilla extract

Directions:
1 In a blender, blend the mango plus the rest of the ingredients, pulse well.
2 Divide into bowls and serve cold.

Nutrition: Calories 122 Fat 4 Fiber 5.3 Carbs 6.6 Protein 4.5

313. Lime Vanilla Fudge

Preparation time: 3 hours
Cooking time: 0 minutes
Servings: 6
Ingredients:
- 1/3 cup cashew butter
- 5 tablespoons lime juice
- ½ teaspoon lime zest, grated
- 1 tablespoons stevia

Directions:
1 In a bowl, mix the cashew butter with the other ingredients and whisk well.
2 Line a muffin tray with parchment paper, scoop 1 tablespoon of lime fudge mix in each of the muffin tins and keep in the freezer for 3 hours before serving.

Nutrition: Calories 200 Fat 4.5 Fiber 3.4 Carbs 13.5 Protein 5

314. Watermelon Cream (FAST)

Preparation Time: 15 minutes
Cooking Time: 0 minutes
Servings: 2
Ingredients:
- 1-pound watermelon, peeled and chopped
- 1 teaspoon vanilla extract
- 1 cup heavy cream
- 1 teaspoon lime juice
- 2 tablespoons stevia

Directions:
1. Pulse the watermelon, cream, and the rest of the ingredients in a bowl put into cups. Keep in the fridge for 15 minutes before serving.

Nutrition: Calories 122 Fat 5.7 Fiber 3.2 Carbs 5.3 Protein 0.4

315. Cocoa Sweet Cherry Cream

Preparation Time: 2 hours
Cooking Time: 0 minutes
Servings: 4
Ingredients:
- ½ cup of cocoa powder
- ¾ cup red cherry jam
- ¼ cup stevia
- 2 cups of water
- 1-pound cherries pitted and halved

Directions:
1. Mix the cherries with the water and the rest of the ingredients in a blender, pulse then put into cups. Cool in the fridge for 2 hours before serving.

Nutrition: Calories 162 Fat 3.4 Fiber 2.4 Carbs 5 Protein 1

316. Papaya Cream (FAST)

Preparation Time: 10 minutes
Cooking Time: 0 minutes
Servings: 2
Ingredients:
- 1 cup papaya, peeled and chopped
- 1 cup heavy cream
- 1 tablespoon stevia
- ½ teaspoon vanilla extract

Directions:
1. Mix the cream with the papaya and the other ingredients in a blender, divide into cups and serve cold.

Nutrition: Calories 182 Fat 3.1 Fiber 2.3 Carbs 3.5 Protein 2

317. Mango Bowls (FAST)

Preparation Time: 30 minutes
Cooking Time: 0 minutes
Servings: 4
Ingredients:
- 3 cups mango, cut into medium chunks
- ½ cup of coconut water

- ¼ cup stevia
- 1 teaspoon vanilla extract

Directions:
1. Mix the mango with the rest of the ingredients in a blender, pulse well, divide into bowls and serve cold.

Nutrition: Calories 122 Fat 4 Fiber 5.3 Carbs 6.6 Protein 4.5

318. Lime Vanilla Fudge

Preparation Time: 3 hours
Cooking Time: 0 minutes
Servings: 6
Ingredients:
- 1/3 cup cashew butter
- 5 tablespoons lime juice
- ½ teaspoon lime zest, grated
- 1 tablespoons stevia

Directions:
1. In a bowl, mix the cashew butter with the other ingredients and whisk well.
2. Line a muffin tray with parchment paper, scoop 1 tablespoon of lime fudge mix in each of the muffin tins and keep in the freezer for 3 hours before serving.

Nutrition: Calories 200 Fat 4.5 Fiber 3.4 Carbs 13.5 Protein 5

319. Blueberry Cake

Preparation Time: 10 minutes
Cooking Time: 30 minutes
Servings: 6
Ingredients:
- 2 cups almond flour
- 3 cups blueberries
- 1 cup walnuts, chopped
- 3 tablespoons stevia
- 1 teaspoon vanilla extract
- 2 eggs, whisked
- 2 tablespoons avocado oil
- 1 teaspoon baking powder
- Cooking spray

Directions:
1. Mix the flour with the blueberries, walnuts, and the other ingredients except for the cooking spray in a bowl, and stir well.
2. Grease a cake pan with the cooking spray, pour the cake mix inside, introduce everything in the oven at 350 degrees F and bake for 30 minutes.
3. Cool the cake down, slice, and serve.

Nutrition: Calories 225 Fat 9 Fiber 4.5 Carbs 10.2 Protein 4.5

320. Blueberry Yogurt Mousse (FAST)

Preparation Time: 30 minutes
Cooking Time: 0 minutes
Servings: 4
Ingredients:
- 2 cups Greek yogurt
- ¼ cup stevia
- ¾ cup heavy cream
- 2 cups blueberries

Directions:
1. In a blender, combine the yogurt with the other ingredients, pulse well, divide into cups, and put in the fridge for 30 minutes before serving.

Nutrition: Calories 141 Fat 4.7 Fiber 4.7 Carbs 8.3 Protein 0.8

321. Almond Peaches Mix (FAST)

Preparation Time: 10 minutes
Cooking Time: 10 minutes
Servings: 4
Ingredients:
- 1/3 cup almonds, toasted
- 1/3 cup pistachios, toasted
- 1 teaspoon mint, chopped
- ½ cup of coconut water
- 1 teaspoon lemon zest, grated
- 4 peaches, halved
- 2 tablespoons stevia

Directions:
1. In a pan, combine the peaches with the stevia and the rest of the ingredients, simmer over medium heat for 10 minutes, divide into bowls and serve cold.

Nutrition: Calories 135 Fat 4.1 Fiber 3.8 Carbs 4.1 Protein 2.3

322. Walnuts Cake

Preparation Time: 10 minutes
Cooking Time: 40 minutes
Servings: 4
Ingredients:
- ½ pound walnuts, minced
- Zest of 1 orange, grated
- 1 and ¼ cups stevia
- Eggs whisked
- 1 teaspoon almond extract
- 1 and ½ cup of almond flour
- 1 teaspoon baking soda

Directions:
1. In a bowl, combine the walnuts with the orange zest and the other ingredients, put into a cake pan lined with parchment paper.

2. Introduce in the oven at 350 degrees F, bake for 40 minutes, cool down, slice, and serve.

Nutrition: Calories 205 Fat 14.1 Fiber 7.8 Carbs 9.1 Protein 3.4

323. Banana-Cinnamon "Ice Cream" (FAST)

Preparation Time: 10 minutes
Cooking Time: 0 minutes
Servings: 4
Ingredients:
- 4 medium frozen bananas, cut into 2-inch chunks
- ¼ cup 100% maple syrup
- 1 teaspoon ground cinnamon

Directions:
1. Allow the frozen banana chunks to rest at room temperature for 5 minutes, then place in a food processor or blender.
2. Add the maple syrup and cinnamon, and purée until well combined.
3. Serve immediately, or store in a freezer-safe container in the freezer until later.

Nutrition: Calories: 159 Total Fat: 0g Saturated Fat: 0g Protein: 1g Carbohydrates: 41 g Fiber: 3g Sodium: 4mg

324. Banana-Oat Walnut Loaf

Preparation Time: 15 minutes
Cooking Time: 25 minutes
Servings: 8
Ingredients:
- Cooking spray
- 2 cups gluten-free rolled oats, plus 2 tablespoons
- 3 ripe bananas, mashed
- 2 large eggs, lightly beaten
- ½ cup honey
- 1 teaspoon baking soda
- ½ cup raw walnuts, chopped

Directions:
1. Preheat the oven to 350°F. Coat an 8-inch loaf pan with cooking spray.
2. In a medium bowl, mix together 2 cups of oats and the mashed bananas, beaten eggs, honey, and baking soda. Gently fold in the walnuts.
3. Pour the mixture into the prepared pan, spreading in an even layer with a spatula. Sprinkle the remaining 2 tablespoons of oats on top of the batter.
4. Bake for about 25 minutes, until the top is golden brown and a toothpick inserted into the center comes out clean. Remove from the oven and allow to cool for 10 minutes. Transfer the bread to a wire rack and let cool for 10 to 15 more minutes, then cut into 1-inch slices.

5. To freeze, place each slice in a resealable plastic bag or wrap them individually in plastic wrap and store the slices in the freezer for up to 2 months. To defrost, refrigerate overnight. The loaf can be eaten at room temperature, warmed in a toaster oven, or reheated in the microwave on high for 20 to 30 seconds. Allow the slices to cool for 2 minutes after reheating in the microwave before eating.

Nutrition: Calories: 205 Total Fat: 6g Saturated Fat: 1g Protein: 4g Carbohydrates: 36g Fiber: 3g Sodium: 122mg

325. Applelicious Apple Crisp

Preparation Time: 15 minutes
Cooking Time: 40 minutes
Servings: 6
Ingredients:
- Cooking spray
- 6 medium apples (like Empire, Honeycrisp, Pink Lady), cored and thinly sliced
- 2 tablespoons honey
- For the topping
- ¾ cup old-fashioned oats
- ¾ cup whole-wheat pastry flour
- ⅓ cup light brown sugar
- 3 tablespoons unsalted butter, at room temperature, cut into pieces
- 3 tablespoons water

Directions:
1. Preheat the oven to 350°F. Coat an 8-by-8-inch baking dish with cooking spray.
2. Place the apples in a medium bowl. Add the honey and toss to coat. Transfer to the prepared baking dish.
3. To make the topping, in a blender, add the oats, flour, brown sugar, butter, and water, and blend until smooth.
4. Use clean fingers to crumble the topping over the apples.
5. Place the baking dish in the middle rack of the oven, and bake for 40 minutes, until the topping is browned and the apples are cooked through.
6. Remove from the oven and allow to cool for at least 10 minutes. Using a spoon, divide the crisp into six portions and serve.

Nutrition: Calories: 268 Total Fat: 7g Saturated Fat: 4g Protein: 3g Carbohydrates: 51 g Fiber: 6g Sodium: 2mg

326. Lemon and Watermelon Granita (FAST)

Preparation Time: 10 minutes
Cooking Time: 0 minutes
Servings: 4

Ingredients:
- 4 cups watermelon cubes
- ¼ cup honey
- ¼ cup freshly squeezed lemon juice

Directions:
1. In a blender, combine the watermelon, honey, and lemon juice. Purée all the ingredients, then pour into a 9-by-9-by-2-inch baking pan and place in the freezer.
2. Every 30 to 60 minutes, run a fork across the frozen surface to fluff and create ice flakes. Freeze for about 3 hours total and serve.

Nutrition: Calories: 153 Protein: 2g Total Carbohydrates: 39g Sugars: 35g Fiber: 1g Total Fat: <1g Saturated Fat: <1g Cholesterol: 0mg Sodium: 7mg

327. Watermelon Bowl

Preparation Time: 1 hour and 10 minutes
Cooking Time: 0 minutes
Servings: 32

Ingredients:
- 1 Watermelon, Halved Lengthwise
- 3 Tablespoons Lime Juice, Fresh
- 1 Cup Sugar
- 1 ½ Cup Water
- 1 ½ Cups Mint Leaves, Fresh & Chopped
- 6 Plums, Pitted & Halved
- 1 Cantaloupe, Small
- 4 Nectarines, Pitted & Halved
- 1 lb. Green Grapes, Seedless

Directions:
1. Mix sugar and water in a two-quart pot and bring it to a boil using medium heat. Stir your sugar in until it dissolves.
2. Mix in your lime juice and mint, and then place it in the fridge until chilled.
3. Chop your watermelon and cantaloupe into bite sized pieces, and then slice the nectarines and plums into wedges.

4. Mix all your fruit together in a large bowl before adding in your grapes.
5. Take the mixture out of the fridge and pour it over the fruit.
6. Mix well, and then cover it with saran wrap.
7. Refrigerate for two hours, and stir occasionally. Serve chilled.

Nutrition: Calories: 111 Protein: 2 Grams Fat: 0 Grams Carbs: 26 Grams Sodium: 7 mg

328. Roasted Plum with Almonds

Preparation Time: 15 minutes
Cooking Time: 30 minutes
Servings: 6

Ingredients:
- 6 Plums, Large, Pitted & Halved
- 3 Tablespoons butter
- 1/3 Cup Brown Sugar
- 2 Cups Fennel, Sliced
- ¼ Cup All Purpose Flour
- 1/3 Cup Almonds, Sliced

Directions:
1. Heat your oven to 425, and then place the plums in a shallow baking dish.
2. Get out a shallow baking dish and place your plums inside.
3. Get out a bowl and mix your brown sugar and butter together until smooth, and blend in your flour. Make sure it's mixed well, and then toss in your almonds.
4. Pour the mixture over the plums evenly, and then bake for twenty-five to thirty minutes. The plums should be tender.

Nutrition: Calories: *204* Protein: 2 Grams Fat: 9 Grams Carbs: 31 Grams Sodium: 64 mg

329. Toasted Rye with Pumpkin Seed Butter (FAST)

Preparation Time: 10 minutes
Cooking Time: 25 minutes and the cooling time
Servings: 4
Ingredients:
- Pumpkin seeds: 220g
- Date nectar: 1 tsp.
- Avocado oil: 2 tbsp.
- Rye bread: 4 slices toasted

Directions:
1. Toast the pumpkin seed on a frying pan on low heat for 5-7 minutes and stir in between
2. Let them turn golden and remove them from the pan
3. Add to the blender when they cool down and make fine powder
4. Add in avocado oil and salt and then again blend to form a paste
5. Add date nectars too and blend
6. On the toasted rye, spread one tablespoon of this butter and serve with your favorite toppings

Nutrition: Carbs: 3 g Protein: 5 g Fats: 10.3 g Calories: 127

330. Steamed Artichokes (FAST)

Preparation Time: 10 minutes
Cooking Time: 15 minutes
Servings: 4
Ingredients:
- 4 medium artichokes
- 1 lemon, halved
- 1 cup water

Directions:
1. To prepare the artichokes, use kitchen shears to trim the spiky tips off all the artichoke leaves. Pull any tough leaves off the very bottom and use a paring knife to trim off the stem. Rub cut parts of the artichoke with the lemon to avoid discoloring.
2. Place a steamer insert or a rack in the pressure cooker pot.
3. Add the water to the pot. Arrange the artichokes in the pressure cooker, stacking them if necessary.
4. Lock lid and set the timer for 15 minutes at high pressure. When the timer is off, quick release the pressure, open the lid, and remove the artichokes with tongs. Serve hot or cool or use in another recipe.

Nutrition: Calories: 27 Carbs: 6g Fat: 0g Protein: 2g

331. Steamed Asparagus, Four Ways (FAST)

Preparation Time: 5 minutes
Cooking Time: 1 minute
Servings: 4
Ingredients:
- ½ cup water
- 1 pound asparagus, trimmed
- 2 tablespoons melted unsalted butter mixed
- ½ teaspoon freshly grated lemon zest
- 2 tablespoons champagne vinaigrette
- 1 tablespoon slivered almonds
- ¼ cup hollandaise sauce
- 1 tablespoon hazelnut oil
- 1 tablespoon chopped hazelnuts
- Salt and pepper

Directions:
1. Place a steamer insert in the pot of a pressure cooker. Add the water to the pot. Place the asparagus in the insert. If the stalks are too long, it's fine to lean them against the sides of the cooker.
2. Lock the lid and then set the timer for 1 minute at high pressure. When the timer is off, quick release the pressure and open the lid. Transfer the asparagus to a plate.
3. Top or toss asparagus with one of the following:
4. 2 tablespoons melted unsalted butter mixed with ½ teaspoon freshly grated lemon zest
5. 2 tablespoons champagne vinaigrette and 1 tablespoon slivered almonds
6. ¼ cup hollandaise sauce
7. 1 tablespoon hazelnut oil and 1 tablespoon chopped hazelnuts. Season with salt and pepper.

Nutrition: Calories: 32 Carbs: 3g Fat: 1g Protein: 5g

332. Pecan and Pear Breakfast (FAST)

Preparation Time: 5 minutes
Cooking Time: 15 minutes
Servings: 4
Ingredients
- cups of water
- ½ teaspoon salt
- 1 cup medium bulgur
- 1 tablespoon vegan margarine

- ripe pears, peeled, cored and chopped
- ¼ cup pecans, chopped

Directions
1. Take a large saucepan, bring water to a boil over high heat
2. Add salt, stir in bulgur
3. Lower heat and simmer for 15 minutes
4. Remove from heat and stir in margarine, pears and pecans
5. Cover and let it sit for 12-15 minutes more
6. Serve and enjoy!

Nutrition: Calories: 255 Fat: 7g Carbohydrates: 45g Protein: 6g

333. Easy Vegan Peanut Butter Overnight Oats (FAST)

Preparation Time: 5 minutes
Cooking Time: 0 minutes
Servings: 1
Ingredients
- ounces of frozen raspberries
- ounces of rolled porridge oats
- 1 teaspoon of maple syrup
- 1 tablespoon of peanut butter

Directions
1. Put the raspberries into a bowl containing the oats, a pinch of salt, and half cup of water. Place in the refrigerator and chill overnight.
2. Add in the maple syrup and top with peanut butter.

Nutrition: Calories: 345 Fat: 12g Carbohydrate: 44g Protein: 11g

334. Super Nutritious Carrot Cake Bites (FAST)

Preparation Time: 10 minutes
Cooking Time: 15 minutes
Servings: 16
Ingredients
- carrots, grated (about 1 1/2 cups)
- 1/4 cup of roughly chopped Medjool dates, softened (about 3 large dates)
- 1/4 cup of coarsely ground flax seed
- 1 cup of rolled oats
- 1/4 cup of plain unsweetened natural style almond butter
- 1/2 cup of raisins
- 1/2 cup of walnut pieces
- 1 1/2 teaspoon of pumpkin pie spice
- 1/2 teaspoon of vanilla extract
- Optional: 1 teaspoon of fresh ginger finely, grated
- Optional: 1 teaspoon of turmeric powder
- 1/2 cup of unsweetened shredded coconut

Directions
1. Microwave the dates in a bowl with one tablespoon of water for about thirty seconds. Transfer all the ingredients minus the coconut into a food processor and blend until blended. Add in water to get a thin consistency.
2. Scoop the mixture into a bowl and chill in the refrigerator to become firm, about thirty minutes. Scoop out the mixture and roll into one-inch balls. Dip each ball in the shredded coconut.

Nutrition: Calories: 101 Carbohydrate: 11g Protein: 2g Fat: 5g

335. Hearty Bran Muffins (FAST)

Preparation Time: 10 minutes
Cooking Time: 20 minutes
Servings: 6
Ingredients
- cups bran flake cereal
- 1 and ½ cups whole wheat flour
- ½ cup raisins
- teaspoons baking powder
- ½ teaspoon cinnamon, ground
- ½ teaspoon salt
- 1/3 cup brown sugar
- ¾ cup fresh orange juice

Directions
1. Preheat your oven to 400 degrees Fahrenheit
2. Take 12-hole muffin tin and lightly grease it
3. Add paper liners
4. Take a large bowl and add bran flakes, flour, raisins, baking powder, cinnamon and salt
5. Take another medium-sized bowl and add orange juice, oil and sugar and mix well
6. Pour wet ingredients into dry ingredients and mix until moist
7. Fill cups about 2/3rd full
8. Bake until golden brown, should take about 20 minutes
9. Serve and enjoy!

Nutrition: Calories: 222 Fat: 11g Carbohydrates: 32g Protein: 6g

336. Harvest Ratatouille (FAST)

Preparation Time: 15 minutes
Cooking Time: 3 minutes
Servings: 4
Ingredients:
- 2 tablespoons extra-virgin olive oil, divided
- 2 large yellow onions, diced
- 1 teaspoon garlic powder
- 1 teaspoon dried thyme
- 1 teaspoon dried oregano
- ½ teaspoon kosher salt, plus more if needed

- 1 eggplant, cut into 1-inch chunks
- 2 red bell peppers, seeded and diced
- 2 summer squash, sliced
- 1 (28-ounce) can whole tomatoes, in juice
- ¼ teaspoon freshly ground black pepper

Directions:

1. With the pressure cooker on the brown or sauté setting, heat 1 tablespoon of olive oil until it shimmers. Add the onions and sauté, stirring frequently, until they are softened and translucent, about 5 minutes. Stir in the garlic powder, thyme, oregano, and salt. Add the eggplant, bell peppers, and squash, and pour the tomatoes and their juices over the vegetables without stirring.
2. Lock the lid, then set the timer for 3 minutes at high pressure. When the timer is off, quick release the pressure. Gently stir the ingredients, drizzling in the remaining 1 tablespoon of olive oil, and season it with salt and pepper if needed. Serve hot or warm.

Nutrition: Calories: 189 Carbs: 15g Fat: 12g Protein: 3g

337. Cauliflower and Potato Hash browns (FAST)

Preparation Time: 5-15 minutes
Cooking Time: 35 minutes
Servings: 4

Ingredients:

- 3 tbsp flax seed powder + 9 tbsp water
- 2 large potatoes, peeled and shredded
- 1 big head cauliflower, rinsed and riced
- ½ white onion, grated
- 1 tsp salt
- 1 tbsp black pepper
- 4 tbsp plant butter, for frying

Directions:

1. In a medium bowl, mix the flaxseed powder and water. Allow thickening for 5 minutes for the flax egg.
2. Add the potatoes, cauliflower, onion, salt, and black pepper to the flax egg and mix until well combined. Allow sitting for 5 minutes to thicken.
3. Working in batches, melt 1 tbsp of plant butter in a non-stick skillet and add 4 scoops of the hashbrown mixture to the skillet. Make sure to have 1 to 2-inch intervals between each scoop.
4. Use the spoon to flatten the batter and cook until compacted and golden brown on the bottom part, 2 minutes. Flip the hashbrowns and cook further for 2 minutes or until the vegetables cook and is golden brown. Transfer to a paper-towel lined plate to drain grease.
5. Make the remaining hashbrowns using the remaining ingredients.
6. Serve warm.

Nutrition: Calories 265 Fats 11. 9g Carbs 36. 7g Protein 5. 3g

VEGAN RECIPES BREAKFAST

338. <u>Veggie Casserole</u>

Preparation Time: 25 minutes
Cooking Time: 45 minutes
Serving: 4
Ingredients:
- 1 lb. okra, trimmed
- 3 tomatoes, cut into wedges
- 3 garlic cloves, chopped
- 1 cup fresh parsley leaves, finely cut

Directions:
1. In a deep ovenproof baking dish, combine okra, sliced tomatoes, olive oil and garlic. Add in salt and black pepper to taste, and toss to combine. Bake in a prepared oven at 350 F for 45 minutes. Garnish with parsley and serve.

Nutrition: 302 calories 13g fat 6g protein

339. <u>Avocado and Olive Paste on Toasted Rye Bread (FAST)</u>

Preparation Time: 5 minutes
Cooking Time: 0 minute
Serving: 4
Ingredients:
- 1 avocado, halved, peeled and finely chopped
- 1 tbsp. green onions, finely chopped
- 2 tbsp. green olive paste
- 4 lettuce leaves
- 1 tbsp. lemon juice

Directions:
1. Crush avocados with a fork or potato masher until almost smooth. Add the onions, green olive paste and lemon juice. Season with salt and pepper to taste. Stir to combine.
2. Toast 4 slices of rye bread until golden. Spoon 1/4 of the avocado mixture onto each slice of bread, top with a lettuce leaf and serve.

Nutrition: 291 calories 13g fat 3g protein

340. <u>Vegan Muffins Breakfast Sandwich (FAST)</u>

Preparation Time: 10 minutes
Cooking Time: 20 minutes
Servings: 2
Ingredients:
- Romesco Sauce: 3-4 tablespoons
- Fresh baby spinach: ½ cup
- Tofu Scramble: 2
- Vegan English muffins: 2
- Avocado: ½ peeled and sliced
- Sliced fresh tomato: 1

Directions:
1. In the oven, toast English muffin
2. Half the muffin and spread romesco sauce
3. Paste spinach to one side, tailed by avocado slices
4. Have warm tofu followed by a tomato slice
5. Place the other muffin half onto the preceding one

Nutrition: Carbs: 18g Protein: 12g Fats: 14g Calories: 276

341. <u>Vegan Breakfast Skillet (FAST)</u>

Preparation Time: 3 minutes
Cooking Time: 5 minutes
Servings: 4
Ingredients:
- 3 tbsp. Olive Oil
- 400 g Firm Tofu, drained and crumbled
- 20 g Chickpeas
- 100 g Spinach
- 1 tbsp. Garlic Powder
- 1 tsp Paprika
- ½ tsp Turmeric Powder
- ¼ tsp Salt
- ¼ tsp Pepper

Directions:
1. Heat olive oil in a skillet.
2. Add crumbled tofu and stir for 2-3 minutes. Stir in all the spices.
3. Add chickpeas and spinach – sauté for another minute. Serve hot.

Nutrition: Calories: 271 / Fat: 19 g / Protein: 18 g / Carbs: 10 g

342. <u>Vegan Breakfast Hash (FAST)</u>

Preparation Time: 15 minutes
Cooking Time: 5 minutes
Servings: 4
Ingredients:
- 1 cup Cooked Quinoa
- 1 cup Shredded Broccoli

- 2 tbsp. Flax Seed
- ½ cup Coconut Flour
- 1 tsp Garlic Powder
- 1 tsp Onion Powder
- 2 tbsp. Coconut Oil

Directions:
1. Stir flax seeds with half a cup of water in a large mixing bowl. Leave for a few minutes. Stir in all remaining ingredients.
2. From the mixture into patties.
3. Heat vegetable oil in a pan.
4. Fry the patties for 2-3 minutes per side.

Nutrition: Calories: 135 / Fat: 10 g / Protein: 3 g / Carbs: 10 g

343. Tofu and Spinach Frittata (FAST)

Preparation Time: 15 minutes
Cooking Time: 5 minutes
Servings: 4
Ingredients:
- 400 g Firm Tofu
- 2 tbsp. tamari
- 2 tbsp. Nutritional Yeast
- 1 tsp Turmeric
- 1 tbsp. Garlic Powder
- 2 cups Baby Spinach, chopped
- 1 Red Bell Pepper, chopped
- 2 tbsp. Olive Oil

Directions:
- Combine tofu, tamari, nutritional yeast, turmeric, and garlic powder in a food processor. Blend until smooth.
- Fold in the spinach and bell pepper into the mixture. Brush an iron skillet with olive oil.
- Pour the mixture into the skillet.
- Bake for 25 minutes at 360F.

Nutrition: Calories: 236 / Fat: 16 g / Protein: 18 g / Carbs: 9 g

344. Cauliflower Fritters

Preparation Time: 10 minutes
Cooking Time: 50 minutes
Servings: 4
Ingredients:
- 30 ounces canned chickpeas, drained and rinsed
- 2 and ½ tablespoons olive oil
- 1 small yellow onion, chopped
- 2 cups cauliflower florets chopped
- 2 tablespoons garlic, minced

Directions:
1. Lay out half of the chickpeas on a baking sheet lined with parchment pepper, add 1

tablespoon oil, season with salt and pepper, toss and bake at 400 degrees F for 30 minutes.
2. Transfer the chickpeas to a food processor, pulse well and put the mix into a bowl.
3. Heat a pan with the ½ tablespoon oil over medium-high heat, add the garlic and the onion and sauté for 3 minutes.
4. Add the cauliflower, cook for 6 minutes more, transfer this to a blender, add the rest of the chickpeas, pulse, pour over the crispy chickpeas mix from the bowl, stir and shape medium fritters out of this mix.
5. Heat a pan with the rest of the oil over medium-high heat, add the fritters, cook them for 3 minutes on each side, and serve breakfast.

Nutrition: 333 calories 12.6g fat 13.6g protein

345. Simple Vegan Breakfast Hash (FAST)

Preparation Time: 10 minutes
Cooking Time: 25 minutes
Servings: 4
Ingredients:
For Potatoes:
- 1 large sweet potato
- 3 medium potatoes
- 1 tablespoon onion powder
- 2 teaspoons sea salt
- 1 tablespoon garlic powder
- 1 teaspoon ground black pepper
- 1 teaspoon dried thyme
- 1/4 cup olive oil

For Skillet Mixture:
1. 1 medium onion
2. 5 cloves of garlic
3. ¼ teaspoon salt
4. ¼ teaspoon black pepper
5. 1 teaspoon olive oil

Directions:
1. Switch on the oven, then set it to 450 degrees F and let it preheat.
2. Meanwhile, take a casserole dish, add all the ingredients for the potatoes, toss, and then cook for 20 minutes, stirring halfway.
3. Meanwhile, take a skillet pan, place it over medium heat, add oil and when hot, cook onion and garlic, for 5 minutes, season well.When potatoes have roasted, add garlic and cooked onion mixture, stir, and serve.

Nutrition: 212 Calories 10g Fat 3g Protein

VEGETARIAN LUNCH

346. Pesto Pearled Barley

Preparation Time: 2 minutes
Cooking Time: 50 minutes
Servings: 4
Ingredients:
- 1 cup dried barley
- 2½ cups vegetable broth
- ½ cup Parm-y Kale Pesto

Directions:
1. In a medium saucepan, combine the barley and broth and bring to a boil. Cover, reduce the heat to low, and simmer for about 45 minutes, until tender. Remove from the stove and let stand for 5 minutes.
2. Fluff the barley, then gently fold in the pesto.
3. Scoop about ¾ cup into each of 4 single-compartment storage containers. Let cool before sealing the lids.

Nutrition: Calories: 237 Total fat: 6g Carbohydrates: 40g Fiber: 11g

347. Celery and Radish Soup (FAST)

Preparation time: 10 minutes
Cooking time: 20 minutes
Servings: 4
Ingredients:
- ½ pound radishes, cut into quarters
- 2 celery stalks, chopped
- 2 tablespoons olive oil
- 4 scallions, chopped
- 1 teaspoon fennel seeds, crushed
- 1 teaspoon coriander, dried
- 6 cups vegetable stock
- Salt and black pepper to the taste
- 6 garlic cloves, minced
- 1 tablespoon chives, chopped

Directions:
1. Heat up a pot with the oil over medium heat, add the celery, scallions and the garlic and sauté for 5 minutes.
2. Add the radishes and the other ingredients, bring to a boil, cover and simmer for 15 minutes.
3. Divide into soup bowls and serve.

Nutrition: calories 120, fat 2, fiber 1, carbs 3, protein 10

348. Watercress Bowls (FAST)

Preparation time: 10 minutes
Cooking time: 0 minutes

Servings: 4
Ingredients:
- 1 cup watercress
- ¼ cup grapes, halved
- ½ cup cherry tomatoes, halved
- 1 tablespoon almonds, chopped
- 1 tablespoon chives, chopped
- ¼ cup baby spinach
- 2 tablespoons avocado oil
- 2 tablespoons lime juice

Directions:
1. In a bowl, combine the watercress with the grapes and the other ingredients, toss well, divide into smaller bowls and serve.

Nutrition: calories 28, fat 1.8, fiber 1, carbs 2.7, protein 1

349. Arugula Tomato Salad (FAST)

Preparation Time: 20 minutes
Servings: 2
Ingredients:
- 4 tablespoons olive oil
- 1 cup cherry tomatoes, halved
- 3 cups arugula, washed, drained
- 1 small red onion, chopped
- 4 tablespoons capers, canned, drained
- 2 tablespoons basil, fresh, chopped

Directions:
1. Add all ingredients into mixing bowl and toss. Serve fresh and enjoy!

Nutritional Values (Per Serving): Calories: 262 Fat: 26.7 g Carbohydrates: 6 g Sugar: 3.1 g Protein: 2.1 g Cholesterol: 0 mg

350. Steamed Cauliflower (FAST)

Preparation Time: 5 minutes
Cooking Time: 10 minutes
Servings: 4
Ingredients:
- 1 large head cauliflower
- 1 cup water
- ½ teaspoon salt
- 1 teaspoon red pepper flakes (optional)

Directions:
1. Remove any leaves from the cauliflower and cut it into florets.
2. In a large saucepan, bring the water to a boil. Place a steamer basket over the water and add the florets and salt. Cover and steam for 5 to 7 minutes, until tender.

3. In a large bowl, toss the cauliflower with the red pepper flakes (if using).
4. Transfer the florets to a large airtight container or 6 single-serving containers. Let cool before sealing the lids.

Nutrition: Calories: 35 Total fat: 0g Carbohydrates: 7g Fiber: 4g

351. Coconut Zucchini Cream (FAST)

Preparation time: 10 minutes
Cooking time: 25 minutes
Servings: 4
Ingredients:
- 1-pound zucchinis, roughly chopped
- 2 tablespoons avocado oil
- 4 scallions, chopped
- Salt and black pepper to the taste
- 6 cups veggie stock
- 1 teaspoon basil, dried
- 1 teaspoon cumin, ground
- 3 garlic cloves, minced
- ¾ cup coconut cream
- 1 tablespoon dill, chopped

Directions:
1. Heat up a pot with the oil over medium high heat, add the scallions and the garlic and sauté for 5 minutes.
2. Add the rest of the ingredients, stir, bring to a simmer and cook over medium heat for 20 minutes more.
3. Blend the soup using an immersion blender, ladle into bowls and serve.

Nutrition: calories 160, fat 4, fiber 2, carbs 4, protein 8

352. Zucchini and Cauliflower Soup (FAST)

Preparation time: 10 minutes
Cooking time: 25 minutes
Servings: 4
Ingredients:
- 4 scallions, chopped
- 1 teaspoon ginger, grated
- 2 tablespoons olive oil
- 1-pound zucchinis, sliced
- 2 cups cauliflower florets
- Salt and black pepper to the taste
- 6 cups veggie stock
- 1 garlic clove, minced
- 1 tablespoon lemon juice
- 1 cup coconut cream

Directions:
1. Heat up a pot with the oil over medium heat, add the scallions, ginger and the garlic and sauté for 5 minutes.

2. Add the rest of the ingredients, bring to a simmer and cook over medium heat for 20 minutes.
3. Blend everything using an immersion blender, ladle into soup bowls and serve.

Nutrition: calories 154, fat 12, fiber 3, carbs 5, protein 4

353. Chard Soup (FAST)

Preparation time: 10 minutes
Cooking time: 25 minutes
Servings: 4
Ingredients:
- 1-pound Swiss chard, chopped
- ½ cup shallots, chopped
- 1 tablespoon avocado oil
- 1 teaspoon cumin, ground
- 1 teaspoon rosemary, dried
- 1 teaspoon basil, dried
- 2 garlic cloves, minced
- Salt and black pepper to the taste
- 6 cups vegetable stock
- 1 tablespoon tomato passata
- 1 tablespoon cilantro, chopped

Directions:
1. Heat up a pan with the oil over medium heat, add the shallots and the garlic and sauté for 5 minutes.
2. Add the Swiss chard and the other ingredients, toss, bring to a simmer and cook over medium heat for 20 minutes more.
3. Divide the soup into bowls and serve.

Nutrition: calories 232, fat 23, fiber 3, carbs 4, protein 3

354. Lime Avocado and Cucumber Soup (FAST)

Preparation time: 5 minutes
Cooking time: 0 minutes
Servings: 4
Ingredients:
- 2 avocados, pitted, peeled and roughly cubed
- 2 cucumbers, sliced
- 4 cups vegetable stock
- Salt and black pepper to the taste
- ¼ teaspoon lemon zest, grated
- 1 tablespoon white vinegar
- 1 cup scallions, chopped
- 1 tablespoon olive oil
- ¼ cup cilantro, chopped

Directions:
1. In a blender, combine the avocados with the cucumbers and the other ingredients,

pulse well, divide into bowls and serve for lunch.

Nutrition: calories 100, fat 10, fiber 2, carbs 5, protein 8

355. Avocado and Kale Soup (FAST)

Preparation time: 5 minutes
Cooking time: 7 minutes
Servings: 4
Ingredients:
- 4 cups kale, torn
- 1 teaspoon turmeric powder
- 1 avocado, pitted, peeled and sliced
- 4 cups vegetable stock
- Juice of 1 lime
- 2 garlic cloves, minced
- 1 tablespoon chives, chopped
- Salt and black pepper to the taste

Directions:
1. In a pot, combine the kale with the avocado and the other ingredients, bring to a simmer, cook over medium heat for 7 minutes, blend using an immersion blender, divide into bowls and serve.

Nutrition: calories 234, fat 12, fiber 4, carbs 7, protein 12

Greens and Vinaigrette (FAST)
Preparation time: 10 minutes
Cooking time: 0 minutes
Servings: 4
Ingredients:
- 1 cup baby kale
- 1 cup baby arugula
- 1 cup romaine lettuce
- 2 tomatoes, cubed
- 1 cucumber, cubed
- 3 tablespoons lime juice
- 1/3 cup olive oil
- 1 tablespoon balsamic vinegar
- Salt and black pepper to the taste

Directions:
1. In a bowl, combine the oil with the vinegar, lime juice, salt and pepper and whisk well.
2. In another bowl, combine the greens with the vinaigrette, toss and serve right away.

Nutrition: calories 112, fat 9, fiber 2, carbs 6, protein 2

356. Mushroom and Mustard Greens Mix (FAST)

Preparation time: 10 minutes
Cooking time: 20 minutes
Servings: 4

Ingredients:
- 1-pound white mushrooms, halved
- 2 cups mustard greens
- 1 tablespoon lime juice
- 3 scallions, chopped
- 2 tablespoons olive oil
- 1 teaspoon sweet paprika
- 1 teaspoon rosemary, dried
- 2 bunches parsley, chopped
- 3 garlic cloves, minced
- Salt and black pepper to the taste

Directions:
1. Heat up a pan with the oil over medium heat, add the scallions, paprika, garlic and parsley and sauté for 5 minutes.
2. Add the mushrooms and the other ingredients, toss, cook over medium heat for 15 minutes, divide between plates and serve.

Nutrition: calories 76, fat 1, fiber 2, carbs 3, protein 3

357. Mustard Greens and Kale Mix (FAST)

Preparation time: 10 minutes
Cooking time: 10 minutes
Servings: 4
Ingredients:
- 1 pound mustard greens
- ½ pound kale, torn
- 2 celery stalks, chopped
- 2 tablespoons avocado oil
- 1 cup tomatoes, cubed
- 2 avocados, peeled, pitted and cubed
- 1 cup coconut cream
- 2 tablespoons lemon juice
- 2 garlic cloves minced
- 2 tablespoons parsley, chopped
- A pinch of salt and black pepper

Directions:
1. Heat up a pan with the oil over medium heat, add the mustard greens, kale, celery and the other ingredients, toss, cook for 10 minutes, divide between plates and serve warm.

Nutrition: calories 200, fat 4, fiber 8, carbs 16, protein 7

358. Mashed Potatoes and Kale with White Beans

Preparation Time: 10 minutes
Cooking Time: 30 minutes
Servings: 4
Ingredients:
- 2 large Russet potatoes
- Pinch salt (optional), plus ½ teaspoon

- ½ cup vegetable broth
- 6 ounces kale, torn into bite-size pieces
- 1 (14.5-ounce) can great northern beans or other white beans, rinsed and drained
- ¼ to ½ teaspoon freshly ground black pepper, to taste

Directions:
1. Wash (but don't peel!) the potatoes, quarter them, then halve each quarter. Place in a large pot and cover with water. Add a pinch of salt (if using) and bring to a boil. Cover, reduce the heat to medium, and cook for about 20 minutes until the potatoes are tender.
2. Drain the potatoes and return to the pot. Pour the vegetable broth over the potatoes. Add the kale and then the beans. Cover and cook on low heat for about 5 minutes, until the kale turns bright green and is lightly wilted.
3. Use a potato masher to mash everything together, and season with ½ teaspoon salt and pepper.
4. Divide the potatoes, kale, and beans evenly among 4 single-serving containers. Let cool before sealing the lids.

Nutrition: Calories: 255 Total fat: 1g Carbohydrates: 53g Fiber: 11g

359. Roasted Jalapeño and Lime Guacamole (FAST)

Preparation Time: 5 minutes
Cooking Time: 10 minutes
Servings: 4
Ingredients:
- 1 to 3 jalapeños (depending on your preferred level of spiciness)
- 1 avocado, peeled and pitted
- 1 tablespoon freshly squeezed lime juice

Directions:
1. Preheat the oven to 400°F. Line a baking sheet with parchment paper.
2. Place the jalapeños on the baking sheet and roast for 8 minutes. (The jalapeño can also be roasted on a grill for 5 minutes if you already have it fired up.)
3. Slice the jalapeños and remove the seeds. Cut the top stem and dice into 1/8-inch pieces. Wash your hands immediately after handling the jalapeños.
4. Use a fork or a masher to mash together the avocado, jalapeño pieces, and lime juice and in a medium bowl. Mash and mix until the

guacamole has the preferred consistency. Then serve and enjoy!

Nutrition: Calories: 77 Total fat: 7g Carbohydrates: 5g Fiber: 3g Protein: 1g

360. Arugula and Artichokes Bowls (FAST)

Preparation time: 5 minutes
Cooking time: 0 minutes
Servings: 4
Ingredients:
- 2 cups baby arugula
- ¼ cup walnuts, chopped
- 1 cup canned artichoke hearts, drained and quartered
- 1 tablespoon balsamic vinegar
- 2 tablespoons cilantro, chopped
- 2 tablespoons olive oil
- Salt and black pepper to the taste
- 1 tablespoon lemon juice

Directions:
1. In a bowl, combine the artichokes with the arugula, walnuts and the other ingredients, toss, divide into smaller bowls and serve for lunch.

Nutrition: calories 200, fat 2, fiber 1, carbs 5, protein 7

361. Spinach and Broccoli Soup (FAST)

Preparation time: 10 minutes
Cooking time: 20 minutes
Servings: 4
Ingredients:
- 3 shallots, chopped
- 1 tablespoon olive oil
- 2 garlic cloves, minced
- ½ pound broccoli florets
- ½ pound baby spinach
- Salt and black pepper to the taste
- 4 cups veggie stock
- 1 teaspoon turmeric powder
- 1 tablespoon lime juice

Directions:
1. Heat up a pot with the oil over medium high heat, add the shallots and the garlic and sauté for 5 minutes.
2. Add the broccoli, spinach and the other ingredients, toss, bring to a simmer and cook over medium heat for 15 minutes.
3. Ladle into soup bowls and serve.

Nutrition: calories 150, fat 3, fiber 1, carbs 3, protein 7

362. Tomato-Pasta (FAST)

Preparation Time: 5 minutes
Cooking Time: 10 minutes
Servings: 4

Ingredients:

- 7 oz. pasta
- 1 diced avocado
- 14 oz. cherry tomatoes halved or quartered
- 4 tbsp. vinaigrette
- 1 clove garlic 7

Directions:

1. Cook pasta base on the instructions of the packaging. Add the garlic to infuse the taste.
2. Drain the pasta slowly and remove the garlic. In a bowl, mix the avocado and tomatoes, and lightly toss in the vinaigrette. Mash the garlic and add it to the avocado mixture.
3. Drizzle a little olive oil all over the pasta. Mix the avocado mixture into the pasta and serve immediately.

Nutrition: Calories: 371 Total fat: 51g Carbohydrates: 11g Fiber: 16g

363. Braised Cabbage (FAST)

Preparation Time: 10 minutes
Cooking Time: 10 minutes
Servings: 3
Ingredients:

- 14 oz. chopped cabbage
- 1 onion cut into rings
- 2 peeled and diced tomatoes
- Olive oil for cooking

Directions:

1. Put olive oil in a frying pan and turn it over medium heat. Sauté the onion rings for 3 minutes until soft and starting to brown.
2. Add the tomatoes and braise for another 3 minutes. Reduce the heat and add the cabbage. Stir fry for another 4 minutes until the cabbage softens.
3. Serve while still warm.

Nutrition: Calories: 90 Total fat: 20g Carbohydrates: 1g Fiber: 1g

364. Veggie Beef Ramen (FAST)

Preparation Time: 10 minutes
Cooking Time: 15 minutes
Servings: 5–6
Ingredients

- 1 package mushroom flavor ramen noodles
- packages chicken flavor ramen noodles
- 1 pound ground beef
- ¼ teaspoon garlic powder
- ¼ teaspoon dried thyme
- cups frozen mixed vegetables
- cups water

Directions

1. Remove the flavor packets from the ramen packs and set aside. Break the noodles into small chunks.
2. Add the beef to a large skillet and stir-cook over medium-high heat until no longer pink.
3. Remove the fat and add the mushroom flavor packet to the skillet; combine and cook for 2 minutes. Set aside the cooked beef mix.
4. Add the water to the skillet and boil it. Add the noodles, thyme, garlic power and veggies along with the chicken flavor packets.
5. Combine and boil the mixture.
6. Turn down heat to low. Cover and allow the mixture to simmer for a few minutes until the pasta is cooked to your satisfaction.
7. Add the beef mix and stir the mixture. Serve warm.

Nutrition: Calories 410 Fat 14 G Carbs 45 G Protein 23 G, Sodium 483 Mg

365. Honey Roasted Cauliflower

Preparation Time: 10 minutes
Cooking Time: 35 minutes
Servings: 4
Ingredients:

- 2 cups cauliflower
- 2 tablespoons diced onion
- 2 tablespoons olive oil
- 1 tablespoon honey
- 1 teaspoon dry mustard
- 1 pinch salt
- 1 pinch ground black pepper

Directions:

1. Preheat oven to 375 degrees F. Lightly coat an 11x7 inch baking dish with non-stick cooking spray.
2. Place cauliflower in a single layer in prepared dish, and top with onion. In a small bowl, combine olive oil, honey, mustard, salt and pepper; drizzle over cauliflower and onion.
3. Bake in the preheated 375 degrees F oven for 35 minutes or until tender, stirring halfway through the cooking time.

Nutrition: Calories 88, Total Fat 7.3g, Saturated Fat 1g, Cholesterol 0mg, Sodium 47mg, Total Carbohydrate 6.4g, Dietary Fiber 0.9g, Total Sugars 5.2g, Protein 0.8g

366. Broccoli Steaks (FAST)

Preparation Time: 10 minutes
Cooking Time: 25 minutes
Servings: 4
Ingredients:

- 1 medium head broccoli
- 3 tablespoons unsalted butter
- 1/4 teaspoon garlic powder

- 1/4 teaspoon onion powder
- 1/8 teaspoon salt
- ¼ teaspoon pepper

Directions:
1. Preheat the oven to 400 degrees F. Please parchment paper on a roasting pan.
2. Trim the leaves off the broccoli and cut off the bottom of the stem. Cut the broccoli head in half. Cut each half into 1 to 3/4-inch slices, leaving the core in place. Cut off the smaller ends of the broccoli and save for another recipe. There should be 4 broccoli steaks.
3. Mix butter, garlic powder, onion powder, salt and pepper.
4. Lay the broccoli on the parchment lined baking sheet. Using half of the butter mixture, brush onto the steaks. Place in the preheated oven for 20 minutes. Remove from the oven and flip the steaks over. Brush steaks with remaining butter and roast for about 20 more minutes, until they are golden brown on the edges.

Nutrition: Calories 86, Total Fat 8.7g, Saturated Fat 5.5g, Cholesterol 23mg, Sodium 143mg, Total Carbohydrate 1.9g, Dietary Fiber 0.7g, Total Sugars 0.5g, Protein 0.8g

367. Broccoli with Garlic Sauce (FAST)

Preparation Time: 10 minutes
Cooking Time: 15 minutes
Servings: 4
Ingredients:
- 2 cups broccoli florets
- 1 garlic clove
- 1/2 tablespoon butter
- 2 teaspoons honey
- 1-1/2 tablespoons apple cider vinegar
- 1 tablespoon fresh parsley

Directions:
1. In a large saucepan with steamer rack, steam broccoli over boiling water 8 to 10 minutes or until crisp-tender (cover with lid while steaming).
2. In a small saucepan, cook minced garlic in butter for 30 seconds then remove pan from heat.
3. Stir in honey, apple cider vinegar and chopped parsley. Return saucepan to heat until sauce is heated.
4. Transfer steamed broccoli to a serving dish.
5. Pour sauce over hot broccoli and toss to coat.

Nutrition: Calories 41, Total Fat 1.6g, Saturated Fat 0.9g, Cholesterol 4mg, Sodium 26mg, Total Carbohydrate 6.2g, Dietary Fiber 1.2g, Total Sugars 3.7g, Protein 1.4g

368. Cranberry Cabbage (FAST)

Preparation Time: 10 minutes
Cooking Time: 15 minutes
Servings: 4
Ingredients:
- 8 ounces canned whole-berry cranberry sauce
- 1 tablespoon fresh lemon juice
- 1/4 teaspoon ground cloves
- 1 medium head red cabbage

Directions:
1. In large pan heat cranberry sauce, lemon juice and cloves together and bring to a simmer.
2. Stir cabbage into melted cranberry sauce, mixing well. Bring mixture to a boil; reduce heat to simmer. Continue cooking until cabbage is tender, stirring occasionally.
3. Serve hot.

Nutrition: Calories 38, Total Fat 0.1g, Saturated Fat 0g, Cholesterol 0mg, Sodium 20mg, Total Carbohydrate 7.9g, Dietary Fiber 2.6g, Total Sugars 3.8g, Protein 1g

369. Larb Salad (FAST)

Preparation Time: 5 Minutes
Cooking Time: 4-5 Minutes
Servings: 4
Ingredients
- 1 teaspoon oil
- 1 package extra-firm tofu, pressed to remove excess water and crumbled
- Juice of 2 limes, divided
- ¼ cup thinly sliced shallots
- 1 scallion, thinly sliced
- cilantro sprigs, sliced
- tablespoons soy sauce
- 1 or 2 mint sprigs, chopped
- ¾ teaspoon ground dried Thai chiles (or red pepper flakes)
- lettuce leaves (iceberg or romaine), for serving

Directions
1. Heat the oil in a medium sauté pan over medium heat. Add the tofu and the juice of ½ lime, and sauté for 4 to 5 minutes, until the tofu is light brown.
2. Place the tofu in a bowl and add the shallots, scallion, cilantro, soy sauce, mint, chiles, and the juice of the 1½ remaining limes. Mix well.
3. Spoon onto lettuce leaves and serve.

Nutrition: Calories: 96 Total fat: 5g Protein: 8g Sodium: 465mg Fiber: 2g

370. Zucchini Fries and Sauce (FAST)

Preparation time: 10 minutes
Cooking time: 25 minutes

Servings: 4

Ingredients:

- 1-pound zucchinis, cut into fries
- 2 tablespoons olive oil
- ½ teaspoon rosemary, dried
- 3 scallions, chopped
- 2 teaspoons smoked paprika
- A pinch of sea salt and black pepper
- 1 cup coconut cream
- 1 tablespoon balsamic vinegar
- ½ teaspoon garlic powder
- 2 tablespoons cilantro, chopped

Directions:

1. Arrange the zucchini fries on a baking sheet lined with parchment paper, add half of the oil, paprika, garlic powder, salt and pepper, toss and bake in the oven at 425 degrees F for 12 minutes.
2. Heat up a pan with the rest of the oil over medium heat, add the scallions and sauté for 3 minutes.
3. Add the cream and the remaining ingredients, toss, and cook over medium heat for 10 minutes more.
4. Divide the zucchini fries between plates, drizzle the sauce all over and serve.

Nutrition: calories 140, fat 5, fiber 2, carbs 20, protein 6

371. Chard and Garlic Sauce (FAST)

Preparation time: 10 minutes
Cooking time: 15 minutes
Servings: 4

Ingredients:

- ½ cup walnuts, chopped
- 4 cups red chard, torn
- 3 tablespoons olive oil
- Juice of 1 lime
- 1 celery stalks, chopped
- 1 cup coconut cream
- 4 garlic cloves, minced
- 1 tablespoon balsamic vinegar
- 2/3 cup scallions, chopped
- A pinch of sea salt and black pepper

Directions:

1. Heat up a pan with the oil over medium heat, add the scallions, garlic and the celery and sauté for 5 minutes.
2. Add the chard and the other ingredients, toss, cook over medium heat for 10 minutes more, divide between plates and serve.

Nutrition: calories 374, fat 34.2, fiber 6.7, carbs 15.4, protein 9

372. Collard Greens and Garlic Mix (FAST)

Preparation time: 10 minutes
Cooking time: 10 minutes
Servings: 4

Ingredients:

- 2 tablespoons avocado oil
- 4 garlic cloves, minced
- 4 bunches collard greens
- 1 tomato, cubed
- A pinch of sea salt and black pepper
- Black pepper to the taste
- 1 tablespoon almonds, chopped

Directions:

1. Heat up a pan with the oil over medium heat, add the garlic, collard greens and the other ingredients, toss well, cook for 10 minutes, divide into bowls and serve.

Nutrition: calories 130, fat 1, fiber 8, carbs 10, protein 6

373. Veggie Hash (FAST)

Preparation time: 10 minutes
Cooking time: 20 minutes
Servings: 4

Ingredients:

- 1 bunch asparagus, chopped
- 2 cups radishes, halved
- ½ cup mushrooms, halved
- 3 tablespoons olive oil
- 1 shallot, chopped
- ½ cup roasted bell peppers, chopped
- 2 garlic cloves, minced
- A pinch of salt and black pepper
- 1 tablespoon chives, chopped
- 1 tablespoon sage, chopped

Directions:

1. Heat up a pan with the oil over medium heat, add the shallot and the garlic and sauté for 5 minutes.
2. Add the mushrooms and sauté for 5 minutes more.
3. Add the rest of the ingredients, toss, cook everything over medium heat for another 10 minutes, divide into bowls and serve.

Nutrition: calories 135, fat 2, fiber 4, carbs 5.4, protein 5

374. Vinegar Cucumber, Olives and Shallots Salad (FAST)

Preparation time: 10 minutes
Cooking time: 0 minutes
Servings: 4

Ingredients:

- 1-pound cucumbers, sliced

- 1 cup black olives, pitted and sliced
- 3 tablespoons shallots, chopped
- ¼ cup balsamic vinegar
- 1 tablespoon dill, chopped
- A pinch of salt and black pepper
- 3 tablespoons avocado oil

Directions:
1. In a bowl, mix the cucumbers with the olives, shallots and the other ingredients, toss well, divide between plates and serve.

Nutrition: calories 120, fat 3, fiber 2, carbs 5, protein 10

375. Lemony Kale Salad

Preparation Time: 10 minutes
Cooking Time: 30 minutes
Servings: 4
Ingredients:
- 2 tablespoons freshly squeezed lemon juice
- ½ tablespoon maple syrup
- 1 teaspoon minced garlic
- 5 cups chopped kale

Directions:
1. Add the lemon juice, maple syrup, and garlic together in a large bowl. Add the kale, massage it in the dressing for 1 to 2 minutes, and serve.
2. Preparation Tip: Make sure to thoroughly massage the kale with the dressing ingredients. This will give the kale a beautiful texture and get the lemon and garlic flavors properly incorporated.

Nutrition: Calories: 51 Fat: 0g Carbohydrates: 11g Fiber: 1g

376. Sautéed Collard Greens (FAST)

Preparation Time: 10 minutes
Cooking Time: 25 minutes
Servings: 4
Ingredients:
- 1½ pounds collard greens
- 1 cup vegetable broth
- ½ teaspoon garlic powder
- ½ teaspoon onion powder
- 1/8 teaspoon freshly ground black pepper

Directions:
1. Remove the hard middle stems from the greens, then roughly chop the leaves into 2-inch pieces.
2. In a large saucepan, mix together the vegetable broth, garlic powder, onion powder, and pepper. Bring to a boil over medium-high heat, then add the chopped greens. Reduce the heat to low and cover.

3. Cook for 20 minutes, stirring well every 4 to 5 minutes, and serve.

Nutrition: Calories: 28 Total fat: 1g Carbohydrates: 4g Fiber: 2g Protein: 3g

377. French Fries

Preparation Time: 10 minutes
Cooking Time: 60 minutes
Servings: 6
Ingredients:
- 2 pounds medium white potatoes
- 1 to 2 tablespoons no-salt seasoning

Directions:
1. Preheat the oven to 400°F. Line a baking sheet with parchment paper.
2. Wash and scrub potatoes and place them on the baking sheet and bake for 45 minutes.
3. Remove potatoes from the oven. Allow to cool in the refrigerator for about 30 minutes, or until you're ready to make a batch of fries.
4. Preheat the oven to 425°F. Line a baking sheet with parchment paper.
5. Slice the cooled potatoes into the shape of wedges or fries, then toss them in a large bowl with the no-salt seasoning.
6. Spread the coated fries out in an even layer on the baking sheet. Bake for about 7 minutes, then remove from the oven, flip the fries over, and redistribute them in an even layer. Bake again for another 8 minutes, or until the fries are crisp and golden brown, and serve.

Nutrition: Calories: 104 Total fat: 0g Carbohydrates: 24g Fiber: 4g Protein: 3g

378. Eggplant and Peppers Soup

Preparation time: 10 minutes
Cooking time: 40 minutes
Servings: 4
Ingredients:
- 2 red bell peppers, chopped
- 3 scallions, chopped
- 3 garlic cloves, minced
- 2 tablespoon olive oil
- Salt and black pepper to the taste
- 5 cups vegetable stock
- 1 bay leaf
- ½ cup coconut cream
- 1-pound eggplants, roughly cubed
- 2 tablespoons basil, chopped

Directions:
1. Heat up a pot with the oil over medium heat, add the scallions and the garlic and sauté for 5 minutes.
2. Add the peppers and the eggplants and sauté for 5 minutes more.
3. Add the remaining ingredients, toss, bring to a simmer, cook for 30 minutes, ladle into bowls and serve for lunch.

Nutrition: calories 180, fat 2, fiber 3, carbs 5, protein 10

379. Eggplant and Olives Stew

Preparation time: 10 minutes
Cooking time: 30 minutes
Servings: 4
Ingredients:
- 2 scallions, chopped
- 2 tablespoons avocado oil
- 2 garlic cloves, chopped
- 1 bunch parsley, chopped
- Salt and black pepper to the taste
- 1 teaspoon basil, dried
- 1 teaspoon cumin, dried
- 2 eggplants, roughly cubed
- 1 cup green olives, pitted and sliced
- 3 tablespoons balsamic vinegar
- ½ cup tomato passata

Directions:
1. Heat up a pot with the oil over medium heat, add the scallions, garlic, basil and cumin and sauté for 5 minutes.
2. Add the eggplants and the other ingredients, toss, cook over medium heat for 25 minutes more, divide into bowls and serve.

Nutrition: calories 93, fat 1.8, fiber 10.6, carbs 18.6, protein 3.4

380. Cauliflower and Artichokes Soup (FAST)

Preparation time: 10 minutes
Cooking time: 25 minutes
Servings: 4
Ingredients:
- 1 pound cauliflower florets
- 1 cup canned artichoke hearts, drained and chopped
- 2 scallions, chopped
- 2 tablespoons olive oil
- 2 garlic cloves, minced
- 6 cups vegetable stock
- Salt and black pepper to the taste
- 2/3 cup coconut cream
- 2 tablespoons cilantro, chopped

Directions:
1. Heat up a pot with the oil over medium heat, add the scallions and the garlic and sauté for 5 minutes.
2. Add the cauliflower and the other ingredients, toss, bring to a simmer and cook over medium heat for 20 minutes more.
3. Blend the soup using an immersion blender, divide it into bowls and serve.

Nutrition: calories 207, fat 17.2, fiber 6.2, carbs 14.1, protein 4.7

381. Avocado, Pine Nuts and Chard Salad (FAST)

Preparation time: 5 minutes
Cooking time: 15 minutes
Servings: 4
Ingredients:
- 1-pound Swiss chard, roughly chopped
- 2 tablespoons olive oil
- 1 avocado, peeled, pitted and roughly cubed
- 2 spring onions, chopped
- ¼ cup pine nuts, toasted
- 1 tablespoon balsamic vinegar
- Salt and black pepper to the taste

Directions:
1. Heat up a pan with the oil over medium heat, add the spring onions, pine nuts and the chard, stir and sauté for 5 minutes.
2. Add the vinegar and the other ingredients, toss, cook over medium heat for 10 minutes more, divide into bowls and serve for lunch.

Nutrition: calories 120, fat 2, fiber 1, carbs 4, protein 8

382. Grapes, Avocado and Spinach Salad (FAST)

Preparation time: 10 minutes
Cooking time: 0 minutes
Servings: 4
Ingredients:
- 1 cup green grapes, halved
- 2 cups baby spinach
- 1 avocado, pitted, peeled and cubed
- Salt and black pepper to the taste
- 2 tablespoons olive oil
- 1 tablespoon thyme, chopped
- 1 tablespoon rosemary, chopped
- 1 tablespoon lime juice
- 1 garlic clove, minced

Directions:
1. In a salad bowl, combine the grapes with the spinach and the other ingredients, toss, and serve for lunch.

Nutrition: calories 190, fat 17.1, fiber 4.6, carbs 10.9, protein 1.7

383. Hot Cranberries and Arugula Mix (FAST)

Preparation time: 10 minutes
Cooking time: 0 minutes
Servings: 4
Ingredients:
*   1 cup cranberries
*   2 cups baby arugula
*   1 avocado, peeled, pitted and cubed
*   1 cucumber, cubed
*   ¼ cup kalamata olives, pitted and sliced
*   1 tablespoon walnuts, chopped
*   2 tablespoons olive oil
*   2 tablespoons lime juice

Directions:
1. In a bowl, combine the arugula with the cranberries and the other ingredients, toss well, divide between plates and serve.

Nutrition: calories 110, fat 4, fiber 2, carbs 10, protein 2

384. Cinnamon Cauliflower Rice, Zucchinis. Spinach (FAST)

Preparation time: 10 minutes
Cooking time: 10 minutes
Servings: 4
Ingredients:
*   1 cup cauliflower rice
*   2 tablespoons olive oil
*   1 zucchini, sliced
*   1 cup baby spinach
*   ½ cup veggie stock
*   ½ teaspoon turmeric powder
*   ¼ teaspoon cinnamon powder
*   A pinch of sea salt and black pepper
*   1/3 cup dates, dried and chopped
*   1 tablespoon almonds, chopped
*   ¼ cup chives, chopped

Directions:
1. Heat up a pan with the oil over medium heat, add the cauliflower rice, dates, turmeric and cinnamon and sauté for 3 minutes.
2. Add the zucchini and the other ingredients, toss, cook the mix for 7 minutes more, divide between plates and serve.

Nutrition: calories 189, fat 2, fiber 2, carbs 20, protein 7

385. Asparagus, Bok Choy and Radish Mix (FAST)

Preparation time: 10 minutes
Cooking time: 12 minutes
Servings: 4
Ingredients:
*   ½ pound asparagus, trimmed and halved
*   1 cup bok choy, torn
*   1 cup radishes, halved
*   2 tablespoons balsamic vinegar
*   2 tablespoons olive oil
*   2 teaspoon Italian seasoning
*   2 teaspoons garlic powder
*   1 teaspoon coriander, ground
*   1 teaspoon fennel seeds, crushed
*   1 tablespoon chives, chopped

Directions:
1. Heat up a pan with the oil over medium heat, add the asparagus, bok choy, the radishes and the other ingredients, toss, cook for 12 minutes, divide between plates and serve.

Nutrition: calories 140, fat 1, fiber 10, carbs 20, protein 8

386. Kale and Cucumber Salad (FAST)

Preparation time: 10 minutes
Cooking time: 0 minutes
Servings: 4
Ingredients:
*   2 cups baby kale
*   2 cucumbers, sliced
*   2 tablespoons avocado oil
*   1 cup coconut cream
*   1 teaspoon balsamic vinegar
*   2 tablespoons dill, chopped

Directions:
1. In a bowl, combine the kale with the cucumbers and the other ingredients, toss and serve.

Nutrition: calories 90, fat 1, fiber 3, carbs 7, protein 2

387. Greens and Olives Pan (FAST)

Preparation time: 10 minutes
Cooking time: 15 minutes
Servings: 4
Ingredients:
*   4 spring onions, chopped
*   2 tablespoons olive oil
*   ½ cup green olives, pitted and halved
*   ¼ cup pine nuts, toasted
*   1 tablespoon balsamic vinegar
*   2 cups baby spinach

- 1 cup baby arugula
- 1 cup asparagus, trimmed, blanched and halved
- Salt and black pepper to the taste

Directions:
1. Heat up a pan with the oil over medium high heat, add the spring onions and the asparagus and sauté for 5 minutes.
2. Add the olives, spinach and the other ingredients, toss, cook over medium heat for 10 minutes, divide between plates and serve for lunch.

Nutrition: calories 136, fat 13.1, fiber 1.9, carbs 4.4, protein 2.8

388. Easy Vegan Pizza Bread (FAST)

Preparation Time: 5 minutes
Cooking Time: 20 minutes
Servings: 4
Ingredients:
- 1 whole-wheat loaf, unsliced
- 1 cup Easy One-Pot Vegan Marinara
- 1 teaspoon nutritional yeast
- ½ teaspoon onion powder
- ½ teaspoon garlic powder

Directions:
1. Preheat the oven to 375°F.
2. Halve the loaf of bread lengthwise. Evenly spread the marinara onto each slice of bread, then sprinkle on the nutritional yeast, onion powder, and garlic powder.
3. Place bread on a baking sheet. Bake for 20 minutes, or until the bread is a light golden brown.

Nutrition: Calories: 230 Total fat: 3g Carbohydrates: 38g Fiber: 7g Protein: 13g

389. Savory Sweet Potato Casserole (FAST)

Preparation Time: 15 minutes
Cooking Time: 30 minutes
Servings: 6
Ingredients:
- 8 sweet potatoes, cooked
- ½ cup vegetable broth
- 1 tablespoon dried sage
- 1 teaspoon dried thyme
- 1 teaspoon dried rosemary

Directions:
1. Preheat the oven to 375°F.
2. Peel the cooked sweet potatoes and put them in a baking dish. Mash sweet potatoes using a fork or potato masher. Then mix it in the broth, sage, thyme, and rosemary.

3. Bake for 30 minutes and serve.

Nutrition: Calories: 154 Total fat: 0g Carbohydrates: 35g Fiber: 6g Protein: 3g

390. White Bean and Chickpea Hummus (FAST)

Preparation Time: 5 minutes
Cooking Time: 30 minutes
Servings: 8
Ingredients:
- 1 (15-ounce) can chickpeas
- 1 (15-ounce) can white beans (cannellini or great northern)
- 3 tablespoons freshly squeezed lemon juice
- 2 teaspoons garlic powder
- 1 teaspoon onion powder

Directions:
1. Prepare the chickpeas and white beans. Make sure to drain and rinse.
2. In a food processor or blender, combine the chickpeas, beans, lemon juice, garlic powder, and onion powder. Process for 1 to 2 minutes, or until the texture is smooth and creamy.
3. Serve right away, or store in a refrigerator-safe container for up to 5 days.

Nutrition: Calories: 69 Total fat: 1g Carbohydrates: 12g Fiber: 4g Protein: 4g

391. Avocado and Cauliflower Hummus (FAST)

Preparation Time: 5 minutes
Cooking Time: 25 minutes
Servings: 2
Ingredients:
- 1 medium cauliflower, stem removed and chopped
- 1 large Hass avocado, peeled, pitted, and chopped
- ¼ cup extra virgin olive oil
- 2 garlic cloves
- 1/2 tbsp. lemon juice
- 1/2 tsp. onion powder
- Sea salt and ground black pepper to taste
- 2 large carrots
- 1/4 cup fresh cilantro, chopped

Directions:
1. Preheat the oven to 450°F, and line a baking tray with aluminum foil.
2. Put the chopped cauliflower on the baking tray and drizzle with 2 tablespoons of olive oil.
3. Roast the chopped cauliflower in the oven for 20-25 minutes, until lightly brown.

4. Remove the tray from the oven and allow the cauliflower to cool down.
5. Add all the ingredients—except the carrots and optional fresh cilantro—to a food processor or blender, and blend the ingredients into a smooth hummus.
6. Transfer the hummus to a medium-sized bowl, cover, and put it in the fridge for at least 30 minutes.
7. Take the hummus out of the fridge and, if desired, top it with the optional chopped cilantro and more salt and pepper to taste; serve with the carrot fries, and enjoy!

Nutrition: Calories 416 Carbohydrates 8. 4 g Fats 40. 3 g Protein 3. 3 g

392. Raw Zoodles with Avocado 'N Nuts

Preparation Time: 10 minutes
Cooking Time: 3-30 minutes
Servings: 2
Ingredients:
- 1 medium zucchini
- 1½ cups basil
- 1/3 cup water
- 5 tbsp. pine nuts
- 2 tbsp. lemon juice
- 1 medium avocado, peeled, pitted, sliced
- Optional: 2 tbsp. olive oil
- 6 yellow cherry tomatoes, halved
- Optional: 6 red cherry tomatoes, halved
- Sea salt and black pepper to taste

Directions:
1. Add the basil, water, nuts, lemon juice, avocado slices, optional olive oil (if desired), salt, and pepper to a blender.
2. Blend the ingredients into a smooth mixture. Add more salt and pepper to taste and blend again.
3. Divide the sauce and the zucchini noodles between two medium-sized bowls for serving, and combine in each.
4. Top the mixtures with the halved yellow cherry tomatoes, and the optional red cherry tomatoes (if desired); serve and enjoy!

Nutrition: Calories 317 Carbohydrates 7. 4 g Fats 28. 1 g Protein 7. 2 g

393. Mushrooms and Chard Soup

Preparation time: 10 minutes
Cooking time: 30 minutes
Servings: 4
Ingredients:
- 3 cups Swiss chard, chopped
- 6 cups vegetable stock

- 1 cup mushrooms, sliced
- 2 garlic cloves, minced
- 1 tablespoon olive oil
- 2 scallions, chopped
- 2 tablespoons balsamic vinegar
- ¼ cup basil, chopped
- Salt and black pepper to the taste
- 1 tablespoon cilantro, chopped

Directions:
1. Heat up a pot with the oil over medium high heat, add the scallions and the garlic and sauté for 5 minutes.
2. Add the mushrooms and sauté for another 5 minutes.
3. Add the rest of the ingredients, toss, bring to a simmer and cook over medium heat for 20 minutes more.
4. Ladle the soup into bowls and serve.

Nutrition: calories 140, fat 4, fiber 2, carbs 4, protein 8

394. Spinach and Mashed Tofu Salad

Preparation Time: 20 minutes
Cooking Time: 3-30 minutes
Servings: 4
Ingredients:
- 2 8-oz. blocks firm tofu, drained
- 4 cups baby spinach leaves
- 4 tbsp. cashew butter
- 1½ tbsp. soy sauce
- 1-inch piece ginger, finely chopped
- 1 tsp. red miso paste
- 2 tbsp. sesame seeds
- 1 tsp. organic orange zest
- 1 tsp. nori flakes
- 2 tbsp. water

Directions:
1. Use paper towels to absorb any excess water left in the tofu before crumbling both blocks into small pieces.
2. In a large bowl, combine the mashed tofu with the spinach leaves.
3. Mix the remaining ingredients in another small bowl and, if desired, add the optional water for a smoother dressing.
4. Pour this dressing over the mashed tofu and spinach leaves.
5. Transfer the bowl to the fridge and allow the salad to chill for up to one hour. Doing so will guarantee a better flavor. Or, the salad can be served right away. Enjoy!

Nutrition: Calories 166 Carbohydrates 5. 5 g Fats 10. 7 g Protein 11. 3 g

VEGAN LUNCH

395. Sweet Potato Quesadillas

Preparation Time: 30 minutes
Cooking Time: 21 minutes
Serving: 3
Ingredients:

- 1 cup dry black beans
- ½ cup dry rice of choice
- 1 large sweet potato, peeled and diced
- ½ cup salsa
- 4 tortilla wraps
- 1 tbsp. olive oil
- ½ tsp. garlic powder
- ½ tsp. onion powder
- ½ tsp. paprika

Directions:

1. Preheat the oven to 350°F.
2. Line a baking pan with parchment paper.
3. Cut the sweet potato into ½-inch cubes and drizzle these with olive oil. Transfer the cubes to the baking pan.
4. Put the pan in the oven and bake the potatoes until tender, for around 1 hour.
5. Allow the potatoes to cool for 5 minutes and then add them to a large mixing bowl with the salsa and cooked rice. Use a fork to smash the ingredients together into a thoroughly combined mixture.
6. Heat a saucepan over medium-high heat and add the potato/rice mixture, cooked black beans, and spices to the pan.
7. Cook everything for about 5 minutes or until it is heated through.
8. Take another frying pan and put it over medium-low heat. Place a tortilla in the pan and fill half of it with a heaping scoop of the potato, bean, and rice mixture.
9. Fold the tortilla in half to cover the filling, and cook the tortilla until both sides are browned—about 4 minutes per side.
10. Serve the tortillas with some additional salsa on the side.

Nutrition: Calories 683, Total Fat 12.7g, Saturated Fat 2.3g, Cholesterol 0mg, Sodium 980mg, Total Carbohydrate 121g, Dietary Fiber 18.5g, Total Sugars 8.3g, Protein 24.9g, Vitamin D 0mcg, Calcium 184mg, Iron 9mg, Potassium 1425mg

396. Satay Tempeh with Cauliflower Rice

Preparation Time: 60 minutes
Cooking Time: 15 minutes
Serving: 4
Ingredients:

- ¼ cup water
- 4 tbsp. peanut butter
- 3 tbsp. low sodium soy sauce
- 2 tbsp. coconut sugar
- 1 garlic clove, minced
- 1 tbsp ginger, minced
- 2 tsp. rice vinegar
- 1 tsp. red pepper flakes
- 4 tbsp. olive oil
- 2 8-oz. packages tempeh, drained
- 2 cups cauliflower rice
- 1 cup purple cabbage, diced
- 1 tbsp. sesame oil
- 1 tsp. agave nectar

Directions:

1. Take a large bowl, combine all the ingredients for the sauce, and then whisk until the mixture is smooth and any lumps have dissolved.
2. Cut the tempeh into ½-inch cubes and put them into the sauce, stirring to make sure the cubes get coated thoroughly.
3. Place the bowl in the refrigerator to marinate the tempeh for up to 3 hours.
4. Before the tempeh is done marinating, preheat the oven to 400°F.
5. Spread the tempeh out in a single layer on a baking sheet lined with parchment paper or lightly greased with olive oil.
6. Bake the marinated cubes until browned and crisp—about 15 minutes.
7. Heat the cauliflower rice in a saucepan with 2 tablespoons of olive oil over medium heat until it is warm.
8. Rinse the large bowl with water, and then mix the cabbage, sesame oil, and agave.
9. Serve a scoop of the cauliflower rice topped with the marinated cabbage and cooked tempeh on a plate or in a bowl and enjoy. Or, store for later.

Nutrition: Calories 554, Total Fat 38.8g, Saturated Fat 7.1g, Cholesterol 0mg, Sodium 614mg, Total Carbohydrate 32.3g, Dietary Fiber 2.1g, Total Sugars 13.9g, Protein 28.1g, Vitamin D 0mcg, Calcium 140mg, Iron 5mg, Potassium 655mg

397. Teriyaki Tofu Wraps

Preparation Time: 30 minutes
Cooking Time: 15 minutes
Serving: 3
Ingredients:
- 1 14-oz. drained, package extra firm tofu
- 1 small white onion, diced
- 1 cup chopped pineapple
- ¼ cup soy sauce
- 2 tbsp. sesame oil
- 1 garlic clove, minced
- 1 tsp. coconut sugar
- 4 large lettuce leaves
- 1 tbsp. roasted sesame seeds
- ¼ tsp Salt
- ¼ tsp pepper

Directions:
1. Take a medium-sized bowl and mix the soy sauce, sesame oil, coconut sugar, and garlic.
2. Cut the tofu into ½-inch cubes, place them in the bowl, and transfer the bowl to the refrigerator to marinate, up to 3 hours.
3. Meanwhile, cut the pineapple into rings or cubes.
4. After the tofu is adequately marinated, place a large skillet over medium heat, and pour in the tofu with the remaining marinade, pineapple cubes, and diced onions; stir.
5. Add salt and pepper to taste, making sure to stir the ingredients frequently, and cook until the onions are soft and translucent — about 15 minutes.
6. Divide the mixture between the lettuce leaves and top with a sprinkle of roasted sesame seeds.
7. Serve right away, or, store the mixture and lettuce leaves separately.

Nutrition: Calories 247, Total Fat 16.2g, Saturated Fat 2.6g, Cholesterol 0mg, Sodium 1410mg, Total Carbohydrate 16.1g, Dietary Fiber 3.1g, Total Sugars 9g, Protein 13.4g, Vitamin D 0mcg, Calcium 315mg, Iron 4mg, Potassium 371mg

398. Mushroom Salad

Preparation time: 10 minutes
Cooking time: 20 minutes
Servings: 2
Ingredients:
- 1 tablespoon butter
- 1/2-pound cremini mushrooms, chopped
- 2 tablespoons extra-virgin olive oil
- Salt and black pepper to taste
- 2 bunches arugula
- 4 slices prosciutto
- 1 tablespoon apple cider vinegar
- 4 sundried tomatoes in oil, drained and chopped
- Fresh parsley leaves, chopped

Directions:
1. Heat a pan with butter and half of the oil.
2. Add the mushrooms, salt, and pepper. Stir-fry for 3 minutes. Reduce heat. Stir again, and cook for 3 minutes more.
3. Add rest of the oil and vinegar. Stir and cook for 1 minute.
4. Place arugula on a platter, add prosciutto on top, add the mushroom mixture, sundried tomatoes, more salt and pepper, parsley, and serve.

Nutrition: Calories: 191 Carbs: 6g Fat: 7g Protein: 17g

399. Tofu Cacciatore

Preparation Time: 45 minutes
Cooking Time: 35 minutes
Serving: 3
Ingredients:
- 1 14-oz. package extra firm tofu, drained
- 1 tbsp. olive oil
- 1 cup matchstick carrots
- 1 medium sweet onion, diced
- 1 medium green bell pepper, seeded, diced
- 1 28-oz. can have diced tomatoes
- 1 4-oz. can tomato paste
- ½ tbsp. balsamic vinegar
- 1 tbsp. soy sauce
- 1 tbsp. maple syrup
- 1 tbsp. garlic powder
- 1 tbsp. Italian seasoning
- ¼ tsp Salt
- ¼ tsp pepper

Directions:
1. Chop the tofu into ¼- to ½-inch cubes.
2. Warmth the olive oil in a large skillet over medium-high heat.
3. Add the onions, garlic, bell peppers, and carrots; sauté until the onions turn translucent, around 10 minutes. Make sure to stir frequently to prevent burning.
4. Now add the balsamic vinegar, soy sauce
5. , maple syrup, garlic powder and Italian seasoning.
6. Stir well while pouring in the diced tomatoes and tomato paste; mix until all ingredients are thoroughly combined.

7. Add the cubed tofu and stir one more time.

8. Cover the pot, turn the heat to medium-low, and allow the mixture to simmer until the sauce has thickened, for around 20-25 minutes.

9. Serve the tofu cacciatore in bowls and top with salt and pepper to taste, or, store for another meal!

Nutrition: Calories 319, Total Fat 12g, Saturated Fat 2.1g, Cholesterol 3mg, Sodium 1156mg, Total Carbohydrate 43.1g, Dietary Fiber 10.4g, Total Sugars 27.1g, Protein 17.6g, Vitamin D 0mcg, Calcium 359mg, Iron 5mg, Potassium 961mg

400. Portobello Burritos

Preparation Time: 50 minutes
Cooking Time: 40 minutes
Serving: 4
Ingredients:
- 3 large portobello mushrooms
- 2 medium potatoes
- 4 tortilla wraps
- 1 medium avocado, pitted, peeled, diced
- ¾ cup salsa
- 1 tbsp. cilantro
- ½ tsp salt
- 1/3 cup water
- 1 tbsp. lime juice
- 1 tbsp. minced garlic
- ¼ cup vegan teriyaki sauce

Directions:
1. Preheat the oven to 400°F.
2. Lightly oil a sheet pan with olive oil (or line with parchment paper) and set it aside.
3. Combine the water, lime juice, teriyaki, and garlic in a small bowl.
4. Slice the portobello mushrooms into thin slices and add these to the bowl. Allow the mushrooms to marinate thoroughly, for up to three hours.
5. Cut the potatoes into large matchsticks, like French fries. Sprinkle the fries with salt and then transfer them to the sheet pan. Place the fries in the oven and bake them until crisped and golden, around 30 minutes. Flip once halfway through for even cooking.
6. Heat a large frying pan over medium heat. Add the marinated mushroom slices with the remaining marinade to the pan. Cook until the liquid has absorbed, around 10 minutes. Remove from heat.

7. Fill the tortillas with a heaping scoop of the mushrooms and a handful of the potato sticks. Top with salsa, sliced avocados, and cilantro before serving.

8. Serve right away, enjoy, or, store the tortillas, avocado, and mushrooms separately for later!

Nutrition: Calories 391, Total Fat 14.9g, Saturated Fat 3.1g, Cholesterol 0mg, Sodium 1511mg, Total Carbohydrate 57g, Dietary Fiber 10.8g, Total Sugars 5.1g, Protein 11.2g, Vitamin D 0mcg, Calcium 85mg, Iron 3mg, Potassium 956mg

401. Mushroom Madness Stroganoff

Preparation Time: 30 minutes
Cooking Time: 25 minutes
Serving: 4
Ingredients:
- 2 cups gluten-free noodles
- 1 small onion, chopped
- 2 cups vegetable broth
- 2 tbsp. almond flour
- 1 tbsp. tamari
- 1 tsp. tomato paste
- 1 tsp. lemon juice
- 3 cups mushrooms, chopped
- 1 tsp. thyme
- 3 cups raw spinach
- 1 tbsp. apple cider vinegar
- 1 tbsp. olive oil
- ¼ tsp Salt
- ¼ tsp pepper
- 2 tbsp. fresh parsley

Directions:
1. Organize the noodles according to the package instructions.
2. Warmth the olive oil in a large skillet over medium heat.
3. Add the chopped onion and sauté until soft—for about 5 minutes.
4. Stir in the flour, vegetable broth, tamari, tomato paste, and lemon juice; cook for an additional 3 minutes.
5. Blend in the mushrooms, thyme, and salt to taste, then cover the skillet.
6. Cook until the mushrooms are tender, for about 7 minutes, and turn the heat down to low.
7. Add the cooked noodles, spinach, and vinegar to the pan and top the ingredients with salt and pepper to taste.
8. Cover the skillet again and let the flavors combine for another 8-10 minutes.

9. Serve immediately, topped with the optional parsley if desired, or, store and enjoy the stroganoff another day of the week!

Nutrition: Calories 240, Total Fat 11.9g, Saturated Fat 1.3g, Cholesterol 0mg, Sodium 935mg, Total Carbohydrate 26.1g, Dietary Fiber 4.3g, Total Sugars 4.9g, Protein 9.9g, Vitamin D 189mcg, Calcium 71mg, Iron 4mg, Potassium 463mg

Preparation Time: 25 minutes

Cooking Time: 21 minutes

Serving: 4

Ingredients:
- 3 cups butternut squash, fresh or frozen, cubed
- 2 tbsp. minced garlic
- 1 tbsp. olive oil
- 1 tsp. red pepper flakes
- 1 tsp. cumin
- 1 tsp. paprika
- 1 tsp. oregano

Crust:
- 2 cups dry French green lentils
- 2 cups water
- 2 tbsp. minced garlic
- 1 tbsp. Italian seasoning
- 1 tsp. onion powder

Toppings:
- 1 tbsp. olive oil
- 1 medium green bell pepper, pitted, diced
- 1 cup chopped broccoli
- 1 small purple onion, diced

Directions:
1. Preheat the oven to 350°F.
2. Prepare the French green lentils according to the method.
3. Add all the sauce ingredients to a food processor or blender, and blend on low until everything has mixed and the sauce looks creamy. Set the sauce aside in a small bowl.
4. Clean the food processor or blender; then add all the ingredients for the crust and pulse on high speed until a dough-like batter has formed.
5. Heat a large deep-dish pan over medium-low heat and lightly grease it with 1 tablespoon of olive oil.
6. Press the crust dough into the skillet until it resembles a round pizza crust and cook until the crust is golden brown—about 5-6 minutes on each side.

7. Put the crust on a baking tray covered with parchment paper.
8. Coat the topside of the crust with the sauce using a spoon, and evenly distribute the toppings across the pizza.
9. Bake the pizza in the oven
10. Slice into 4 equal pieces and serve, or store.

Nutrition: Calories 258, Total Fat 9.2g, Saturated Fat 1.2g, Cholesterol 2mg, Sodium 21mg, Total Carbohydrate 38.3g, Dietary Fiber 9.7g, Total Sugars 6.2g, Protein 9g, Vitamin D 0mcg, Calcium 111mg, Iron 4mg, Potassium 838mg

402. Lasagna Fungo

Preparation Time: 20 minutes

Cooking Time: 40 minutes

Serving: 8

Ingredients:
- 10 lasagna sheets
- 2 cups matchstick carrots
- 1 cup mushrooms, sliced
- 2 cups raw kale
- 1 14-oz. package extra firm tofu, drained
- 1 cup hummus
- ½ cup nutritional yeast
- 2 tbsp. Italian seasoning
- 1 tbsp. garlic powder
- 1 tbsp. olive oil
- 4 cups marinara sauce
- 1 tsp. salt

Directions:
1. Preheat the oven to 400°F.
2. Cook the lasagna noodles or sheets according to method.
3. Take a large frying pan, put it over medium heat, and add the olive oil.
4. Throw in the carrots, mushrooms, and half a teaspoon of salt; cook for 5 minutes.
5. Add the kale, sauté for another 3 minutes, and remove the pan from the heat.
6. Take a large bowl, crumble in the tofu, and set the bowl aside for now.
7. Take another bowl and add the hummus, nutritional yeast, Italian seasoning, garlic, and ½ teaspoon salt; mix everything.
8. Coat the bottom of an 8x8 baking dish with 1 cup of the marinara sauce.
9. Cover the sauce with a couple of the noodles or sheets, and top these with the tofu crumbles.
10. Add a layer of the vegetables on top of the tofu.

11. Continue to build up the lasagna by stacking layers of marinara sauce, noodles or sheets, tofu, and vegetables, and top it off with a cup of marinara sauce.

12. Cover the lasagna with aluminum foil, and bake in the oven for 20-25 minutes.

13. Take away the foil and put back in the oven for an additional 5 minutes.

14. Allow the lasagna to sit for 10 minutes before serving, or store for another day!

Nutrition: Calories 491, Total Fat 13.1g, Saturated Fat 2.2g, Cholesterol 30mg, Sodium 959mg, Total Carbohydrate 73.5g, Dietary Fiber 9g, Total Sugars 13.3g, Protein 23.3g, Vitamin D 32mcg, Calcium 176mg, Iron 5mg, Potassium 903mg

403. Vegan Olive Pasta (FAST)

Preparation Time: 10 minutes
Cooking Time: 5 minutes
Servings: 4
Ingredients:
- 4 cups whole grain penne pasta
- 1/2 cup olives, sliced
- 1 tbsp capers
- 1/4 tsp red pepper flakes
- 3 cups of water
- 4 cups pasta sauce, homemade
- 1 tbsp garlic, minced
- Pepper
- Salt

Directions:
1. Add all fixings into the pot and stir well, then cook on high within 5 minutes. Stir and serve.

Nutrition: Calories 441 Fat 10.1 g Carbohydrates 77.3 g Sugar 24.1 g Protein 11.8 g Cholesterol 5 mg

404. Lebanesen Delight

Preparation Time: 10 minutes
Cooking Time: 15 minutes
Servings: 5
Ingredients:
- 1 Tablespoon Olive Oil
- 1 Cup Vermicelli (Can be Substituted for Thin Spaghetti) Broken into 1 to 1 ½ inch Pieces
- 3 Cups Cabbage, Shredded
- 3 Cups Vegetable Broth, Low Sodium
- ½ Cup Water
- 1 Cup Instant Brown Rice
- ¼ Teaspoon Sea Salt, Fine
- 2 Cloves Garlic
- ¼ Teaspoon Crushed Red Pepper
- ½ Cup Cilantro Fresh & Chopped
- Lemon Slices to Garnish

Directions:
1. Get out a saucepan and then place it over medium-high heat. Add in your oil and once it's hot you will need to add in your pasta. Cook for three minutes or until your pasta is toasted. You will have to stir often in order to keep it from burning.

2. Add in your cabbage, cooking for another four minutes. Continue to stir often.

3. Add in your water and rice. Season with salt, red pepper and garlic before bringing it all to a boil over high heat. Stir, and then cover. Once it's covered turn the heat down to medium-low. Allow it all to simmer for ten minutes.

4. Remove the pan from the burner and then allow it to sit without lifting the lid for five minutes. Take the garlic cloves out and then mash them using a fork. Place them back in, and stir them into the rice. Stir in your cilantro as well and serve warm. Garnish with lemon wedges if desired.

Nutrition: Calories: 259 Protein: 7 Grams Fat: 4 Grams Carbs: 49 Grams Sodium: 123 mg

405. Sweet and Sour Tofu

Preparation Time: 40 minutes
Cooking Time: 21 minutes
Serving: 4
Ingredients:
- 14-oz. package extra firm tofu, drained
- 2 tbsp. olive oil
- 1 large red bell pepper, pitted, chopped
- 1 medium white onion, diced
- 2 tbsp. minced garlic
- ½-inch minced ginger
- 1 cup pineapple chunks
- 1 tbsp. tomato paste
- 2 tbsp. rice vinegar
- 2 tbsp. low sodium soy sauce
- 1 tsp. cornstarch
- 1 tbsp. cane sugar
- ¼ tsp Salt
- ¼ tsp pepper

Directions:
1. whisk together the tomato paste, vinegar, soy sauce, cornstarch, and sugar in a bowl.

2. Cut the tofu into ¼-inch cubes, place in a medium bowl, and marinate in the soy sauce mixture until the tofu has absorbed the flavors (up to 3 hours).

3. Heat 1 tablespoon of the olive oil in a frying pan over medium-high heat.

4. Add the tofu chunks and half of the remaining marinade to the pan, leaving the rest for later.
5. Stir frequently until the tofu is cooked golden brown, approximately 10-12 minutes. Remove the tofu from the heat and set aside in a medium-sized bowl.
6. Add the other tablespoon of olive oil to the same pan, then the garlic and ginger; heat for about 1 minute.
7. Add in the peppers and onions. Mix until the vegetables have softened, about 5 minutes.
8. Pour the leftover marinade into the pan with the vegetables and heat until the sauce thickens while continuously stirring, around 4 minutes.
9. Add the pineapple chunks and tofu cubes to the pan while stirring and cook for 3 minutes.
10. Serve and enjoy right away, or, let the sweet and sour tofu cool down and store for later!

Nutrition: Calories 290, Total Fat 16.9g, Saturated Fat 2.6g, Cholesterol 0mg, Sodium 512mg, Total Carbohydrate 19.5g, Dietary Fiber 3.3g, Total Sugars 9.1g, Protein 15.9g, Vitamin D 0mcg, Calcium 138mg, Iron 1mg, Potassium 434mg

406. Barbecued Greens & Grits

Preparation Time: 60 minutes
Cooking Time: 35 minutes
Serving: 4
Ingredients:
- 1 14-oz. package tempeh
- 3 cups vegetable broth
- 3 cups collard greens, chopped
- ½ cup vegan BBQ sauce
- 1 cup gluten-free grits
- ¼ cup white onion, diced
- 2 tbsp. olive oil
- 2 garlic cloves, minced
- 1 tsp. salt

Directions:
1. Preheat the oven to 400°F.
2. Sliced the tempeh into thin slices and combine it with the vegan BBQ sauce in a shallow baking dish. Set aside and let marinate for up to 3 hours.
3. Heat 1 tablespoon of olive oil in a frying pan over medium heat and then add the garlic and sauté until it is fragrant.
4. Add the collard greens and ½ teaspoon of salt and cook until the collards are wilted and dark. Remove the pan from the heat and set aside.
5. Cover the tempeh and vegan BBQ sauce mixture with aluminum foil. Put the baking dish into the oven and bake the ingredients for 15 minutes. Reveal and continue to bake for another 10 minutes, until the tempeh is browned and crispy.
6. While the tempeh cooks, heat the remaining tablespoon of olive oil in the previously used frying pan over medium heat.
7. Cook the onions until brown and fragrant, around 10 minutes.
8. Pour in the vegetable broth, bring it to a boil; then turn the heat down to low.
9. Slowly whisk the grits into the simmering broth. Add the remaining ½ teaspoon of salt before covering the pan with a lid.
10. Let the ingredients simmer for about 8 minutes, until the grits are soft and creamy.
11. Serve the tempeh and collard greens on top of a bowl of grits and enjoy, or store for later!

Nutrition: Calories 374, Total Fat 19.1g, Saturated Fat 3.5g, Cholesterol 0mg, Sodium 1519mg, Total Carbohydrate 31.1g, Dietary Fiber 2g, Total Sugars 9g, Protein 23.7g, Vitamin D 0mcg, Calcium 163mg, Iron 4mg, Potassium 645mg

407. Potato Soup (FAST)

Preparation time: 5 minutes
Cooking time: 12 minutes
Servings: 2
Ingredients:
- 2 potatoes, peeled, cubed
- 1/3 teaspoon salt
- 1 1/2 cup vegetable broth
- 3/4 cup of water
- 1/8 teaspoon ground black pepper
- 1 tablespoon Cajun seasoning

Directions:
1. Take a small pan, place potato cubes in it, cover with water and vegetable broth, and then place the pan over medium heat.
2. Boil the potato until cooked and tender, and when done, remove the pan from heat and blend the mixture by using an immersion blender until creamy.
3. Return pan over medium-low heat, add remaining Ingredients: stir until mixed and bring it to a simmer.

4. Taste to adjust seasoning, then ladle soup into bowls and then serve.

Nutrition: Calories: 203 Carbs: 5g Fat: 6g Protein: 37g

408. Teriyaki Eggplant (FAST)

Preparation time: 5 minutes
Cooking time: 15 minutes
Servings: 2
Ingredients:
- 1/2-pound eggplant
- 1 green onion, chopped
- 1/2 teaspoon grated ginger
- 1/2 teaspoon minced garlic
- 1/3 cup soy sauce
- 1 tablespoon coconut sugar
- 1/2 tablespoon apple cider vinegar
- 1 tablespoon olive oil

Directions:
1. Prepare vegan teriyaki sauce and for this, take a medium bowl, add ginger, garlic, soy sauce, vinegar, and sugar in it and then whisk until sugar has dissolved completely.
2. Cut eggplant into cubes, add them into vegan teriyaki sauce, toss until well coated and marinate for 10 minutes.
3. When ready to cook, take a grill pan, place it over medium-high heat, grease it with oil, and when hot, add marinated eggplant.
4. Cook for 3 to 4 minutes per side until nicely browned and beginning to charred, drizzling with excess marinade frequently and transfer to a plate.
5. Sprinkle green onion on top of the eggplant and then serve.

Nutrition: Calories: 132 Carbs: 4g Fat: 4g Protein: 13g

409. Sweet Potato Sushi

Preparation Time: 90 minutes
Cooking Time: 35 minutes
Serving: 3
Ingredients:
- 1 14-oz. package silken tofu, drained
- 3 nori sheets
- 1 large sweet potato, peeled
- 1 medium avocado, pitted, peeled, sliced
- 1 cup water
- ¾ cup dry sushi rice
- 1 tbsp. rice vinegar
- 1 tbsp. agave nectar
- 1 tbsp. amino acids

Directions:
1. Preheat the oven to 400°F / 200°C.
2. Stir the amino acids (or tamari) and agave nectar together in a small bowl until it is well combined and set aside.
3. Cut the sweet potato into large sticks, around ½-inch thick. Place them on a baking sheet lined with parchment and coat them with the tamari/agave mixture.
4. Bake the sweet potatoes in the oven until softened—for about 25 minutes—and make sure to flip them halfway so the sides cook evenly.
5. Meanwhile, bring the sushi rice, water, and vinegar to a boil in a medium-sized pot over medium heat, and cook until liquid has evaporated, for about 10 minutes.
6. While cooking the rice, cut the block of tofu into long sticks. The sticks should look like long, thin fries. Set aside.
7. Remove the pot from heat and let the rice sit for 10-15 minutes.
8. Cover your work area with a piece of parchment paper, clean your hands, wet your fingers, and lay out a sheet of nori on the parchment paper.
9. Cover the nori sheet with a thin layer of sushi rice, while wetting the hands frequently. Leave sufficient space for rolling up the sheet.
10. Place the roasted sweet potato strips in a straight line across the width of the sheet, about an inch away from the edge closest to you.
11. Lay out the tofu and avocado slices right beside the potato sticks and use the parchment paper as an aid to roll up the nori sheet into a tight cylinder.
12. Slice the cylinder into 8 equal pieces and refrigerate. Repeat the process for the remaining nori sheets and fillings.
13. Serve chilled, or, store to enjoy this delicious sushi later!

Nutrition: Calories 467, Total Fat 17.1g, Saturated Fat 3.4g, Cholesterol 0mg, Sodium 81mg, Total Carbohydrate 64g, Dietary Fiber 7.6g, Total Sugars 11g, Protein 15.4g, Vitamin D 0mcg, Calcium 78mg, Iron 6mg, Potassium 921mg

410. Brown Basmati Rice Pilaf (FAST)

Preparation Time: 10 minutes
Cooking Time: 3 minutes
Serving: 2

Ingredients:
- ½ tablespoon vegan butter
- ½ cup mushrooms, chopped
- ½ cup brown basmati rice
- 3 tablespoons water
- 1/8 teaspoon dried thyme
- Ground pepper to taste
- ½ tablespoon olive oil
- ¼ cup green onion, chopped
- 1 cup vegetable broth
- ¼ teaspoon salt
- ¼ cup chopped, toasted pecans

Directions:
1. Place a saucepan over medium-low heat. Add butter and oil.
2. When it melts, add mushrooms and cook until slightly tender.
3. Stir in the green onion and brown rice. Cook for 3 minutes. Stir constantly.
4. Stir in the broth, water, salt and thyme.
5. When it begins to boil, lower heat and cover with a lid. Simmer until rice is cooked. Add more water or broth if required.
6. Stir in the pecans and pepper.
7. Serve.

Nutrition: Calories 256, Total Fat 8.8g, Saturated Fat 1.3g, Cholesterol 0mg, Sodium 318mg, Total Carbohydrate 39.8g, Dietary Fiber 1.6g, Total Sugars 1g, Protein 4.5g, Vitamin D 63mcg, Calcium 26mg, Iron 1mg, Potassium 144mg

411. Avocado Toast with Chickpeas (FAST)

Preparation time: 5 minutes
Cooking time: 5 minutes
Servings: 2

Ingredients:
- 1/2 of avocado, peeled, pitted
- 4 tablespoons canned chickpeas, liquid reserved
- 1 tablespoon lime juice
- 1 teaspoon apple cider vinegar
- 2 slices of bread, toasted
- 1/4 teaspoon salt
- 1/4 teaspoon paprika
- 1 teaspoon olive oil

Directions:
1. Take a medium skillet pan, place it over medium heat, add oil and when hot, add chickpeas and cook for 2 minutes.
2. Sprinkle 1/8 teaspoon each salt and paprika over chickpeas, toss to coat, and then remove the pan from heat.

3. Place avocado in a bowl, mash by using a fork, drizzle with lime juice and vinegar and stir until well mixed.
4. Spread mashed avocado over bread slices, scatter chickpeas on top and then serve.

Nutrition: Calories: 235 Carbs: 5g Fat: 5g Protein: 31g

412. Vegan Mushroom Pho

Preparation Time: 10 minutes
Cooking Time: 30 minutes
Serving: 3

Ingredients:
- 14-oz. block firm tofu, drained
- 6 cups vegetable broth
- 3 green onions, thinly sliced
- 1 tsp. minced ginger
- 1 tbsp. olive oil
- 3 cups mushrooms, sliced
- 2 tbsp. hoisin sauce
- 1 tbsp. sesame oil
- 2 cups gluten-free rice noodles
- 1 cup raw bean sprouts
- 1 cup matchstick carrots
- 1 cup bok choy, chopped
- 1 cup cabbage, chopped
- ¼ tsp Salt
- ¼ tsp pepper

Directions:
1. Cut the tofu into ¼-inch cubes and set it aside.
2. Take a deep saucepan and heat the vegetable broth, green onions, and ginger over medium high heat.
3. Boil for 1 minute before reducing the heat to low; then cover the saucepan with a lid and let it simmer for 20 minutes.
4. Take another frying pan and heat the olive oil in it over medium-high heat.
5. Add the cut-up mushrooms to the frying pan and cook until they are tender, for about 5 minutes.
6. Add the tofu, hoisin sauce, and sesame oil to the mushrooms.
7. Heat until the sauce thickens (around 5 minutes), and remove the frying pan from the heat.
8. Prepare the gluten-free rice noodles according to the package instructions.
9. Top the rice noodles with a scoop of the tofu mushroom mixture, a generous amount of broth, and the bean sprouts.
10. Add the carrots, and optional cabbage and bok choy (if desired), right before serving.

11. Top with salt and pepper to taste and enjoy, or, store ingredients separately!

Nutrition: Calories 610, Total Fat 18.9g, Saturated Fat 3.5g, Cholesterol 0mg, Sodium 2098mg, Total Carbohydrate 83g, Dietary Fiber 5.4g, Total Sugars 9.4g, Protein 29.6g, Vitamin D 252mcg, Calcium 366mg, Iron 7mg, Potassium 1132mg

413. Ruby Red Root Beet Burger

Preparation Time: 20 minutes
Cooking Time: 21 minutes
Serving: 6
Ingredients:
- 1 cup dry chickpeas
- ½ cup dry quinoa
- 2 large beets
- 2 tbsp. olive oil
- 2 tbsp. garlic powder
- 1 tbsp. balsamic vinegar
- 2 tsp. onion powder
- 1 tsp. fresh parsley, chopped
- ¼ tsp Salt
- ¼ tsp pepper
- 2 cups spinach, fresh or frozen, washed and dried
- 6 buns or wraps of choice

Directions:
1. Preheat the oven to 400°F.
2. Peel and dice the beets into ¼-inch or smaller cubes, put them in a bowl, and coat the cubes with 1 tablespoon of olive oil and the onion powder.
3. Spread the beet cubes out across a baking pan and put the pan in the oven.
4. Roast the beets until they have softened, approximately 10-15 minutes. Take them out and set aside so the beets can cool down.
5. After the beets have cooled down, transfer them into a food processor and add the cooked chickpeas and quinoa, vinegar, garlic, parsley, and a pinch of pepper and salt.
6. Pulse the ingredients until everything is crumbly, around 30 seconds.
7. Use your palms to form the mixture into 6 equal-sized patties and place them in a small pan.
8. Put them in a freezer, up to 1 hour, until the patties feel firm to the touch.
9. Heat the remaining 1 tablespoon of olive oil in a skillet over medium-high heat and add the patties.

10. Cook them until they're browned on each side, about 4-6 minutes per side.
11. Store or serve the burgers with a handful of spinach, and if desired, on the bottom of the optional bun.
12. Top the burger with your sauce of choice.

Nutrition: Calories 353, Total Fat 9.2g, Saturated Fat 1.5g, Cholesterol 0mg, Sodium 351mg, Total Carbohydrate 57.8g, Dietary Fiber 9g, Total Sugars 9.2g, Protein 13.9g, Vitamin D 0mcg, Calcium 103mg

414. Green Onion Soup (FAST)

Preparation time: 5 minutes
Cooking time: 12 minutes
Servings: 2
Ingredients:
- 6 green onions, chopped
- 7 ounces diced potatoes
- 1/3 teaspoon salt
- 2 tablespoons olive oil
- 1 1/4 cup vegetable broth
- 1/4 teaspoon ground white pepper
- 1/4 teaspoon ground coriander

Directions:
1. Take a small pan, place potato in it, cover with water, and then place the pan over medium heat.
2. Boil the potato until cooked and tender, and when done, drain the potatoes and set aside until required.
3. Return saucepan over low heat, add oil and add green onions and cook for 5 minutes until cooked.
4. Season with salt, pepper, and coriander, add potatoes, pour in vegetable broth, stir until mixed and bring it to simmer.
5. Then remove the pan from heat and blend the mixture by using an immersion blender until creamy.
6. Taste to adjust seasoning, then ladle soup into bowls and then serve.

Nutrition: Calories: 191 Carbs: 1g Fat: 1g Protein: 15g

415. Fresh Dal

Preparation time: 15 minutes
Cooking time: 5 hours
Servings: 11
Ingredients:
- 1 teaspoon cumin
- 1 oz. mustard seeds
- 10 oz. lentils
- 1 teaspoon fennel seeds
- 7 cups water
- 6 oz. tomato, canned

- 4 oz. onion
- ½ teaspoon fresh ginger, grated
- 1 oz. bay leaf
- 1 teaspoon turmeric
- 1 teaspoon salt
- 2 cups rice

Directions:
1. Peel the onion. Chop the onion and tomatoes and place them in a slow cooker.
2. Combine the cumin, mustard seeds, and fennel seeds in a shallow bowl.
3. Add the bay leaf and mix. Sprinkle the vegetables in the slow cooker with the spice mixture.
4. Add salt, turmeric, and grated fresh ginger. Add rice and mix.
5. Add the lentils and water. Stir gently.
6. Then close the slow cooker lid and cook Dal for 5 hours on LOW.
7. When the dish is done, stir and transfer to serving plates. Enjoy!

Nutrition: Calories: 102g, Fat: 22g, Carbs: 5g, Protein: 34g,

416. Pepper & Kale   (FAST)

Preparation Time: 5 minutes
Cooking Time: 15 minutes
Serving: 4
Ingredients
- 2 cans chickpeas
- 4 cloves garlic
- 1 large sweet onion
- 4 tbsp olive oil
- 2 red peppers
- 6 cups kale

Direction
1. Heat BBQ and prepare a greased BBQ basket or pan.
2. Meanwhile, mix together chickpeas, garlic, onion, red peppers and olive oil in a bowl and add to the BBQ basket and place on the grill. Stir regularly.
3. When almost ready to serve add kale and stir constantly until the kale is slightly wilted. Serve with garlic toast, pita bread or rice.

Nutrition: 520 Calories 16g Fiber 18g Protein 111.

417. Caesar Pasta   (FAST)

Preparation Time: 10 minutes
Cooking Time: 0 minute
Serving: 1
Ingredients
- 2 cups chopped romaine lettuce

- 2 tablespoons Vegan Caesar Dressing
- ½ cup cooked pasta
- ½ cup canned chickpeas
- 2 additional tablespoons Caesar Dressing

Direction
1. Blend the lettuce, dressing, (if using).
2. Add the pasta, chickpeas, and additional dressing. Toss to coat.

Nutrition: 415 Calories 9g Protein 13g Fiber   9g

418. Quinn-Otto with Dried Tomatoes

Preparation Time: 10 minutes
Cooking Time: 30 min
Serving: 2
Ingredients
- 3 cups vegetable broth
- 2 cloves garlic, minced
- ½ cup quinoa
- ¼ cup sun-dried tomatoes in oil
- 1 teaspoon parsley
- 1 small onion, minced
- 1 ½ tablespoons olive oil
- 2 tablespoons basil

Direction
1. Place a saucepan over medium heat. Add oil. Once heated, sauté onion and garlic.
2. Cook the quinoa: Cook 2/3 cup uncooked quinoa in water, according to package directions.
3. Add a cup of broth and mix well. Season.
4. Add some more broth, tomatoes and herbs. Mix well. Cook until nearly dry.
5. Repeat adding the broth, a little at a time and cook until nearly dry each time, add cooked quinoa. Stir often.

Nutrition: 402 Calories 13g Fat 11g Protein

419. Rainbow Taco Boats (FAST)

Preparation Time: 10 minutes
Cooking Time: 0 minutes
Servings: 4
Ingredients:
- 1 head romaine lettuce, destemmed
For the Filling:
- 1/2 cup alfalfa sprouts
- 1 medium avocado, peeled, pitted, cubed
- 1 cup shredded carrots
- 1 cup halved cherry tomatoes
- 3/4 cup sliced red cabbage
- 1/2 cup sprouted hummus dip
- 1 tablespoon hemp seeds
For the Sauce:
- 1 tablespoon maple syrup

- 1/3 cup tahini
- 1/8 teaspoon sea salt
- 2 tablespoons lemon juice
- 3 tablespoons water

Directions:
1. Prepare the sauce and for this, take a medium bowl, add all the ingredients in it and whisk until well combined.
2. Assemble the boats and for this, arrange lettuce leaves in twelve portions, top each with hummus, and the remaining ingredients for the filling.
3. Serve with prepared sauce.

Nutrition: 314 Cal 23.6 g Fat 4 g Saturated Fat 23.2 g Carbohydrates 9.3 g Fiber 6.2 g Sugars 8 g Protein;

420. Eggplant Sandwich (FAST)

Preparation Time: 10 minutes
Cooking Time: 25 minutes
Servings: 4
Ingredients:
For the Sandwich:
- 2 ciabatta buns
- 1 medium eggplant, peeled, sliced, soaked in salted water
- 1 medium tomato, sliced
- 1/2 of a medium cucumber, sliced
- 1/2 cup arugula
- 4 tablespoons mayo

For the Marinade:
- 1 teaspoon agave syrup
- 1/4 teaspoon salt
- 1/4 teaspoon ground black pepper
- 1 teaspoon smoked paprika
- 1 tablespoon soy sauce
- 1 tablespoon olive oil

Directions:
1. Switch on the oven, then set it to 350 degrees F and let it preheat.
2. Prepare the marinade and for this, take a small bowl, place all the ingredients in it and whisk until combined.
3. Drain the eggplant slices, pat dry with a kitchen towel, and brush with prepared marinade, arrange them on a baking sheet and then bake for 20 minutes until done.
4. Assemble the sandwich and for this, slice the bread in half lengthwise, then spread mayonnaise in the bottom half of the bun and top with baked eggplant slices, tomato, and cucumber slices, and sprinkle with salt and black pepper.

5. Top with arugula leaves, cover with the top half of the bun, and then cover with aluminum foil.
6. Preheat the grill over medium-high heat setting and when hot, place prepared sandwiches and grill for 3 to 5 minutes until toasted.
7. Cut each sandwich through the foil into half and serve.

Nutrition: 688 Cal 15 g Fat 2 g Saturated Fat 118 g Carbohydrates 7 g Fiber 7 g Sugars 21 g Protein;

421. Flavorful Refried Beans

Preparation Time: 15 Minutes
Cooking Time: 8 hours
Servings: 8
Ingredients:
- 3 cups of pinto beans, rinsed
- 1 small jalapeno pepper, seeded and chopped
- 1 medium-sized white onion, peeled and sliced
- 2 tablespoons of minced garlic
- 5 teaspoons of salt
- 2 teaspoons of ground black pepper
- 1/4 teaspoon of ground cumin
- 9 cups of water

Directions:
1. Using a 6-quarts slow cooker, place all the ingredients: and stir until it mixes properly.
2. Cover the top, plug in the slow cooker; adjust the cooking time to 6 hours, let it cook on high heat setting and add more water if the beans get too dry.
3. When the beans are done, drain them and reserve the liquid.
4. Mash the beans using a potato masher and pour in the reserved cooking liquid until it reaches your desired mixture.
5. Serve immediately.

Nutrition: Calories: 198 Carbs: 22g Fat: 7g Protein: 19g

422. Smoky Red Beans and Rice

Preparation Time: 15 Minutes
Cooking Time: 5 hours
Servings: 8
Ingredients:
- 30 ounces of cooked red beans
- 1 cup of brown rice, uncooked
- 1 cup of chopped green pepper
- 1 cup of chopped celery
- 1 cup of chopped white onion
- 1 1/2 teaspoon of minced garlic
- 1/2 teaspoon of salt

- 1/4 teaspoon of cayenne pepper
- 1 teaspoon of smoked paprika
- 2 teaspoons of dried thyme
- 1 bay leaf
- 2 1/3 cups of vegetable broth

Directions:

1. Using a 6-quarts slow cooker, all the ingredients are except for the rice, salt, and cayenne pepper.
2. Stir until it mixes appropriately and then cover the top.
3. Plug in the slow cooker; adjust the cooking time to 4 hours, and steam on a low heat setting.
4. Then pour in and stir the rice, salt, cayenne pepper and continue cooking for an additional 2 hours at a high heat setting.

Nutrition: Calories: 234 Carbs: 13g Fat: 7g Protein: 19g

423. Spicy Black-Eyed Peas

Preparation Time: 15 Minutes
Cooking Time: 60 Minutes
Servings: 8
Ingredients:

- 32-ounce black-eyed peas, uncooked
- 1 cup of chopped orange bell pepper
- 1 cup of chopped celery
- 8-ounce of chipotle peppers, chopped
- 1 cup of chopped carrot
- 1 cup of chopped white onion
- 1 teaspoon of minced garlic
- 3/4 teaspoon of salt
- 1/2 teaspoon of ground black pepper
- 2 teaspoons of liquid smoke flavoring
- 2 teaspoons of ground cumin
- 1 tablespoon of adobo sauce
- 2 tablespoons of olive oil
- 1 tablespoon of apple cider vinegar
- 4 cups of vegetable broth

Directions:

1. Place a medium-sized non-stick skillet pan over an average temperature of heat; add the bell peppers, carrot, onion, garlic, oil and vinegar.
2. Stir until it mixes properly and let it cook for 5 to 8 minutes or until it gets translucent.
3. Transfer this mixture to a 6-quarts slow cooker and add the peas, chipotle pepper, adobo sauce and the vegetable broth.
4. Stir until mixes properly and cover the top.

5. Plug in the slow cooker; adjust the cooking time to 8 hours and let it cook on the low heat setting or until peas are soft.

Nutrition: Calories: 211 Carbs: 22g Fat: 7g Protein: 19g

424. Lentil, Cauliflower and Grape Salad (FAST)

Preparation Time: 10 minutes
Cooking Time: 25 minutes
Servings: 4
Ingredients:

- For the Cauliflower:
- 1 medium head of cauliflower, cut into florets
- 1/4 teaspoon sea salt
- 1 1/2 tablespoons curry powder
- 1 1/2 tablespoons melted coconut oil

For the Tahini Dressing:

- 2 tablespoons tahini
- 1/8 teaspoon salt
- 1.8 teaspoon ground black pepper
- 4 1/2 tablespoons green curry paste
- 1 tablespoon maple syrup
- 2 tablespoons lemon juice
- 2 tablespoons water

For the Salad:

- 1 cup cooked lentils
- 4 tablespoons chopped cilantro
- 1 cup red grapes, halved
- 6 cups mixed greens

Directions:

1. Switch on the oven, then set it to 400 degrees F and let it preheat.
2. Prepare the cauliflower and for this, take a medium bowl, place cauliflower florets in it, drizzle with oil, season with salt and curry powder, toss until mixed.
3. Take a baking sheet, line it with parchment sheet, spread cauliflower florets in it, and then bake for 25 minutes until tender and nicely golden brown.
4. Meanwhile, prepare the tahini dressing and for this, take a medium bowl, place all of its ingredients and whisk until combined, set aside until required.
5. Assemble the salad and for this, take a large salad bowl, add roasted cauliflower florets, lentils, grapes, and mixed greens, drizzle with prepared tahini dressing and toss until well combined.
6. Serve straight away.

Nutrition: 420 Cal 14 g Fat 5 g Saturated Fat 37.6 g Carbohydrates 9.8 g Fiber 12.8 g Sugars 10.8 g Protein;

425. Loaded Kale Salad

Preparation Time: 10 minutes
Cooking Time: 30 minutes
Servings: 4
Ingredients:
- 1 ½ cup cooked quinoa

For The Vegetables:
- 1 whole beet, peeled, sliced
- 4 large carrots, peeled, chopped
- 1/2 teaspoon curry powder
- 1/8 teaspoon sea salt
- 2 tablespoons melted coconut oil

For The Dressing:
- ¼ teaspoon of sea salt
- 2 tablespoons maple syrup
- 3 tablespoons lemon juice
- 1/3 cup tahini
- 1/4 cup water

For the Salad:
- 1/2 cup sprouts
- 1 medium avocado, peeled, pitted, cubed
- 1/2 cup chopped cherry tomatoes
- 8 cups chopped kale
- 1/4 cup hemp seeds

Directions:
1. Switch on the oven, then set it to 375 degrees F and let it preheat.
2. Take a baking sheet, place beets and carrots on it, drizzle with oil, season with curry powder and salt, toss until coated, and then bake for 30 minutes until tender and golden brown.
3. Meanwhile, prepare the dressing and for this, take a small bowl, place all the ingredients in it and whisk until well combined, set aside until required.
4. Assemble the salad and for this, take a large salad bowl, place kale leaves in it, add remaining ingredients for the salad along with roasted vegetables, drizzle with prepared dressing and toss until combined.
5. Serve straight away.

Nutrition: 472 Cal 22.8 g Fat 3.8 g Saturated Fat 58.7 g Carbohydrates 12.5 g Fiber 9.2 g Sugars 14.6 g Protein;

426. Sabich Sandwich (FAST)

Preparation Time: 10 minutes
Cooking Time: 10 minutes
Servings: 4
Ingredients:
- 1/2 cup cooked white beans

- 2 medium potatoes, peeled, boiled, ½-inch thick sliced
- 1 medium eggplant, destemmed, ½-inch cubed
- 4 dill pickles, ¼-inch thick sliced
- ¼ teaspoon of sea salt
- 2 tablespoons olive oil
- 1/4 teaspoon harissa paste
- 1/2 cup hummus
- 1 tablespoon mayonnaise
- 4 pita bread pockets
- 1/2 cup tabbouleh salad

Directions:
1. Take a small frying pan, place it over medium-low heat, add oil and wait until it gets hot.
2. Season eggplant pieces with salt, add to the hot frying pan and cook for 8 minutes until softened, and when done, remove the pan from heat.
3. Take a small bowl, place white beans in it, add harissa paste and mayonnaise and then stir until combined.
4. Assemble the sandwich and for this, place pita bread on clean working space, smear generously with hummus, then cover half of each pita bread with potato slices and top with a dill pickle slices.
5. Spoon 2 tablespoons of white bean mixture on each dill pickle, top with 3 tablespoons of cooked eggplant pieces and 2 tablespoons of tabbouleh salad and then cover the filling with the other half of pita bread.
6. Serve straight away.

Nutrition: 386 Cal 13 g Fat 2 g Saturated Fat 56 g Carbohydrates 7 g Fiber 3 g Sugars 12 g Protein;

427. Chickpea and Mayonnaise Salad Sandwich (FAST)

Preparation Time: 10 minutes
Cooking Time: 0 minutes
Servings: 4
Ingredients:
For the mayonnaise:
- 1/3 cup cashew nuts, soaked in boiling water for 10 minutes
- ½ teaspoon ground black pepper
- 1 teaspoon salt
- 6 teaspoons apple cider vinegar
- 2 teaspoon maple syrup
- 1/2 teaspoon Dijon mustard

For the chickpea salad:

- 1 small bunch of chives, chopped
- 1 ½ cup sweetcorn
- 3 cups cooked chickpeas

To serve:
- 4 sandwich breads
- 4 leaves of lettuce
- ½ cup chopped cherry tomatoes

Directions:
1. Prepare the mayonnaise and for this, place all of its ingredients in a food processor and then pulse for 2 minutes until smooth, scraping the sides of the container frequently.
2. Take a medium bowl, place chickpeas in it, and then mash by using a fork until broken.
3. Add chives and corn, stir until mixed, then add mayonnaise and stir until well combined.
4. Assemble the sandwich and for this, stuff sandwich bread with chickpea salad, top each sandwich with a lettuce leaf, and ¼ cup of chopped tomatoes and then serve.

Nutrition: 387 Cal 19 g Fat 5 g Saturated Fat 39.7 g Carbohydrates 7.2 g Fiber 4.6 g Sugars 10 g Protein;

428. Veggie Noodles (FAST)

Preparation Time: 10 minutes
Cooking Time: 5 minutes
Servings: 2
Ingredients:
- tablespoons vegetable oil
- spring onions, divided
- 1 cup snap pea
- tablespoons brown sugar
- oz. dried rice noodles, cooked
- garlic cloves, minced
- carrots, cut into small sticks
- tablespoons soy sauce

Directions:
1. Heat vegetable oil in a skillet over medium heat and add garlic and 3 spring onions.
2. Cook for about 3 minutes and add the carrots, peas, brown sugar and soy sauce.
3. Add rice noodles and cook for about 2 minutes.
4. Season with salt and black pepper and top with remaining spring onion to serve.

Nutrition: Calories: 25; Fat: 2.0g Protein: 5.2g Carbohydrates: 5.3g Fiber: 4g; Sodium: 18mg

429. Pesto Quinoa with White Beans (FAST)

Preparation Time: 5 minutes

Cooking Time: 15 minutes
Servings: 4
Ingredients:
- 12 ounces cooked white bean
- 3 ½ cups quinoa, cooked
- 1 medium zucchini, sliced
- ¾ cup sun-dried tomato
- ¼ cup pine nuts
- 1 tablespoon olive oil

For the Pesto:
- 1/3 cup walnuts
- 2 cups arugula
- 1 teaspoon minced garlic
- 2 cups basil
- ¾ teaspoon salt
- ¼ teaspoon ground black pepper
- 1 tablespoon lemon juice
- 1/3 cup olive oil
- 2 tablespoons water

Directions:
1. Prepare the pesto, and for this, place all of its ingredients in a food processor and pulse for 2 minutes until smooth, scraping the sides of the container frequently and set aside until required.
2. Take a large skillet pan, place it over medium heat, add oil and when hot, add zucchini and cook for 4 minutes until tender-crisp.
3. Season zucchini with salt and black pepper, cook for 2 minutes until lightly brown, then add tomatoes and white beans and continue cooking for 4 minutes until white beans begin to crisp.
4. Stir in pine nuts, cook for 2 minutes until toasted, then remove the pan from heat and transfer zucchini mixture into a medium bowl.
5. Add quinoa and pesto, stir until well combined, then distribute among four bowls and then serve.

Nutrition: 352 Cal 27.3 g Fat 5 g Saturated Fat 33.7 g Carbohydrates 5.7 g Fiber 4.5 g Sugars 9.7 g Protein;

430. Pumpkin Risotto (FAST)

Preparation Time: 5 minutes
Cooking Time: 20 minutes
Servings: 4
Ingredients:
- 1 cup Arborio rice
- ½ cup cooked and chopped pumpkin
- 1/2 cup mushrooms
- 1 rib of celery, diced

- ½ of a medium white onion, peeled, diced
- ½ teaspoon minced garlic
- ½ teaspoon salt
- 1/3 teaspoon ground black pepper
- 1 tablespoon olive oil
- ½ tablespoon coconut butter
- 1 cup pumpkin puree
- 2 cups vegetable stock

Directions:
1. Take a medium saucepan, place it over medium heat, add oil and when hot, add onion and celery, stir in garlic and cook for 3 minutes until onions begin to soften.
2. Add mushrooms, season with salt and black pepper and cook for 5 minutes.
3. Add rice, pour in pumpkin puree, then gradually pour in the stock until rice soaked up all the liquid and have turned soft.
4. Add butter, remove the pan from heat, stir until creamy mixture comes together, and then serve.

Nutrition: 218.5 Cal 5.2 g Fat 1.5 g Saturated Fat 32.3 g Carbohydrates 1.3 g Fiber 3.8 g Sugars 6.3 g Protein;

431. Gear Up Lentils

Preparation Time: 5 minutes
Cooking Time: 40 minutes
Serving: 6
Ingredients
- 5 cups water
- 2¼ cups brown lentils
- 3 teaspoons minced garlic
- 1 bay leaf
- ½ teaspoon dried basil
- ½ teaspoon dried oregano
- ½ teaspoon dried rosemary
- ½ teaspoon dried thyme

Direction:
1. Boil water, lentils, garlic, bay leaf, basil, oregano, rosemary, and thyme. Decrease heat to low, and simmer for 35 minutes. Drain any excess cooking liquid.
2. Transfer to a container, or scoop 1 cup of lentils into each of 6 storage containers. Let cool before sealing the lids.

Nutrition: 257 Calories 1g Fat 19g Protein

432. Boulders Bean Burgers (FAST)

Preparation Time: 10 minutes
Cooking Time: 10 minutes
Serving: 4

Ingredients
- 1 tablespoon olive oil
- ¼ cup couscous
- ¼ cup boiling water
- 1 (15-ounce) can white beans
- 2 tablespoons balsamic vinegar
- 2 tablespoons chopped sun-dried tomatoes or olives
- ½ teaspoon garlic powder
- ½ teaspoon salt
- 4 burger buns

Direction
1. Preheat the oven to 350°F.
2. Grease rimmed baking sheet with olive oil or line it with parchment paper. Mix couscous and boiling water.
3. Cover and set aside for about 5 minutes. Once the couscous is soft and the water is absorbed, fluff it with a fork. Add the beans, and mash them to a chunky texture. Add the vinegar, olive oil, sun-dried tomatoes, garlic powder, and salt; stir until combined but still a bit chunky.
4. Portion mixture into 4, and shape each into a patty. Put the patties on the prepared baking sheet, and bake for 25 to 30 minutes. Alternatively, heat some olive oil in a large skillet over medium heat, then add the patties, making sure each has oil under it.
5. Fry for about 5 minutes. Flip, adding more oil as needed, and fry for about 5 minutes more. Serve.

Nutrition: 315 Calories 12g Fiber 16g Protein

433. Black Bean Pizza Plate (FAST)

Preparation Time: 10 minutes
Cooking Time: 20 minutes
Serving: 2
Ingredients
- 2 prebaked pizza crusts
- ½ cup Spicy Black Bean Dip
- 1 tomato, thinly sliced
- 1 carrot, grated
- 1 red onion
- 1 avocado

Direction
1. Preheat the oven to 400°F.
2. Lay the two crusts out on a large baking sheet. Spread half the Spicy Black Bean Dip on each pizza crust.
3. Then layer on the tomato slices with a pinch pepper if you like. Sprinkle the

grated carrot with the sea salt and lightly massage it in with your hands.

4.   Spread the carrot on top of the tomato, then add the onion.

5.   Pop the pizzas in the oven for 10 to 20 minutes, or until they're done to your taste. Top the cooked pizzas with sliced avocado and another sprinkle of pepper.

Nutrition: 379 Calories 15g Fiber 13g Protein

434. Tomato Basil Spaghetti (FAST)

Preparation Time: 5 minutes
Cooking Time: 20 minutes
Servings: 4
Ingredients:

- 15-ounce cooked great northern beans
- 10.5-ounces cherry tomatoes, halved
- 1 small white onion, peeled, diced
- 1 tablespoon minced garlic
- 8 basil leaves, chopped
- 2 tablespoons olive oil
- 1-pound spaghetti

Directions:

1.   Take a large pot half full with salty water, place it over medium-high heat, bring it to a boil, add spaghetti and cook for 10 to 12 minutes until tender.

2.   Then drain spaghetti into a colander and reserve 1 cup of pasta liquid.

3.   Take a large skillet pan, place it over medium-high heat, add oil and when hot, add onion, tomatoes, basil, and garlic and cook for 5 minutes until vegetables have turned tender.

4.   Add cooked spaghetti and beans, pour in pasta water, stir until just mixed and cook for 2 minutes until hot.

5.   Serve straight away.

Nutrition: 147 Cal 5 g Fat 0.7 g Saturated Fat 21.2 g Carbohydrates 1.5 g Fiber 5.4 g Sugars 3.8 g Protein;

435. Bean and Rice Burritos (FAST)

Preparation Time: 10 minutes
Cooking Time: 20 minutes
Servings: 6
Ingredients:

- 32 ounces refried beans
- 2 cups cooked rice
- 2 cups chopped spinach
- 1 tablespoon olive oil
- 1/2 cup tomato salsa
- 6 tortillas, whole-grain, warm
- Guacamole as needed for serving

Directions:

1.   Switch on the oven, then set it to 375 degrees F and let it preheat.

2.   Take a medium saucepan, place it over medium heat, add beans, and cook for 3 to 5 minutes until softened, remove the pan from heat.

3.   Place one tortilla on clean working space, spread some of the beans on it into a log, leaving 2-inches of the edge, top beans with spinach, rice and salsa, and then tightly wrap the tortilla to seal the filling like a burrito.

4.   Repeat with the remaining tortillas, place these burritos on a baking sheet, brush them with olive oil and then bake for 15 minutes until golden.

5.   Serve burritos with guacamole.

Nutrition: 421 Cal 9 g Fat 2 g Saturated Fat 70 g Carbohydrates 11 g Fiber 3 g Sugars 15 g Protein;

436. Avocado and Chickpeas Lettuce Cups (FAST)

Preparation Time: 10 minutes
Cooking Time: 0 minutes
Servings: 4
Ingredients:

- 2 small avocados, peeled, pitted, diced
- 8 ounces hearts of palm
- ¾ cup cooked chickpeas
- 1/2 cup cucumber, diced
- 1 tablespoon minced shallots
- 2 cups mixed greens
- 1 tablespoon Dijon mustard
- 1 lime, zested, juiced
- 2 tablespoons chopped cilantro and more for topping
- 2/3 teaspoon salt
- 1/3 teaspoon ground black pepper
- 1 tablespoon apple cider vinegar
- 2 ½ tablespoons olive oil

Directions:

1.   Take a medium bowl, add shallots and cilantro in it, stir in salt, black pepper, mustard, vinegar, lime juice, and zest until just mixed and then slowly mix in olive oil until combined.

2.   Add cucumber, hearts of palm and chickpeas, stir until mixed, fold in avocado and then top with some more cilantro.

3.   Distribute mixed greens among four plates, top with chickpea mixture and then serve.

Nutrition: 280 Cal 12.6 g Fat 1.5 g Saturated Fat 32.8 g Carbohydrates 9.3 g Fiber 1.2 g Sugars 7.6 g Protein;

437. Minted Peas (FAST)

Preparation Time: 5 minutes
Cooking Time: 5 minutes
Serving: 4
Ingredient:
- 1 tablespoon olive oil
- 4 cups peas, fresh or frozen (not canned)
- ½ teaspoon sea salt
- Freshly ground black pepper
- 3 tablespoons chopped fresh mint

Direction:
1. In a large sauté pan, cook olive oil over medium-high heat until hot. Add the peas and cook, about 5 minutes. Remove the pan from heat. Stir in the salt, season with pepper, and stir in the mint. Serve hot.

Nutrition: 90 Calories 5g Fiber 8g Protein

438. Glazed Curried Carrots (FAST)

Preparation Time: 5 minutes
Cooking Time: 15 minutes
Serving: 6
Ingredient:
- 1-pound carrots
- 2 tablespoons olive oil
- 2 tablespoons curry powder
- 2 tablespoons pure maple syrup
- Juice of ½ lemon

Direction
1. Cook carrots with water over medium-high heat for 10 minutes. Drain and return them to the pan over medium-low heat.
2. Stir in the olive oil, curry powder, maple syrup, and lemon juice. Cook, stirring constantly, until the liquid reduces, about 5 minutes. Season well and serve immediately.

Nutrition: 91 Calories 5g Fiber 9g Protein

439. Sautéed Citrus Spinach (FAST)

Preparation Time: 10 minutes
Cooking Time: 10 minutes
Serving: 4
Ingredient:
- 2 tablespoons olive oil
- 1 shallot, chopped
- 2 garlic cloves, minced
- 10 ounces' baby spinach
- Zest and juice of 1 orange

Direction
1. Cook olive oil over medium-high heat. Cook the shallot for 3 minutes. Cook garlic for 30 seconds.
2. Add the spinach, orange juice, and orange zest. Cook for 2 minutes. Season with salt and pepper. Serve warm.

Nutrition: 91 Calories 4g Fiber 7g Protein

440. Baked Zucchini Chips

Preparation Time: 20 minutes
Cooking Time: 2 hours 45 minutes
Servings: 10
Ingredients:
- 2 medium zucchinis, sliced with a mandolin
- 1 tbsp. olive oil
- 1/2 tsp salt

Directions:
1. Preheat your oven to 200 degrees F.
2. Prepare your baking sheets by lining with parchment paper.
3. Add all ingredients to a large mixing bowl and toss to coat the zucchini with oil and salt thoroughly.
4. Arrange the zucchini slices in a single layer on the baking sheet. They can touch but they should not overlap.
5. Bake for 2 and a half hours or until the zucchini chips are golden and crispy.
6. Turn off the oven and allow them to cool with the oven door cropped slightly open. This will allow the zucchini chips to crisp up even more as they cool.

Nutrition: Total fat: 1.5g / Cholesterol: 0mg / Sodium: 120mg / Total carbohydrates: 1.3g Dietary fiber: 0.4g / Protein: 0.5g / Calcium: 6mg / Potassium: 103mg / Iron: 0mg

VEGETARIAN DESSERT

441. Avocado Pudding ,Chia (FAST)

Preparation Time: 10-20 minutes
Cooking Time: 10 minutes
Servings: 4
Ingredients:
- 2 large avocados, pee led, pitted
- 40ml unsweetened cacao
- 45g coconut cream
- 15ml coconut oil, melted
- 30g vanilla flavored rice protein powder
- 4 drops Stevia
- 15g Chia seeds

Directions:
1. In a food blender, combine avocados, cacao, coconut cream, coconut oil, Vanilla WPI, and Stevia.
2. Blend until smooth.
3. Divide among four serving bowls.
4. Refrigerate 10 minutes.
5. Sprinkle with chia seeds and serve.

Nutrition: Calories 278 Total Fat 22.6g Total Carbohydrate 16.2g Dietary Fiber 11.4g Total Sugars 0.6g Protein 12.1g

442. Apple Mix

Preparation Time: 10 minutes
Cooking Time: 4 hours
Servings: 6
Ingredients
- 6 apples, cored, peeled and sliced
- 1 and ½ cups almond flour
- Cooking spray
- 1 cup coconut sugar
- 1 tablespoon cinnamon powder
- ¾ cup cashew butter, melted

Directions
1. Add apple slices to your slow cooker after you've greased it with cooking spray
2. Add flour, sugar, cinnamon and coconut butter, stir gently, cover, cook on High for 4 hours, divide into bowls and serve cold.

Nutrition: Calories 200 fat 5 fiber 5 carbs 8 protein 4 g

443. Pears and Dried Fruits Bowls

Preparation Time: 10 minutes
Cooking Time: 4 hours
Servings: 12

Ingredients
- 3 pears, cored and chopped
- ½ cup raisins
- 2 cups dried fruits
- 1 teaspoon ginger powder
- ¼ cup coconut sugar
- 1 teaspoon lemon zest, grated

Directions
1. In your slow cooker, mix pears with raisins, dried fruits, ginger, sugar and lemon zest, stir, cover, cook on Low for 4 hours, divide into bowls and serve cold.

Nutrition: Calories 140 fat 3 fiber 4carbs 6 protein 6

444. Pears and Orange Sauce

Preparation Time: 10 minutes
Cooking Time: 4 hours
Servings: 4
Ingredients
- 4 pears, peeled and cored
- 2 cups orange juice
- ¼ cup maple syrup
- 2 teaspoons cinnamon powder
- 1 tablespoon ginger, grated

Directions
1. In your slow cooker, mix pears with orange juice, maple syrup, cinnamon and ginger, cover and cook on Low for 4 hours.
2. Divide pears and orange sauce between plates and serve warm. !

Nutrition: Calories 140 fat 1 fiber 2 carbs 3 protein 4

445. Almond Cookies

Preparation Time: 10 minutes
Cooking Time: 2 hours and 30 minutes
Servings: 12
Ingredients
- 1 tablespoon flaxseed mixed with 2 tablespoons water
- ¼ cup coconut oil, melted
- 1 cup coconut sugar
- ½ teaspoon vanilla extract
- 1 teaspoon baking powder
- 1 and ½ cups almond meal
- ½ cup almonds, chopped

Directions
1. In a bowl, mix oil with sugar, vanilla extract and flax meal and whisk.

2   Add baking powder, almond meal and almonds and stir well.

3   Line your slow cooker with parchment paper, spread cookie mix on the bottom of the pot, cover and cook on Low for 2 hours and 30 minutes.

4   Leave cookie sheet to cool down, cut into medium pieces and serve.

5   Enjoy!

Nutrition: Calories 220 fat 2 fiber 1 carbs 3 protein 6

446.   Pumpkin Cake

Preparation Time: 10 minutes
Cooking Time: 2 hours and 20 minutes
Servings: 10
Ingredients
- 1 and ½ teaspoons baking powder
- Cooking spray
- 1 cup pumpkin puree
- 2 cups almond flour
- ½ teaspoon baking soda
- 1 and ½ teaspoons cinnamon, ground
- ¼ teaspoon ginger, ground
- 1 tablespoon coconut oil, melted
- 1 tablespoon flaxseed mixed with 2 tablespoons water
- 1 tablespoon vanilla extract
- 1/3 cup maple syrup
- 1 teaspoon lemon juice

Directions
1   In a bowl, flour with baking powder, baking soda, cinnamon and ginger and stir.

2   Add flaxseed, coconut oil, vanilla, pumpkin puree, maple syrup and lemon juice, stir and pour in your slow cooker after you've sprayed it with cooking spray and lined with parchment paper.

3   Cover pot and cook on Low for 2 hours and 20 minutes.

4   Leave cake to cool down, slice and serve.

5   Enjoy!

Nutrition: Calories 182 fat 3 fiber 2 carbs 3 protein 1

447.   Salted Caramel Coconut Balls

Preparation Time: 15 minutes
Cooking Time: 25 minutes
Servings: 12 balls
Ingredients:
- 1 cup pitted dates
- 1 cup almonds
- ¼ cup coconut flakes
- ¼ tsp. salt

Directions:
1.   Blend the dates, almonds, and salt until a sticky dough forms in your food processor.

2.   Divide dough into 12. Roll this to make balls. Roll the balls in the coconut flakes, making sure they're completely covered, and serve.

Nutrition: Calories: 33 Total fat: 3g Carbohydrates: 1g Protein: 0g

448.   Baked Pears (FAST)

Preparation Time: 5 minutes
Cooking Time: 25 minutes
Servings: 2
Ingredients:
- 2 halved pears
- 1 tsp dark syrup
- Cinnamon

Directions:
1.   Preheat the oven to 350 F.

2.   Scoop the seeds out of your pears and place them in your baking tray. Drizzle with syrup and sprinkle with cinnamon.

3.   Bake for 20 - 25 minutes and serve while warm.

Nutrition: Calories: 208 Total fat: 498g Carbohydrates: 3g Protein: 0g

449.   No Bake Apple Pie (FAST)

Preparation Time: 5 minutes
Cooking Time: 0 minutes
Servings: 2
Ingredients:
- 2 chopped red apples
- ¼ cup chopped almonds
- ¼ cup sultanas
- 2 tsp. lemon juice
- ½ tsp. cinnamon

Directions:
1.   In a bowl, mix the almonds, sultanas, lemon juice, and cinnamon. Toss the apples in the mixture, making sure the apples are completely covered.

2.   Plate the dessert, top with a dollop of chilled coconut cream, garnish with some chopped almonds and serve.

Nutrition: Calories: 300 Total fat: 13g Carbohydrates: 17g Protein: 2g

450.   Spiced Dutch Cookies   (FAST)

Preparation Time: 10-20 minutes
Cooking Time: 8 minutes
Servings: 6

Ingredients:
- 180g almond flour
- 55ml coconut oil, melted
- 60g rice protein powder, vanilla flavor
- 1 banana, mashed
- 40g Chia seeds
- Spice mix:
- 15g allspice
- 1 pinch white pepper
- 1 pinch ground coriander seeds
- 1 pinch ground mace

Directions:
1. Preheat oven to 190C/375F.
2. Soak chia seeds in ½ cup water. Place aside 10 minutes.
3. Mash banana in a large bowl.
4. Fold in almond flour, coconut oil, protein powder, and spice mix.
5. Add soaked chia seeds and stir to combine.
6. Stir until the dough is combined and soft. If needed add 1-2 tablespoons water.
7. Roll the dough to 1cm thick. Cut out cookies.
8. Arrange the cookies onto baking sheet, lined with parchment paper.
9. Bake 7-8 minutes.
10. Serve at room temperature.

Nutrition: Calories 278 Total Fat 20g Total Carbohydrate 13.1g Dietary Fiber 5.9g Total Sugars 2.4g Protein 13.1g

451. Stewed Rhubarb

Preparation Time: 10 minutes
Cooking Time: 7 hours
Servings: 4
Ingredients
- 5 cups rhubarb, chopped
- 2 tablespoons coconut butter
- 1/3 cup water
- 2/3 cup coconut sugar
- 1 teaspoon vanilla extract

Directions
1 Put rhubarb in your slow cooker.
2 Add water and sugar, stir gently, cover and cook on Low for 7 hours.
3 Add coconut butter and vanilla extract, stir and keep in the fridge until it's cold.
4 Enjoy!

Nutrition: Calories 120 fat 2 fiber 3 carbs 6 protein 1

452. Warming Baked Apples

Preparation Time: 10 minutes
Cooking Time: 2 hours and 10 minutes
Servings: 5

Ingredients:
- 4 medium-sized apples
- 1/2 cup of granola
- 4 teaspoon of maple syrup
- 2 tablespoons of melted vegan butter, unsalted

Directions:
1. Cut off the top of the apple and remove the core from each apple using a measuring spoon.
2. Fill the center of each apple with 1/8 cup of granola and place it in a 4-quarts slow cooker.
3. Drizzle with butter and then sprinkle with a teaspoon maple syrup over each apple.
4. Cover the top, plug in the slow cooker; adjust the cooking time to 2 hours and let it cook on the high heat setting or until it gets tender. Serve right away.

Nutrition: Calories: 162 Carbohydrates: 42g Protein: 0.5g Fats: 0.3g

453. Poached Plums

Preparation Time: 10 minutes
Cooking Time: 3 hours
Servings: 6
Ingredients
- 14 plums, halved
- 1 and ¼ cups coconut sugar
- 1 teaspoon cinnamon powder
- ¼ cup water

Directions
1 Arrange plums in your slow cooker, add sugar, cinnamon and water, stir, cover, cook on Low for 3 hours, divide into cups and serve cold. Enjoy!

Nutrition: Calories 150 fat 2 fiber 1 carbs 2 protein 3

454. Bananas and Agave Sauce

Preparation Time: 10 minutes
Cooking Time: 2 hours
Servings: 4
Ingredients
- Juice of ½ lemon
- 3 tablespoons agave nectar
- 1 tablespoon coconut oil
- 4 bananas, peeled and sliced diagonally
- ½ teaspoon cardamom seeds

Directions
1 Arrange bananas in your slow cooker, add agave nectar, lemon juice, oil and cardamom, cover and cook on Low for 2 hours.
2 Divide bananas on plates, drizzle agave sauce all over and serve. Enjoy!

Nutrition: Calories 120 fat 1 fiber 2 carbs 8 protein 3

VEGAN DESSERT

455. Coconut Cacao Bites

Preparation Time: 1 hour and 10 minutes
Cooking Time: 0 minute
Servings: 20
Ingredients:
- 1 1/2 cups almond flour
- 3 dates, pitted
- 1 1/2 cups shredded coconut, unsweetened
- 1/4 teaspoons ground cinnamon
- 2 Tablespoons flaxseed meal
- 1/16 teaspoon sea salt
- 2 Tablespoons vanilla protein powder
- 1/4 cup cacao powder
- 3 Tablespoons hemp seeds
- 1/3 cup tahini
- 4 Tablespoons coconut butter, melted

Directions:
1. Place all the ingredients in a food processor and pulse for 5 minutes until the thick paste comes together.
2. Drop the mixture in the form of balls on a baking sheet lined with parchment sheet, 2 tablespoons per ball and then freeze for 1 hour until firm to touch.
3. Serve straight away.

Nutrition: Calories: 120 Cal / Fat: 4.5 g / Carbs: 15 g / Protein: 4 g / Fiber: 2 g

456. Wonderful Peanut Butter Mousse (FAST)

Preparation Time: 2 to 5 minutes
Cooking Time: 0 minutes
Servings: 4
Ingredients:
- 4 tablespoons natural unsweetened peanut butter
- ½ can coconut cream
- 1 ½ teaspoons stevia

Directions:
1. First of all, please check that you've all the ingredients obtainable. Now combine all ingredients & whip for one minute, until mixture forms peaks.
2. Finally, chill for at least three hours or until a mousse texture is achieved.

Nutrition: Calories: 206 / Protein: 5 g / Fat: 18 g / Carbs: 6 g

457. Watermelon Mint Popsicles

Preparation Time: 8 hours and 5 minutes
Cooking Time: 0 minute
Servings: 8
Ingredients:
- 20 mint leaves, diced
- 6 cups watermelon chunks
- 3 tablespoons lime juice

Directions:
1. Add watermelon in a food processor along with lime juice and then pulse for 15 seconds until smooth.
2. Pass the watermelon mixture through a strainer placed over a bowl, remove the seeds and then stir mint into the collected watermelon mixture.
3. Take eight Popsicle molds, pour in prepared watermelon mixture, and freeze for 2 hours until slightly firm.
4. Then insert popsicle sticks and continue freezing for 6 hours until solid.
5. Serve straight away

Nutrition: Calories: 90 Cal Fat: 0 g Carbs: 23 g Protein: 0 g Fiber: 0 g

458. Brownie Energy Bites

Preparation Time: 1 hour and 10 minutes
Cooking Time: 0 minute
Servings: 2
Ingredients:
- 1/2 cup walnuts
- 1 cup Medjool dates, chopped
- 1/2 cup almonds
- 1/8 teaspoon salt
- 1/2 cup shredded coconut flakes
- 1/3 cup and 2 teaspoons cocoa powder, unsweetened

Directions:
1. Place almonds and walnuts in a food processor and pulse for 3 minutes until the dough starts to come together.
2. Add remaining ingredients, reserving ¼ cup of coconut and pulse for 2 minutes until incorporated.
3. Shape the mixture into balls, roll them in remaining coconut until coated, and refrigerate for 1 hour.
4. Serve straight away

Nutrition: Calories: 174.6 Cal Fat: 8.1 g Carbs: 25.5 g Protein: 4.1 g Fiber: 4.4 g

459. Tantalizing Apple Pie Bites (FAST)

Preparation Time: 20 minutes
Cooking Time: 0 minutes
Servings: 4
Ingredients

- 1 cup chopped walnuts - ½ a cup of coconut oil
- ¼ cup of ground flaxseed - ½ ounce of frozen, dried apples
- 1 teaspoon of vanilla extract
- 1 teaspoon of cinnamon - Liquid Stevia

Directions
1. Melt the coconut oil until it is liquid
2. Take your blender and add walnuts, coconut oil, and process well
3. Add flaxseeds, vanilla, and Stevia
4. Keep processing until a fine mixture form
5. Stop and add crumbled dried apples
6. Process until your desired texture appears
7. Portion the mixture amongst muffin molds and allow them to chill

Nutrition: Calories: 194 / Fat: 19g / Carbs: 2g / Protein: 2.3g

460. Vintage Moist Almond Cake

Preparation Time: 1 hour
Cooking Time: 30 minutes
Servings: 8
Ingredients:

- 5 oz. sugar
- 1 cup Greek yogurt, vanilla (full fat)
- 1 cup almond flour
- 1 ½ teaspoons baking powder
- 1 egg
- ¼ teaspoons baking soda
- 1 ½ teaspoons vanilla
- ¼ teaspoons salt
- 2 oz. butter (soft)
- ½ teaspoon cinnamon powder

Directions:
1. First of all, please confirm you've all the ingredients accessible. Grease a 0- inch

layer cake tin and sprinkle with a little almond flour. Heat oven to about 3600 F. to 3700 F.
2. Now sift your salt, cinnamon powder, baking soda, baking powder, almond flour, & sugar in a large bowl. Stir to combine, and set aside.
3. This step is essential. Place in a blender, banana, egg, butter, sugar, and vanilla.
4. Then blend for about 2 minutes at super-speed; consistency should be smooth.
5. Pour blended mixture into almond flour mixture & mix thoroughly.
6. One thing remains to be done. Pour and scrape into the greased tin.
7. Finally, place in oven and bake for about 25 to 30 minutes. Cool & serve.

Nutrition: Calories: 157 / Protein: 2.3 g / Fat: 8 g / Carbs: 19.5 g

461. Iconic Braised Endives

Preparation Time: 20 to 25 minutes
Cooking Time: 35 minutes
Servings: 2
Ingredients:

- 1 ¾ oz. Butter
- Salt and pepper to taste
- 1 tablespoon Lemon juice
- 3 Endives (chopped lengthwise, brown bruised bits discarded)
- 3 ½ tablespoon Water

Directions:
1. First of all, please check that you've all the ingredients out there. Melt the butter in a non-stick place the endives in it.
2. Then season with salt and pepper & sprinkle the lemon juice on top.
3. One thing remains to be done. Now please leave to brown for about 5 to 10 minutes and then flip.
4. Finally, add a little water to the pan & cook covered for about 20 to 25 minutes.

Nutrition: Calories: 225 / Protein: 3 g / Fat: 21 g / Carbs: 9 g

BONUS INSTANT POT RECIPES

462. <u>Amaranth Banana Breakfast Porridge</u>

Preparation Time: 10 minutes
Cooking Time: 25 minutes
Servings: 8
Ingredients
- cup amaranth
- cinnamon sticks
- bananas, diced
- Tbsp chopped pecans
- cups water

Directions
1. Combine the amaranth, water, and cinnamon sticks, and banana in a pot. Cover and let simmer around 25 minutes.
2. Remove from heat and discard the cinnamon. Places into bowls, and top with pecans.

Nutrition: Calories 330 Carbohydrates 62 g Fats 6 g Protein 10 g

463. <u>Mango-Lime Rice (FAST)</u>

Preparation Time: 5 minutes
Cooking Time: 10 minutes
Servings: 2
Ingredients:
- ½ cup brown rice
- 1 cup water
- ¼ tablespoon fresh lime juice
- 1/8 cup chopped fresh rosemary
- ¼ mango, peeled, pitted, and cut into 1/2-inch cubes

Directions:
1. Combine water, brown rice, and lime juice, mango in an Instant Pot.
2. Close the pressure-release valve. Select Manual and set the pot at High Pressure for 10 minutes. At the end of the cooking time, allow the pot to sit undisturbed for 10 minutes, then release any remaining pressure.
3. Serve with fresh rosemary.
4. Enjoy.

Nutrition: Calories 210 Fat 2g Cholesterol 0mg Carbohydrate 45.2g Fiber 3.9g

464. <u>Parsley Hummus Pasta (FAST)</u>

Preparation Time:05 minutes
Cooking Time: 05 minutes
Servings: 2
Ingredients:
- ½ cup chickpeas

- 1/8 cup coconut oil
- ½ fresh lemon
- 1/8 cup tahini
- ½ teaspoon garlic powder
- 1/8 teaspoon cumin
- 1/4 teaspoon salt
- 1 green onions
- 1/8 bunch fresh parsley, or to taste
- 1 cup pasta
- Enough water

Directions:
1. Drain the chickpeas and add them to a food processor along with the coconut oil, juice from the lemon, tahini, garlic powder, cumin, and salt. Pulse the Ingredients, adding a small amount of water if needed to keep it moving, until the hummus is smooth.
2. Slice the green onion (both white and green ends) and pull the parsley leaves from the stems. Add the green onion and parsley to the hummus in the food processor and process again until only small flecks of green remain. Taste the hummus and adjust the salt, lemon, or garlic if needed.
3. Add pasta, water into Instant Pot. Place lid on pot and lock into place to seal. Pressure Cook on High Pressure for 4 minutes. Use Quick Pressure Release.
4. In Sauté mode add hummus to pasta. When it mixes turn off the switch of Instant Pot.
5. Serve and enjoy.

Nutrition: Calories 582, Total Fat 26. 3g, Cholesterol 47mg, Sodium 338mg, Total Carbohydrate 71g, Dietary Fiber 10. 8g, Total Sugars 6. 1g, Protein 19. 9g

465. <u>Cabbage and Noodles (FAST)</u>

Preparation Time: 5 minutes
Cooking Time: 5 minutes
Servings: 2
Ingredients:
- 1 cup wide egg noodles
- 1 1/2 tablespoon butter
- 1small onion
- 1/2 head green cabbage, shredded
- Salt and pepper to taste

Directions:
1. Add egg noodles, butter, water, onion, green cabbage, pepper, and salt to Instant Pot. Place lid on Instant Pot and lock into place to seal.

Pressure Cook on High Pressure for 4 minutes. Use Quick Pressure Release.
2. Serve and enjoy.

Nutrition: Calories183 Fat 6.8g Cholesterol 31mg Carbohydrate 27.2g Fiber 5.9g

466. Japanese Sushi Rice (FAST)

Preparation Time: 5 minutes
Cooking Time: 20 minutes
Servings: 2
Ingredients:
- 2 cups water
- 1 teaspoon salt
- 1 teaspoon honey
- ½ sheet nori
- 1 cup uncooked white rice (sushi rice)

Directions:
1. In an Instant Pot, combine the water, salt, honey, and nori. Bring to a boil and add the rice.
2. Close the pressure-release valve. Select Manual and set the pot at High Pressure for 10 minutes. At the end of the cooking time, allow the pot to sit undisturbed for 10 minutes, then release any remaining pressure.
3. Serve and enjoy.

Nutrition: Calories 340 Fat 0.6g Cholesterol 0mg Carbohydrate 76.8g Fiber 1.5g

467. Zucchini Noodles (FAST)

Preparation Time: 10 minutes
Cooking Time: 15 minutes
Servings: 2
Ingredients:
- 2 zucchinis, peeled
- Marinara sauce of your choice
- Any other seasonings you wish to use

Directions:
1. Peel & spiralizer your zucchini into noodles.
2. Add some of your favorite sauce to Instant Pot, hit "Sauté" and "Adjust," so it's on the "More" or "High" setting.
3. Once the sauce is boiling, add now the noodles to the pot. Toss the noodles in the sauce and allow them to heat up and soften for a few minutes for about 2-5 minutes.
4. Serve in the bowls and top with grated parmesan, if desired.
5. Enjoy!

Nutrition: Calories 86 Fat 2g Cholesterol 1mg Carbohydrate 15.2g Fiber 3.8g

468. Mexican Beans

Preparation Time: 15 minutes
Cooking Time: 35 minutes
Servings: 2
Ingredients:
- ½ cup dried pinto beans
- 2 cups water
- 1 small onion, chopped
- 1 medium ripe tomato, chopped
- 1 fresh bell pepper, chopped
- 1 tablespoon fresh cilantro, chopped

Directions:
1. Select the High Sauté setting on the Instant Pot, add pinto beans, water, onion, ripe tomato, and bell pepper. Secure the lid. Press the Cancel button to reset the program, then select the Pressure Cook or Manual setting and set the cooking time for 35 minutes at High Pressure.
2. Let the pressure release naturally; this will take 10 to 20 minutes.
3. Garnish with fresh cilantro.

Nutrition: Calories 212 Fat 0.9g Cholesterol 0mg Carbohydrate 40.4g Fiber 9.8g

469. Maple & Vanilla Toast (FAST)

Preparation time: 5 minutes
Cooking Time: 2 minutes
Serving: 2
Ingredients:
- 2 tbsp maple syrup
- 1 tsp vanilla extract
- 2 bread slices
- 2 tbsp vegan butter

Direction:
1. Combine the vanilla and syrup to brush over the slices of bread—all sides.
2. Warm up the Instant Pot using the sauté function. Melt the butter and add the prepared bread slices.
3. Sauté the bead for two minutes on each side.
4. Serve with your favorite toppings.

Nutrition: Calories 224, Carbohydrates 25.3 g, Fats 0.8 g, Protein 2.3 g

470. Vanilla Quinoa (FAST)

Preparation time: 5 minutes
Cooking Time: 1 minutes
Serving: 3
Ingredients:
- 1 cup uncooked quinoa
- 2 cups water

- 1.5 tbsp maple syrup
- 2 tbsp cinnamon powder
- 1 tsp vanilla
- 1 pinch salt

Toppings:
- Crushed almonds, cherries, fresh berries

Direction:
1. Add the quinoa, water, maple syrup, cinnamon powder, vanilla, and salt into the Instant Pot.
2. Set the pressure manually for 1 minute.
3. When done, let it do a natural release for 10 minutes. Then, quick release the remainder of the pressure and serve with toppings.

Nutrition: Calories 280, Carbohydrates 47 g, Fats 4 g, Protein 9 g

471. Sweet Potato Toast (FAST)

Preparation time: 10 minutes
Cooking time: 10 minutes
Serving: 4
Ingredients:
- 3 tbsp vegan butter
- 2 sweet potatoes
- 1 tsp turmeric powder

Direction:
1. Peel the potatoes and slice.
2. Warm up the Instant Pot using the sauté function. Add one tbsp of the butter. Add 1/3 of the slices into the pot and sauté until browned on each side.
3. Continue until all of the potatoes are done.
4. Sprinkle the toasts with the turmeric and garnish with your favorite toppings such as coconut cream and veggies.

Nutrition: Calories 140, Carbohydrates 27 g, Fats 4 g, Protein 2.5 g

472. Butternut Squash Risotto (FAST)

Preparation time: 5 minutes
Cooking Time: 16 minutes
Serving: 8
Ingredients:
- 2 cups Arborio rice
- 4 cups butternut squash, peeled, seeded and diced
- 5-ounces baby spinach
- 8-ounce Baby Bella mushrooms, sliced
- 4 cups vegetable broth

Direction:
1. Switch on the instant pot, pour water in the inner pot, press the sauté/simmer button, then adjust cooking time to 5 minutes and let preheat.
2. Add squash, stir well and continue cook for 2 minutes.
3. Then add mushrooms, cook for another minute, add 1 tablespoon minced garlic, stir well and cook for 3 minutes.
4. Then add rice, stir until combined, season rice with 1 teaspoon salt, 1/3 teaspoon black pepper and 1/4 teaspoon Italian seasoning.
5. Pour in the broth, stir well to remove browned bits from the bottom of the pot and press the cancel button.
6. Top rice mixture with spinach, then secure instant pot with its lid in the sealed position, press the manual button, adjust cooking time to 6 minutes, select high-pressure cooking and let cook until instant pot buzz.
7. Then slowly blend in water until pesto is blended to desired consistency.
8. When instant pot buzzes, press the cancel button and do quick pressure release until pressure knob drops down.
9. Then carefully open the instant pot, stir risotto, transfer into bowls and serve.
10. Serve the risotto with pesto.

Nutrition: Calories 342, Carbohydrates 58 g, Fats 9.1 g, Protein: 9 g

473. Quinoa Burrito Bowls

Preparation time: 10 minutes
Cooking Time: 26 minutes
Serving: 4
Ingredients:
- 1 cup quinoa, rinsed
- 1 1/2 cups cooked black beans
- 1/2 of medium red onion, peeled and diced
- 1 medium bell pepper, cored and diced
- 1 cup tomato salsa, and more for serving

Direction:
1. Switch on the instant pot, grease the inner pot with 1 teaspoon olive oil, press the sauté/simmer button, then adjust cooking time to 5 minutes and let preheat.
2. Add onion and pepper and cook for 8 minutes or until softened, then season with 1/2 teaspoon salt and 1 teaspoon ground cumin and cook for 1 minute or until fragrant.
3. Add quinoa and beans, then pour in salsa and 1 cup water, stir until mixed and press the cancel button.

4. Secure instant pot with its lid in the sealed position, then press the rice button, adjust cooking time to 12 minutes, select low-pressure cooking and let cook until instant pot buzz.
5. Instant pot will take 10 minutes or more to build pressure, and when it buzzes, press the cancel button and do natural pressure release for 10 minutes or more until pressure knob drops down.
6. Then carefully open the instant pot, fluff quinoa with a fork and ladle into bowls.
7. Serve with guacamole, salsa, and lemon wedges.

Nutrition: Calories 657.7, Carbohydrates 95 g, Fats 17.4 g, Protein: 34.1 g

474. Breakfast Potatoes

Preparation time: 10 minutes
Cooking Time: 35 minutes
Serving: 5
Ingredients:
- 6 medium potatoes, peeled and ½-inch cubed
- 1 medium white onion, peeled and ½-inch cubed
- 1 medium green bell pepper, ½-inch cubed
- 3/4 cup vegetable broth

Direction:
1. Switch on the instant pot, add 3 tablespoons coconut oil in the inner pot, press the sauté/simmer button, then adjust cooking time to 5 minutes and let preheat.
2. Then add potatoes and cook for 3 minutes or until sauté.
3. Sprinkle potatoes with ¾ teaspoon salt, 1/3 teaspoon black pepper, ¼ teaspoon paprika and 1 tablespoon nutritional yeast, cook for 4 minutes and then press the cancel button.
4. Secure instant pot with its lid in the sealed position, then press the manual button, adjust cooking time to 1 minute, select high-pressure cooking and let cook until instant pot buzz.
5. Instant pot will take 10 minutes or more to build pressure, and when it buzzes, press the cancel button and do quick pressure release until pressure knob drops down.
6. Carefully open the instant pot, gently stir the potatoes, then transfer into a bowl and let refrigerate until cooked.
7. Then place a skillet pan over medium heat, grease with oil and when hot, add onion and pepper and cook for 10 minutes or until softened.
8. Transfer vegetables to a plate, add potatoes into the pan and cook for 10 to 15 minutes or until potatoes are crispy and nicely browned.
9. Return vegetables into the pan, stir well and cook for 1 minute or until thoroughly heated.
10. Serve immediately.

Nutrition: Calories 157, Carbohydrates 30 g, Fats 2.5 g, Protein 4.6 g

475. Papaya Stuffed Acorn Squash (FAST)

Preparation time: 5 minutes
Cooking Time: 3 minutes
Serving: 4
Ingredients:
- 2 cups of water
- 4 tsp maple syrup
- 2 tsp vegan butter
- 1 acorn squash, halved and deseeded
- 1 cup chopped peeled papaya
- A pinch cinnamon powders

Direction:
1. Open the instant pot, pour in the water, and fit in the trivet.
2. Put the maple syrup and vegan butter in a safe microwave bowl and melt together in the microwave for 20 seconds.
3. In another medium bowl, mix the papaya with the cinnamon and spoon the mixture into the squash halves.
4. Drizzle the syrup mixture over the stuffing and place the squash halves on the trivet.
5. Close the pot's lid, secure the pressure valve, and select Steam mode. Set the timer for 3 minutes.
6. When ready, perform a quick pressure release, and open the lid.
7. Remove the squash onto a serving plate, allow cooling for 1 to 2 minutes.

Nutrition: Calories 123, Carbohydrates 21.9 g, Fats 3.9 g, Protein 1.6 g

476. Sweet Potato Hash Brown Bowls (FAST)

Preparation time: 8 minutes
Cooking Time: 23 minutes
Serving: 4
Ingredients:
- 1 cup water
- 1 ½ lb. sweet potatoes, cubed
- 2 tbsp vegetable oil

- 1 large red onion, peeled and diced
- ¼ sliced white mushrooms
- 1 red bell pepper, deseeded and diced
- 1 garlic clove, minced
- Salt and black pepper to taste
- 1 tsp sweet paprika
- 1 tsp hot sauce
- 1 (8 oz) black beans, drained and rinsed
- 1 tbsp freshly chopped parsley
- 1 tsp dried oregano

Serving:
- 1 avocado, pitted and chopped
- Chopped parsley to garnish

Direction:
1. Turn on and open the instant pot; add the water into the pot.
2. Pour the potatoes into a steamer basket and fit the basket into the pot over the water.
3. Close the lid, secure the pressure valve, and select Manual mode on high pressure. Set the timer for 12 minutes.
4. Once the pot beeps, do a natural pressure release for 15 to 20 minutes, and then open the lid.
5. Carefully remove the steamer basket and set aside the potatoes to cool. Discard the water in the pot and select Sauté mode.
6. Pour the oil into the pot to heat and add the onion, mushrooms, and red bell pepper. Stir-fry until the vegetables have softened, 7 minutes.
7. Add the potatoes, garlic, salt, black pepper, paprika, hot sauce, black beans, parsley, and oregano. Stir and cook the ingredients until the flavors adequately incorporate, 4 minutes.
8. Adjust the taste with salt and black pepper and turn the pot off. Spoon the dish into serving bowls and garnish with avocado and parsley.

Nutrition: Calories 256, Carbohydrates 27.8 g, Fats 15.9 g, Protein 8.5 g

477. Carrots and Pineapple Muffins (FAST)

Preparation time: 20 minutes
Cooking Time: 8 minutes
Serving: 4
Ingredients:
- 2 tbsp flaxseed meal + 6 tbsp water
- 2/3 cup vegetable oil
- 1 tsp vanilla extract
- 1 cup beet sugar

- 1 ½ cups plain flour
- 1 tsp baking soda
- 1 tsp cinnamon powder
- ¼ tsp salt
- 2 tsp baking powder
- 1 cup chopped pineapple, crushed
- 1 cup grated carrots
- 2 cups of water

Direction:
1. In a small bowl, whisk the flaxseed meal with water and allow sitting for 15 minutes to combine properly. After, whisk in the vegetable oil and vanilla.
2. In a medium bowl, combine the beet sugar, flour, baking soda, cinnamon powder, salt, and baking powder. Beat in the flax egg mixture until adequately combined and fold in the carrots and pineapples.
3. Spoon the mixture into a 12-holed silicon egg mold.
4. Open the instant pot and pour in the water. Fit in a trivet and place the egg molds on top. Cover with aluminum foil.
5. Close the lid, secure the pressure valve, and select Manual mode on high pressure. Set the timer for 8 minutes.
6. Once done baking, perform a natural pressure release for 10 minutes, then a quick pressure release to let out the remaining steam, and open the lid.
7. Take out the egg mold and remove the foil. Pop out each muffin from the frame and transfer to a wire rack to cool. Serve the muffins slightly cooled.

Nutrition: Calories 642, Carbohydrates 74 g, Fats 36.7 g, Protein 5.3 g

478. Arugula Quinoa Breakfast

Preparation time: 7 minutes
Cooking Time: 2 minutes
Serving: 6
Ingredients:
- 4 ounces arugula
- 2 blood oranges, peeled and segment separated
- 1 ½ cups quinoa
- 2 ¼ cups water
- ¼ teaspoon cinnamon, ground
- 1 tablespoon olive oil
- 3 ounces walnuts, chopped
- Salt to taste

Direction:
1. Take your Instant Pot; open the top lid and plug it on.
2. Add the water with quinoa, cinnamon, and salt; gently stir to combine.
3. Properly close the top lid; make sure that safety valve is properly locked.
4. Press "manual" cooking function; set timer to 1-2 minutes. Then, set pressure level to "high".
5. Allow the pressure to build to cook the ingredients.
6. After cooking time is over press "cancel" setting. Find and press "NPR" for natural pressure release; it takes around 10 minutes to release pressure slowly.
7. Open the top lid, arugula, and oil; divide the cooked recipe in serving containers.
8. Top with the walnut and orange; serve warm.

Nutrition: Calories 127, Carbohydrates6 g, Fats 6 g, Protein 3 g

479. Classic Cinnamon Quinoa (FAST)

Preparation time: 5 minutes
Cooking Time: 1 minutes
Serving: 6
Ingredients:
- 2 ¼ cups water
- ¼ teaspoon cinnamon, ground
- ½ teaspoon vanilla
- 1 ½ cups quinoa
- 2 tablespoons maple syrup
- A pinch of salt
- Sliced almond and/apples for serving

Direction:
1. Take your Instant Pot; open the top lid and plug it on.
2. Add the water with maple syrup, quinoa, cinnamon, vanilla, and salt; gently stir to combine.
3. Properly close the top lid; make sure that safety valve is properly locked.
4. Press "manual" cooking function; set timer to 1-2 minutes. Then, set pressure level to "high".
5. Allow the pressure to build to cook the ingredients.
6. After cooking time is over press "cancel" setting. Find and press "NPR" for natural pressure release; it takes around 10 minutes to release pressure slowly.
7. Open the top lid, arugula, and oil; divide the cooked recipe in serving containers.

8. Serve warm with the sliced almond and/or apple slices on top.

Nutrition: Calories 126, Carbohydrates 21 g, Fats 11 g, Protein

480. Quinoa Veggie Morning (FAST)

Preparation time: 5 minutes
Cooking Time: 3 minutes
Serving: 4
Ingredients:
- Juice from 1 lime
- 1 bunch parsley, chopped
- 1 tomato, chopped
- 1 cup black quinoa
- 1 ½ cups water
- A pinch of salt
- Zest from 1 lime, grated
- ½ cup green olives, pitted and sliced
- 1 yellow bell pepper, chopped
- 1 cucumber, chopped

Direction:
1. Take your Instant Pot; open the top lid and plug it on.
2. Add the quinoa with water, salt and lime zest; gently stir to combine.
3. Properly close the top lid; make sure that safety valve is properly locked.
4. Press "manual" cooking function; set timer to 3 minutes. Then, set pressure level to "high".
5. Allow the pressure to build to cook the ingredients.
6. After cooking time is over press "cancel" setting. Find and press "QPR" for quick pressure release
7. Open the top lid, drain the liquid; add the lime juice, parsley, tomato, olives, bell pepper, and cucumber.
8. Toss the mixture and divide the cooked recipe in serving containers. Serve warm.

Nutrition: Calories 163, Carbohydrates 26 g, Fats 3 g, Protein 8 g

481. Instant Peas Risotto (FAST)

Preparation Time: 10 minutes
Cooking Time: 10 minutes
Servings: 3
Ingredients:
- 1 cup baby green peas
- 1 cup Arborio rice
- 2 cloves garlic, diced
- 3 tablespoons olive oil
- 1 brown onion, diced

- ½ teaspoon salt
- 2 celery sticks, make small cubes
- ½ teaspoon pepper
- 2 tablespoons lemon juice
- 2 cups vegetable stock

Directions:
1. Take your Instant Pot and place it on a clean kitchen platform. Turn it on after plugging it into a power socket.
2. Put the pot on "Sauté" mode. In the pot, add the oil, celery, onions, pepper, and salt; cook for 4-5 minutes until the ingredients become soft.
3. Mix in the zest, stock, garlic, peas, and rice. Stir the ingredients.
4. Close the lid and lock. Ensure that you have sealed the valve to avoid leakage.
5. Press "Manual" mode and set timer for 5 minutes. It will take a few minutes for the pot to build inside pressure and start cooking.
6. After the timer reads zero, press "Cancel" and quick release pressure.
7. Carefully remove the lid, add the lemon juice and serve warm!

Nutrition: Calories - 362 Fat – 13g Carbohydrates – 52.5g Fiber – 3g Protein – 8g

482. Mushroom Bean Farro

Preparation Time: 8-10 minutes
Cooking Time: 30 minutes
Servings: 3-4
Ingredients:
- 3 cups mushrooms, chopped
- 1 seeded jalapeno pepper, chopped
- 1 tablespoon shallot powder
- 2 tablespoons barley
- 1 tablespoon red curry paste
- ½ cup farro
- 1 cup navy beans, dried
- 2 tablespoons onion powder
- 9 garlic cloves, minced
- 2 tomatoes, diced
- Pepper and salt as needed

Directions:
1. Take your Instant Pot and place it on a clean kitchen platform. Turn it on after plugging it into a power socket.
2. Open the lid from the top and put it aside; start adding the beans, faro, barley, mushrooms, garlic, jalapeno, curry paste, shallot and onion powder, pepper and salt.

3. Add water to cover all the ingredients; gently stir them.
4. Close the lid and lock. Ensure that you have sealed the valve to avoid leakage.
5. Press "Manual" mode and set timer for 30 minutes. It will take a few minutes for the pot to build inside pressure and start cooking.
6. After the timer reads zero, press "Cancel" and naturally release pressure. It takes about 8-10 minutes to naturally release pressure.
7. Carefully remove the lid and add the tomatoes.
8. Sprinkle cilantro and scallions; serve warm!

Nutrition: Calories 238 Fat 6.5g Carbohydrates 38g Fiber 1.5g Protein 11g

483. Squash Eggplant Mania (FAST)

Preparation Time: 8-10 minutes
Cooking Time: 20 minutes
Servings: 4
Ingredients:
- 14 ounces eggplant, chopped
- 2 yellow onions, chopped
- 14 ounces squash, chopped
- 4 tomatoes, chopped
- 1 tablespoon olive oil, extra virgin
- 3 garlic cloves, finely minced
- ½ teaspoon thyme, dried
- 1 red capsicum, chopped
- 1 green capsicum, chopped
- 2 teaspoons dried basil
- Black pepper and salt as needed

Directions:
1. Take your Instant Pot and place it on a clean kitchen platform. Turn it on after plugging it into a power socket.
2. Put the pot on "Sauté" mode. In the pot, add the oil, garlic, and onion; cook for 3-4 minutes until the ingredients become soft.
3. Add the squash, eggplant, both capsicum, tomatoes, thyme, salt, pepper and basil; stir well.
4. Close the lid and lock. Ensure that you have sealed the valve to avoid leakage.
5. Press "Manual" mode and set timer for 10 minutes. It will take a few minutes for the pot to build inside pressure and start cooking.
6. After the timer reads zero, press "Cancel" and naturally release pressure. It takes about 8-10 minutes to naturally release pressure.
7. Carefully remove the lid and serve warm!

Nutrition: Calories 152 Fat 10g Carbohydrates 11.5g Fiber 3g Protein 2g

484. Potato Mustard Salad (FAST)

Preparation Time: 8-10 min.
Cooking Time: 10 min.
Servings: 6
Ingredients:
- 1 celery stalk, chopped
- 1 cup water
- 3 teaspoons dill, finely chopped
- 1 small yellow onion, chopped
- 1 teaspoon cider vinegar
- 3 ounces vegan mayo
- 6 red potatoes
- 1 teaspoon mustard
- Black pepper and salt as needed

Directions:
1. Take your Instant Pot and place it on a clean kitchen platform. Turn it on after plugging it into a power socket.
2. Open the lid from the top and put it aside; add the potatoes and water.
3. Close the lid and lock. Ensure that you have sealed the valve to avoid leakage.
4. Press "Manual" mode and set timer for 3 minutes. It will take a few minutes for the pot to build inside pressure and start cooking.
5. After the timer reads zero, press "Cancel" and quick release pressure.
6. Carefully remove the lid and chop the potatoes.
7. In a bowl of medium size, thoroughly mix the onion, potatoes, celery, salt, pepper, and dill.
8. Add the vegan mayo, vinegar, and mustard; stir well. Serve warm!

Nutrition: Calories 141 Fat 2g Carbohydrates 22.5g Fiber 2g Protein 4g

485. Chickpea Burger (FAST)

Preparation Time: 8-10 minutes
Cooking Time: 20 minutes
Servings: 5-6
Ingredients:
- 1 teaspoon cumin
- 2 bay leaves
- 1 cup chickpeas (dried), soaked for 4 hours
- 1 teaspoon thyme, dried
- 3 tablespoons tomato paste
- ½ cup whole wheat flour
- 1 teaspoon salt
- 1 teaspoon garlic powder
- Pepper as needed

Directions:
1. Take your Instant Pot and place it on a clean kitchen platform. Turn it on after plugging it into a power socket.
2. Open the lid from the top and put it aside; add the chickpeas and enough water to cover them.
3. Add the cumin powder, bay leaves, garlic powder, thyme, onion salt and pepper. Gently stir them.
4. Close the lid and lock. Ensure that you have sealed the valve to avoid leakage.
5. Press "Manual" mode and set timer for 15 minutes. It will take a few minutes for the pot to build inside pressure and start cooking.
6. After the timer reads zero, press "Cancel" and quick release pressure.
7. Carefully remove the lid. Discard bay leaves and drain water.
8. Transfer the mixture in a blender; blend to make it smooth. Add the flour and tomato paste; blend again.
9. Make 5 burger patties from the mix and grill them until turn golden on both sides.
10. Add them to the burger buns and add your favorite veggies and vegan mayo. Enjoy!

Nutrition: Calories 109 Fat 2g Carbohydrates 20g Fiber 4.5g Protein 5g

486. Spinach Pasta Treat (FAST)

Preparation Time: 5 min.
Cooking Time: 15 min.
Servings: 4
Ingredients:
- 2 garlic cloves, crushed
- 2 garlic cloves, chopped
- 1 pound spinach
- 1 pound fusilli pasta
- A drizzle of olive oil
- ¼ cup pine nuts, chopped
- Black pepper and salt to taste

Directions:
1. Take your Instant Pot and place it on a clean kitchen platform. Turn it on after plugging it into a power socket.
2. Put the pot on "Sauté" mode. In the pot, add the oil, garlic, and spinach; cook for 6-7 minutes until the ingredients become soft.
3. Add the pasta, salt, and pepper; add water to cover the pasta.
4. Close the lid and lock. Ensure that you have sealed the valve to avoid leakage.

5. Press "Manual" mode and set timer for 6 minutes. It will take a few minutes for the pot to build inside pressure and start cooking.
6. After the timer reads zero, press "Cancel" and quick release pressure.
7. Carefully remove the lid; mix the chopped garlic and pine nuts.
8. Serve warm!

Nutrition: Calories 198 Fat 1g Carbohydrates 6.5g Fiber 1g Protein 7g

487. Mexican Style Vegan Rice (FAST)

Preparation Time: 5 minutes
Cooking Time: 8-10 minutes
Servings: 5-6
Ingredients:
- ½ piece chopped white onion
- 2 cups water
- 2 cups white rice, long-grain
- 3 cloves minced garlic
- 1 jalapeño, optional
- ½ cup tomato paste
- 2 teaspoon salts

Directions:
1. Take your Instant Pot and place it on a clean kitchen platform. Turn it on after plugging it into a power socket.
2. Put the pot on "Sauté" mode. In the pot, add the oil, garlic, onion, rice, and salt; cook for 3-4 minutes until the ingredients become soft.
3. Mix the tomato paste, pepper and water; stir well.
4. Close the lid and lock. Ensure that you have sealed the valve to avoid leakage.
5. Press "Manual" mode and set timer for 4 minutes. It will take a few minutes for the pot to build inside pressure and start cooking.
6. After the timer reads zero, press "Cancel" and naturally release pressure. It takes about 8-10 minutes to naturally release pressure.
7. Carefully remove the lid, fluff the mix and serve warm!

Nutrition: Calories 521 Fat 1.5g Carbohydrates 39g Fiber 3g Protein6g

488. Perfect Herb Rice (FAST)

Preparation Time: 10 minutes
Cooking Time: 4 minutes
Servings: 4
Ingredients:
- 1 cup brown rice, rinsed
- 1 tbsp olive oil
- 1 1/2 cups water
- 1/2 cup fresh mix herbs, chopped

- 1 tsp salt

Directions:
1. Put all fixings into the pot and stir well. Cook on high for 4 minutes. Stir well and serve.

Nutrition: Calories 264 Fat 9.9 g Carbohydrates 36.7 g Sugar 0.4 g Protein 7.3 g Cholesterol 0 mg

489. Belly-Filling Cajun Rice & Chicken (FAST)

Preparation Time: 15 minutes
Cooking Time: 20 minutes
Servings: 6
Ingredients:
- 1 tablespoon oil
- 1 onion, diced
- 3 cloves of garlic, minced
- 1-pound chicken breasts, sliced
- 1 tablespoon Cajun seasoning
- 1 tablespoon tomato paste
- 2 cups chicken broth
- 1 ½ cups white rice, rinsed
- 1 bell pepper, chopped

Directions:
1. Press the Sauté on the Instant Pot and pour the oil.
2. Sauté the onion and garlic until fragrant.
3. Stir in the chicken breasts and season with Cajun seasoning.
4. Continue cooking for 3 minutes.
5. Add the tomato paste and chicken broth. Dissolve the tomato paste before adding the rice and bell pepper.
6. Close the lid and press the rice button.
7. Once done cooking, do a natural release for 10 minutes.
8. Then, do a quick release.
9. Once cooled, evenly divide into serving size, keep in your preferred container, and refrigerate until ready to eat.

Nutrition: Calories per serving: 337 Carbohydrates: 44.3g Protein: 26.1g Fat: 5.0g

490. Rosemary Beef Chuck Roast

Preparation Time: 5 minutes
Cooking Time: 45 minutes
Servings: 5-6
Ingredients:
- 3 pounds chuck beef roast
- 3 garlic cloves
- ¼ cup balsamic vinegar
- 1 sprig fresh rosemary
- 1 sprig fresh thyme
- 1 cup of water
- 1 tablespoon vegetable oil
- Salt and pepper to taste

Directions:
1. Cut slices in the beef roast and place the garlic cloves in them.
2. Coat the roast with the herbs, black pepper, and salt.
3. Preheat your instant pot using the sauté setting and add the oil.
4. When warmed, add the beef roast and stir-cook until browned on all sides.
5. Add the remaining ingredients; stir gently.
6. Seal the lid and cook on high pressure for 40 minutes using the manual setting.
7. Let the pressure release naturally, about 10 minutes.
8. Uncover the instant pot; transfer the beef roast the serving plates, slice and serve.

Nutrition: Calories: 542 Protein: 55.2 g Fat: 11.2 g Carbohydrates: 8.7 g

491. Pork Chops and Tomato Sauce (FAST)

Preparation Time: 10 minutes
Cooking Time: 20 minutes
Servings: 4
Ingredients:
- 4 pork chops, boneless
- 1 tablespoon soy sauce
- ¼ teaspoon sesame oil
- 1 and ½ cups tomato paste
- 1 yellow onion
- 8 mushrooms, sliced

Directions:
1. In a bowl, mix pork chops with soy sauce and sesame oil, toss and leave aside for 10 minutes.
2. Set your instant pot on sauté mode, add pork chops and brown them for 5 minutes on each side.
3. Add onion, stir and cook for 1-2 minutes more.
4. Add tomato paste and mushrooms, toss, cover and cook on high for 8-9 minutes.
5. Divide everything between plates and serve.
6. Enjoy!

Nutrition: Calories: 300 Protein: 4 g Fat: 7 g Carbohydrates: 18 g

492. Pork Potato (FAST)

Preparation Time: 8-10 minutes
Cooking Time: 25 minutes
Servings: 4
Ingredients:
- 10 ounces pork neck, fat remove and make small pieces
- 1 medium sweet potato, chopped
- 1 tablespoon oil

- 3 cups beef stock, Low – sodium
- 1 onion, chopped (finely)

Directions:
1. Take your pot and place over dry kitchen surface; open its top lid and switch it on.
2. Press "sauté". Grease the pot with some Cooking oil.
3. Add the onions; cook for 2 minutes until turn translucent and softened.
4. Add the meat; stir-cook for 4-5 minutes to evenly brown.
5. Mix in the stock and potatoes.
6. Close its top lid and make sure that its valve it closed to avoid spillage.
7. Press "Manual". Adjust the timer to 20 minutes.
8. Pressure will slowly build up; let the added ingredients to cook until the timer indicates zero.
9. Press "CANCEL". Now press "NPR" for natural release pressure. Instant pot will gradually release pressure for about 8-10 minutes.
10. Open the top lid transfer the cooked recipe in serving plates.
11. Serve the recipe warm.

Nutrition: Calories: 278 Protein: 18 g Fat: 18 g Carbohydrates: 12 g

493. Garlic Pulled Pork

Preparation Time: 5 minutes
Cooking Time: 1 hour and 40 minutes
Servings: 12
Ingredients:
- 4-pounds pork shoulder, boneless and cut into 3 pieces
- 2 tablespoons soy sauce
- 2 tablespoons brown sugar
- 1 cup chicken broth
- 10 cloves garlic, finely chopped
- 2 tablespoons butter, melted at room temperature

Directions:
1. In a mixing bowl, combine the broth, soy sauce, and brown sugar. Add the garlic and stir to combine.
2. Preheat your instant pot using the sauté setting and add the butter.
3. When warmed, add the pork pieces and stir-cook until browned on all sides.
4. Add the soy mix; stir gently.
5. Seal the lid and cook on high pressure for 90 minutes using the manual setting.
6. Let the pressure release naturally, about 10 minutes.

7. Uncover the instant pot; take out the meat and shred it using a fork.
8. Return the shredded meat to the instant pot and stir the mixture well.
9. Transfer to serving plates and serve.

Nutrition: Calories: 142 Protein: 11.2 g Fat: 8.2 g Carbohydrates: 3.5 g

494. Shrimp, Mushroom, and Broccoli (FAST)

Preparation Time: 15 Minutes
Cooking Time: 8 Minutes
Servings: 2
Ingredients
- 1 pound of shrimp
- 2 garlic, minced
- 1 cup broccoli
- 2 tablespoons of soy sauce
- 1teaspoon of stevia
- oil spray, for greasing
- 1 tablespoon of lemon juice
- ½ pound of shitake mushroom

Directions
1. Preheat the air fryer by selecting air fry mode for 5 minutes at 350 degrees F.
2. Select start/pause to begin the preheating process.
3. Once preheating is done, press start/pause.
4. Take a bowl and add the shrimp, minced garlic, soy sauce, and stevia.
5. Then add lemon juice and vegetables.
6. Toss all the ingredients well
7. Add it to the air fryer basket that is greased with oil spray.
8. Set it to air fry mode at 390 degrees F, for 8 minutes.
9. Once done, take out the ingredients and serve.

Nutrition: Calories 259 | Fat 4.6g| Sodium 1744mg | Carbs 23.5g | Fiber 3.7g | Sugar 5.3g | Protein 55.8g

Fahrenheit	Celsius		Imperial	Metric
225	107		1/2 oz.	14 g
250	121		1 oz.	28 g
275	135		2 oz.	57 g
300	149		3 oz.	85 g
325	163		4 oz.	113 g
350	177		5 oz.	142 g
375	190		6 oz.	170 g
400	204		7 oz.	199 g
425	218		8 oz.	227 g
450	238		9 oz.	255 g
475	246		10 oz.	284 g
			12 oz	340 g
			1 lb.	454 g
			1 ½ lb.	680 g
			2 lb.	907 g
			2.2 lb.	1 kg

Fluid Ounces	Cups	Milliliters	Liters
2	1/4	59	.059
4	1/2	118	.118
8	1	237	.237
16	2	473	.473
24	3	710	.71
32	4	946	.946
33.6	4.22	1000	1

Fluid Ounces	Cups	Milliliters	Liters
2	1/4	59	.059
4	1/2	118	.118
8	1	237	.237
16	2	473	.473
24	3	710	.71
32	4	946	.946
33.6	4.22	1000	1

INDEX

CONCLUSION AND BONUS

Dear reader, I would appreciate it if you would just spend a minute of your time and post a short review on AMAZON to let other users know how this experience was and what you liked most about the book.

Maybe you have a recipe that you particularly liked and want to let us know.

Also, as of recently **(07/2022)** I have decided to do a giveaway to all our readers, yes, I want to give you a **gift.**

You will have more *300 recipes* at your disposal!

Below you will find a QR CODE that will give you direct access to this bonus (PDF file to download directly to your device) *without having to subscribe to any mailing list or having to leave your personal data.* **We hope you enjoy it**

In addition, as a publishing house, we have many more books and audiobooks that perhaps might be of interest to you or your loved ones in various genres (for example, parenting).

If you would like a copy or would like to share your feedback with us directly, we would be happy to: please write to us at **author.author1001@gmail.com** A friendly greeting, we wish you the best

Made in United States
Orlando, FL
07 October 2022

23082760R00109